Y0-BDH-053

NAG HAMMADI STUDIES

VOLUME IV

NAG HAMMADI STUDIES

EDITED BY

MARTIN KRAUSE - JAMES M. ROBINSON
FREDERIK WISSE

IN CONJUNCTION WITH

ALEXANDER BÖHLIG – JEAN DORESSE – SØREN GIVERSEN
HANS JONAS – RODOLPHE KASSER – PAHOR LABIB
GEORGE W. MACRAE – JACQUES-É. MÉNARD – TORGNY SÄVE-SÖDERBERGH
WILLEM CORNELIS VAN UNNIK – R. MCL. WILSON
JAN ZANDEE

IV

GENERAL EDITOR OF THE COPTIC GNOSTIC LIBRARY

JAMES M. ROBINSON

LEIDEN
E. J. BRILL
1975

THE COPTIC GNOSTIC LIBRARY

EDITED WITH ENGLISH TRANSLATION, INTRODUCTION AND NOTES

published under the auspices of

THE INSTITUTE FOR ANTIQUITY AND CHRISTIANITY

NAG HAMMADI CODICES

III, *2* AND IV, *2*

THE GOSPEL OF THE EGYPTIANS

(THE HOLY BOOK OF THE GREAT INVISIBLE SPIRIT)

EDITED WITH TRANSLATION AND COMMENTARY BY

ALEXANDER BÖHLIG AND FREDERIK WISSE

in cooperation with

PAHOR LABIB

published under the auspices of

THE GERMAN ARCHAEOLOGICAL INSTITUTE

LEIDEN

E. J. BRILL

1975

ISBN 90 04 04226 1

PRINTED IN BELGIUM

CONTENTS

FOREWORD

The Coptic Gnostic Library is a complete edition of the Nag Hammadi codices and of Codex Berolinensis 8502, comprising a critical text with English translation, introductions to each codex and tractate, notes and indices. Its aim is to present these texts in a uniform edition that will promptly follow the appearance of *The Facsimile Edition of the Nag Hammadi Codices* and that can be a basis for more detailed technical and interpretive investigations. Further studies of this sort are expected to appear in the monograph series *Nag Hammadi Studies* of which the present edition is a part.

The gnostic religion is a significant religious position in its own right, besides being a force that interacted with early Christianity and Judaism in their formative periods. This modern realization has until recently been seriously impeded by the scarcity of original source material. Now this situation has been decisively altered. It is thus under a sense of obligation imposed by the discovery of these largely unique documents that the present edition has been prepared.

The Coptic Gnostic Library is a project of the Institute for Antiquity and Christianity, Claremont, California. The translation team consists of Alexander Böhlig, James Brashler, Roger A. Bullard, C. J. de Catanzaro, Peter A. Dirkse, Søren Giversen, Charles W. Hedrick, Bentley Layton, George W. MacRae, Jacques-E. Ménard, Dieter Mueller, William Murdock, Douglas M. Parrott, Birger Pearson, Malcolm L. Peel, James M. Robinson, William C. Robinson, Jr., William R. Schoedel, John Sieber, John D. Turner, Francis E. Williams, R. McL. Wilson, Orval Wintermute, Frederik Wisse and Jan Zandee. The project was initiated in 1966 on a more limited basis, but rapidly developed as the texts became increasingly available. Its early history may be traced in the preliminary announcements in *New Testament Studies*, 16 (1969/70) 185-190 and in *Essays on the Coptic Gnostic Library* (an off-print from *Novum Testamentum*, 12, published by E. J. Brill, 1970), 83-85. As now envisaged, the full scope of the edition is eleven volumes. These correspond to the volumes of the facsimile edition, except in the case of Codices II-V, where three sets of parallel texts will be edited in the form of synopses. The remaining tractates of Codices II-V will appear in two further volumes, the one containing II, *2-7* and III, *5*, and the other containing V, *2-5*, all of Codex VI, and BG 8502, *1* and *4*.

The team research of the project has been supported primarily by the National Endowment for the Humanities, the American Philosophical Society, the John Simon Guggenheim Memorial Foundation and the Institute for Antiquity and Christianity of Claremont Graduate School. Members of the project have participated in the restoration work of the Technical Sub-Committee of the International Committee for the Nag Hammadi Codices, at the Coptic Museum in Cairo, under the sponsorship of the Arab Republic of Egypt and UNESCO. This extensive work in the reassembly of fragments, reconstitution of pagination and first-hand collation of the Coptic text not only served the immediate needs of the facsimile edition, but also provided a basis for a critical edition. Without such generous support and such mutual cooperation of all parties concerned this edition could hardly have been prepared. Therefore we wish to express our sincere gratitude to all who have been involved.

An especial word of thanks is due the Egyptian and UNESCO officials through whose assistance the work has been carried on: Gamal Mokhtar, President of the Egyptian Antiquities Organization, our gracious and able host in Egypt; Pahor Labib, Director Emeritus, and Victor Girgis, Director, of the Coptic Museum, who together have guided the work on the manuscript material; Samiha Abd El-Shaheed, Curator for Manuscripts at the Coptic Museum, who is personally responsible for the codices and was constantly by our side in the Library of the Coptic Museum. And, at UNESCO, N. Bammate, Director of the Department of Culture, who has guided the UNESCO planning since its beginning, and Dina Zeidan, specialist in the Arab Program of the Division of Cultural Studies, who has always proved ready with gracious assistance and helpful advice.

We also gratefully acknowledge the continued interest and support of F. C. Wieder, Jr., Director, and T. A. Edridge, Assistant Manager, of E. J. Brill.

With regard to the present volume, we wish to express our gratitude to Alexander Böhlig, Pahor Labib and Frederik Wisse as well as to the Cairo section of the German Archaeological Institute for their willingness to alter previous publication plans for *The Gospel of the Egyptians* so that it could become not only a part of this edition, but might also be its distinguished opening volume.

James M. Robinson

PREFACE

The so-called Gospel of the Egyptians, of which two independent versions are extant among the Nag Hammadi papyri in the Coptic Museum of Old Cairo, is unrelated to the apocryphal Christian Gospel of the same name. The edition had its beginning in the agreement between Alexander Böhlig and Pahor Labib in the fall of 1963. During the spring of 1964 Böhlig made a transcription of the version contained in Codex III, and he used it as the basis for the placement of the main fragments of the version in Codex IV, of which then a transcription was made. For political and personal reasons the work on the originals had to be discontinued until 1967; in the meantime the work on the edition proceded on the basis of photographs. When James M. Robinson asked Böhlig in 1966 to allow an English version of his translation of GEgypt to be included in a reader of Coptic Gnostic tractates being planned in Claremont, California, Böhlig agreed to this, but later came to the conviction that it would be advantageous to publish the entire edition in English in order to make it accessible to a wider public. Thus in 1968 he invited Frederik Wisse to become co-editor with equal responsibility. Wisse was at that time preparing, on the basis of photographs, a translation of GEgypt for the Coptic Gnostic project of the Institute for Antiquity and Christianity in Claremont, California. Beginning in 1969 joint working sessions were held in Claremont and Tübingen; in addition an extensive exchange of manuscripts and comments took place. The many difficulties in the tractate called for frequent reconsideration of the text, translation and interpretation. From 1970 on, it was possible for Wisse to work also with the originals in connection with the preparations for the UNESCO facsimile edition of the Nag Hammadi codices. In the course of restoring Codex IV he was able to verify the fragments already identified on the basis of the photographs and to place further ones.

The commentary and the introductory chapters intend to facilitate the reading of the tractate, and to show that we are not dealing here with a conglomerate of abstruse mythologumena, but rather with a definite line of argument, although one which makes use of a frame of reference to which we are not accustomed.

Special mention needs to be made of the Sonderforschungsbereich 13

"Orientalistik" at the University of Göttingen, which included the work on the proofs in its program, since the text belongs to the material which is basic for its research. Furthermore thanks are due to the institutions which have provided the necessary travel and research grants: the Deutsche Forschungsgemeinschaft, the Deutsche Archäologische Institut, the American Philosophical Society, the Morse Fund of Yale University and the Institute for Antiquity and Christianity in Claremont, California. We would also like to express our gratitude to Dr. Gertrud Böhlig, Lenore Brashler and James A. Brashler for their assistance in preparing the manuscript.

Tübingen, November 1973

Alexander Böhlig
Frederik Wisse

TABLE OF TRACTATES

The following table lists for the thirteen Nag Hammadi Codices and the Berlin Codex 8502 the Codex and tractate numbers, the tractate titles as used in this edition (the titles found in the tractates themselves, often simplified and standardized, or, when the tractate bears no surviving title, one supplied by the editors), and the abbreviations of these titles.

I,*1*	The Apocryphon of James	ApocryJas
I,*2*	The Gospel of Truth	GTr
I,*3*	The Treatise on the Resurrection	OnRes
I,*4*	The Tripartite Tractate	TriTrac
I,*5*	The Prayer of the Apostle Paul	PrPaul
II,*1*	The Apocryphon of John	ApocryJn
II,*2*	The Gospel of Thomas	GTh
II,*3*	The Gospel of Philip	GPh
II,*4*	The Nature of the Archons	NatArch
II,*5*	On the Origin of the World	OnOrgWld
II,*6*	The Exegesis on the Soul	ExSoul
II,*7*	The Book of Thomas the Contender	ThCont
III,*1*	The Apocryphon of John	ApocryJn
III,*2*	The Gospel of the Egyptians	GEgypt
III,*3*	Eugnostos the Blessed	Eug
III,*4*	The Sophia of Jesus Christ	SJC
III,*5*	The Dialogue of the Saviour	DialSav
IV,*1*	The Apocryphon of John	ApocryJn
IV,*2*	The Gospel of the Egyptians	GEgypt
V,*1*	Eugnostos the Blessed	Eug
V,*2*	The Apocalypse of Paul	ApocPaul
V,*3*	The First Apocalypse of James	1 ApocJas
V,*4*	The Second Apocalypse of James	2 ApocJas
V,*5*	The Apocalypse of Adam	ApocAd
VI,*1*	The Acts of Peter and the Twelve Apostles	AcPetTwAp
VI,*2*	The Thunder : Perfect Mind	Thund
VI,*3*	Authoritative Teaching	AuthTeach
VI,*4*	The Concept of our Great Power	GrPow

SIGLA

.	A subscript dot placed under a letter indicates that the letter is visually uncertain, even if the context seems to make the reading certain. Visual certainty does not depend upon the amount of surviving ink but upon the exclusion of all other alternatives than the one presented in the transcription. Dots on the line indicate the number of missing letters of which ink vestiges survive when letters are not restored.
[ ]	Square brackets indicate a lacuna in the manuscript, where lettering once occurred but is now completely absent, due either to a hole through the papyrus or a deterioration only on the surface. When the text cannot be restored with reasonable probability, the number of missing letters is indicated by [......].
< >	Pointed brackets indicate the editor has either inserted letters omitted unintentionally by the scribe or replaced letters erroneously inserted by the scribe with what the scribe presumably intended to write. In the latter case a footnote records the actual reading.
{ }	Braces indicate cancellations by the editor of dittography or other material erroneously interpolated by the scribe.
\ /	High strokes indicate a scribal insertion above the line.
( )	Parentheses in the translation indicate material useful to the English text but not explicitly present in the Coptic; Greek words are included in the translation in parentheses.
III,*2*	Roman numerals are used to number codices and Arabic numerals in italics to number tractates.

ABBREVIATIONS

A	Achmimic
A²	Subachmimic
B	Bohairic
II J	The Second Book of Yeu
PS	The Pistis Sophia
S	Sahidic
sa	The Sahidic version of the New Testament
U	Untitled Treatise from Codex Brucianus

THE MANUSCRIPTS

Two versions of GEgypt have been preserved in the Coptic Gnostic library from Nag Hammadi. One is the second of the five tractates of Codex III, the other is the second of the two tractates in Codex IV. Codex III, *2* originally comprised pages 40-69, and Codex IV, *2* included pages 50-81. Both versions have suffered considerable loss. Of III, *2*, pages 40-44 have lost the inside margin and part of the text, pages 45-48 are completely missing, pages 49-54 lack the inside top corner with almost all the text surviving, and the inside half of pages 57-58 has broken off and is lost. IV, *2* is much more fragmentary, although every page is represented. Only pages 50-53, 59-66 and 71-78 contain more than half of their original text. Of the original tractate more than 90 percent survives in one or the other of the two versions.

The physical dimensions of Codices III and IV have been described by MARTIN KRAUSE.[1] He also presents on Plate 5 of his volume a photo of III 40, which contains the end of ApocryJn and the beginning of GEgypt.[2] Thus far no plates have been published of IV, *2*.[3]

Codex III, *2*

Of the original thirty pages twenty-six have been partly or completely preserved. Their original size was 15,5 × 25,5 cm, and the average column of writing measures 11 × 20 cm. The pages were numbered above the middle of the column.[4] Numbers are partly

---

[1] *Die drei Versionen des Apokryphon des Johannes im Koptischen Museum zu Alt-Kairo,* ADAIK, Kopt. Reihe 1 (Wiesbaden 1962) pp. 17-22.

[2] A photographic reproduction of III 40 can also be found in "Les papyrus gnostiques coptes" by PAHOR LABIB, *La Revue du Caire,* 197 (1956), 227 and in "Le Livre sacré du grand Esprit invisible" by JEAN DORESSE, *Journal Asiatique* 254 (1966), Plate 1. In the same article DORESSE presents III 69 on Plate 2. Pages 69 and 67 can be found in DORESSE's "A Gnostic Library from Upper Egypt," *Archaeology* III (1950), 72. This plate was also published in "The Gnostic Library of Chenoboskion" by VICTOR R. GOLD, *The Biblical Archaeologist* XV (1952), 75.

[3] Some pages of IV, *1* have been published by KRAUSE in: *Die drei Versionen,* Plates 16-24.

[4] Also the Subachmimic Codices I, X and XI (first hand) in the library have the numbers above the middle of the column. Codices IV-IX and XI (second hand) have been numbered above the outside of the writing column.

or completely visible on pages 40, 42, 44, 54-56 and 60-69. The even-numbered pages have horizontal fibers and the odd pages have vertical fibers. No fragments belonging to III, *2* have been found.

The scribe of the codex did not write any of the other Nag Hammadi codices. The codex is written in a casual, flowing uncial script, evidently by an experienced scribe. Noteworthy is the ϭ with its long sweeping top stroke which continues over one or more of the following letters.[1] The left margin is straight and some effort has also been made to keep a straight right margin, if necessary by means of line fillers.[2] In some places where a word division would have been awkward, letters have been crowded at the end of a line.

The scribe regularly placed a dot above the right side of a ⲡ or ⲧ when it is the final letter of a word, and above the first ⲅ of a double gamma combination.[3] There are also a few instances where a dot was placed on the ⲧ in ⲉⲧ-, ⲁⲧ- and ⲙⲛ̄ⲧ-.[4] Evidently this constitutes a development towards word and syllable division.[5] In Codices IV, V, VI, VIII and IX the final ⲡ and ⲧ of a word or syllable are marked by means of a backstroke or "flag" instead of a dot. In Codices VII and XI (second hand) only the ⲧ has the backstroke pointing mark. Codices II and XIII have a more developed pointing system. They use a mark which looks like an apostrophe or small diagonal stroke where Codex III has a dot.[6]

Most of the inconsistencies in pointing by the scribe of III, *2* can be readily explained. The final ⲧ of ϣⲟⲙⲛⲧ has in most cases

---

[1] There are several instances where the top stroke of the ϭ serves simultaneously as the superlinear stroke over a following ⲛ (40,13; 49,23; 51,3; 63,21).

[2] Line fillers were used only on pages 41, 42, 52, 55 and 69. Apparently only a half-hearted attempt was made to regulate the right margin, perhaps after the Codex was finished. Besides Codex III only Codex XII uses line fillers.

[3] In most instances (57,9; 58,8; 60,3; 61,21; 62,15; 69,12) the mark over the ⲅ is not a dot but a small circumflex. This "circumflex" is also found in other tractates in the codex and is used in Codices IV-VI, VIII and IX.

[4] The instances are: ⲁⲧ- 41,4.20; 42,17; 44,11; 49,24; 64,8; 66,25 and 68,18; ⲙⲛ̄ⲧ- 64,4; ⲉⲧ- 68,22. Occasionally there is also a dot on the article ⲡ when it precedes a noun beginning with the letter ⲡ or on the article ⲧ before a noun beginning with a ⲧ.

[5] The reason for pointing final letters of a word or syllable is most likely an effort to facilitate reading aloud. Since the ⲡ and ⲧ as articles are often the first letter of a word the need for word division would be especially felt with these letters. This would explain the instance in 65,7 where the dots were placed both above the ⲧ and ⲡ in ⲥⲱⲧⲡ. At first the scribe thought the ⲡ belonged with the following word and thus placed the dot on the ⲧ. When he noticed his mistake he placed another dot above the ⲡ.

[6] The apostrophe is also used in a few instances in Codex VII after ⲙ and ⲗ.

not been pointed. Apparently the scribe confused the ending with the prefix ⲘⲚ̄Ⲧ- which he normally does not point. He usually does not point the final ⲡ and ⲧ when they fall at the end of a line.[1] This is consistent with the function of pointing as word division. Pointing cannot always be easily distinguished from punctuation. Particularly in Codices I, II and III the pointing mark is easily confused with the full stop (στιγμή). This has led to the unfortunate conclusion that punctuation in Coptic manuscripts is of little or no help to the modern editor. However, when justice is done to the pointing conventions of, for example, Codices II and III, the punctuation can be distinguished and generally makes good sense.[2] A paragraphos in the left margin has been used at the end of the tractate (69,5) and again at the end of the colophon (69,17).[3]

An unusual feature in III, *2* is the use of ⲛ̄ before ⲡ as in 40, 16 ⲛ̄ⲡⲟⲩⲟⲉⲓⲛ. There are twenty-three instances in the tractate where the normal assimilation to ⲙ̄ has not occurred. III, *2*, in contrast to many other tractates in the library, has very few doublings of the ⲛ before vowels.[4] Also the use of ⲡⲓ, ϯ and ⲛⲓ is sparse. The few occurrences may have a demonstrative force. It is worthy of note that the plural definite article form ⲛⲉⲛ- occurs once at 64,22.

Codex III shares with Codex II a peculiar policy for the superlinear strokes on the final two consonants of a word. Strokes appear only when the last letter is ⲃ,ⲙ,ⲛ,ⲥ or ⲣ such as in ϩⲱⲧ̄ⲃ, ⲥⲱⲧ̄ⲙ, ⲱϫ̄ⲛ, ϩⲱⲃ̄ⲥ and ϩⲱⲧ̄ⲣ. When the final two consonants of a word end in ⲕ,ⲡ,ⲧ,ϣ,ϥ,ϩ or ϫ such as in ⲱⲙⲕ, ϩⲱⲧⲡ, ⲙⲟⲩϫⲧ, ⲡⲱⲣϣ, ⲟⲩⲱⲥϥ, ⲱⲛϩ and ⲡⲱⲣϫ there is no superlinear stroke.[5] This policy is so consistently followed that it must have a firm phonetic basis.[6]

The verb ⲉⲓ only rarely received a "circumflex", and ϩⲓ never.[7] Most proper names have not been marked with the usual long super-

---

[1] The four remaining instances where the pointing is missing must be oversights (51,8; 57,4; 63,22; 67,1).

[2] The published editions of Codices II and III made an attempt at reproducing pointing and punctuation but failed to distinguish between them.

[3] The paragraphos was also used by the scribe of Codices IV-VI and VIII-IX.

[4] There are only four instances: 41,20; 49,14; 55,19 and 62,14.

[5] When the final letter is the suffix ⲕ or ϥ the combination normally does have a superlinear stroke. This is not the case in Codex II.

[6] It appears that the superlinear stroke is used only when the second consonant functions as a sonant.

[7] III 49,15 and 65,18. A slightly curved stroke or circumflex on ⲉ͡ⲓ n ϩ͡ⲓ is normal for Codices IV-IX and XI (second hand).

linear stroke. If a pattern can be observed at all it is that the more important and familiar heavenly beings are the more likely ones to have a superlinear stroke. Generally the strokes are used only in the first couple of occurrences of a name.[1] This suggests that once the reader could be assumed to be familiar with the name the superlinear stroke was left out. Also the particle of relation ⲛ̄ linking an adjective with the following noun is often not present before proper names, e.g. III 52, 22f. 24f. 26; 62, 19.

Corrections in III, *2* are frequent. They were made by writing over the error or by crossing it out and writing above the line. The written-over readings cannot always be recovered with certainty, since they have often been erased by washing out the ink. A number of the corrections were definitely made by the scribe himself, and possibly all of them were. However, many of the corrections involve a change of meaning and cannot be explained as corrections of scribal errors. Thus either the scribe of the codex made changes in substance after copying the tractate or this was done by another scribe whose hand cannot be readily distinguished from the copyist of the codex. There are a number of apparent corrections by means of over-writing which on close examination proved to be blottings from the facing page.

The following list of references is made up of corrections which do not involve a change of meaning; details are given in the notes to the transcription: 42, 5; 43, 2.3 (bis).12.13; 44, 24; 49, 20; 51, 8; 53, 12.23; 55, 6.13.24; 56, 3.9.22; 57, 11.25; 58, 14.20; 59, 6; 60, 1.13.16; 61, 15.20; 62, 6.15.23; 63, 7.16.19.20.22.24; 64, 3; 65, 26; 66, 3.9.23. 24.26; 67, 1.15; 68, 4.7; 69, 12. Most of these are mistakes which were noticed immediately by the scribe and corrected before he finished the line. These scribal errors include omitted letters, haplography, dittography and misassociation with a word or phrase in the immediate context.

The following list of references is made up of corrections which do or may involve a change of meaning; details are given in the notes to the transcription and translation: 41, 20; 44, 17; 49, 22; 51, 1; 52, 5; 53, 11 (bis); 54, 8; 59, 9; 62, 13; 64, 23; 65, 5; 66, 2.7; 67, 14. Several of these, such as the change from "seventy-fourth" to "fourth" in 54, 8, cannot be explained as scribal errors. These may be from the hand of another scribe. In 59, 9 the scribe wrote inadvertently "the first man" instead of "the first creature". He noticed his mistake

[1] The name ⲥⲏⲑ has a superlinear stroke only in five of its twenty-four occurrences (51,20; 54,11; 60,9; 62,4; 68,2).

immediately, crossed out ⲣⲱⲙⲉ, and followed it with the correct word. Since this did not result in an extra long line, the scribe could not have followed the column of the Coptic model he was copying. This is confirmed by other corrections, and by the fact that the several extensive cases of homoioteleuton did not result in fewer lines per column.

In spite of the many corrections, many scribal errors requiring emendation remain. In the following cases a word was misspelled due to haplography, dittography, omitted letters or scrambled letters; details are given in the notes to the transcription: 41, 19; 52, 6.13; 54, 8; 55, 3.14.21; 56, 19; 58, 5; 59, 17.22; 62, 11; 65, 4; 66, 26; 68, 13.19.

A second category of emendations involves ⲛ̄- and ⲙⲛ̄-. The scribe is particularly inaccurate at this point.[1]

40, 18	ⲛ̄ⲡⲉⲓⲱⲧ	for	ⲙⲛ̄ ⲡⲉⲓⲱⲧ	(IV 50, 9).
40, 19	ⲙ̄ⲧⲙⲏⲉ	for	ⲙⲛ̄ ⲧⲙⲏⲉ	(IV 50, 10).
52, 12	ⲙ̄ⲟⲩⲟⲉⲓⲛ	for	ⲛ̄ⲟⲩⲟⲉⲓⲛ.	
53, 9	ⲙ̄ⲡⲙⲉϩϥⲧⲟⲟⲩ	for	ⲡⲙⲉϩϥⲧⲟⲟⲩ.	
53, 23	ⲙ̄ⲡϣⲟⲙⲛ̄ⲧ	for	ⲙⲛ̄ ⲡϣⲟⲙⲛ̄ⲧ	(IV 65, 17).
54, 5	ⲙ̄ⲛⲓⲁⲓⲱⲛ	for	ⲙⲛ̄ ⲛⲓⲁⲓⲱⲛ	(IV 65, 24).
60, 8	ⲧⲉⲥⲡⲟⲣⲁ	for	ⲛ̄ⲧⲥⲡⲟⲣⲁ.	
60, 21	ⲛ̄ⲑⲉ ⲛ̄ⲙⲓⲥⲥⲁ	for	ⲙⲛ̄ ⲑⲉⲙⲓⲥⲥⲁ	(III 62, 20 and IV 72, 3).
64, 24	ⲡⲛⲟϭ	for	ⲙ̄ⲡⲛⲟϭ	(IV 76, 15).

The remaining emendations are more extensive and thus more controversial; details are given in the notes to the transcription: 40, 12; 42, 5; 52, 20; 55, 15; 60, 6; 62, 24f.

Both the corrections and emendations indicate that the accuracy of the scribe of III, *2* left much to be desired. This conclusion is supported by his spelling of proper names.[2]

Finally there are some unattested forms which may be due to scribal error: 43,7 (ⲕⲟⲟⲩⲛ⸗ for ⲕⲟⲩⲟⲩⲛ⸗); 51, 12 (ⲧⲟⲩⲛ⸗ for ⲧⲱⲟⲩⲛ⸗); 54, 15 (ⲉⲥⲏⲧⲉ for ⲉⲥⲏⲧ); 56, 7.7-8 (ⲙⲉⲉⲩⲉ for ⲙⲁⲁⲩ); 60, 12.15 (ϩⲟⲉⲓⲛ for ϩⲟⲉⲓⲛⲉ); 62, 6 (ⲙⲁϩⲧⲉ for ⲉⲙⲁϩⲧⲉ); 63, 8 (ⲛⲟⲩϩⲙ̄-); 41, 19 (ⲙⲉϥ- for ⲙⲉϩ-), cf. Kahle, Bala'izah I, p. 145.

It is questionable, however, whether this is a matter of spelling errors. These forms can also be explained as dialectical or orthogra-

---

[1] See also the corrections in 51,1; 52,5 and 66,2.

[2] See *infra*, pp. 16f.

phical peculiarities. ⲙⲉⲉⲩⲉ for ⲙⲁⲁⲩ and ϩⲟⲉⲓⲛ for ϩⲟⲉⲓⲛⲉ are very well possible, since an ⲉ can readily be attached to sonants, cf. in Sahidic ⲛⲏⲩⲉ for ⲛⲏⲩ, ⲗⲁⲁⲩⲉ for ⲗⲁⲁⲩ, and on the other hand, ⲙⲉⲉⲩ for ⲙⲉⲉⲩⲉ. Such an ⲉ also occurs with non-sonant sounds; thus ⲉⲥⲏⲧⲉ would be confirmed by ⲟⲩⲱϣⲉ, which occurs along side of ⲟⲩⲱϣ in this text.[1] ⲙⲁϩⲧⲉ is possible in light of the fact that the form ⲙⲁϩⲉ is attested in Sahidic. ⲛⲟⲩϩⲙ̄- would here be an instance of *status absolutus* being used for *status constructus*, a phenomenon that is not found elsewhere in III, *2*, but that is possible in the dialectical or non-standardized form of Sahidic. The remaining forms, ⲧⲟⲩⲛ⸗ and ⲕⲟⲟⲩⲛ⸗ can also be permitted to stand without emendation when one considers that for both words the spellings vary considerably.

The few forms which depart from standardized Sahidic can be grouped as follows:

1. Orthographical peculiarities:
   a) Single instead of double vowel: ⲙⲟⲛⲉ 60, 13; ⲙⲁϫⲉ 68, 9.
   b) ⲙⲉⲛ for ⲙ̄ⲛ 53, 14; reversed ⲣ̄ⲛ⸗ for ⲣⲉⲛ⸗ 60, 18.
   c) ⲏⲟⲩ instead of ⲏⲩ; ⲉⲣⲏⲟⲩ 49, 19 and ⲉⲟⲩ instead of ⲉⲩ: ⲙⲉⲟⲩⲉ 68, 19.
   d) ⲣⲱⲭϩ 61, 5 alongside of ⲣⲱⲕϩ 63, 6.

2. AA[2] vocalization in a few places:
   a) ⲁ for ⲟ: ⲛⲁⲙⲧⲉ 50, 22.
      ⲛⲁϭ 66, 22.
   b) ⲉ for ⲁ: ⲉⲙⲁϩⲧⲉ 54, 1; 55, 23.
      ⲙⲉⲉⲩ(ⲉ) 56, 6.7 (bis).
      ⲡⲉϊ, ⲡⲉⲉⲓ, ⲛⲉⲉⲓ 49, 5; 66, 4; 67, 7.
      ⲣⲉⲛ 68, 7; 69, 12.
      ϩⲉⲡ 63, 7.

3. Forms that correspond to A, A[2] or B:
   ⲁⲛⲏϩⲉ 50, 22; 60, 22; 66, 19; 68, 24.
   ⲥϩⲏⲧ⸗ 69, 10. (It is to be noted that earlier at 68, 2.10 ⲥⲁϩ⸗ occurred. Perhaps this shows that the translators of the colophon and the tractate were not the same person.)
   ⲧⲟⲩⲃⲟ or ⲧⲟⲩⲃⲟ⸗ 64, 18; 67, 20.
   ⲙⲏⲉ 40, 19; 55, 6; 64, 15; 65, 14.

---

[1] P. E. Kahle, *Bala'izah* (London 1954) I, p. 64f.

4. ϫⲱ instead of ϫⲟ. Cf. Kahle, *Bala'izah* I, p. 82.
Variations between ϫⲓⲛ ⲛ̄ alongside of ϫⲛ̄ ⲛ̄ and ϩⲁⲣⲉϩ alongside of ϩⲁⲣⲏϩ occur.

Most of these forms which appear to be non-Sahidic are in reality early spellings of the pre-classical period. Thus what appear to be Subachmimic intrusions are actually forms which are regularly found in the Sahidic tractates of the Nag Hammadi library and other Sahidic manuscripts of the same period. This is confirmed by Rodolphe Kasser's *Compléments au Dictionnaire Copte de Crum.*

There are almost no unusual or non-Sahidic grammatical features in the tractate. The Perfect Relative is normally ⲛ̄ⲧⲁ⸗ but twice ⲉⲧⲁ⸗ (59, 12; 63, 22) and once ⲉⲣ- (60, 26). ϫⲉⲕⲁⲁⲥ is used with III Fut. (51, 7f. 12.13f.; 59, 17; 68, 19) and II Fut. (50, 24f.; 51, 9f.; 54, 6f.). ϫⲉ is used once with II Fut. (67, 25). Only once is a Greek verb introduced by ⲣ̄- (67, 13). A unique expression for the passive by means of an impersonal third person feminine singular instead of the usual third person plural occurs. This construction, which also is found in III, *1*, is in a relative clause both times (III, *2*, 66, 6 and III, *1*, 33, 17).

Codex IV, *2*

Few Nag Hammadi codices have gotten into as much disarray as Codex IV.[1] Although parts of all its eighty-one inscribed pages have been preserved, the majority of them are extant only in fragmentary form and these fragments were thoroughly mixed up by the time they were put in plexiglass containers by Martin Krause. By eliminating all the fragments which Krause had identified as belonging to IV, *1*, the remainder could be presumed to belong to IV, *2*. The main clue to the order and position of the fragments had to be found in the parallel version in Codex III. The situation was far more difficult than with IV, *1*, however, since the versions of ApocryJn in Codices II and IV are almost identical and the former was well preserved except for the first four pages.[2] Consequently even small

---

[1] Only Codex X rivals it. Unfortunately the tractates in Codex X have no parallel versions, as do those in Codex IV, to bring order to the confusion.

[2] An almost complete text of these first pages was available in the Codex Berolinensis 8502. Walter C. Till, *Die gnostischen Schriften des koptischen Papyrus Berolinensis*

fragments of IV, *1* could be identified with certainty. In contrast the two versions of GEgypt are independent translations from the Greek which differ widely in wording, syntax, and sometimes meaning.[1] Compounding the problem are the lacunae in the first half of III, *2* and the lack of pages 45-48. The recurring liturgical formulae of the tractate proved to be of great help in restoring the pages of IV, *2* for which no parallel was available. Only a number of small fragments remain unidentified.[2] Some of the text of several pages of Codex IV has flaked-off lettering. Reconstruction on the basis of traces of letters proved generally successful.

In preparing this edition an attempt has been made to do justice to even the smallest trace of a letter. When a letter is certain, independent of the context, even though it is partly in a lacuna, no dot has been used under the letter. A dot has been placed under all letters of which the traces of ink were ambiguous. With a parallel text available it proved useful to fill in as many of the lacunae as possible. The available space in the line and the linguistic characteristics of the tractate were usually sufficiently known to make the reconstruction valuable. As a result it was often possible to ascertain whether the two versions differed in the passage in question. If no parallel text had been available it would have been little more than a fatuous exercise in Coptic composition.

Martin Krause reports that IV, *2* consisted of pages 50-83 with page 84 empty.[3] James M. Robinson, on the other hand, lists pages 50, 1-82, top.[4] However, there is no evidence of writing beyond page 81. Only a fragment of the top of pages 81 and 82 is extant. Of page 81 the left half of the first line and the top of the second line is visible, but the top of page 82 is blank. Page 81 could readily have contained the last part of the tractate up to the colophon. This means that either page 82 was empty and IV, *2* lacked the colophon, or the colophon was written on page 82 but began at a lower point on the page. Since the colophon is clearly secondary there is no need to assume that

8502 (*Texte und Untersuchungen zur Geschichte der altchristlichen Literatur* 60^2, 2 ed. by H.-M. Schenke, Berlin 1972), pp. 78-195.

[1] See *infra*, pp. 11-15.

[2] Their identification depends on a prior successful reconstruction of the place where the fragment belongs. Thus at best they only help to confirm the text. Some of the small fragments may actually belong to IV, *1* or to another codex.

[3] *Die drei Versionen*, p. 21.

[4] "The Coptic Gnostic Library Today," *NTS* XIV (1968), 395. He changed this to 50,1-81 end in "The Coptic Gnostic Library," *Novum Testamentum* 12 (1970), 83.

IV, *2* had the colophon. The codex has a front flyleaf and a blank protective sheet in the center, between pages 42 and 43. It is not clear whether the protective sheet extended over the full width. Whether the end papers belonged to the original quire, as they do in Codex VII, can no longer be ascertained. Not counting the end papers this adds up to a quire of twenty-three sheets. The last two folios of the second half of the quire appear to have been uninscribed. Fragments of these blank pages have been identified. Due to the fragmentary state of the codex and the inferior quality of the papyrus the extent of the rolls or strips from which the sheets of the quire were cut could not be established with certainty.

The original size of the pages was 13,2 × 23,3 cm and the average column of writing measures 9,5 × 19,5 cm. The pages were numbered above the outside edge of the writing column. Numbers are partially or completely visible on pages 71-78. The even-numbered pages have vertical fibers and the odd-numbered pages have horizontal fibers.

The hand of Codex IV is very similar to those of Codices V, VI, VIII and IX. The codex is written in a handsome, regular uncial script. Its regularity, clarity and lack of errors indicate a careful and experienced scribe. The left margin is reasonably straight; less care has been taken with the right margin. There are no line fillers and there is little crowding of letters. The superlinear strokes are remarkably precise, running from the middle of a letter to the middle of the next when two consonants form a syllable.[1] All proper names except place names have been marked with a long superlinear stroke. The only apparent exceptions are ⲆⲞⳌⲞⲘⲈⲆⲰⲚ and ⲈⲆⲞⲔⲖⲀ. Perhaps they were not considered beings but places.

The final ⲡ or ⲧ of a word as well as the ⲧ in ⲉⲧ-, ⲁⲧ- and ⲘⲚ̄Ⲧ-[2] are consistently marked by means of a backstroke or "flag." The purpose is clearly the same as the pointing in Codex III. The verb ⲉ͡ⲓ and the syllable ϩ͡ⲓ have a slightly rounded superlinear stroke

---

[1] The same is true for the most beautiful hand in the library found in Codices VII and the second half of XI. In contrast the superlinear strokes in Codices II and XII are much less accurate. In Codex II the stroke on the final letter of a construct form does not connect the last two consonants of that form but rather the last letter of the construct with the first letter of its complement. In Codex XII the scribe placed the stroke too far to the right.

[2] The exception is when the superlinear stroke runs only over the Ⲙ and Ⲛ rather than over all three letters (e.g. Ⲙ̄ⲚⲦⲘⲈ).

or circumflex.[1] Since most of the superlinear strokes are somewhat rounded, it is difficult to say whether the scribe intended to distinguish between the stroke on ⲉ͡ⲓ and ϩ͡ⲓ and the normal superlinear stroke. A diaeresis is used on the initial iota or upsilon of names. Paragraphing is accomplished by placing the first letter of the new paragraph in the margin (67, 2),[2] and by means of a colon (78, 10; 80, 25).

There are only four corrections in the extant text (54, 26; 57, 11; 59, 20 and 77, 1; see notes *in loco*). Emendations are necessary only in the following places (see the transcription notes for details): 62, 2; 63, 4; 72, 2; 74, 8.17; 75, 3 and 79, 11. However, IV is not without omissions. Instances of homoioteleuton occur at 52, 17 and 67, 27, and something has also been left out before 79, 17.

The tractate conforms to standard Sahidic spelling. It generally uses one form of a word consistently even when the Sahidic has several options. There are some minor exceptions as well as some pre-classical and unattested spellings. ⲉ† is used instead of ⲟ† as in many other Nag Hammadi texts; ⲛ̄ⲧⲱ⸗ (B) in 64, 25 against otherwise ⲛ̄ⲧⲁ⸗; ⲕⲟⲩⲟⲩⲛ̄ϥ in 75, 9 against four times ⲕⲟⲩⲛ⸗; ⲉⲧⲃⲏⲧ⸗ 63, 4 for ⲉⲧⲃⲏⲏⲧ and ⲁϩⲱⲣ instead of ⲁϩⲱⲱⲣ, 56, 15; 60, 17; ⲛ̄ⲙ- in 73, 11 against ⲙ̄ⲛ-; ⲙⲉϩϣⲟⲙⲉⲧ 64, 5; 68, 4; 77, 16 against otherwise ⲙⲉϩϣⲟⲙ̄ⲧ. ⲥⲟⲧ⸗ 71, 1 in place of ⲥⲁⲧ⸗ may be seen as an overly correct form. ⲛⲉⲁ⸗ in 74, 4; 75, 10 agrees with V 46, 10 etc. The form ⲧⲱⲱⲛ̄ϥ in 76, 11 is unattested, while ϣⲧ̄ⲣⲧ̄ⲣ in 66, 1 is also found in A^2 and Bodmer VI. In 78, 6 ⲥⲟⲩⲱⲛ- is used as *status constructus*.[3]

The articles ⲡⲓ, ϯ and ⲛⲓ are used very frequently, although not consistently. In IV 55, 3 it is striking that, contrary to the normal usage, the plural article ⲛⲓ is used before the number ϣⲙ̄ⲧ, although this may be explained as an error resulting from the frequent use of the plural article in the context. Noteworthy in this tractate is the almost exclusive use of ⲛ̄ⲧⲉ for the genitive. The ⲛ̄ is generally doubled before ⲁ, ⲉ and ⲟⲩ, and ⲁⲩⲱ is used to connect adjectives. ϣⲁ ⲉⲛⲉϩ with the exception of 65, 1 is not linked to the preceding noun with the normal adjectival ⲛ̄. Greek verbs are introduced by ⲣ̄-.

[1] Also the Greek vocative particle ὦ receives such a stroke but it does not occur in IV, *2*.

[2] The first letter of 51,1 is in the margin but it appears that this is due to the fact that the scribe had first written the ⲉ on the last line of page 50 but changed his mind after he had already written the ⲃⲟⲗ on 51,1.

[3] It may or may not be accidental that these forms occur mostly in the last part of the tractate.

The prefix ϭιⲛ-builds a masculine noun as in Bohairic (51, 6). The normal Perfect Relative is ⲉⲧⲁ, but also ⲉⲛⲧⲁ⸗ is used (58, 5; 62, 15).[1] The relative substantives are introduced by the demonstrative pronouns ⲡⲏ, ⲧⲏ, ⲛⲏ, as in Bohairic. There are only three definite cases where ⲡⲁϊ is the antecedent of the relative construction (53, 25; 55, 13 and 60, 4). Otherwise ⲡⲁϊ, ⲧⲁϊ and ⲛⲁϊ are used in ⲉⲧⲉ ⲡⲁϊ ⲡⲉ and when no relative construction is involved. ⲉⲧⲁ- functions as a Temporal after ϩⲟⲧⲁⲛ in 66, 2. Final clauses are constructed with ϩⲓⲛⲁ and the conjunctive,[2] and once with ϫⲉⲕⲁⲁⲥ and the II Future (63, 8). The tractate frequently uses the verbal prefix ⲉⲁ⸗ (51, 15; 52, 12.19; 59, 2.4.29; 61, 9.16; 63, 22; 64, 13; 66, 29; 78, 8; 80, 10). The parallel passages in III, *2*, when extant, use the I Perfect.[3] Most likely it is the use of the Perfect Circumstantial which here does not have the usual circumstantial function but rather continues a preceding I Perfect (STERN, *Kopt. Gram.* § 423).

The two Coptic versions of GEgypt are independent translations of basically the same Greek text, as is the case with the two versions of ApocryJn found in BG 8502 and III, *1*. The extent to which the numerous differences between III, *2* and IV, *2* go back to variants in the Greek *Vorlagen* or to the Coptic textual tradition must be investigated for each particular case and can not be established with certainty. The reader is referred to the commentary on the particular passages. That these manuscripts are copies of earlier Coptic manuscripts can be clearly demonstrated in the case of III. For instance this is seen first at III 55, 21-22 where two lines of the *Vorlage* have been omitted due to homoioteleuton, and secondly at III 63, 2 where ⲡⲛⲟⲩⲧⲉ instead of ⲡϯ is found.[4] In IV 52, 17 a similar case of homoioteleuton, where a complete line is apparently missing, suggests that IV too is a copy of a Coptic manuscript. If one assumes that the Coptic text of III has been frequently copied and either interpreted or even changed with more or less success, then a considerable

---

[1] The ⲛ̄ⲧⲁ in 51,18 and 53,1 appears to be II Perfect rather than the Perfect Relative.

[2] The third person singular is spelled ⲛ̄ⲧⲉϥ in 63, 2 and perhaps 63, 6, as in Bohairic. The third person singular feminine is spelled ⲛ̄ⲧⲁⲥ in 63,4 but this should be emended to ⲛ̄ⲧⲉⲥ. The other examples of the conjunctive conform to standard Sahidic.

[3] The two exceptions are III 52,2 (ϣⲁⲥ) and III 66,6 (Conjunctive following II Future).

[4] Cf. *infra*, p. 191.

number of the variants can be attributed to developments within the Coptic textual tradition. Similarly, unstandardized texts such as the old Syriac and old Latin textual traditions of the New Testament, as well as the Coptic translations of the book of Proverbs reflect the rather wide divergences typical for this period.

Initially the most striking difference between III, *2* and IV, *2* concerns translation policies. Although both versions are translations into the Sahidic dialect, the diction of III, *2* is strikingly different from that of IV, *2*. In III the translation is rather free, whereas IV reflects a concerted effort to render the Greek as faithfully as possible; for example, ⲣ̄ϣⲃⲏⲣ ⲛ̄ϯⲙⲉⲧⲉ for *συνευδοκεῖν*, ⲣ̄ⲁⲓⲧⲓ ⲛ̄ϣⲟⲣⲡ for *προαιτεῖν* (ⲁⲓⲧⲓ in III); ⲉⲟⲩⲉϩ̄ⲙ ϫⲡⲟ for *ἀναγεννᾶν* (ϫⲡⲟ in III). In IV 75, 19 ⲁϥⲟⲩⲟⲥϥⲟⲩ is a very literal translation of *ἐκύρωσεν*, "to make motionless" (cf. *infra*, p. 193f.). The use of Greek words is especially striking, since there are twice as many in III, *2* as in IV, *2*. In this respect also the relationship of these two manuscripts corresponds to that between III, *1* and BG ApocryJn. The following table provides a list of the corresponding Greek and Coptic terms used in both versions. The Coptic or Greek equivalents have been added in parentheses if they are used elsewhere in the tractate in question.

III	IV
ἄγειν (ⲉⲓⲛⲉ)	ⲉⲓⲛⲉ
ἀγέννητος	ⲁⲧⲙⲓⲥⲉ
ἅγιον (ⲉⲧⲟⲩⲁⲁⲃ)	ⲉⲧⲟⲩⲁⲁⲃ
ἄδηλος (ⲁⲧϣⲁϫⲉ ⲙ̄ⲙⲟ⸗)	ⲁⲧϣⲁϫⲉ ⲙ̄ⲙⲟ⸗
αἰών (ⲙ̄ⲛ̄ⲧϣⲁ ⲉⲛⲉϩ)	ⲉⲛⲉϩ (normally *αἰών*)
ἄκλητος (-*ν*)	ⲁⲧϫⲁϩⲙ⸗
ἀλήθεια (ⲙⲏⲉ, ⲙⲉ)	ⲙⲉ (*ἀλήθεια*)
ἀληθὲς ἀληθῶς	ϩⲛ̄ ⲟⲩⲙⲛ̄ⲧⲙⲉ ⲛⲁⲙⲉ
ἀληθῶς ἀληθῶς	ϩⲛ̄ ⲟⲩⲙⲛ̄ⲧⲙⲉ ⲛⲁⲙⲉ
ἀνάπαυσις	ⲙ̄ⲧⲟⲛ
ἀόρατος (-*ν*) (ⲁⲧⲛⲁⲩ ⲉⲣⲟ⸗)	ⲁⲧⲛⲁⲩ ⲉⲣⲟ⸗
ἀπάγειν (ϫⲓ)	ϫⲓ
ἀπερινόητος	ⲁⲧⲣ̄ϫⲓⲟⲟⲣ ⲙ̄ⲙⲟ⸗
ἄρρητος (ⲁⲧϣⲁϫⲉ ⲙ̄ⲙⲟ⸗)	ⲁⲧϣⲁϫⲉ ⲙ̄ⲙⲟ⸗
ἀρσενική (ϩⲟⲟⲩⲧ)	ϩⲟⲟⲩⲧ
ἀσήμαντος	ⲁⲧϯ ϣⲱⲗ̄ϩ ⲉⲣⲟ⸗, ⲙ̄ⲙⲁⲉⲓⲛ ⲁⲛ

αὐτογενής	ϫⲡⲟ ⲉⲃⲟⲗ ⲙ̄ⲙⲟ⸗ ⲙⲁⲩⲁⲁ⸗ (normally *αὐτογενής*)
αὐτογένιος	ϫⲡⲟ ⲉⲃⲟⲗ ⲙ̄ⲙⲟ⸗ ⲙⲁⲩⲁⲁ⸗
ἀφθαρσία	ⲁⲧϫⲱϩⲙ̄, ⲙⲛ̄ⲧⲁⲧϫⲱϩⲙ̄
ἄφθαρτος (-*ν*)	ⲁⲧϫⲱϩⲙ̄
βάπτισμα (ϫⲱⲕ̄ⲙ)	ϫⲱⲕ̄ⲙ, ⲱⲙ̄ⲥ
βίβλος (ϫⲱⲱⲙⲉ)	ϫⲱⲱⲙⲉ
γεννητός (ϫⲡⲟ)	ϫⲡⲟ
ⲥⲟⲟⲩⲛ	*γνῶσις* (ⲥⲟⲟⲩⲛ)
δύναμις (ϭⲟⲙ)	ϭⲟⲙ
ⲇⲟⲝⲟⲙⲉⲇⲱⲛ	ⲣⲉϥϯ ⲉⲟⲟⲩ
ἐπιγέννιος (ⲡⲓⲣⲉ ⲉⲃⲟⲗ)	ⲡⲓⲣⲉ ⲉⲃⲟⲗ ⲙ̄ⲙⲟ⸗ ⲙⲁⲩⲁⲁ⸗
ἐπίκλητος	ⲧⲱϩ̄ⲙ
ἐπιτροπή	ⲟⲩⲁϩ ⲥⲁϩⲛⲉ
ⲁⲧⲟⲩⲁϩⲙ⸗ (-*ἑρμηνεύειν*)	-*ἑρμηνεύειν*
-*εὐαγγελίζεσθαι*	ⲁⲧⲧⲁϣⲉ ⲟⲉⲓϣ ⲙ̄ⲙⲟ⸗
εὐδοκεῖν	ϯ ⲙⲉⲧⲉ
εὐδοκία	ϯ ⲙⲉⲧⲉ
θέλημα (ⲟⲩⲱϣ, ⲟⲩⲱϣⲉ)	ⲟⲩⲱϣ, ⲟⲩⲱϣⲉ
ϫⲉⲕⲁⲁⲥ	*ἵνα* (ϫⲉⲕⲁⲁⲥ)
ἱερά (ⲉⲧⲟⲩⲁⲁⲃ)	ⲉⲧⲟⲩⲁⲁⲃ
καιρός (ⲟⲩⲟⲉⲓϣ)	ⲟⲩⲟⲉⲓϣ
καταλύειν	ⲃⲱⲗ ⲉⲃⲟⲗ
κατανεύειν	ϯ ⲙⲉⲧⲉ
κεραννύναι	ϭⲱⲣ̄ϭ
κόλπος (ⲕⲟⲩⲟⲩⲛⲧ⸗)	ⲕⲟⲩⲛ⸗, ⲕⲟⲩⲟⲩⲛ⸗
κρίνειν (ϩⲁⲡ)	ϯ ϩⲁⲡ
κυροῦν (ⲧⲁϫⲣⲟ)	ⲧⲁϫⲣⲟ, ⲟⲩⲟⲥϥ⸗
λογογενής	ϫⲡⲟ ⲛ̄ϣⲁϫⲉ ϫⲡⲟ⸗ ϩ̄ⲛ ⲟⲩϣⲁϫⲉ
λόγος (ϣⲁϫⲉ)	ϣⲁϫⲉ
λοιμός (ⲙⲟⲩ)	ⲙⲟⲩ
ⲕⲟⲩⲟⲩⲛⲧ⸗	*μήτρα* (ⲕⲟⲩⲛ⸗, ⲕⲟⲩⲟⲩⲛ⸗)
μνήμη (ⲙⲉⲉⲩⲉ)	ⲙⲉⲉⲩⲉ
μορφή (ⲉⲓⲛⲉ)	ⲉⲓⲛⲉ (*μορφή*)
ὀνομάζειν, -*ὀνομάζειν* (ϯ ⲣⲁⲛ)	ϯ (ⲣⲁⲛ), ⲁⲧϯ ⲣⲁⲛ ⲉⲣⲟ⸗
ὁπλίζειν	ϩⲱⲱⲕ
παραστάτης	ⲉⲧⲁϩⲉⲣⲁⲧ⸗
πλανᾶν	ⲥⲱⲣ̄ⲙ
ϫⲱⲕ (*πλήρωμα*)	*πλήρωμα*

πρόγνωσις	ϭⲓⲛⲣ̄ϣⲟⲣⲡ̄ ⲛ̄ⲥⲟⲟⲩⲛ
προελθεῖν (ⲉ͡ⲓ ⲉⲃⲟⲗ)	ⲉ͡ⲓ ⲉⲃⲟⲗ, ⲣ̄ϣⲟⲣⲡ̄ ⲛ̄ⲉ͡ⲓ ⲉⲃⲟⲗ ⲣ̄ϣⲟⲣⲡ̄ ⲛ̄ⲟⲩⲱⲛ̄ϩ ⲉⲃⲟⲗ
ⲕⲁⲣⲱϥ (*σιγή*)	*σιγή* (ⲕⲁⲣⲱϥ)
σιγή (ⲕⲁⲣⲱϥ)	ⲕⲁⲣⲱϥ (*σιγή*)
ϫⲟ (normally *σπορά*)	*σπορά*
σταυροῦν	ⲉⲓϣⲉ
σύνεσις (ⲥⲟⲟⲩⲛ)	ⲥⲟⲟⲩⲛ
συνευδοκεῖν	ⲣ̄ϣⲃⲏⲣ ⲛ̄ϯ ⲙⲉⲧⲉ
τελεία (ϫⲏⲕ ⲉⲃⲟⲗ)	ⲉⲧϫⲏⲕ ⲉⲃⲟⲗ
ὑστέρημα	ϩⲁⲉ
φρόνησις	ⲥⲃⲱ
φωνή (ⲥⲙⲏ)	ⲥⲙⲏ
ⲟⲩⲟⲉⲓⲛ (*φωστήρ*)	*φωστήρ* (ⲟⲩⲟⲉⲓⲛ)
χάρις (ϩⲙⲟⲧ)	ϩⲙⲟⲧ
ⲟⲩⲟⲉⲓϣ (*χρόνος*)	*χρόνος* (ⲟⲩⲟⲉⲓϣ)
χωρεῖν	ϣ⟨ⲱ⟩ⲡ (*χωρεῖν*)
ⲛ̄ⲑⲉ	*ὡς* (ⲛ̄ⲑⲉ)

The list demonstrates the remarkable fact that the large number of Greek words in III did not cause an appreciable reduction in the Coptic vocabulary used in the tractate. For elsewhere in the tractate III uses the Coptic equivalent found in IV of half of its Greek vocabulary. In other words, in a large number of cases the use of Greek words in III is not due to the lack of an appropriate Coptic equivalent nor to uncertainty about the exact meaning of the Greek word. Here, as is generally the case with the Greek words in Coptic texts, it is not a matter of *whether* Greek words have been used in the Coptic translation, but *how many*.

Some reasons for the large number of Greek words in III are apparent. Greek in titles as well as words or phrases which have become or were in the process of becoming *termini technici* are preferred. Thus III retains the Greek words for "holy" only in the title and in "holy Spirit." Also such words as *αὐτογενής*, *αἰών*, *ἀνάπαυσις*, *ἀφθαρσία*, *δύναμις*, *ἐξουσία*, etc., fall into this category. On this point III shows more sensitivity to Gnostic religious idiom than IV. III does not have a consistent policy on the "negative" divine attributes.

There appears to be a tendency on the part of the Coptic-speaking Gnostic to appropriate for his own the Greek terminology of Gnosticism. This is especially strong in the untitled tractate from Codex

Brucianus. It is not necessary to assume that the Coptic translators of GEgypt were not able to translate certain words. Rather, to the extent that such words were not already present in vernacular Coptic, they intended to make a creative contribution to the language by importing Greek words. This was nothing unusual, since a great many Greek words had already been taken up into the vernacular. The fact that in certain places the translator of III allowed the feminine ending of the adjective to stand need not indicate lack of skill.[1] This phenomenon probably has been occasioned by the fact that the Greek expression formed a conceptual unit, for example, *ἀρσενικὴ παρθένος, πνευματικὴ ἐκκλησία, ἱερὰ βίβλος, ὑλικὴ σοφία*. The last expression does not even conform to Coptic grammar. In none of these expressions is there any reason to make corrections.

The appropriation of liturgical formulae in III betrays the same tendency as the appropriation of gnostic terminology. *εἶ ὃ εἶ, εἶ ὃς εἶ* in III and IV were taken over untranslated. In addition III has also left *εἶ ἕν* and *αἰὼν ὁ ὤν* untranslated. One should recall that the Coptic liturgy retains entire Greek sentences. It is also possible that the Coptic translators did not recognize these phrases to be Greek, since they are found in conjunction with unintelligible speech.

The places in which IV has a Greek word which differs from III need mentioning. In IV *ἀερόδιος* is not used but instead it is replaced by the genitival attribute ⲙ̄ⲡⲁⲏⲣ. *ἀλλογένιος* is replaced by the more frequently used word *ἀλλογενής*. In III *ἀποτάσσεσθαι* and *ἀπόταξις* occur, while IV has the synonym *ἀποταγή*. Furthermore IV has once *ἐπειδή* for *γάρ* and *οὔτε* for *οὐδέ*. III 54, 13 ff. has a main clause with *τότε* where IV 66, 2ff. has a dependent clause with *ὅταν*.

Scribal errors have also occured in Greek words, e.g. III has ⲁⲛⲁⲩⲡⲁⲩⲥⲓⲥ for ⲁⲛⲁⲡⲁⲩⲥⲓⲥ, ⲁⲡⲫⲁⲣⲧⲟⲥ (both an error and an unorthographic spelling) for ⲁⲫⲑⲁⲣⲧⲟⲥ, ⲅⲉⲛⲁ for ⲅⲉⲛⲉⲁ, and ⲥⲧⲣⲁⲅⲏⲧⲟⲥ for ⲥⲧⲣⲁⲧⲏⲅⲟⲥ. That IV has both ⲡⲁⲣⲁⲗⲏⲙⲡⲧⲱⲣⲟⲥ and ⲡⲁⲣⲁⲗⲏⲙⲁⲱⲣⲟⲥ is to be explained phonetically, as is ⲁⲡⲟⲣⲣⲟⲓⲁ with a single ⲣ. Also ⲡⲁⲣⲉⲥⲧⲁⲧⲏⲥ in III for ⲡⲁⲣⲁⲥⲧⲁⲧⲏⲥ need not be a mistake. ⲡⲗⲁⲥⲥⲁ in III instead of ⲡⲗⲁⲥⲥⲉ is also found in BG ApocryJn and SJC (cf. index s.v.).

[1] Cf. A. Böhlig, *Die griechischen Lehnwörter im sahidischen und bohairischen Neuen Testament* (München [2]1958), pp. 124ff.

It can be viewed as a change into another conjugation, especially when one considers that the form ⲉⲩⲭⲁⲣⲓⲥⲧⲁ is formed from ⲉⲩⲭⲁⲣⲓⲥⲧⲉⲓ. The use of itacistic spellings and the like are not uncommon in IV (e.g. ⲉⲱⲛ), but III is also not free from them (ⲕⲉⲣⲟⲥ, ⲉⲥⲑⲏⲥⲓⲥ). Thus it is not possible to deduce the quality of the texts from the orthography of the Greek words.

The proper names should be discussed along with the Greek words. They were not part of the vernacular, and a large number of them look like artificial formulations which must not have been known to all Gnostics. This made errors possible. A number of itacistic spellings and the like occur in IV, where III, apart from obvious misspellings, reflects the *Vorlage*. ⲥⲉⲗⲙⲉⲭⲉⲗ for ⲥⲉⲗⲙⲉⲗⲭⲉⲗ and the lack of ⲃⲁⲣ in ⲥⲉⲥⲉⲅⲅⲉⲛⲫⲁⲣⲁⲅⲅⲏⲥ appear to be errors in III, for example. ⲥⲁⲙⲗⲱ instead of ⲥⲁⲙⲃⲗⲱ could be a sound-spelling. There are also differences in endings between the two versions. The spelling ⲃⲁⲣⲃⲏⲗⲟⲛ (III, *2*) corresponds to that of III, *1* over against ⲃⲁⲣⲃⲏⲗⲱ in IV, *2* and ApocryJn II, *1*; IV, *1*; BG 8502. The "great James" stands over against the "great Jacob." Though in the New Testament the Greek ending is only used when naming contemporary persons, and ⲓⲁⲕⲱⲃ is used for the patriarch, one does not expect a reference to Jacob here.[1] Rather it should be noted that the Greek ending was not added when the name was mentioned in a ceremonial tone as is the case here. Why the attribute "the great" occurs instead of "the just" is not clear. Is James "the great" being contrasted with James "the less" (Bauer, *Lexicon*, s.v.) or has James, who still bears Jewish-Christian traits in the two apocalypses named after him in Codex V, become one among other great bringers of salvation? That would fit well with the advanced pluralism in Gnosticism as it is attested in the Nag Hammadi library. For Peter stands along side of James in ApocryJas, and ApocPaul is found in the same codex as I and II ApocJas.

For ⲓ̈ⲉⲥⲥⲉⲩⲥ ⲙⲁⲍⲁⲣⲉⲩⲥ ⲓ̈ⲉⲥⲥⲉⲇⲉⲕⲉⲩⲥ, as in ApocAd V 85, 30f., the hymn in III 66, 8-22 has the vocative ⲓ̈ⲉⲥⲥⲉⲩ ⲙⲁⲍⲁⲣⲉⲩ ⲓ̈ⲉⲥⲥⲉⲇⲉⲕⲉⲩ while IV uses the nominative of the second declension, ⲓ̈ⲉⲥⲥⲉⲟⲥ etc.[2] On the other hand both manuscripts have the accusative -ⲉⲁ in a place where the accusative may have occurred in the *Vorlagen*. The accusative also remains with other names:

---

[1] Blass-Debrunner § 53,2.

[2] Cf. Böhlig, *Lehnwörter*, pp. 117ff.

ⲁⲕⲣⲁⲙⲁⲛ (III, IV) ⲙⲓⲕⳓⲁⲛⲑⲏⲣⲁ (IV), ⲙⲓⲭⲁⲛⲟⲣⲁ (III, IV), ⲙⲓⲭⲉⲁ (III, IV), ⲥⲟⲇⲟⲙⲏⲛ (III, IV). The nominative of these words occurs in ⲙⲓⳓⲁⲛⲑⲏⲣ (III), ⲙⲓⲭⲉⲩⲥ (III, but IV ⲙⲓⲥⲉⲩⲥ).[1] In IV 76, 4 ⲙⲛⲏⲥⲓⲛⲟⲩ could be ⲙⲛⲏⲥⲓⲛⲟⲩⲛ (III has ⲙⲛⲏⲥⲓⲛⲟⲩⲥ). The ⲛ falls away easily, especially here at the end of the line, where it can be indicated by a stroke over the last letter which could have been combined with the stroke used over the proper name. The name *Μνησινοῦς* is a typical Greek compound word. The forms for Sodom are especially interesting. To protect the final consonant an ⲁ had become attached as in *Ἱεροσόλυμα* : *Σόδομα* III 56, 10; 60, 18; IV 71, 30. This word, inflected as a plural neuter noun, has followed the pattern of *Γομόρρα*, while until now only the reverse phenomenon was known.[2] In both instances of the accusative *Σοδόμην* in III, the corresponding place in IV has the nominative *Σοδόμη*. It remains a question whether this had already developed in Greek or is a construction of the Coptic translator. The occurrences of *Σόδομα* speak for the latter. Perhaps in IV the final ⲛ has fallen away because the next word begins with ⲛ̄.

A peculiarity of IV lies in the attempt to translate *Δοξομέδων* once with ⲣⲉϥϯ ⲉⲟⲟⲩ. Although IV as a rule strives to be faithful to the Greek text, the translator was not able to avoid mistranslations completely. IV 52, 17 renders *δόξα* by means of ⲥⲟⲟⲩⲛ, although here it should certainly be translated by ⲉⲟⲟⲩ as in III. When IV 76, 27 speaks of the "slain souls" in contrast to III 65, 7 "souls of the elect", the different translations of the Greek word *ἐξαιρηθείς* (Aorist passive participle of *ἐξαιρεῖν* "to slay" or *ἐξαιρεῖσθαι* "to elect") could have been in the *Vorlagen*. Likewise III 61, 17f. and IV 73, 1 can go back to the different meanings of *ἀμφιβολία*, just as ⲧⲱϩⲙ̄ in IV 75, 7 may well render *ἐπίκλητος*. Real misunderstanding seems to occur in III 60, 21. Furthermore, there are in III a considerable number of misinterpretations, secondary expansions as well as omissions. In light of this, III must be considered the inferior version. (See commentary for particulars).

---

[1] ⲙⲓⲥⲉⲩⲥ is not a misspelling but goes back to palatalization, cf. *κασία* for *κακία* (E. Schwyzer, *Griechische Grammatik* I, p. 160). Cf. also Rev 18:13 ⲥⲓⲛⲁⲙⲱⲙⲟⲛ (sa) for *κιννάμωμον*.

[2] Blass-Debrunner § 38 and 57.

THE TITLE

Ever since JEAN DORESSE's brief description of III, *2* in "Trois livres gnostiques inédits: Évangile des Égyptiens, Épître d'Eugnoste, Sagesse de Jésus Christ" [1] the tractate has been known as "The Gospel of the Egyptians". This is the name given to the tractate at the beginning of the scribal colophon in III 69, 6. The formal title of the tractate as stated at the end of the colophon III 69, 16-17 and again, with the usual decorations, directly below the colophon (III 69, 18-20) reads ⲧⲃⲓⲃⲗⲟⲥ ⲧϩⲓⲉⲣⲁ ⲙ̄ⲡⲛⲟϭ ⲛ̄ⲁϩⲟⲣⲁⲧⲟⲛ ⲙ̄ⲡⲛⲉⲩⲙⲁ (69, 17 ⲡ̄ⲛ̄ⲁ̄) ϩⲁⲙⲏⲛ.[2] The title "The Holy Book of the Great Invisible Spirit" should have been preferred but DORESSE's title is now too well established to change it.[3]

Strictly speaking, the colophon does not read "The Gospel of the Egyptians" but "The Egyptian Gospel" (ⲡⲉⲩⲁⲅⲅⲉⲗⲓⲟⲛ ⲛ̄ⲣ̄ⲙ̄ⲛ̄ⲕⲏⲙⲉ).[4] However, the adjective in this context would be most unusual if not unprecedented. All parallel expressions, such as the Gospel of Peter, of Mary, of the Hebrews, of the Ebionites, etc., refer to persons either as the users of the gospel or as the alleged authors. Such titles as the Gospel of Truth or the Gospel of Perfection refer either to the subject matter or make a value judgement about the book. Therefore, the adjective "Egyptian" with "gospel" should be rejected as rendering a most unlikely, if not impossible, meaning. Either the scribe skipped one of the three ⲛ's or the plural article was left out, as is done more often with the names of nations in the genitive case.[5] The German translation "Ägypterevangelium" allows one to skirt the problem.[6]

---

1 *Vigiliae Christianae* II (1948), 137-143.

2 The ϩⲁⲙⲏⲛ in 69,17 closes the colophon and should not be considered a part of the title. The final decorated title in 69,18-20 is a copy of the title at the end of the colophon and it consequently retained the ϩⲁⲙⲏⲛ. A jagged line is placed directly under the title decoration perhaps to prevent further writing on the page.

3 DORESSE himself now uses the double title "Le Livre sacré du grand Esprit invisible" ou "L'Évangile des Égyptiens," in his publication of the text and translation of III, *2* in *Journal Asiatique* 254 (1966), 317-435 (appeared early 1968).

4 ⲣ̄ⲙ̄ⲛ̄ⲕⲏⲙⲉ is the usual adjective of ⲕⲏⲙⲉ, see CRUM, *Dict.* p. 110a.

5 See HANS QUECKE, *Das Markusevangelium Saïdisch, Text der Handschrift PPalau Rib. Inv.-Nr. 182 mit den Varianten der Handschrift M 569* (Barcelona 1972), pp. 46f.

6 This is the title used by ALEXANDER BÖHLIG in his publication of a tentative translation and short commentary of III 40,12 - 55,16 and its parallel IV 50,1 - 67,1 in "Die himmlische Welt nach dem Ägypterevangelium von Nag Hammadi," *Le Muséon*

The question which remains is where the two titles came from. Martin Krause believes that the formal title at the end is an abbreviation of the full title given in the colophon : ⲡⲉⲩⲁⲅⲅⲉⲗⲓⲟⲛ ⲛ̄ⲣ̄ⲙ̄ⲛ̄ⲕⲏⲙⲉ ⲧⲃⲓⲃⲗⲟⲥ ⲛ̄ⲥϩⲁï ⲛ̄ⲛⲟⲩⲧⲉ ⲧϩⲓⲉⲣⲁ ⲉⲧϩⲏⲡ (69, 6-8).[1] This is unlikely, not only because it is difficult to see 69, 16-17 and 18-20 as an abbreviation of 69, 6-8, but because the formal title is obviously taken from the incipit to the tractate (III 40,12f. = IV 50,1-3).

Many of the titles in the Nag Hammadi library prove to be secondarily developed from the incipit to the tractate. In the earliest stage no title is present but the incipit lends itself to an easy identification of the tractate. The Gospel of Truth (I, *2*) is the most obvious example of this. One step removed from this is the title of VI, *7* where the first part of the incipit "This is the Prayer that they spoke" has been made into a title by means of some decorative lines and diples. In the next development a phrase or abbreviation of the incipit has been made into the formal title either at the beginning or at the end of the tractate. Indentation and decorative marks clearly separate it from the body of the tractate. Tractates in this category are: the Hypostasis of the Archons (II, *4*), the Apocalypse of Adam (V, *5*), the Paraphrase of Shem (VII, *1*), and the Three Steles of Seth (VII, *5*).[2] The formal title at the end of III, *2* clearly belongs with this group.

In the next group the title is formed by means of a short interpretative rephrasing of the incipit. In this category belong the Apocryphon of John (II, *1*; III, *1*; IV, *1*), the Gospel of Thomas (II, *2*), the Book of Thomas the Contender (II, *7*), the Letter of Eugnostos the Blessed (III, *3*; V, *1*), the Apocalypse of Paul (V, *2*), the Apocalypse of James (V, *3*), the Apocalypse of James (V, *4*), and the Letter of Peter which he sent to Philip (VIII, *2*). A closer look at these titles reveals that there was more involved than the need for a short and memorable phrase. What stands out is that the canonical terms "gospel", "letter" and "apocalypse" have been introduced even

---

LXXX (1967), 5-26 and 365-377, and by Hans-Martin Schenke for his German translation, based on Doresse's transcription, in "Das Ägypter-Evangelium aus Nag-Hammadi-Codex III," *NTS* XVI (1969/70), 196-208.

[1] *Die drei Versionen*, p. 19 n. 7.

[2] Zost (VIII, *1*) probably also belongs to this category. VII, *1* has its title at the beginning, II, *4* and VII, *5* at the end, and V, *5* both at the beginning and at the end of the tractate.

though these designations were not used in the tractate itself. These secondary titles betray a Christianization process.

It appears now that the title at the beginning of the colophon in III, *2* is such a Christianization of the first line of the incipit. The uncertainty is due to the unfortunate lacunae at the beginning of both versions. The general structure of the incipit is clear. After the designation "holy book" there follow two clauses. Using the evidence of both versions the following reconstruction can be considered certain:

III ⲡϫⲱⲱⲙⲉ ⲛ̄ⲧϩ[ⲓⲉ]ⲣ̣[ⲁ ⲛ̄ⲧⲉ ⲛ.......] ⲛ̄ⲧⲉ ⲡⲓⲛⲟϭ ⲛⲁⲧⲛⲁⲩ ⲉⲣ[ⲟϥ ⲙ̄ⲡⲛⲁ·]
IV [ⲡϫⲱⲱⲙⲉ ⲉⲧⲟⲩⲁ]ⲁ̣ⲃ ⲛ̄ⲧⲉ ⲛⲓ[....... ⲛ̄ⲧⲉ] ⲡ̣ⲓⲛⲟϭ ⲛ̄ⲛⲁ-[ⲧⲛⲁⲩ ⲉⲣⲟϥ ⲙ̄ⲡⲛⲁ·]

It is immediately apparent that the title in III 69, 18-20 is taken from the incipit, combining the introductory phrase "the holy book" with the second attribute introduced by ⲛ̄ⲧⲉ.[1] All that remains of the word following the first ⲛ̄ⲧⲉ is the plural article in Codex IV. Fortunately there is a close parallel to the opening lines of GEgypt. The incipit of 3StSeth (VII, *5*) reads ⲡⲟⲩⲱⲛ̄ϩ ⲉⲃⲟⲗ (= ἡ *ἀποκάλυψις*) ⲛ̄ⲧⲉ ⲇⲱⲥⲓⲑⲉⲟⲥ ⲛ̄ⲧⲉ ϯϣⲟⲙⲧⲉ ⲛ̄ⲥⲧⲏⲗⲏ ⲛ̄ⲧⲉ ⲥⲏ̄ⲑ̄.[2] The ⲡⲟⲩⲱⲛ̄ϩ ⲉⲃⲟⲗ is parallel to the "the holy book". The first ⲛ̄ⲧⲉ introduces the person with whom the tractate is associated, in this case the mythological author, and the second ⲛ̄ⲧⲉ introduces the main subject matter. Thus the parallel in VII, *5* strongly suggests that the word in the lacuna refers to persons. If the ⲡⲉⲩⲁⲅⲅⲉⲗⲓⲟⲛ ⟨ⲛ̄⟩ⲛ̄ⲣ̄ⲙ̄ⲛ̄ⲕⲏⲙⲉ is derived from the incipit then these persons must be the Egyptians. A careful measurement of the available space shows that ⲣ̄ⲙ̄ⲛ̄ⲕⲏⲙⲉ fits very well in both cases.

The colophon has a much more Christian character than the tractate

---

[1] Translations of some of the titles are often left partly or completely in Greek. Examples of this are:

IV, *1* ⲕⲁⲧⲁ ⲓ̈ⲱ[ⲁⲛ]ⲏⲛ ⲁⲡⲟⲕⲣⲩⲫⲟⲛ (49,27f.)
VI, *3* ⲁⲩⲑⲉⲛⲧⲓⲕⲟⲥ ⲗⲟⲅⲟⲥ (35,23f.)
VII, *2* ⲇⲉⲩⲧⲉⲣⲟⲥ ⲗⲟⲅⲟⲥ ⲧⲟⲩ ⲙⲉⲅⲁⲗⲟⲩ ⲥⲏⲑ (70,11-12)
VII, *3* ⲁⲡⲟⲕⲁⲗⲩⲯⲓⲥ ⲡⲉⲧⲣⲟⲩ (70,13; 84,14)
XIII, *1* ⲡⲗⲟⲅⲟⲥ ⲛ̄ⲧⲉⲡⲓⲫⲁⲛⲓⲁ ⲅ̄, ⲡⲣⲱⲧⲉⲛⲛⲟⲓⲁ ⲧⲣⲓⲙⲟⲣⲫⲟⲥ ⲅ̄, ⲁⲅⲓⲁ ⲅⲣⲁⲫⲏ ⲡⲁⲧⲣⲟⲅⲣⲁⲫⲟⲥ ⲉⲛ ⲅⲛⲱⲥⲉⲓ ⲧⲉⲗⲉⲓⲁ (50, 18-21).

[2] VII 118,10-12.

itself, which can at best only be called marginally Christian. This is especially seen in the presence of the Christian confession *Ἰησοῦς Χριστὸς θεοῦ υἱὸς σωτήρ* followed by the ⲒⲬⲐⲨⲤ monogram (69, 14f.). Therefore, just as the term *εὐαγγέλιον* in the title of the Gospel of Thomas appears to be an apologetic adaptation of "the secret words" in the incipit [1], so the word *εὐαγγέλιον* in the colophon of III, *2* can be seen as a Christianizing interpretation of "the holy book" in the incipit. Also the second line of the colophon reflects the content of the tractate. ⲦⲂⲒⲂⲖⲞⲤ ⲚⲤϨⲀÏ ⲚⲚⲞⲨⲦⲈ ⲦϨⲒⲈⲢⲀ ⲈⲦϨⲎⲠ (69, 7f.) refers to the authorship of the book by Seth who hid it in high mountains on which the sun has not risen.[2]

The mythological heavenly Seth inspired by God was the author of this writing. When one considers the fact that Seth was made the father of the seed of the primal Father, then he can also be assigned by the primal Father to write a holy book. The meaning of the phrase introduced by ⲚⲦⲈ is difficult. Is it a subjective or objective genitive? Is it a holy book which the Egyptians possess and which is about the great invisible Spirit or which originates from the invisible Spirit? If one feels obliged to see an exact parallelism to the title of 3StSeth, then the first meaning would be fitting. If one considers the circumstance that in Greek, and correspondingly in Coptic, the genitive occurred, one should be conscious of its ambiguity. One could consider it to be a genitive of relation which is also possible in the case of 3StSeth. Such a genitive can mean "pertaining to", that is, either "belonging to" or "concerning".[3] Perhaps the ambiguity is intended for the Gnostic reader.

Why did the author of the colophon re-name the writing a gospel? One could, of course, be satisfied with seeing a mechanical process in this re-naming, since in this case "holy book" could mean "gospel", assuming the Christianizing tendency. A scribe familiar with the title of the Christian apocryphal Gospel of the Egyptians would have been especially tempted to replace "holy book" with "gospel".

But one can also argue on the basis of the content and not only on the basis of the title. Then it would be well to proceed from the passages in which Jesus and Christ occur in this writing. Christ is a figure in heaven and Jesus is the embodiment of Seth on earth.

---

[1] II 32,10f.

[2] III 68,1-4.

[3] Cf. in Coptic ⲠⲀ-, ⲦⲀ-, ⲚⲀ-.

The central position occupied by Seth in the work makes it not difficult to see it as a gospel of Seth, since the creation of Seth is presented in the framework of the creation of the heavenly and lower world. To be sure, a gospel for the Gnostics is not only a report about the work and words of the historical Jesus, and not a literary genre as in the ecclesiastical formation of the canon, but a view of the history of the world *sub specie aeternitatis* in which the way of those to be redeemed and the way of the redeemer is presented. For this an explanation of their origin was necessary, and therefore, a description of the light-world. The other Gnostic gospels also can only be understood on the basis of a real Gnostic-cosmic view. The Gospel of Thomas, which has only sayings, is only understandable against the background of this cosmic view. The Gospel of Philip employs mythological conceptions. In the Gospel of Truth Jesus is pictured as the redeemer in a cosmic framework. In the present document the Christianization process is completed by the writer of the colophon who explains the book as a gospel on the basis of the identification of Seth with Jesus. It is to be assumed that the colophon did not exist in IV, *2*.

It remains a question why the writing was connected with the Egyptians. This could point to an origin in Egypt. One can, however, just as legitimately accept the explanation that the naming was done by non-Egyptians who wanted to see in it references to Egypt. With great caution can one infer a connection with Egypt on the basis of the name Seth alone. Perhaps in Egypt someone may have connected the Seth of the Old Testament with the Egyptian god Seth.[1] Although Seth is often seen as an evil god, there were strong tendencies in the later period to remove this onus from him. In magical texts he is designated as the god who hates evil.[2] It is even said of him that he did *not* injure his brother. A change in evaluation of a being from negative to positive is moreover very common in Gnosticism.[3] One encounters a typical example in GEgypt, where Sodom and Gomorrah are seen not as cities of sin but as holy cities.[4] When one considers that the Egyptian god Seth was accused of sodomy, it is a short step to see GEgypt as an attempt to change the role of the Egyptian Seth

---

[1] Cf. HERMANN KEES, "Seth" in *Pauly-Wissowa RE* 2.R., 2.Hbd., col. 1896-1922; cf. also HANS BONNET, *Reallexikon der ägyptischen Religionsgeschichte* (Berlin 1952), Art. Seth, col. 702-715.

[2] Cf. KEES, col. 1921.

[3] ALEXANDER BÖHLIG, *Mysterion und Wahrheit* (Leiden 1968), pp. 82f.

[4] III 56,8-13 (IV is lost); III 60,9-18 = IV 71,18-30.

or to surpass him with Seth, the son of Adam. The Egyptian Seth who was a well-known and powerful god, and who was incarnate in the Pharaoh,[1] is then changed into the biblical Seth of the Gnostics who was revealed in Jesus. The Sethians thereby claim to have the correct theology of Seth.[2]

The issue remains of the strange ⲧ of ⲛ̄ⲧϩⲓⲉⲣⲁ in III 40, 12. It should be kept in mind that the twice-stated title at the end of the tractate as well as the incipit of IV, *2* support the reading "the holy book". Secondly, the Coptic translator of III, *2*, who also translated the colophon and the title, has in the three parallel occurrences of the word (69, 6f. 16.19) translated word for word : ἡ βίβλος ἡ ἱερά = ⲧⲃⲓⲃⲗⲟⲥ ⲧϩⲓⲉⲣⲁ. The colophon has the typical style of an interlinear version, thereby showing its origin from a Greek *Vorlage*. The first two words of the incipit were in the same way literally translated but the Greek ἡ βίβλος was substituted by ⲡϫⲱⲱⲙⲉ, ἡ ἱερά was retained, however, in spite of the difference of gender, and preceded by ⲛ̄. Can one perhaps suppose that ⲧϩⲓⲉⲣⲁ was seen as one word and that ⲛ̄ is a connective particle indicating the adjective? Although this construction is not attested, the alternative of assuming that the title in III, *2* differed from the title in IV, *2* is more difficult. Therefore, the text has been emended.

---

[1] Cf. Kees, col. 1905-1908; 1911.

[2] On the problem of identifying Sethian teaching see "The Sethians and the Nag Hammadi Library" by Frederik Wisse in *Society of Biblical Literature 1972 Proceedings* Vol. 2, pp. 601-607.

THE CONTENT

The so-called Gospel of the Egyptians is a typical work of mythological Gnosticism. In spite of the basic work of HANS JONAS,[1] writings of this kind still do not receive their due appreciation. They too have a situation in life (*Sitz im Leben*) — indeed, a situation in intellectual life. To view ourselves only as the heirs of the classical period of Greek philosophy, to devaluate other ancient ways of thought, and to discard what is different is too easy a solution. It is not the task of a historian to become a Gnostic himself, but he must make a serious effort to discern the peculiar inner logic of each text. He may not terminate the investigation with the assertion that the text is abstruse.

The question must be asked why a confusing abundance of mythological names and events are offered in a text which in the colophon is even designated as a gospel. Does this literature emerge out of theological and philosophical thought or is it the result of a partly magical, partly fanciful degeneration? Magical currents, however, are to be found in Neoplatonists worthy of serious consideration (Iamblichus), and the use of myth (*Mythos*) was a legitimate means of philosophical presentation since Plato. The combination of dialogue and myth he used has been retained in those Gnostic writings in which a mythological main part serves to answer a question, such as II, *5*, for example, where Hesiod's thesis of the origin of the world from chaos provides the point of departure for the discussion. Another example is found in Eugnostos, the Blessed (III, *3*; V, *1*) where the problems of pagan philosophers are answered with a mythological presentation. Likewise in the Exegesis on the Soul (II, *6*) the opinions of "the wise" serve as the starting point of the writing. Thus the disparagement of mythological Gnosticism because of its use of myths is unfounded.

Another question is whether the mythological presentation so predominates that it becomes an end in itself and eclipses the main thought with the result that the logical structure of the work is no longer apparent. As a parallel one could cite the relationship of theology and liturgy in the liturgies of the eastern churches. According to contemporary opinion the influence of arithmology led to an uncon-

---

[1] HANS JONAS, *Gnosis und spätantiker Geist* (3 ed. Göttingen 1964).

trolled overgrowth. At least concerning the Pythagoreans it has been claimed that "the oddities of symbolic explanation (*Deuterei*) into which they fell should not cause us to overlook that thereby the attempt was made to recognize an enduring conceptual order of things and to find their ultimate basis in mathematical relationships".[1] The same allowance should be made for the Gnostics, for whom numerical harmony also played an important role.

Likewise, the thought pattern of a prototype and its counterpart (*Urbild-Abbild*), which already in an older form came out of Pythagoreanism, required a considerable expansion of the mythology. For the cosmic world must indeed have its prototype in the heavenly world. The Gnostics wanted to have information about this heavenly world, irrespective of whether the supreme, unknowable God was assumed to be within the heavenly world or to exist above it. Furthermore, some Gnostics made another distinction within the world itself by separating cosmic prototype from an earthly counterpart. Such speculation can likewise be explained, particularly since the dualism in these Gnostic systems is a prominent factor as is also the astrological view of the world.

The discussion of man and his soul is actually the main theme of Gnosticism. The cosmogonic and cosmological constructions of Gnosticism form the logical presuppositions for its anthropology and psychology. The myth (*Mythos*) of Greek philosophy is combined with the view of the history of salvation as it was developed by Judaism and taken up by Christianity. Such a constructed myth (*Kunstmythos*) made use of individual myths circulating in the Near East. The syncretistic multiplicity and frequent parallel arrangement and combination cause the picture to appear kaleidoscopic and confusing for the non-specialist. However, when one investigates the relationship of the religious content to the form of expression, a definite structure can generally be discerned. To see mythological Gnosticism as a degeneration would be a misunderstanding of its method. For even Christocentric Gnosticism such as that of the Gospel of Thomas, the Gospel of Philip, the Gospel of Truth, and the Treatise on the Resurrection can really be understood only in terms of a mythological understanding of existence, and presents a less perplexing picture only because Jesus Christ is so much in the foreground. Some of the

---

[1] W. Windelband, *Lehrbuch der Geschichte der Philosophie*, ed. H. Heimsoeth (15th ed. Tübingen 1957), p. 41.

Nag Hammadi writings are difficult to understand because they are compilations of various pieces of tradition. Yet the fact that such a compilation has not always been successfully carried out does not contradict that Gnosticism was able to communicate by means of mythology, as the following analysis of the content of GEgypt will attempt to make clear.

The tractate can be divided into four main sections.

I. The origin of the heavenly world: III 40, 12-55, 16 = IV 50, 1-67, 1.
II. The origin, preservation and salvation of the race of Seth: III 55, 16-66, 8 = IV 67, 2-78, 10.
III. The hymnic section: III 66, 8-67, 26 = IV 78, 10-80, 15.
IV. The concluding section dealing with the origin and transmission of the tractate: III 68, 1-69, 17 = IV 80, 15-81 end.

I. The supreme God dwells in solitary height. He is light and silence, and he is primarily described by means of negative attributes. His Pronoia still lives within him. He does not emanate a divine being in order to beget a third being with her, but rather evolves in such a way that a trinity made up of Father, Mother and Son comes forth. At the same time, the Domedon (Lord of the house) comes into being who is usually called Doxomedon (Lord of glory). He can be considered to be the aeon which envelops the world of light. Over against the alien, supreme God, he may be regarded as a kind of second God. After the main description,[1] this evolutionary development is mentioned once more, this time from a viewpoint which takes the members of the trinity to be ogdoads. The first ogdoad, the Father, is made up of *ἔννοια, λόγος, ἀφθαρσία*, eternal life, *θέλημα, νοῦς, πρόγνωσις* and Father.[2] The second ogdoad, the Mother, also bears the name Barbelo. Her parts are complex mythological entities which are hard to identify, partly due to the lacunae in both versions. The third ogdoad, the Son, is made up of himself together with the seven voices.[3]

After the detailed description of the ogdoads follows a section in which the Doxomedon-aeon is pictured, now in greater detail, as a heavenly throne room. A plaque has been attached to the throne with an inscription on it made up of all the vowels of the Greek alphabet with each vowel listed twenty-two times — the total number of letters in the Semitic alphabet.

[1] III 41,7-23 = IV 50,23 - 51,15.

[2] Cf. *infra*, pp. 171f.

[3] III 41,23 - 43,8 = IV 51,15 - 53,3.

Having provided a picture of the genesis of the heavenly primal powers, the text continues with their liturgical activities. Presentations of praise and accompanying requests for the sending forth of a new power are now typical for the further development of the action, particularly in the first section, although this literary device is also used in the second section.

1. The primal trinity turns to the great invisible Spirit and the Barbelo. As a consequence the thrice-male child fills the Doxomedon-aeon.

2. The thrice-male child — now shown to belong to the great Christ — in turn makes a request of the great invisible Spirit and the Barbelo. The male virgin Youel comes into being. Next the Splenditenens Esephech appears. The thrice-male child, Youel and Esephech are considered the five seals of the primal trinity and together they form its completion.[1]

3. There is a presentation of praise, of which the subject has to be inferred,[2] on the bottom fragment of IV 57.[3] In IV 59 we find a female being (probably *πρόνοια*) who, while passing through the aeons, establishes angelic powers which are to praise the trinity and its pleroma. The pleroma seems to be made up of the five seals and is also referred to here as the great Christ. After the great Christ comes the great Logos, the divine *αὐτογενής*. The Logos functions next as the heavenly creator.

4. The Logos offers praise to the great invisible Spirit. As a result Mirothoe appears, a great cloud of light, who begets the Light-Adamas. The supreme God appears in Adamas in order to eliminate the deficiency in the lower regions. The Logos and the Light-Adamas are united.

5. The Logos and Adamas offer praise and pray together for the pleroma of the lights. Adamas, on his own, requests that he may beget his son Seth. As a fulfillment of the request, the lights Harmozel, Oroiael, Davithe and Eleleth are begotten, and likewise the great Seth. The four lights, together with the perfect hebdomad, form eleven ogdoads. It is not further specified with what kind of hebdomad we are dealing here. The lights are complemented with consorts

[1] They add up to eight although this is not mentioned.

[2] The fragmentary state of IV 57-58 and the complete loss of the corresponding pages in Codex III leaves the total number of the presentations of praise uncertain.

[3] IV 57,13ff.

(χάρις, αἴσθησις, σύνεσις, φρόνησις) and thus become themselves an ogdoad. Added to these is another ogdoad made up of ministers and their consorts: Gamaliel, Gabriel, Samblo and Abrasax with μνήμη, ἀγάπη, εἰρήνη and Eternal Life. These two ogdoads, together with the three ogdoads of the Father, the Mother and the Son form a quintet of ogdoads, a total of forty heavenly beings.

6. The Logos and the pleroma of the four lights give praise and request that the Father may be called the fourth in respect to the incorruptible race, and that the seed of the Father may be called the seed of the great Seth. In response to this prayer the thrice-male child appears together with the great Christ who creates a church of angelic beings which praises the trinity of Father, Mother and Son, and their pleroma. This church has the task of bringing the revelation to those who are worthy. The section ends with "amen", indicating that the first main part has come to an end.[1]

II. The second main section is dominated by the work of Seth. As the son of Adamas, he was one of the lower powers of the world of light. Through him, the light in the lower world is connected with the supreme God. The fact that the church of angelic beings was created in answer to the request to call the children of the Father the seed of Seth, is probably an indication that this church of angelic beings, which has been begotten by the thrice-male child and Christ and thus is the seed of the Father, now represents the heavenly prototype of the race of Seth.

Also in this section of the tractate presentations of praise with prayer and response are used twice as a stylistic device. However, this time Seth performs the action. The first prayer begins the section which deals with the creation of the seed, i.e. the race of Seth. In the second prayer Seth asks God for guards for his seed. A third segment of this section then describes how Seth himself performs the work of salvation.

In answer to the first prayer Plesithea, the virgin with the four breasts, comes into being. She is the "mother of the angels, the mother of the lights, the glorious mother".[2] She produces the seed of Seth out of Sodom and Gomorrah, and Seth accepts it with great joy and places it in the four aeons, in the third phoster Davithe.

---

[1] III 55,16 = IV 67,1.

[2] III 56,6ff. (IV is lost).

Following this presentation, a description of the origin of the creator of the world is inserted to clarify the background of the work of Seth and his race in the world. His origin goes back to the wish of the light Eleleth, who thinks it appropriate that after 5000 years a ruler over chaos and the underworld should come into being. Gamaliel, the minister of the light Oroiael, speaks the creative word upon which the hylic Sophia, who already has come forth, divides herself into two parts, the second of which becomes the angel Saklas. Together with the demon Nebruel, he creates twelve angelic assistants and orders them to become rulers over their worlds. Upon completion of the world he finally says in mistaken self-confidence, "I am a jealous God, and apart from me, nothing has come into being".[1] This claim is refuted by a voice from heaven which rebukes him with the words, "The Man exists and the Son of Man".[2] Along with the voice, an image appears which presents the occasion for the creation of the first creature (*πλάσμα*). In order to help him, the *μετάνοια* appears. On account of God's approval (*εὐδοκία*) of the race of the sons of Seth, he sends the *μετάνοια* to eliminate the *ὑστέρημα*. She prayed for (the repentance of) the children of the evil Archon as well as those of Adam and Seth.

After this cosmogonic section the author returns to the creation of the seed of Seth. A new mythological figure, the angel Hormos, appears. He creates the seed of Seth in a *λογογενὲς σκεῦος* through the Holy Spirit, although by means of mortal maidens. The great Seth sows his seed into the created aeons. Again Sodom and Gomorrah are mentioned. It is the place of the planting, or the place of origin. Still a third origin of the seed of Seth is reported. Through a word, Edokla gives birth to truth and justice, the beginning of the seed of life eternal and of all those who persevere because they know their heavenly origin, i.e. the children of Seth. Thus they are scattered over both the heavenly and the lower world. The problem lies in their existence in the world, for there they are exposed to dangers. Flood, fire, starvation and pestilence threaten them, afflictions which occur because of them. The devil is considered the originator of these afflic-

---

[1] III 58,25f. (IV is lost).

[2] III 59,2ff. (IV is lost). As an answer to the arrogance of Ialdabaoth this voice is also mentioned in OnOrWld II 103 (151), 19f. where it refers to the immortal man of light. The reference to the existence of Man and the Son of Man also occurs in ApocryJn (II 14,14f. = III 21,17f. = BG 47,15f.), but there it is directed toward Pistis Sophia.

tions. He is characterized by his many guises and the strife within his realm. Therefore Seth raises his voice in presentation of praise and prayer for the protection of his seed. In response, 400 angels come forth under the leadership of Aerosiel and Selmelchel to guard the men of Seth. The earthly history of the children of Seth begins after the creation of *ἀλήθεια* and *θέμισσα* and continues until the end of the world, when the judgment of the present aeon and its archons will take place.

The picture would be incomplete if the saving work of Seth in the world were left unmentioned. Seth cannot leave his children alone. In accordance with the will of the great invisible Spirit, he is sent down by the heavenly world to do this task. For the sake of pacifying the cosmos, he also suffers the hostilities that are connected with earthly existence; for that precisely is the means of redeeming the race that has gone astray. He brings baptism as a rite for rebirth through the Holy Spirit. To accomplish his mission, he puts on the living Jesus as a garment. Salvation is accomplished by a reconciliation of the world with itself, by a denial of the world and the god of the thirteen aeons, and by the convocation of the saints and the heavenly beings, in particular the pre-existent Father. Seth-Jesus is established as Lord over the cosmic powers.

Upon the description of the works of Seth follows a catalog of all the powers who dispense salvation,[1] beginning with Yesseus, Mazareus, Yessedekeus up to the great invisible Spirit. At the end of the enumeration the specific means of salvation are dealt with again. Yoel is listed as a pre-existent heavenly being who corresponds to John the Baptist in the world. Then a time reference is given: "from now on ...".[2] From that time stems the gnosis of those who are to be redeemed through the incorruptible person Poimael and those that are worthy of the baptism. The section closes with the promise that the saved ones will not taste death.

III. The hymnic part appears to have two sections of hymns. The reconstruction of the meter is greatly complicated by the fact that we are dealing with a Coptic translation from the Greek. A guarded attempt has been made in the commentary to argue for two hymns made up of five strophes with four lines each. It is unclear to whom

[1] III 64,9 - 65,26 = IV 75,24 - 77 end.

[2] III 65,26 (IV is lost).

the first hymn is addressed. It could refer to Jesus. In the second hymn the worshipper is addressing a trinity or a tetrad consisting of the supreme God as the Father, the Mother, Jesus as the Son, and another light-being. In this way he expresses the ecstatic-mystical experience of the Gnostic believer.

IV. The final section [1] consists of several, originally independent units. First Seth is designated as the author of the book.[2] The first part mentions[3] that Seth had placed this book on very high mountains so that it has remained unknown up to now. Neither the prophets nor primitive Christianity were familiar with it.

Also in the second part [4] the authorship is attributed to Seth. A time of 130 years is indicated for the writing.[5] This time the mountain on which the book was placed is mentioned by name: Charaxio. The book will reveal at the end of time the race of Seth and its adherents who belong to the invisible Spirit, his *μονογενής*-son and the Barbelo. This section ends with "amen".[6]

Finally a colophon follows.[7] In it the tractate is given the name "The Egyptian Gospel" or "The Gospel of the Egyptians". The author — who must be one of the copyists of the tractate — asks for himself and his fellow lights *χάρις, σύνεσις, αἴσθησις* and *φρόνησις*. The prayer is addressed to *Ἰησοῦς χριστὸς θεοῦ υἱὸς σωτήρ* whose monogram ΙΧΘΥС is added. The author himself mentions both his spiritual name, Eugnostos, and his name in the flesh, Gongessos.

In the reconstruction of the principal ideas, the preceding sketch of the content was based upon the version which appeared to be correct or the one which was extant. Therefore, the details and the differences between the versions could not be dealt with. These will be treated in the commentary. However, again and again it becomes obvious that an adequate interpretation without the version contained in Codex IV is not possible since it seems to have been based on a

---

[1] III 68,1-69,17 = IV 80,14-81 end.

[2] III 68,2 = IV 80,15f.; III 68,10f. = IV 80,26-81,1.

[3] III 68,1-9 = IV 80,15-25.

[4] III 68,10 - 69,5 = IV 80,26-81 end.

[5] The 130 years are identical to the time which passed, according to the Hebrew tradition, before Adam became father of Seth (Gen 5:3).

[6] III 69,5.

[7] III 69,6-17 (lost or not originally present in IV).

better Greek original and also contains less errors and misunderstandings than III.

The tractate belongs to those texts which are grouped as writings of Seth in *Koptisch-gnostische Apokalypsen aus dem Codex V von Nag Hammadi* by A. Böhlig - P. Labib, p. 87. Though direct access to these texts has cast doubt upon the Sethian character of some of them[1], in the present work we are dealing with a writing of Seth in the fullest sense of the word. If we accept the title "Gospel of the Egyptians", then we have a Sethian gospel because in it Seth's work of salvation in behalf of his children takes the central place. But it has been combined with Barbelo-Gnostic material in which the creation of Seth is mentioned. Thus the heavenly prologue could be given. For this one should compare ApocryJn, which comes from a similar tradition. Also there, the invisible, virginal Spirit, whose uniqueness is best expressed by means of negative attributes, stands at the head of the pantheon.[2] Barbelo, his *ἔννοια*, emanates from him as a feminine complement. In accordance with the trinity of Father, Mother and Son, which was current at that time in the East Mediterranean area, she also gives birth to a spark of light, a *μονογενής*. The great invisible Spirit anoints him and makes him *χριστός*. The emanation in ApocryJn is complicated by the insertion of beings such as Nous, Will, Understanding, etc., into the order of emanation. In contrast to ApocryJn, GEgypt presents the trinity of Father, Mother and Son as an evolution of the great invisible Spirit. Its description is more disciplined. The understanding of the individual beings of the trinity as ogdoads is a new element. The Doxomedon-aeon and the five seals are also not present in ApocryJn.

The *λόγος*, the divine *αὐτογενής*, plays a much greater role in GEgypt than in ApocryJn. In the latter tractate he has moved to the background in favor of Christ. Christ is the divine *αὐτογενής* who has created the world through the *λόγος*. In GEgypt, Christ has only a peripheral role. Both texts know about his anointing by the great invisible Spirit.[3] Another important difference is found in the time of the creation of the four lights. In ApocryJn they come forth from the light, which is identified with Christ. In GEgypt they appear upon the request of the Logos and Adamas.[4] Here the Logos is given a

---

1 See F. Wisse, "The Sethians and the Nag Hammadi Library".

2 BG 22,17ff. = II 2,26ff.

3 III 44,23f. = IV 55,12f.; BG 30,14ff. = III 9,24ff. = II 6,23ff.

4 BG 32,19ff. = III 11,15ff. = II 7,30ff.; III 50,17ff. = IV 62,16ff.

considerably larger role; he practically takes the place of the Christ in ApocryJn. However, Christ precedes him.[1] This Christ belongs to the second group of the pantheon, which is only attested in GEgypt: the thrice-male child, the virgin Youel and the Splenditenens Esephech. The mentioning of Christ appears to be secondary; it could be an interpretative gloss. The four lights in ApocryJn have not been complemented by consorts to become an ogdoad, but are surrounded by twelve (4 × 3) aeons. Yet the female consorts, as described in GEgypt, are also mentioned in ApocryJn, although rather abruptly.[2] Also the ogdoad of their ministers is missing. The creation of Adam in ApocryJn takes place after that of the lights but also through the *αὐτογενής*. However, in ApocryJn he is identified as Christ, whereas in GEgypt he is identified as Logos. Furthermore, in GEgypt the work of Mirothoe has been inserted, while in ApocryJn we find the *πρόγνωσις* and the perfect *νοῦς*. The difference in the characterization of Adamas is also of interest. In ApocryJn he is the perfect, true human being, while in GEgypt he originates from Man. This latter formulation thus presents the concept of the God "Anthropos". All the more interesting in both versions is the ascription of praise to the supreme God as he through whom and to whom everything was created. In GEgypt this refers to "Man", while in ApocryJn it is spoken by Adamas as a presentation of praise to the invisible Spirit. In both texts Seth is the son of Adamas. Although ApocryJn also speaks of the descendants of Seth and specifies their dwelling place — this occurs in GEgypt in a different context — the problematic behind the petition in III 54, 6ff. is absent. However, it is a characteristic element of the theme of GEgypt.

The problematic of the second main section of GEgypt is completely different from the section that follows in ApocryJn.[3] Yet the story of Sophia and her son, which is treated at great length in ApocryJn, is also used in GEgypt, though in a very abbreviated form.[4] The fall of Sophia is not mentioned here, for the creation of a ruler of the world is due to a decision of the heavenly realm. Eleleth expresses the wish that a ruler be created, perhaps due to the fact that he stands closest to the lower region, as the dwelling place of the more susceptible

---

1 IV 60, 7f. The corresponding page in III is lost.

2 BG 33,6f. = III 11,22f. = II 8,3f.

3 BG 36,16ff. = III 14,9ff. = II 9,25ff.

4 III 56,26ff. = IV 68,9 (the rest is lost).

souls. A descending hierarchy of lights, moreover, seems to be indicated in Zost (VIII, *1*) where, similar to ApocryJn, Adamas and Seth appear subsequent to the lights.[1] In contrast, the hierarchy in GEgypt puts a special emphasis on Seth.

For the birth of the seed of Seth, its dwelling place, preservation and salvation as presented in the second main section of GEgypt there are parallels available in some other writings in the Nag Hammadi library. Particularly relevant are ApocAd (V, *5*), Zost (VIII, *1*) and TriProt (XIII, *1*). The Codex Brucianus should also be mentioned at this point. In GEgypt as well as ApocryJn, Zost and Codex Brucianus, Seth belongs to the heavenly world. This is also the case in the ApocAd, yet here the double appearance of Seth and his seed in heaven and on earth is explained through a clever dialectic. Adam calls the son who takes the place of Abel, Seth. This is the name of the heavenly progenitor of the great race, who was given the knowledge (*γνῶσις*) which Adam and Eve lost.[2] In GEgypt the heavenly Seth is the son of the heavenly Adamas. But his relationship to the world and his work of salvation are achieved through his descent into the world, where he appears as Jesus. For the mythological details of the creation of the children of Seth, we have, unfortunately, no parallels available up to now. Even though the mythological repertoire must have been familiar to the author of Zost, the references there are either on fragmentary pages or so short that no further conclusions can be drawn from them. The threat of the flood and the fire to the race of Seth are described in detail in ApocAd. While in ApocAd the race of Seth is removed by angels,[3] in GEgypt there are only hints of this, such as the report that guardians will guard them. Some of the mythological beings who are enumerated at the end of the second main part are also mentioned in ApocAd, Zost and Codex Brucianus.

One could describe GEgypt as a work in which the Sethians portrayed their salvation history. That could have been the basis for the name "gospel" in the colophon. If one extends the term gospel somewhat beyond its use in the New Testament, this characterization is certainly legitimate. Just as the Gospels of the New Testament describe the life of Jesus from the history preceding his birth — and in the Gospel of John from his pre-existence in heaven — through his words

---

[1] VIII 29 and 30.

[2] V 64,29ff.

[3] V 69,19ff.; 76,17ff.

and works to death and resurrection, so too, in GEgypt, the life of Seth is presented: his pre-history, the origin of his seed, its preservation by the heavenly powers and the coming of Seth into the world, and his work of salvation, especially through baptism. If one takes into account that liturgical acts have an important role in the unfolding cosmic drama, then it is perfectly understandable that the experience of salvation is expressed in a hymnic section. It is Seth himself who puts the account about himself in writing. The presence of hymns brings to mind the presentations of praise in 3StSeth (VII, *5*).[1]

The mystery character of GEgypt stems from the fact that the book has long been hidden. It also fits well with the nature of Gnostic sects. The name "Gospel of the Egyptians" leads also to a further suggestion. It is possible that this title was given to the book by non-Egyptians because they knew that the book had been transmitted by Egyptians or that it was especially liked in Egypt. But in that case there must be a special feature, which forms the basis for this popularity. Only one comes to mind: Seth, who is a central figure in the tractate.[2] Gnosticism is fond of interpreting as good what traditionally was considered evil, e.g. the serpent in paradise. Thus it is possible that the Egyptian god Seth — or Set — was reinterpreted in terms of Seth, the son of Adam. Perhaps this was done by the Sethians for missionary purposes,[3] for we know of attempts to rehabilitate the Egyptian god Seth from magical texts.[4] They call him a god who hates evil, and they deny that he injured his brother. Since he is connected in this tractate with Sodom and Gomorrah, which have been reinterpreted as the home of the good seed of Seth, one is reminded that the Egyptian Seth was accused of sodomy. Furthermore, the use of the symbol of the fish may also relate to this, for the fish was a typhonian animal.[5] At the same time *ἰχθύς* was a monogram for Christ (*Ἰησοῦς χριστὸς θεοῦ υἱὸς σωτήρ*) which is attested in Egypt in *The Tutor* (*Παιδαγωγός*)[6] of Clement of Alexan-

---

1 VII 118,10 - 127,27.

2 For the original location and the interpretation of the Nag Hammadi library it is important to know whether the place name ϢЄΝЄСΗΤ could mean "the trees of Seth," since this place is located near Nag Hammadi. Cf. H. Kees, "Seth" (in *Pauly-Wissowa*, RE), col. 1903.

3 Cf. *supra*, pp. 22f.

4 Cf. H. Kees, "Seth", col. 1896-1922, especially 1921.

5 Cf. H. Kees, "Seth", col. 1901-1902.

6 *Paed.* III 11,59,2 (= ed. Stählin, p. 270,8).

dria. Perhaps the monogram in the colophon was deliberately used. In that case Egypt may be the place of origin of the tractate.

The work cannot be considered a unity, for it appears to incorporate several groups of traditions. The first part, which is related to ApocryJn, must be considered a typical product of "Barbelo-Gnostic" speculation. Yet the grouping according to ogdoads could be evidence of Valentinian influence. Even though the redaction appears to be very skillful, it is evident that older pieces of traditional material were used. Thus the tractate gives a simple description of the trinity at first, but later it presents an expanded interpretation which uses the schema of ogdoads. This further description need not be attributed to the compiler, since it could just as well have been a piece of tradition which circulated on the subject. Indeed, such a compilation of pieces of tradition helps to explain the variation in the order of creation between GEgypt and ApocryJn.

Even more than the first section, the second section is characterized by a compilation of disparate pieces. The birth and settlement of the seed of Seth is made up of three mythologumena designed to make different contributions to the story and to form a unified account. The first describes the birth through Plesithea. Also Zost presents her as the mother of the angels,[1] thus indicating that the heavenly part of the race of Seth is being described. Since the children of Seth are not cosmic beings by nature, they receive a place in heaven in the third light Davithe. Consequently this first report precedes that of the creation of the world. But the same tradition teaches that the children of Seth appear in the world. In ApocAd this happens rather unexpectedly; nothing is said about a connection with the human form.[2] The second mythologumenon which follows upon the creation story, seems to deal with that question. Here the angel Hormos clothes the seed of Seth in human form, and they are brought by Seth into the created aeons. In both mythologumena, the story has been connected with Sodom and Gomorrah as the dwelling place of the seed of Seth. How the opinions of the Gnostics differed becomes apparent in Codex III 60, 12ff.,[3] where competing views are placed directly next to each other.

---

1 VIII 53,12f.

2 V 71,10ff.

3 IV 71,21ff. does not present these alternatives. Yet it is best to assume that they were already present in the Greek *Vorlage* of III.

The third mythologumenon deals with the race of Edokla. This must refer to the seed of Seth called here the seed of eternal life. Through her creation of truth and justice she establishes the beginning of a new epoch.[1] The time span from "truth and justice" until the end is the earthly time.

If one assumes a compilation of pieces of tradition, it will also be easier to separate Christian from pre-Christian material. First of all, the colophon belongs to the Christianized parts since it speaks of Jesus Christ, while the two preceding conclusions are pieces of tradition which, in connection with the composition of the book, speak only of Seth. The teaching of the appearance of Seth as Jesus, which presupposes familiarity of the Sethians with Christianity,[2] is extensively developed in GEgypt. Jesus is also seated in heaven with Seth. Furthermore the hostile attitude toward the law is significant. What is in the law is crucified. This is probably due to Pauline influence.[3] Christ is not mentioned very often. Apart from the occurrence in the colophon [4] the "great Christ" appears six times.[5] In all cases the context leaves no doubt that ⲭ̅ⲥ̅ (IV) or ⲭ̅ⲣ̅ⲥ̅ (III) indicates *χριστός* and not *χρηστός*. It is problematic how far the thrice-male child has been identified with Christ[6]. This is in itself further evidence for the secondary role given to Christ in the tractate.

Some allusions to the New Testament are evident. In the soteriological passage 2 Cor 5: 19 has been reinterpreted,[7] and at the end of the passage there is a reference to John 8 : 52. In the description of the angels Eph 2 : 2 seems to have been reinterpreted. For the crucifixion of that which is in the law, Gal 6 : 14; Eph 2 : 15f. and Col 2 : 14 come to mind. The interpretation of the cross as a sign of victory fully agrees with the Gnostic way of thinking and was favored by Origen as well. The formula *ἄρχων τοῦ αἰῶνος τούτου* can be found in Ignatius [8] and corresponds to *ὁ ἄρχων τοῦ κόσμου (τούτου)* in John 12 : 31; 14 : 30; 16 : 11 and *ὁ θεὸς τοῦ αἰῶνος τούτου* in 2 Cor 4 : 4. We also meet the term *διάβολος*. As in other Gnostic texts, baptism is mentioned, but it has not been spiritualized as in ApocAd.

[1] III 62,19ff. = IV 74,4ff.

[2] EPIPHANIUS, *Panarion* 39.1,2-3 (ed. HOLL, p. 72).

[3] Cf. *infra*, p. 196.

[4] III 69,14 (not present in IV).

[5] IV [55,6]; IV 55,12=III 44,22; IV [56,27]; 59,17; 60,8; IV 66,8 = III 54,20.

[6] Cf. *infra*, p. 45.

[7] Cf. *infra*, p. 192.

[8] IGNATIUS, *Eph.* 17,1 *et al.*

It functions instead as a symbol of the Spirit. Thus Christian elements are found throughout the tractate. This would indicate a composition date in the second or third century if we can assume that the tractate in its present form is a compilation. Yet some of the pieces of tradition may well be considerably older and, as in the case of other Nag Hammadi tractates, go back to a Gnosticism which preceeds the development of Christian Gnosticism.

THE PRESENTATIONS OF PRAISE

Presentations of praise and prayers play an important role in the development of the narrative in GEgypt. The same phenomenon can be observed in ApocryJn and the Manichaean literature.[1] In these acts of worship the whole pantheon is recounted as far as it has been developed at that point in the narrative. In order to consider these mythological figures and their characteristics in greater detail and to simplify the discussion in the commentary, the relevant material has been brought together into one chapter.

The presentations of praise in III, *2* are introduced by ϯ ⲛ̄ⲟⲩⲥⲙⲟⲩ[2] and once by ϯ ⲥⲙⲟⲩ.[3] IV, *2* on the other hand, uses ⲉⲓⲛⲉ ⲉϩⲣⲁ̈ⲓ̈ ⲛ̄ⲟⲩⲥⲙⲟⲩ.[4] Usually the presentation of praise is followed by a petition.[5]

The following beings are the recipients of the presentations of praise:

1. the great invisible Spirit,
2. the male virgin Barbelo,
3. the great Doxomedon-aeon,
4. the thrice-male child,
5. the male virgin Youel,
6. Esephech, the Splenditenens,
7. the ethereal earth.

1. The great invisible Spirit is the supreme deity who can only be described by means of negative attributes. Such a description has been employed in GEgypt as well as in the extensive introductory sections of ApocryJn and SJC. Instances of this are presented in the presentations of praise as well as in some other places. The tractate

---

[1] *Kephalaia* II (Lfg. 11-12) ed. A. Böhlig (Stuttgart 1966), p. 271,26ff. See also A. Böhlig, "Neue Kephalaia des Mani", in *Mysterion und Wahrheit* (Leiden 1968), p. 257

[2] III [44,25]; 49,23; 50,17f. where it refers back to the previous instance; 53,15f. 55,18; 61,23f.

[3] III 44,10.

[4] IV 54,14f.; 55,15f.; 56,7f.; 57,13; 60,22; 61,24; [62,16] where it refers back to the previous instance; 65,8f.; 67,3f.; 73,7f.

[5] In III, *2* it is introduced by ⲁⲓⲧⲓ: 44,13; 50,21; 51,6; 56,3; 62,12, and in IV, *2* by ⲣ̄ⲁⲓⲧⲓ: 54,20; 56,8; [62,19f. 31]; 73,25.

has been named after this being "the holy book of the great invisible Spirit". In all the presentations of praise he is called great (ⲚⲞϬ) and invisible (ⲀϨⲞⲢⲀⲦⲞⲚ in III,*2*, ⲀⲦⲚⲀⲨ ⲈⲢⲞϤ in IV,*2*).[1] The predicate "virginal" (ⲠⲀⲢⲐⲈⲚⲒⲔⲞⲚ) is missing in one instance.[2] Four times the additional predicates "uncallable" [3] and "unnameable"[4] have been used. Once the predicate "incomprehensible" (ⲀⲦⲦⲀϨⲞϤ) occurs.[5] Outside of the presentations of praise the great invisible Spirit is also called "Father".[6]

2. After the Father comes the male virgin Barbelo. She is found in six of the seven presentations of praise. The name Barbelo in most cases has been left out in III, *2*.[7] Such differences between the versions may go back to the Greek *Vorlagen*. In III 44, 27 the male virgin is called ⲒⲰ[ⲎⲖ].[8] Since the male virgin Youel does not appear on the scene until IV 56, 20 — the text is uncertain due to lacunae in IV, *2* and missing pages in III, *2* — Yoel was most likely mistakenly written for Barbelo. There is no reference to the male virgin in IV 60, 24f.[9]

In one place Barbelo is called "Mother".[10] She is the female complement of the Father. However, we are dealing here with a higher form of existence which is difficult to grasp in terms of human concepts. She is not simply the divine consort of mythology. She is a virgin just as the great invisible Spirit is "virginal". The predicate "male" indicates her truly divine character. For the essence of divine per-

---

[1] III 44,11.26; 49,23; 53,16; 55,19 (ⲀϨⲞⲢⲀⲦⲞⲤ). 61,24 ⲀϨⲞⲢⲀⲦⲞⲚ is missing; probably the scribe skipped a line. IV 54,16; 55,17; 60,23 (the parallel in III is lost); 61,25; 65,10; 67,5; 73,9.

[2] III 44,26 = IV 55,17.

[3] ⲀⲔⲖⲎⲦⲞⲚ in III 44,12; 53,17; 55,19 (ⲀⲔⲖⲎⲦⲞⲤ); 61,24. All the parallel occurrences in IV are partly or completely in lacunae. There is a question about the way IV has translated ἄκλητον. The ⲀⲔⲖⲎⲦⲞⲚ in III 65,10 has for its parallel in IV 77,5 ⲀⲦϪⲀϨⲘ[ⲈϤ] (but not in a presentation of praise). Since in IV 54,16 ⲀⲦϪ[is visible it is possible that the translator of IV, *2* consistently mistranslated ἄκλητον by ⲀⲦϪⲀϨⲘ̄Ϥ [65,10; 67,5; 73,8].

[4] III 44,11 ⲀⲦϪⲰ ⲘⲠ[ⲈϤⲢⲀⲚ]; 55,20 ⲀⲦⲞⲚⲞⲘⲀⲌⲈ ⲘⲘⲞϤ; IV: ⲀⲦϮ ⲢⲀⲚ ⲈⲢⲞϤ 54,17; 65,11 (missing in the parallel III 53, 16ff.); 67,6. It probably also occurs in IV 73,9f., but IV has a lacuna and III appears to have skipped a line.

[5] III 49,24. The parallel in IV 61,25 is in a lacuna.

[6] III 40,13f. = IV 50,3 etc.

[7] It is spelled ⲂⲀⲢⲂⲎⲖⲞⲚ in III 42,12; 62,1; 69,3. This same spelling is found in ApocryJn (III, *1*). IV, *2* reads ⲂⲀⲢⲂⲎⲖⲰ in [52,4; 54,20; 61,27] and 73,12.

[8] The parallel in IV 55,17f. is in a lacuna.

[9] The parallel in III is lost.

[10] III 42,12 = IV 52,4.

fection is that unity in which male and female are united.[1] Barbelo possesses precisely those characteristics which belong to the highest deity. Like the great invisible Spirit, she too is uninterpretable, ineffable and self-begotten.[2] According to Irenaeus,[3] as well as the Gnostic writing Apocry Jn, the so-called Barbelo-Gnostics made Barbelo their characteristic deity.

The meaning of the name Barbelo remains an open question.[4] One wonders whether barbēʿ ʾelōh ("in four is God") is related to the *τετρακτύς* of Greek philosophy. The sporadic use of the name Barbelo in GEgypt may be due to the fact that the tractate has borrowed from Barbelo-Gnosticism yet does not belong to it but wants to go beyond it.

3. The position of the third being in the order of the recipients of the presentations of praise varies. Only in one of the four occurrences does the Doxomedon-aeon appear in the third place.[5] In the other cases he is preceded by the thrice-male child, Youel and Esephech.[6] However, since the Doxomedon-aeon appears upon the scene first [7] and proves to be the resting place of the thrice-male child,[8] he ought to be discussed third even if he is last in the original sequence.

The alternate name of this being is *Δομέδων Δοξομέδων*. This double designation is rare.[9] Probably the first part is the more original one, meaning "Lord of the House",[10] which then was reformulated to "Lord of Glory" in a light-realm theology. Except for the first two instances, where the double designation Domedon Doxomedon

---

[1] Cf. ApocAd V 64,6ff.; 1 ApocJas V 41,16ff.; GPh II 68,23-26; 70,9-17 (logia 71 and 78); 2 Clem. 12,2; Clem. *Strom.* III 9,63 (from the apocryphal Gospel of the Egyptians). Furthermore it should be remembered that Philo considered the change from female to male necessary. Cf. R. A. Baer, *Philo's Use of the Categories Male and Female* (Leiden 1970).

[2] III 42,16ff. = IV 52,8-12.

[3] *Adv. Haer.* I, 29.

[4] Cf. H. Leisegang, *Die Gnosis* (4 ed. Stuttgart 1955), p. 186.

[5] III 53,19f. = IV 65,13f.

[6] III 50,4f. = IV 62,4; III 56,1 (IV is lost); III 62,8f. = IV 73,19f.

[7] III 41,13ff. = IV 51,2-5.

[8] III 43,15f. = IV 53,13ff.

[9] III 41,14f. = IV 51,2f.; III 43,9f. (the parallel in IV 53,5 reads only ⲇⲟⲝⲟⲙⲉⲇⲱⲛ).

[10] The name Domiel found in Jewish literature must be closely related to this meaning, and was probably judaized by means of the "-el" which gives the being its heavenly character. Cf. G. Scholem, *Jewish Gnosticism, Merkabah Mysticism, and Talmudic Tradition* (New York 1960), p. 33.

is found, the title "the great Doxomedon-aeon" is used.[1] Several occurrences of this title are in the plural, i.e. the great Doxomedon-aeons.[2] Once IV translates Doxomedon into Coptic as ⲣⲉϥϯ ⲉⲟⲟⲩ.[3] This being is further described as "the aeon of the aeons".[4]

The question remains who this being is and what he signifies. The fluctuation between singular and plural would indicate a collective being. Also the fact that he is described as a spacial entity points in this direction. He is pictured as a throne surrounded by powers. The relation with the trinity of Father, Mother and Son [5] on the one hand, and with the thrice-male child on the other, make him a manifestation of the Father of light who rests in secrecy and suddenly appears with his light. For this he needs an aeon in which he presents himself as a second god or as a being who encompasses the heavenly realm. He is the great throne room of the god who appeared in the realm of light. This description reminds one of the Jewish concept of the מעשׂה מרכבה. On the other hand, the presentation in terms of an aeon also comes into play. In Hermeticism the aeon has the position of a second god just as it does here. [6] Here too he could be the totality of the revealed god. The Doxomedon-aeon would be meaningless and inconceivable if he were not filled. That is why he should not be pictured as a personal being, which is supported by the fact that he does not speak. It is also insufficient to see him as ruler surrounded by hosts of ministering angels, for he is filled by the child of light and the light beings who belong to him.

It is uncertain whether the name placed on the throne refers to Doxomedon or to the male child.[7] Grammatically both are possible. The spacial description of the Doxomedon-aeon explains why he is listed once before the male child and the other times after Esephech. The male child, the male virgin and Esephech are closely connected with Doxomedon. Perhaps it stems from this trinitarian notion that the

---

[1] III 43,15 = IV 53,12f.; III 44,20 = IV 55,8f.; III 50,4f. = IV 62,4; III 53,19f. = IV 65,13f.; III 56,1 (IV is lost); III 62,8f. = IV 73,19f. The two exceptions are III 41,14f. = IV 51,2f. and III 43,9f. = IV 53,5. These also happen to be the two instances where III has the double name ⲇⲟⲙ̣ⲉⲇⲱⲛ ⲇⲟⲝⲟⲙⲉⲇⲱⲛ.

[2] IV 62,4 (III 50,5f. has the singular); IV 65,13f. (III 53,19f. has the singular but the following pronoun refers to him in the plural); III 56,1 (IV is lost).

[3] IV 73,19f.

[4] III 41,15 = IV 51,4; III 43,10 = IV 53,5f.

[5] III 41,17ff. = IV 51,7-10.

[6] This agrees with Melch (IX 6,1; 16,30) where Doxomedon is called the first born Aeon

[7] III 43,17-20 = IV 53,15-19.

trinity of Father, Mother and Son are added to him.[1] In that case the first three beings are the content of the Doxomedon, the fourth is the Son, the fifth the Mother and the sixth the Father.

It is tempting to identify Yeu (ιεογ) of PS and the Books of Yeu with Doxomedon. However, two difficulties arise which run counter to this suggestion. First, Yeu does not occur in any of the texts from Nag Hammadi. Secondly, the spelling ιεογ found in PS does not correspond with ιηογ in III, *2* and IV, *2*. The second objection is not very strong, because η and ε are interchangeable, e.g. ηληληθ along side of ηλεληθ. The first argument has more weight, although to be sure, precisely the transformation of Yeu into Doxomedon could have been the basis for the lack of any other reference to his name.

Yeu is closely connected with the light, and since he himself brings forth a plurality of Yeu's, he too becomes a collective entity. In the First Book of Yeu he is designated as the god of truth who has emanated from the highest god and appears in manifold form. In the Second Book of Yeu he is described as belonging to the external treasures.[2] He is the external form of the unapproachable God. In PS he is said to be the overseer of the light.[3] His origin is traced back to the pure light of the first tree. His primacy comes from his function as the emissary of the light [4] and as the primal man.[5] He also has duties with respect to the realm of the angels and the archons. Yeu has a wide range of responsibilities. He is the second god who orders the cosmic world. His tasks exceed those of the Doxomedon while at the same time including them. It is important for the event of salvation that the souls go to their rest inside of him.[6]

4. In response to the request of the three powers which form the trinity, the thrice-male child comes into being.[7] The expression πϣομ̄ν̄τ ν̄ϩοογτ ν̄αλογ in III or πιϣ̄μ̄τ ϩοογτ ν̄αλογ in IV is open to two interpretations. The question is whether the ϣομ̄ν̄τ modifies αλογ or ϩοογτ, i.e. "three male children" or "thrice-male child". The first interpretation is supported by the

---

[1] III 41,13-19 = IV 51,2-10.

[2] II J 307,30 transl. Schmidt-Till.

[3] PS 15,30; 20,38 etc. transl. Schmidt-Till.

[4] PS 125,23f.; 208,25 transl. Schmidt-Till.

[5] PS 185,4; 208,25; 215,29.30 transl. Schmidt-Till.

[6] II J 307,32ff. transl. Schmidt-Till.

[7] III 44,18f. = IV 55,3ff. The passage is seriously obscured by lacunae in both versions.

occurrence of the plural ⲛⲓϣⲙ̄ⲧ ϩⲟⲟⲩⲧ [ⲛⲓ]ϣⲙ̄[ⲧ ⲅⲉ]ⲛⲟⲥ[1] which is an exception to the rule that in Coptic numerals take a singular article.[2] III, *2* in one place has the accompanying verb in the plural.[3] The second interpretation is supported by the predominant use of the singular with the verbs, and the occurrence of adjectives formed with *τρι(σ)*- for intensification, especially in Gnostic and Hermetic literature, e.g. *τρισμέγιστος*, *τριδύναμος*,[4] *τριπνεύματος*. Also *τρισάρσης* occurs: "But (*δέ*) the tenth Father has a thrice-male (*τρισάρσης*) face, an Adamas face and a pure (*εἰλικρινής*) face".[5] In other Coptic-Gnostic tractates *τρισάρσης* is found in translation. In 3StSeth (VII, *5*) the ⲅⲉⲣⲁⲇⲁⲙⲁⲥ, the father of Seth, is called thrice-male.[6] In ApocryJn it is said of the Barbelo that "she became a first man, which is the virginal Spirit, the thrice-male, the one with the three powers, the three names, the three creatures, the ageless aeon".[7] The version in Codex II also describes her as the *μητροπάτωρ* of everything, yet with the same characteristic description. In SJC the spirit of Sophia, who is the female complement of the perfect Man, is called "thrice-male".[8] Although 3StSeth and SJC show that intensification is the primary meaning of the expression, yet ApocryJn offers at the same time a strong emphasis on three aspects so that trinity and unity do not exclude each other.[9]

The question remains whether the occurrences in GEgypt present a sufficient basis to establish the meaning of the expression. Most of the instances in the lists of the members of the pantheon are of no further help.[10] However, one instance reads ⲡⲓϩⲟⲟⲩⲧ ⲛ̄ⲁⲗⲟⲩ[11] against ⲡϣⲟⲙⲛ̄ⲧ ⲛ̄ϩⲟⲟⲩⲧ ⲛ̄ⲁⲗⲟⲩ.[12] This is possibly, though not

[1] IV 55,3.

[2] Cf. Walter C. Till, *Koptische Grammatik*, § 162.

[3] III 54,13f. The parallel in IV 66,2f. is of no help since the verbal prefix precedes the noun. In III the noun stands in extraposition, and the verbal prefix is in the plural as is the rule when the subject is a numeral. Cf. L. Stern, *Koptische Grammatik*, § 486.

[4] Cf. the Pistis Sophia (PS), the Books of Yeu (J) and the untitled treatise from Codex Brucianus (U). Indices are available in the editions of Schmidt-Till and C. Baynes.

[5] U 341,8 transl. Schmidt-Till.

[6] VII 120,29; 121,8.

[7] BG 27,17 - 28,3 = III 7,23-8,4. The parallel passage in II 5,5-11 is considerably different.

[8] BG 96,3 = III 102,12f. It is lacking in Eug (III, *3*) due to homoioteleuton.

[9] BG 27,19ff. = III 7,23ff.; cf. II 5,6ff.

[10] III 49,26 = IV 61,28; III 53,23f. = IV 65,17f.; III 55,⟨21⟩ = IV 67,8.

[11] IV 73,12f.

[12] III 62,2.

necessarily, an error. In another place preserved only in IV ⲡⲁⲗⲟⲩ ⲛ̄ⲛⲁ[ⲧ]ϫ[ⲱϩ̄ⲙ] occurs.[1] In both cases the expression introduces the name Telmael Telmachael Eli Eli Machar Machar Seth. The thrice-male child offered praise and prayed.[2] He came forth because of the first ogdoad, the one of the Father.[3] He rests himself in the Doxomedon-aeon.[4] Four times he is linked to the great Christ to whom he apparently belongs.[5] His appearance is related in time to the appearance of Christ: "When the thrice-male child came from above down to ... there came forth the great one who possesses all greatnesses of the great Christ".[6] The parallel passage in III reads: "Then the three male children came forth from above to the below ... (and) there came forth the greatness, the whole greatness of the great Christ".[7] Just before this passage the Father has been called the fourth,[8] perhaps by adding one to a trinity to form a tetrad. This tetrad may also be involved in the name which is given to the thrice-male child, ⲧⲉⲗⲙⲁⲏⲗ ⲧⲉⲗⲙⲁⲭⲁⲏⲗ ⲏⲗⲓ ⲏⲗⲓ ⲙⲁⲭⲁⲣ ⲙⲁⲭⲁⲣ ⲥⲏⲑ.[9] Seth is added to the names of the thrice-male child, because the race of God is also his race.[10] The presence of the name Seth could indicate that the trinity of the child combined with Seth has become a divine tetrad.[11] That we are dealing here with a trinity, or a tetrad, in a unity is clear from IV 59, 17f. Although the expression is in the singular, the threefold child together with Seth must be meant since the names follow. The same expression is found in III 56, 16f.[12] without the names. Here Seth acknowledges the creation of his seed as a gift granted him by "the incorruptible child".

This seemingly confusing mythology is nonetheless meaningful throughout. It is meant to make plausible the light-origin of the

---

[1] IV 59,18f.

[2] IV 56,6-9.

[3] III 42,5ff. = IV 51,22ff.

[4] III 43,15ff. = IV 53,12-15.

[5] IV [55,6]; III 44,22f. = IV 55,11f.; IV 59,16-21; III 54,13-20 = IV 66,2-8.

[6] IV 66,2-8.

[7] III 54,13-20.

[8] III 54,7f. IV 65,26f. is obscured by lacunae.

[9] IV 59,18-21 (III is lost); III 62,2ff. = IV 73,12ff.; III 65,8f. = IV 77,2ff. (See also the commentary p. 190).

[10] Cf. III 54,6ff. = IV 65,25ff.

[11] It is possible that the *topos* of the three young men in the fiery oven and their angel (3 + 1) did play a role in the formation of this formulation.

[12] IV is lost.

seed of Seth. The thrice-male child originates from the supreme God. This explains his connection with the first ogdoad-Father. The child forms a tetrad with Seth who is also a light-being. Even during the time that Seth is not yet a historical being he is customarily mentioned together with the names of the child. The passages in which the child is connected with the great Christ appear to be secondary. The tendency would be to identify Christ with the child and thus the separate mentioning of Christ appears to be evidence of a mythologumenon which was already present beforehand. The identification of Jesus with a child or youth is known from Christian-Gnostic texts. While in the Actus Vercellenses [1] and the Acts of John [2] he has a manifold appearance, in ApocPaul he is a youth [3], and in ApocryJn he states unambiguously that he is at the same time father, mother and son.[4] Earlier in ApocryJn it was mentioned that he revealed himself as a child, an old man and a servant.[5] Yet this connection between Jesus and the child appears to be a secondary development. Also in Manichaeism the child appears alone [6] and together with Jesus.[7] The child is also known from the untitled work from Codex Brucianus.[8] In the latter case he is an ἐπίσκοπος and presides over a place which does not belong to the true depth but forms a more accessible entity. In Zost (VIII, *1*) the child possesses a special aspect of perfection and he is a transcendent being.[9] He is also called "the perfect child who is higher than God".[10] Thus the concept of the child indicates a being which evolved from the light. He occupies a special position depending on the form of the myth and the penetration into Gnosticism of the person of Jesus or Christ with whom he was connected. His threefold character is explained by the fact that he is one being which contains three persons.

5. In response to the prayer of the thrice-male child "the male virgin Youel" appears.[11] She follows him in the order of the presen-

---

1 Hennecke-Schneemelcher, *The New Testament Apocrypha* II, p. 304 [209].

2 *Ibid.*, II, p. 225 [151].

3 V 18,7.

4 BG 21,19ff. = II 2,13ff.

5 BG 21,3ff. = II 2,2ff.

6 See the index to the Manichaean Psalmbook.

7 *Keph.* 35,27 and *Mitteliranische Manichaica aus Chinesisch-Turkestan* III, ed. Andreas-Henning (Berlin 1934), pp. 38ff. [878].

8 U 338,39; 339,12 transl. Schmidt-Till.

9 VIII 2,9.

10 VIII 13,4f.

11 IV 56,11-20. The text is obscured by lacunae.

tations of praise.[1] The name Youel is already known from the untitled treatise from Codex Brucianus.[2] The meaning of the name given there, "God forever",[3] has no philological basis. The name refers to the *παμμήτωρ*. This leads to a difficulty which is also found in GEgypt. For in one place the Barbelo, who is in our text the universal mother, is called ϊωηλ,[4] probably a variant of ϊογηλ. Considering their characteristics, an interchange of Barbelo and Youel can easily be understood. Thus just as Valentinianism has two Sophia figures, so GEgypt has two virgins, the second of which has not been relegated to an inferior status, however. In Zost she is also designated as virginal [5] and as "mother of glory".[6] At the same time she is viewed as a female *δοξοκράτωρ* (ϯρεϥⲁ[ⲙⲁϩⲧε] ⲙ̄πεοογ),[7] "the (f.) male and virginal possessor of glories" (τⲁ [ⲛιεο]ογ ⲛ̄ϩοογτ ⲁγω ⲙ̄[πⲁρθ]εⲛικοⲛ)[8] and "she who possesses all the glories" (τⲁ ⲛ̄εο[ογ] τηρογ).[9] That means that she has the character of the being who follows her in the presentations of praise in GEgypt. She also possesses *δοξοκρατία* which in the untitled treatise from Codex Brucianus is attributed to the *παμμήτωρ* among others.[10]

Thus in the second series of light-beings in our text there is a correspondence of the second person to the second person of the first trinity. The character of the light-virgin can also be illustrated from other Gnostic texts. Well-known is the characterization of the light-virgin in PS as a judge who resides in the intermediate region.[11] In Manichaeism she is with Jesus in the ship of the moon and her function is that of purification.[12] In II, *5* she forms a trinity with Sabaoth and Jesus.[13] Jesus sits to the right of Sabaoth and she, carrying the name

[1] τⲁρcεⲛικη ⲛ̄πⲁρθεⲛοc ϊογηλ in III, ϯϩοογτ ⲙ̄πⲁρθεⲛοc ϊογηλ in IV. III 50,1f. = IV 61,29; III 53,24f. = IV 65,18f.; III 55,21f. = IV 67,9; III 62,5f. = IV 73,16.

[2] U 339,33; 355,2f. transl. Schmidt-Till.

[3] U 355,2f. transl. Schmidt-Till.

[4] III 44,27 = IV 55,18. This variant is also found in Zost (VIII 59,13 and 64,11).

[5] VIII 59,15.

[6] VIII 56,16.

[7] VIII 56,15.

[8] VIII 59,13.

[9] VIII 55,14; 64,11; 65,10.

[10] U 354,36 transl. Schmidt-Till.

[11] PS 153f. transl. Schmidt-Till.

[12] For his role as *σοφία* see Schmidt-Polotsky, *Ein Mani-Fund in Ägypten* (Berlin 1933), p. 68.

[13] II 105 (153),29f.

"virgin of the holy Spirit", to the left. We are probably already here dealing with two concepts of the trinity, that of Father - Mother - Son, and that of Father - Son - Spirit. The connection between the two is that in certain systems the Mother is thought of as both virgin and spirit. The characterization as judge, which may have come from the Iranian concept of the *daēna*, is not present in GEgypt.

6. Without a further request the appearance of Youel is followed by that of ⲎⲤⲎⲪⲎⲬ.[1] He follows her in the order of the presentations of praise.[2] He is identified as ⲡⲉⲧⲉⲙⲁϩⲧⲉ ⲙ̄ⲡⲉⲟⲟⲩ (III,*2*) or ⲡⲓⲣⲉϥⲁⲙⲁϩⲧⲉ ⲙ̄ⲡⲉⲟⲟⲩ (IV,*2*). This expression corresponds with the Manichaean term *φεγγοκάτοχος* or Splenditenens. This being in Manichaean mythology functions as the first son of the living Spirit.[3] The exact counterpart is *δοξοκράτωρ* which is found in the untitled treatise from Codex Brucianus.[4] The name is difficult to interpret. The designation "the child of the child" (ⲡⲁⲗⲟⲩ ⲙ̄ⲡⲁⲗⲟⲩ) has been added to the name.[5]

In PS "child of the child" refers to the twin-savior.[6] In the second Book of Yeu it refers to a being other than the twin-savior who is mentioned immediately following it.[7] In the same tractate it appears also without any reference to the twin-savior in the context.[8] The connection with the twin-savior is perhaps nothing more than an interpretation of the name and would indicate that the one child belongs to the other. Otherwise these instances tell us little about the origin and meaning of this mythologumenon. GEgypt may have given us a starting point. For if it is legitimate to see a second trinity of father, mother and son in the thrice-male child, Youel and Esephech, then the child Esephech is the child of the thrice-male child.

The praise is also offered to "the crown of his glory".[9] This could

---

1 IV 56,20ff. The spelling in GEgypt is consistently with an Ⲭ. In Zost it differs between Ⲭ (VIII 45,11) and Ⲕ (VIII 45,2).

2 III 50,2ff. = IV 62,1ff.; III 53,25 - 54,3 = IV 65,19ff.; III 55,22ff. (IV is lost); III 62,6ff. = IV 73,17ff.

3 Cf. F. Cumont, *La cosmogonie manichéenne* (Bruxelles 1908), pp. 22ff., and the Coptic Manichaean texts.

4 U 355,10 transl. Schmidt-Till.

5 IV [56,21f.] and 59,25 (III is lost); III 50,3 = IV 62,2f.; III 54,1f. (missing in IV 65,20); III 55,24 (IV is lost). In III 62,7 = IV 73,18 it is missing in both versions.

6 PS 125,3; 147,38 transl. Schmidt-Till.

7 II J 316,1 transl. Schmidt-Till.

8 II J 306,11 transl. Schmidt-Till.

9 IV 59,26 (III is lost); III 50,4 = IV 62,3; III 54,2f. = IV 65,21; III 55,23f. where it precedes "the child of the child" (IV is lost); III 62,7f. = IV 73,18f.

be a cosmic reference to the stars. However, the more literal meaning would suffice. The Splenditenens is, of course, surrounded by light which adorns him like a crown.

7. Only once has the "ethereal earth" been added at the end (ⲡⲕⲁϩ ⲛ̄ⲁⲉⲣⲟⲇⲓⲟⲥ[1] = ⲡⲕⲁϩ ⲙ̄ⲡⲁⲏⲣ)[2]. The intention of the writer is to contrast the earth where mankind lives with a heavenly model because it is inhabited by the men of light, probably to be understood as the race of Seth. The author strongly asserts here his belief in the special nature of the Gnostics. That "ethereal earth" is a secondary addition to the presentation of praise is suggested by the fact that the pleroma is mentioned twice. The phrase "and the whole pleroma which I have mentioned before",[3] which really belongs at the end of the description of the Doxomedon-aeon, has been repeated with variations after the description of the ethereal earth.[4] The question arises whether, at least at a later point, the pleroma in its own right was taken up secondarily as part of the list of the presentations of praise. Especially those places where the Doxomedon-aeon stands at the end make a reference to the pleroma in the conclusion of the presentation of praise easy to understand. Just before mention is made of the place which embraces the realm of light, and it follows the final summary in the pleroma which includes everything that has been said about the realm of light, i.e. "which I have described before" or "which I have mentioned before".[5] It is, of course, also possible to relate this sentence to the pleroma of the Doxomedon-aeon. In that case it would refer back to his description in the beginning of the tractate. In the presentation of praise which has the Doxomedon-aeon before the thrice-male child,[6] the pleroma was not moved with it. We may take this as an indication that even if the pleroma is not a being in its own right, it is seen as the conclusion and summary of the presentation of praise. Perhaps after the transposition it was felt that the mentioning of the pleroma had become unconnected and therefore it was further elaborated. The fact that this time there is no reference to things which have been mentioned

[1] III 50,10.

[2] IV 62,9.

[3] III 50,8ff. = IV 62,7f.

[4] III 50,16f. = IV 62,14ff.

[5] III 50,16f. = IV 62,14f; III 56,2f. (IV is lost); III 62,11f. = IV 73,23f.

[6] III 53,19-24 = IV 65,13-18.

before supports the assumption that it originally referred to the pleroma of the Doxomedon-aeon.

The discussion of the presentations of praise is not complete without a word about the form of the list in relation to the structure of the tractate as a whole. Most likely the list was originally a piece of traditional material which existed well before the composition and redaction of GEgypt. The problems discussed above which arose because of the change of the sequence and because of additions witness to this. Originally the list had another purpose than it has at present within the tractate. The sequence was most likely the following:

1. the great invisible Spirit,
2. Barbelo,
3. the thrice-male child,
4. Youel,
5. Esephech,
6. Doxomedon-aeon.

From this sequence the parallelism with the trinity of the so-called Barbelo-Gnostics is even more apparent. According to this list the trinity of Father, Mother and Son would correspond to the first three beings in the presentations of praise. However, this is not the case in GEgypt. There a special trinity of Father, Mother and Son comes into being from the great invisible Spirit, not through emanation but through evolution. The Father and the Son remain anonymous and only the Mother is identified, as Barbelo. The fact that the lists of beings who are praised retain the traditional form witnesses to their original character. As can be seen from the placing together of the trinity and the five seals,[1] GEgypt has regrouped them. Here a new and second trinity is formed which consists of five persons. When they — the thrice-male child, Youel and Esephech — are described as five seals, this is to express their character as the "image" of the first trinity. The Doxomedon-aeon forms the spacial framework, which is, as the embodiment of the emanations, indeed the second God.

[1] IV 56,24f.

THE GOSPEL OF THE EGYPTIANS

TEXT AND TRANSLATION

The Introduction: III 40,12-41,7

III 40,12 ⲡϫⲱⲱⲙⲉ ⲛ̄{ⲧ}ϩ[ⲓⲉ]ⲣ̣[ⲁ ⲛ̄ⲧⲉ ⲛ̄ⲣ̄ⲙ̄ⲛ̄ⲕⲏⲙⲉ]
ⲛ̄ⲧⲉ ⲡⲓⲛⲟϭ ⲛⲁⲧⲛⲁⲩ ⲉⲣ̣[ⲟϥ ⲙ̄ⲡⲛ̄ⲁ̄ ⲡⲉⲓ]
14 ⲱⲧ̇ ⲛ̄ⲁⲧϫⲱ ⲙ̄ⲡⲉϥⲣⲁ[ⲛ ⲡⲉⲛⲧⲁϥⲉⲓ ⲉ]
ⲃⲟⲗ ϩ̄ⲛ̄ ⲛⲉⲧϫⲟⲥⲉ ⲛ̄ⲧ[ⲉ ⲡⲓϫⲱⲕ ⲡⲟⲩ]
16 ⲟⲉⲓⲛ ⲛ̄ⲡⲟⲩⲟⲉⲓⲛ ⲛ̄ⲛ[ⲓⲁⲓⲱⲛ ⲛ̄ⲟⲩⲟ]
ⲉⲓⲛ · ⲡⲟⲩⲟⲉⲓⲛ ⲛ̄ⲧⲉ ⲧ[ⲥⲓⲅⲏ ⲛ̄ⲧⲡⲣⲟ]
18 ⲛⲟⲓⲁ ⟨ⲙ⟩ⲛ̄ ⲡⲉⲓⲱⲧ̇ ⲛ̄ⲧⲥⲓⲅ̣ⲏ̣ ⲡ̣[ⲟⲩⲟⲉⲓⲛ]
ⲙ̄ⲡϣⲁϫⲉ ⲙ̣̄⟨ⲛ⟩ ⲧⲙⲏⲉ · ⲡⲟⲩⲟ̣[ⲉⲓⲛ ⲛ̄ⲛⲓ]

41 [ⲙⲁ]
[ⲁⲫⲑⲁ]ⲣⲥ̣ⲓ̣[ⲁ· ⲡⲟ]ⲩⲟⲉⲓⲛ ⲉⲧⲉ ⲙ̄ⲛ̄ ⲁⲣⲏϫ̄ϥ·
2 [ⲡ̈]ⲡ̣ⲉⲓⲣⲉ ⲉⲃⲟⲗ ϩ̄ⲛ̄ ⲛⲓⲁⲓⲱⲛ ⲛ̄ⲟⲩⲟⲉⲓⲛ
ⲛⲧⲉ ⲡⲉⲓⲱⲧ̇ ⲛ̄ⲁⲧ̇ⲟⲩⲱⲛϩ ⲉⲃⲟⲗ ⲛ̄ⲁⲥⲏ
4 ⲙⲁⲛⲧⲟⲥ ⲛ̄ⲁⲧϩⲁⲗⲗⲟ ⲛ̄ⲁⲧ̇ⲉⲩⲁⲅ̇ⲅⲉⲗⲓ ⲙ̄ⲙⲟϥ
ⲡⲁ̣[ⲓ]ⲱⲛ ⲛ̄ⲛⲓⲁⲓⲱⲛ ⲛ̄ⲁⲩⲧⲟⲅⲉⲛⲏⲥ ⲛ̄

40,12 See *supra*, p. 20 and 23.
41, 5 Perhaps emend to ⟨ⲡ⟩ⲁⲩⲧⲟⲅⲉⲛⲏⲥ (IV 50,18).

The [holy (ἱερά)] book [of the Egyptians] / about the great invisible [Spirit (πνεῦμα), the] Father / whose name cannot be uttered [, he who came] / 15 forth from the heights of [the perfection, the] light / of the light of the [aeons (αἰών) of light], / the light of the [silence (σιγή) of the] providence (πρόνοια) / <and> the Father of the silence (σιγή), the [light] / of the word and the truth, the light [of the] // *41* [incorruptions (ἀφθαρσία), the] infinite light, / [the] radiance from the aeons (αἰών) of light / of the unrevealable, unmarked (ἀσήμαντος), / ageless, unproclaimable (-εὐαγγελίζεσθαι) Father, / 5 the aeon (αἰών) of the aeons (αἰών), autogenes (αὐτογενής), /

The Introduction: IV 50,1-23

IV 50 [ⲛ̄]
[ⲡϫⲱⲱⲙⲉ ⲉⲧⲟⲩⲁ]ⲁ̣ⲃ ⲛ̄ⲧⲉ ⲛⲓ
2 [ⲣ̄ⲙ̄ⲛ̄ⲕⲏⲙⲉ ⲛ̄ⲧⲉ] ⲡ̣ⲓⲛⲟϭ ⲛ̄ⲛⲁ
[ⲧⲛⲁⲩ ⲉⲣⲟϥ ⲙ̄ⲡ̄ⲛ̄ⲁ̄] ⲡⲓⲱⲧ̀ ⲛ̄ⲁⲧ̀
4 [ϫⲱ ⲙ̄ⲡⲉϥⲣⲁⲛ ⲉⲧⲁ]ϥⲣ̄ϣⲟⲣⲡ̄ ⲛ̄
[ⲉ͡ⲓ ⲉⲃⲟⲗ ϩ̄ⲛ̄ ⲛⲓ]ϫⲓⲥⲉ · ⲡⲟⲩⲟ
6 [ⲉⲓ]ⲛ ⲛ̄ⲧ̣ⲉ [ⲡⲓ]ϫ̣ⲱⲕ · ⲡⲟⲩⲟⲉⲓⲛ
ϣⲁ ⲉⲛⲉϩ ⲛ̄ⲧⲉ ⲛⲓⲉⲛⲉϩ · ⲡⲟⲩⲟ
8 [ⲉ]ⲓ̣ⲛ ϩ̄ⲛ̄ ⲟⲩⲥⲓⲅⲏ ϩ̄ⲛ̄ ⲟⲩⲡⲣⲟⲛⲟⲓⲁ
ⲙ̣̄ⲛ̄ ⲟⲩⲥⲓⲅⲏ ⲛ̄ⲧⲉ ⲡⲓⲱⲧ̀ · ⲡⲟⲩⲟ
10 [ⲉⲓ]ⲛ ϩ̄ⲛ̄ ⲟⲩϣⲁϫⲉ ⲙ̄ⲛ̄ ⲟⲩⲙ̄ⲛ̣̄ⲧ̣ⲙⲉ ·
[ⲡⲟ]ⲩ̣ⲟⲉⲓⲛ ⲛ̄ⲛⲁⲧ̀ϫⲱϩ̄ⲙ̄ ⲡⲟⲩⲟ
12 [ⲉⲓⲛ] ⲛ̄ⲛⲁⲧ̀ϫ̣ⲓⲟⲟⲣ ⲙ̄ⲙⲟϥ · ⲡⲟⲩ
[ⲟⲉⲓ]ⲛ̣ ⲉⲧⲁϥⲣ̄ϣⲟⲣⲡ̄ ⲛ̄ⲉ͡ⲓ ⲉⲃⲟⲗ ϣⲁ
14 [ⲉⲛⲉϩ] ⲛ̄ⲧⲉ ⲛⲓⲉⲛⲉϩ ⲛ̄ⲧⲉ ⲡⲓⲱⲧ̀
[ⲛ̄ⲛ]ⲁⲧ̀ϣⲁϫⲉ ⲙ̄ⲙⲟϥ ⲁⲩ̣ⲱ ⲛ̄
16 [ⲛⲁⲧ̀]ϯ ϣⲱⲗ̄ϩ ⲉⲣⲟϥ ⲁⲩⲱ ⲛ̄ⲛⲁⲧ̀
[ⲧⲁ]ϣⲉ ⲟⲉⲓϣ ⲙ̄ⲙⲟϥ ⲡⲉⲱⲛ ⲛ̄
18 [ⲧⲉ] ⲛ̣ⲉ̣ⲱⲛ · ⲡⲓϫⲡⲟ ⲉⲃⲟⲗ ⲙ̄ⲙⲟϥ

50, 2 See *supra*, p. 20.

[The] holy [book] of the / [Egyptians about the] great / [invisible Spirit (πνεῦμα),] the Father whose / [name can]not [be uttered, he who] / [came forth from the] heights, the light / of [the] perfection, the eternal light / of the eternities, the light / in silence (σιγή), in the providence (πρόνοια) / and silence (σιγή) of the Father, the light / in word and truth, / [the] incorruptible light, the / inaccessible light, the / eternal [light] / of the eternities, which has come forth, of the / ineffable and / [un]marked and / unproclaimable Father, the aeon (αἰών) / [of] the aeons (αἰών), he who begets /

50,8.10 "in" or "from" see commentary.

III 41, 6 [ⲁⲩ]ⲧ̣ⲟⲅⲉⲛⲓⲟⲥ ⲛ̅ⲉⲡⲓⲅⲉⲛⲛⲓⲟⲥ ⲛ̅ⲁⲗⲗⲟⲅⲉ[ⲛ]ⲓ̣ⲟⲥ ⲡⲁⲓⲱⲛ ⲛ̅ⲙⲉ ⲁⲗⲏⲑⲱⲥ

self-begotten (αὐτογένιος), self-producing (ἐπιγέννιος), alien (ἀλλογένιος), / the really (ἀληθῶς) true aeon (αἰών).

The appearance of the three powers: III 41,7 - 12

ⲁⲩⲡⲣⲟ[ⲉⲗⲑ]ⲉ ⲉⲃⲟⲗ ⲛ̅ϩⲏⲧ̅ϥ̅ · ⲛ̅ϭⲓ ϣⲟⲙⲧⲉ ⲛ̅ϭⲟⲙ [ⲉⲛ]ⲁⲓ̈ ⲛⲉ ⲡⲉⲓⲱⲧ ⲧⲙⲁⲁⲩ ⲡϣⲏⲣⲉ ⲉ[ⲃⲟⲗ] ϩ̣ⲛ̅ ⲧⲥⲓⲅⲏ ⲉⲧⲟⲛϩ̅ ⲡ̈ⲡⲓⲣⲉ ⲉⲃⲟⲗ ϩ̅ⲙ̅ [ⲡⲉⲓ]ⲱⲧ ⲛ̅ⲁⲫⲑⲁⲣⲧⲟⲥ ⲛⲁⲓ̈ ⲛ̅ⲧⲁⲩⲉⲓ ⲉ[ⲃⲟⲗ ϩ]ⲛ̅ ⲧⲥⲓ̣ⲅⲏ ⲇⲉ ⲙ̅ⲡⲓⲁⲇⲏⲗⲟⲥ ⲛ̅ⲉⲓⲱⲧ

Three / powers came forth (προελθεῖν) from him; / they are the Father, the Mother (and) the Son, / from the living silence (σιγή), what came forth from / the incorruptible (ἄφθαρτος) Father. These (+δέ) came / [forth from] the silence (σιγή) of the unknown (ἄδηλος) Father. /

IV 50 [ⲙⲁⲩⲁ]ⲁϥ · ⲁⲩⲱ ⲡⲓⲡⲓⲣⲉ ⲉⲃⲟⲗ

[ⲙ̄ⲙⲟϥ] ⲙⲁⲩⲁⲁϥ · ⲁⲩⲱ ⲙ̄ⲛ̄ ⲡⲓ

[ⲁⲗ]ⲗⲟ̣ⲅ̣ⲉⲛ̣ⲏⲥ ϯϭⲟⲙ ⲛ̄ⲛⲁⲧⲣ̄ϩⲉⲣ

[ⲙ]ⲏ̣ⲛⲉⲩⲉ ⲙ̄ⲙⲟⲥ ⲛ̄ⲧⲉ ⲡⲓⲱⲧ̓

[ⲛ̄ⲛ]ⲁⲧ̓ϣⲁϫⲉ ⲙ̄ⲙⲟϥ ·

himself, and he who comes forth from / [20] himself, and the / alien one (ἀλλογενής), the uninterpretable (-ἑρμηνεύειν) power / of the ineffable / Father.

The appearance of the three powers: IV 50,23 - 51,2

ⲁⲩⲉ͡ⲓ

[ⲉⲃ]ⲟⲗ ⲙ̄ⲙⲟϥ ⲛ̄ϭⲓ ϣⲟⲙⲧⲉ ⲛ̄ϭⲟⲙ

[ⲉ]ⲧⲉ ⲛⲁⲓ̈ ⲛⲉ· ⲡⲓⲱⲧ̓ ⲧⲙⲁ

[ⲁⲩ] ⲡϣⲏⲣⲉ ⲛⲓⲡⲓⲣⲉ ⲉⲃⲟⲗ ⲙ̄

[ⲙⲟ]ⲟⲩ ⲙⲁⲩⲁⲁⲩ ⲉⲃⲟⲗ ϩⲛ̄ ⲟⲩ

[ⲥⲓⲅ]ⲏ ⲉⲥⲟⲛ[ϩ̄] ⲛ̣̄ⲧⲉ ⲡⲓⲱⲧ̓ ⲛ̄ⲁⲧ̓

[ϫ]ⲱ̣ϩⲙ̄ · ⲛⲁⲓ̈ [ⲁ]ⲩ̣ⲣ̄ϣⲟⲣⲡ̄̓ ⲛ̄ⲉ͡ⲓ

51 [ⲛ̄ⲁ]

ⲉⲃⲟⲗ ϩⲛ̄ ⲟⲩⲥⲓ[ⲅⲏ ⲛ̄ⲧⲉ ⲡⲓⲱⲧ̓ ⲛ̄ⲛⲁⲧ̓]

ϣⲁϫⲉ ⲙ̄ⲙⲟ̣[ϥ

Three / powers came forth from him; / [25] they are the Father, the Mother / (and) the Son, they who came forth from / themselves, from the / living [silence (σιγή)] of the incorruptible Father. / These came // *51* forth from the silence (σιγή) [of the] ineffable / [Father.]

The composition of the realm of light: III 41,13-23

III 41 [ⲁⲩⲱ] ⲉⲃⲟ̣[ⲗ ϩ]ⲙ̅ ⲡⲙⲁ ⲉⲧⲙ̅ⲙⲁⲩ ⲁϥⲡⲣⲟ
[ⲉⲗⲑⲉ ⲉⲃⲟⲗ ⲛ̅]ϭ[ⲓ] ⲇ̣ⲟⲙⲉⲇⲱⲛ ⲇⲟⲝⲟⲙⲉ
[ⲇⲱⲛ ⲡⲁⲓⲱⲛ ⲛ̅]ⲧ̣ⲉ ⲛⲓⲁⲓⲱⲛ ⲁⲩⲱ ⲡⲟⲩ
[ⲟⲉⲓⲛ ⲛ̅ⲧⲉ ⲧⲟⲩ]ⲉ̣ⲓ ⲧⲟⲩⲉⲓ ⲛ̅ⲛ̅ϭⲟⲙ ⲛ̅
[ⲧⲁⲩ · ⲁⲩⲱ ⲛ̅ⲧ]ⲉ̣ⲓ̣ϩⲉ ⲡϣⲏⲣⲉ ⲁϥⲉⲓ
[ⲉⲃⲟⲗ ⲙ̅ⲙ]ⲉ̣ϩϥⲧⲟⲟⲩ ⲧⲙⲁⲁⲩ ⲛ̅ⲙⲉϩ
[ϯⲉ ⲡⲉⲓⲱ]ⲧ̇ ⲙ̅ⲙⲉϥⲥⲟⲟ{ⲟ}ⲩ ⲛⲉϥⲟ
[ ] ⲁⲗⲗⲁ ⲛ̅ⲛⲁⲧ̇ϯ ⲥⲟⲉⲓⲧ̇
[ⲉⲣⲟϥ ⲡⲁϊ]ⲉⲧⲉⲩⲁⲥⲏⲙⲁⲛⲧⲟⲥ ⲡⲉ ϩ̅ⲛ̅
[ⲛⲓϭⲟⲙ ⲧⲏ]ⲣⲟⲩ ⲛⲓⲉⲟⲟⲩ ⲙ̅ⲛ̅ ⲛⲓⲁ
[ⲫⲑⲁⲣ]ⲥ̣ⲓⲁ

41,18f. The reconstructions are 2 letters shorter than expected perhaps due to an imperfection in the papyrus.
20 Corr. ⲁⲗ over ⲡⲉ.

[And] from that place / Domedon Doxomedon came [forth] (*προελθεῖν*), / [the aeon (*αἰών*) of] the aeons (*αἰών*) and the [light] / [of] each one of [their] powers. / [And] thus the Son came / [forth] fourth; the Mother [fifth;] / [the Father] sixth. He was / [ ] but (*ἀλλά*) unheralded / [; it is he] who is unmarked (*ἀσήμαντος*) among / all [the powers], the glories and the / [incorruptions (*ἀφθαρσία*)].

The composition of the realm of light: IV 51,2-15

IV 51, 2 . . .]. ⲛ̄ⲧ[. . . . ⲇⲟ]
ⲝⲟⲙⲉⲇⲱ̣[ⲛ . . ⲇⲟ]ⲙⲉⲇ̣[ⲱⲛ
ⲡⲓⲉⲱⲛ ⲛ̄[ⲧⲉ ⲛⲓⲉⲱ]ⲛ · ⲡⲟ̣[ⲩⲟⲉⲓⲛ ⲁϥ]
ⲣ̄ϣⲟⲣⲡ̄' ⲛ̄ⲉ͡ⲓ ⲉⲃⲟ[ⲗ ⲙ̄]ⲙ̣ⲁ̣[ⲩ ⲉⲧⲉ ⲡⲁ̈ⲓ]
ⲡⲉ ⲡϭⲓⲛⲉ͡ⲓ ⲉⲃⲟⲗ ⲛ̄[ⲧⲉ ⲧⲟⲩⲉ͡ⲓ ⲧⲟⲩ]
ⲉ͡ⲓ ⲛ̄ⲧⲉ ⲛⲉⲩϭⲟⲙ · [ⲁⲩⲱ ⲛ̄ϯϩⲉ ⲡϣⲏ]
ⲣⲉ ⲁϥⲉ͡ⲓ ⲉⲃⲟⲗ ⲉⲡⲙⲉ[ϩϥⲧⲟⲟⲩ]
ⲧⲙⲁⲁⲩ ⲇⲉ ⲉⲥⲉ ⲙ̄ⲙ[ⲉϩϯⲉ]
ⲡⲓⲱⲧ' ⲇⲉ ⲉ̣[ϥⲉ ⲙ̄ⲙⲉϩⲥⲟⲟⲩ]
ϩ[̄. . . .]ⲁⲉ[ⲁⲗⲗⲁ]
[ⲟ]ⲩⲁⲧⲙⲁⲉⲓ̣[ⲛ ⲡⲉ ⲡⲁ̈ⲓ ⲇⲉ ⲛⲉϥ]
ⲉ ⲙ̄ⲙⲁⲉⲓⲛ ⲁⲛ [ϩ̄ⲛ ϩⲉ]ⲛ̣ϭ̣[ⲟⲙ]
ⲧⲏⲣⲟⲩ · ϩⲉⲛⲉ̣[ⲟ]ⲟ̣ⲩ ⲛ̄ⲁ[ⲧ'ϫⲱ]
ϩ̄ⲙ

51, 2 The letter before ⲛ̄ⲧ is ⲁ or ⲗ.
14 No superlin. stroke is visible on ⲛ.

[ ] Doxomedon / [Domedon] / the aeon (αἰών) [of the aeons (αἰών)], the [light] / [5] came forth from [there, i.e.] / the coming forth of [each one] / of their powers. [And thus the Son] / came forth [fourth], / and (δέ) the Mother is [the fifth,] / [10] and (δέ) the Father [is the sixth.] / [but (ἀλλά)] / [he is] without mark [, and (δέ) he was] / unmarked [among] all [powers,] / incorruptible glories. /

The three ogdoads: III 41,23 - 43,8

a) Their appearance: III 41,23 - 42,4

III 41 ⲉⲃⲟⲗ ϩ̅ⲙ ⲡⲙⲁ ⲉⲧ̅ⲙ̅ⲙⲁⲩ

24 [ⲁⲩⲉⲓ ⲉ]ⲃⲟⲗ ⲛ̅ϭⲓ ⲧϣⲟⲙⲧⲉ ⲛ̅ϭⲟⲙ·

42 ⲙⲃ

ⲧϣⲟⲙⲧⲉ ⲛ̅ϩⲟⲅ̣ⲇⲟ̣ⲁ̣ⲥ̣ ⲉⲧ̣ⲉ̣ [ⲡⲉⲓⲱⲧ̇]

2 ϩ̅ⲛ ⲟⲩⲥⲓⲅⲏ ⲙ̅ⲛ ⲧⲉϥⲡⲣⲟⲛⲟⲓ̣ⲁ̣ [ⲉⲓⲛⲉ]

ⲙ̅ⲙⲟⲟⲩ ⲉⲃⲟⲗ ϩ̅ⲛ ⲕⲟⲩⲟⲩⲛⲧ̅ϥ · ⲉⲧⲉ ⲛ̅

4 ⲧⲟⲟⲩ ⲡⲉⲓⲱⲧ̇ ⲧⲙⲁⲁⲩ ⲡϣⲏⲣⲉ·

From that place / the three powers [came] forth, // *42* the three ogdoads (ὀγδοάς) that [the Father] / [brings] forth, in silence (σιγή) with his providence (πρόνοια), / from his bosom, i.e. / the Father, the Mother (and) the Son.

b) The first ogdoad: III 42,5-11

ⲧϣⲟ⟨ⲣⲡ⟩ⲉ ⲛ̅ϩⲟⲅⲇⲟⲁⲥ ⲉⲧⲉ ⲉⲧⲃ[ⲏ]ⲏ̣ⲧ̣̅[ⲥ̅]

6 ⲁⲡϣⲟⲙ̅ⲛ̅ⲧ̅ ⲛ̅ϩⲟⲟⲩⲧ̇ ⲛ̅ⲁⲗⲟⲩ ⲡ[ⲣⲟ]

ⲉⲗⲑⲉ ⲉⲃⲟⲗ · ⲉⲧⲉ ⲧⲉⲛⲛⲟⲓⲁ ⲧⲉ ⲙ̅ⲛ [ⲡⲗⲟ]

8 ⲅⲟⲥ ⲙ̅ⲛ ⲧⲁⲫⲑⲁⲣⲥⲓⲁ ⲙ̅ⲛ ⲡⲱ[ⲛ̅ϩ ⲛ̅]

ϣⲁ ⲉⲛⲉϩ· ⲡⲉⲑⲉⲗⲏⲙⲁ ⲡⲛⲟ[ⲩⲥ]

10 ⲙ̅ⲛ ⲧⲉⲡⲣⲟⲅⲛⲱⲥⲓⲥ ⲡϩⲟⲟⲩⲧ [ⲥϩⲓ]

ⲙⲉ ⲛ̅ⲉⲓⲱⲧ̇·

42, 5 Corr. ϣ over ⲉ ? The scribe wrote ⲧϣⲟⲙⲧⲉ perhaps under the influence of 42,1.

/[5] The <first> ogdoad (ὀγδοάς), because of which / the thrice-male child came forth (προελθεῖν), / which is the thought (ἔννοια), and [the] word (λόγος), / and the incorruption (ἀφθαρσία), and the eternal / [life], the will (θέλημα), the mind (νοῦς), / [10] and the foreknowledge (πρόγνωσις), the androgynous / Father.

The three ogdoads: IV 51,15 - 53,3

a) Their appearance: IV 51,15 - 22

IV 51 ⲉⲁⲩⲣ̄ϣⲟⲣⲡ̄ʼ ⲛ̄ⲉ͡ⲓ ⲉ̣[ⲃⲟⲗ]
16 ⲙ̄ⲙⲟϥ ⲛ̄ϭⲓ ϣⲟⲙⲧⲉ ⲛ̄ϭ[ⲟⲙ ·]
ⲉⲧⲉ ϣⲟⲙⲧⲉ ⲛⲉ ⲛ̄ⲟⲅ[ⲇⲟⲁⲥ]
18 ⲛⲁï ⲛ̄ⲧⲁⲡⲓⲱⲧʼ ⲛ̄ⲧⲟ̣[ⲩ ⲉⲃⲟⲗ]
ϩ̄ⲛ ⲕⲟⲩⲛ̄ϥ ϩ̄ⲛ ⲟⲩⲥ̣ⲓⲅ̣ⲏ̣ [ⲙ̄ⲛ]
20 ⲟⲩⲡⲣⲟⲛⲟⲓⲁ · ⲉⲧⲉ ⲛⲁ̣[ï ⲛⲉ]
ⲡⲓⲱⲧʼ ⲧⲙⲁⲁⲩ [ⲡϣⲏ]
22 ⲣⲉ ·

[15] There came [forth] / from him three [powers,] / which are three ogdoads (ὀγδοάς) / which the Father brought [forth] / from his bosom in silence (σιγή) [and] / [20] providence (πρόνοια), which [are] / the Father, the Mother (and) [the] / [Son].

b) The first ogdoad: IV 51,22 - 52,2

22 ϯϣⲟⲣⲡ̄ʼ ⲛ̄ⲟⲅⲇⲟⲁⲥ ⲧ̣[ⲏ]
ⲉⲧⲁⲡⲓϣ̄ⲙ̄ⲧ̄ʼ ϩⲟⲟⲩⲧʼ ⲛ̄ⲁⲗⲟ[ⲩ]
24 ⲉ͡ⲓ ⲉⲃⲟⲗ ⲉⲧⲃⲏⲏⲧ̄ⲥ ⲉ[ⲧⲉ ⲧⲁï]
ⲧⲉ ϯⲉⲛⲛⲟⲓⲁ ⲙ̄ⲛ̣ ⲡⲓϣⲁ[ϫⲉ ⲙ̄ⲛ]
26 ⲡⲓⲱⲛ̄ϩ ⲛ̄ⲛⲁ[ⲧ]ϫⲱϩ̄ⲙ ϣ̣[ⲁ ⲉ]
ⲛⲉϩ · ⲟⲩⲱϣ̣· ⲟⲩⲛⲟⲩ[ⲥ·]
52 [ⲛ̅ⲃ̅]
[ⲙ̄ⲛ ⲟⲩϭⲓⲛⲣ̄ϣⲟ]ⲣⲡ̄ʼ ⲛ̄ⲥⲟⲟⲩⲛ
2 [ⲡⲓⲱ]ⲧ̣ʼ ⲛ̄ϩ[ⲟⲟⲩⲧʼ ⲥ]ϩ͡ⲓⲙⲉ

52, 2 Superlin. stroke on ⲛ is in the lacuna.

The first ogdoad (ὀγδοάς), the [one] / because of which the thrice-male child / came forth, [which] / [25] is the thought (ἔννοια), and the word, [and] / the eternal, incorruptible life, / will, mind (νοῦς), // *52* [and] foreknowledge, / [the] androgynous [Father].

c) The second ogdoad: III 42,11-21

III 42 ⲧⲙⲉϩⲥ̄ⲛⲧⲉ ⲛ̄ϭⲟ̣[ⲙ ⲛ̄]
12 ϩⲟⲅⲇⲟⲁⲥ ⲧⲙⲁⲁⲩ ⲧⲃⲁ̣[ⲣⲃ]ⲏ̣ⲗⲟⲛ [ⲙ̄ⲡⲁⲣ]
ⲑⲉⲛⲟⲥ ⲉⲡⲓ̄ⲧⲓ̄ⲧⲓ̄ⲱⲭ[.] ̄. [
14 ⲁ̄ⲓ · ⲙⲉⲙⲉ̄ⲛⲉ̄ⲁⲓ̄ⲙⲉⲛ̣[ⲡⲉ]
ⲧϩⲓⲭ̄ⲛ ⲧⲡⲉ· ⲕⲁⲣⲃ[
16 ⲧϭⲟⲙ ⲛ̄ⲁⲑⲉⲣⲙⲏ̣[ⲛⲉⲩⲉ ⲙ̄ⲙⲟⲥ]
ⲧⲙⲁⲁⲩ ⲛ̄ⲁⲧ̇ϣⲁⲭ̣ⲉ̣ [ⲙ̄ⲙⲟⲥ ⲁⲥⲡⲉⲓ]
18 ⲣⲉ ⲉⲃⲟⲗ ϩⲁⲣⲓϩⲁⲣⲟⲥ ϩ[
ⲙ̄ⲙⲟⲥ ⲁⲥⲡⲣⲟⲉⲗⲑⲉ ⲉ̣[ⲃⲟⲗ · ⲁⲥⲉⲩ]
20 ⲇⲟⲕⲉⲓ ⲙ̄ⲛ̄ ⲡⲉⲓⲱⲧ̇ ⲙ̄[ⲡⲓⲕⲁⲣⲱϥ ⲛ̄]
ⲕⲁⲣⲱϥ

The second ogdoad (*ὀγδοάς*)-/ power, the Mother, the virginal (*παρθένος*) Barbelon / ⲉⲡⲓⲧⲓⲧⲓⲱⲭ[ ] / ⲁⲓ, ⲙⲉⲙⲉⲛⲉⲁⲓⲙⲉⲛ [who] / 15 presides over the heaven, ⲕⲁⲣⲃ[ ] / the uninterpretable (-*ἑρμηνεύειν*) power, / the ineffable Mother [. She originated] / from herself [ ]; / she came forth (*προελθεῖν*); [she] / 20 agreed (*εὐδοκεῖν*) with the Father [of the] silent / [silence].

c) The second ogdoad: IV 52,2-14

IV 52, 2 ϯϭⲟⲙ
[ⲙ̅ⲙ]ⲉϩⲥ̅ⲛ̅[ⲧⲉ ⲉⲩⲟ]ⲅ̣ⲇⲟⲁⲥ ⲧⲉ
[ⲧⲙⲁ]ⲁⲩ ϯ[ⲃⲁⲣⲃⲏⲗ]ⲱ ⲙ̅ⲡⲁⲣⲑⲉⲛⲟⲥ
[ⲛ̅ϩⲟ]ⲟ̣ⲩ[ⲧ̀ . .] .ⲕⲁⲃⲁ · ⲁⲇⲱⲛⲉ·
[ ] ⲡⲏ ⲉⲧ̀ⲕⲏ ϩ͡ⲓϫ̅ⲛ̅ ⲧⲡ̣ⲉ
[ ] . [.]ⲁⲕⲣⲱⲃⲱⲣⲓⲁⲱⲣ
[. . .]. ϯϭ̣ⲟⲙ ⲛ̅ⲛⲁⲧⲣ̅ϩ̅ⲉ̅ⲣ̣ⲙⲏ
[ⲛⲉⲩⲉ] ⲙ̣̅ⲙ̣ⲟ̣[ⲥ] ⲁⲩⲱ ⲛ̅ⲛⲁ̣ⲧ̀
[ϣⲁϫⲉ ⲙ̅ⲙⲟⲥ] ⲧⲁï .ⲣ̅ⲙ. [
[ ]ⲕ ⲁ[ⲥⲡⲓ]ⲣ̣[ⲉ]
[ⲉⲃⲟⲗ ⲙ̅ⲙⲟⲥ ⲙⲁ]ⲩ̣ⲁⲁⲥ ⲉⲁⲥ
[ⲣ̅ϣⲟⲣⲡ̅ ⲛ̅ⲉ͡ⲓ ⲉ]ⲃⲟⲗ · ⲁⲥϯ ⲙⲉⲧⲉ
[ⲙ̅ⲛ̅] ⲡⲓⲱⲧ̣̀ [ⲛ̅]ⲧⲉ ϯⲥⲓⲅⲏ ⲉⲧⲟⲛ̣ϩ̣

52, 5 Trace appears to be ⲏ.
6 There is a faint ⲉ at the end of the line, perhaps erased.
11 There may be too little room for ⲥⲡⲓ in the lacuna.

The / second power [which] is [an] ogdoad (*ὀγδοάς*), / [the] Mother, the [male] virgin (*παρθένος*) [Barbelo] / [ ].ⲕⲁⲃⲁ, ⲁⲇⲱⲛⲉ / [ ] he who presides over the heaven / [ ]ⲁⲕⲣⲱⲃⲱⲣⲓⲁⲱⲣ / [,] the uninterpretable (-*ἑρμηνεύειν*) / and in[effable] power, / she ... / [ ]. She originated / [from] herself, and she / [came] forth. She agreed / [with] the Father of the living silence (*σιγή*). /

d) The third ogdoad: III 42,21 - 43,4

III 42 ⲧⲙⲉϩϣⲟⲙⲧⲉ̣ [ⲛ̅ϭⲟⲙ ⲛ̅ϩⲟ]
22 ⲅⲗⲟⲁⲥ ⲡϣⲏⲣⲉ ⲛ̅ⲧⲥ[ⲓⲅⲏ ⲛ̅ⲥⲓⲅⲏ]
ⲙⲛ̅ ⲡⲉⲕⲗⲟⲙ ⲛ̅ⲧⲥⲓⲅⲏ ⲛ̅ⲥⲓ[ⲅⲏ ⲙⲛ̅]
24 ⲡⲉⲟⲟⲩ ⲙ̅ⲡⲉⲓⲱⲧ̇ ⲙⲛ̅ ⲧⲁⲣⲉ̣[ⲧⲏ ⲛ̅ⲧ]
43 [ⲙⲅ]
[ⲙⲁⲁⲩ ·] ⲡ̣ⲁⲓ̈ ⲉ̣ϥⲉⲓⲛⲉ ⲉⲃⲟⲗ ϩⲛ̅ ⲛ̅ⲕⲟⲗ
2 [ⲡⲟⲥ] ⲛ̅ⲧⲥⲁϣϥⲉ ⲛ̅ϭⲟⲙ ⲙ̅ⲡⲛⲟϭ ⲛ̅
[ⲟⲩⲟ]ⲉⲓⲛ ⲛ̅ⲧⲥⲁϣϥⲉ ⲛ̅ⲥⲙⲏ ⲁⲩⲱ ⲡϣⲁ
4 [ϫⲉ ⲡ]ⲉ ⲡⲉⲩϫⲱⲕ

42,23 **ⲏ and ⲛ̅ are connected by a down-sloping diagonal stroke.**
43, 2 Corr. ⲥ over ⲁ.
3 Corr. ⲙ over erasure. ⲁ in ⲁⲩⲱ over ⲓ ?

The third ogdoad (ὀγδοάς) - / [power], the Son of the [silent (σιγή) silence (σιγή)], / and the crown of the silent (σιγή) silence (σιγή), [and] / the glory of the Father, and the virtue (ἀρετή) [of the] // *43* [Mother. He] brings forth from the bosom (κόλπος) / the seven powers of the great / light of the seven voices, and the word / [is] their completion.

e) The summary: III 43,4-8

4 ⲛⲁⲓ̈ ⲛⲉ ⲧϣⲟⲙⲧⲉ ⲛ̅
[ϭⲟⲙ] ⲧϣⲟⲙⲧⲉ ⲛ̅ϩⲟⲅⲇⲟⲁⲥ ⲛ̅ⲧⲁⲡⲉⲓ

These are the three / [5] [powers], the three ogdoads (ὀγδοάς) that the Father /

d) The third ogdoad: IV 52,15-24

IV 52 [ϯ⟨ⲙⲉϩ⟩ϣ]ⲟⲙⲧⲉ ⲇⲉ ⲛ̄ϭⲟⲙ ⲉⲩⲟⲅⲇ[ⲟⲁⲥ]
16 [ⲧⲉ] ⲡ̣[ⲓ]ϣⲏⲣⲉ ⲛ̄ⲧⲉ ϯⲥⲓⲅⲏ ⲙ̄ⲛ
[ⲟⲩⲕⲁⲣ]ⲱϥ · ⲙ̄ⲛ ⲟⲩⲥⲟⲟⲩⲛ ⲛ̣̄
18 [ⲧⲉ ⲡⲓⲱ]ⲧ̣ ⲙ̄ⲛ ⲟⲩⲁⲣⲉⲧⲏ ⲛ̄ⲧⲉ̣
[ⲧⲙ]ⲁⲁⲩ· ⲡⲁï ⲉⲁϥⲣ̄ϣⲟⲣⲡ̄ ⲛ̣̄
20 [ⲉⲓⲛⲉ ⲉ]ⲃ̣ⲟ̣ⲗ ϩ̄ⲛ̣ ⲕⲟⲩⲛ̄ϥ ⲛ̄ⲥⲁϣϥⲉ̣
[ⲛ̄ϭ]ⲟ̣ⲙ ⲛ̄ⲧ̣ⲉ ⲡⲓⲛⲟϭ ⲛ̄ⲟⲩⲟⲉⲓⲛ
22 [ⲛ̄]ⲧⲉ ϯⲥⲁϣϥⲉ ⲛ̄ⲥⲙⲏ ⲉⲧ[ⲉⲩ]
[ⲉⲃ]ⲟⲗ ⲙ̄ⲙⲟ̣ⲟⲩ ⲡⲉ ⲡϣⲁϫⲉ
24 [ⲛ̄ⲧⲉ] ⲡⲉⲩⲡⲗⲏⲣⲱⲙⲁ ·

52,15 There is not enough room for ϯⲙⲉϩϣ in the lacuna.
16 ⲓ̄ has flaked off. Perhaps homoioteleuton: ϯⲥⲓⲅⲏ ⲙ̄ⲛ ⟨ⲡⲓⲕⲗⲟⲙ ⲛ̄⟩ⲟⲩⲕⲁⲣⲱϥ, or a whole line dropped out: ⲟⲩⲕⲁⲣⲱϥ ⲙ̄ⲛ ⲡⲓⲕⲗⲟⲙ ⲛ̄.

[15] And (δέ) the third power which [is] an ogdoad (ὀγδοάς), / the Son of the silence (σιγή) and / <silence, and the crown of the> silence, and the knowledge / [of the Father], and the virtue (ἀρετή) of / [the] Mother, who [brought] / [20] [forth] from his bosom seven / powers of the great light / of the seven voices from / which is the word / [of] their completion (πλήρωμα).

e) The summary: IV 52,24 - 53,3

24 ⲉⲧⲉ
[ⲛⲁï] ⲛ̣ⲉ ϣⲟⲙ̣ⲧ̣ⲉ ⲛ̄ϭⲟⲙ · ⲉⲧⲉ
26 [ϣⲟ]ⲙⲧⲉ ⲛ̄ⲟ̣[ⲅ]ⲇⲟⲁⲥ ⲛⲉ ⲛⲁ[ï]

These / [25] are three powers, i.e. / three ogdoads (ὀγδοάς), these //

III 43,6 [ⲱⲧ̇ ϩ]ⲛ̄ ⲧⲉϥⲡⲣⲟⲛⲟⲓⲁ ⲉⲓⲛⲉ ⲙ̄ⲙⲟⲟⲩ
[ⲉⲃⲟⲗ] ϩⲛ̄ ⲕⲟⲟⲩⲛⲧ̄ϥ · ⲁϥⲉⲓⲛⲉ ⲙ̄ⲙⲟⲟⲩ
8 [ⲉⲃⲟⲗ] ϩⲙ̄ ⲡⲙⲁ ⲉⲧⲙ̄ⲙⲁⲩ

43,6-8 Doresse was still able to read all except the first letter of each line (*JA* 254, 1966, p. 340).

[through] his providence (*πρόνοια*) brought / [forth] from his bosom. He brought them / [forth] at that place.

The description of the Doxomedon-aeon: III 43,8 - 44,9

8 ⲁϥⲡⲣⲟⲉⲗ
[ⲑⲉ ⲉ]ⲃⲟⲗ ⲛ̄ϭⲓ ⲇⲟⲙⲉⲇⲱⲛ ⲇⲟⲝⲟⲙⲉ
10 [ⲇⲱⲛ] ⲡⲁⲓⲱⲛ ⲛ̄ⲛⲓⲁⲓⲱⲛ ⲙⲛ̄ ⲡⲉ
[ⲑⲣⲟ]ⲛ̣ⲟⲥ ⲉⲧⲛ̄ϩⲏⲧ̄ϥ · ⲙⲛ̄ ⲛ̄ⲇⲩⲛⲁⲙⲓⲥ
12 [ⲉⲧⲕ]ⲱⲧ[ⲉ ⲉⲣ]ⲟ̣ϥ ⲛⲓⲉⲟⲟⲩ ⲙⲛ̄ ⲛⲓⲁ
[ⲫⲑⲁ]ⲣⲥ̣[ⲓⲁ · ⲡⲉ]ⲓ̣ⲱⲧ̇ ⲙ̄ⲡⲛⲟϭ ⲛ̄ⲟⲩⲟ
14 [ⲉⲓⲛ ⲛ̄ⲧⲁϥⲉⲓ ⲉⲃ]ⲟⲗ ϩⲙ̄ ⲡⲓⲕⲁⲣⲱϥ · ⲡⲉ
[ⲡⲛⲟϭ ⲛ̄ⲇⲟⲝⲟⲙ]ⲉⲇⲱⲛ ⲛⲁⲓⲱⲛ ⲉⲧⲉ
16 [ⲡϣⲟⲙⲛ̄ⲧ ⲛ̄ϩⲟ]ⲟ̣ⲩⲧ̇ ⲛ̄ⲁⲗⲟⲩ ⲙ̄ⲧⲟⲛ
[ⲙ̄ⲙⲟⲟⲩ ⲙ̄ⲙ]ⲟ̣ϥ ⲁⲩⲱ ⲁⲩⲧⲁϫⲣⲟ ⲛ̄

43,9-12 Doresse was still able to read all except the first letter of 10 and the first two letters of 9, 11 and 12 (*JA* 254, 1966, p. 340).
12 Corr. ⲁ over ?
13 Corr. ⲟ in ⲟⲩ over ⲉ.
14f. Stop after ϥ is unusually high and large. Perhaps it is not a punctuation mark. Alternate reconstr. ⲡⲉⲉⲓⲛⲟϭ.
17 ⲙ̄ⲙⲟⲟⲩ preferable to ⲙ̄ⲙⲟϥ to account for the available space.

Domedon / Doxomedon came forth (*προελθεῖν*), / [10] the aeon (*αἰών*) of the aeons (*αἰών*), and the / [throne (*θρόνος*)] which is in him, and the powers (*δύναμις*) / [which surround] him, the glories and the / [incorruptions (*ἀφθαρσία*). The] Father of the great light / [who came] forth from the silence, he is / [15] [the great] Doxomedon-aeon (*αἰών*) in which / [the thrice-] male child rests. / And the throne (*θρόνος*) /

IV 53 [ⲛ̄ⲅ̄]

ⲛ̄ⲧⲁⲡⲓⲱⲧ' [ⲛ̄ⲧⲟⲩ ⲉⲃⲟⲗ ϩⲛ̄ ⲕⲟⲩ]
ⲛ̄ϥ ϩⲛ̄ ⲟⲩⲥⲓ̣[ⲅⲏ ⲙⲛ̄ ⲟ]ⲩⲡⲣ̣[ⲟⲛⲟⲓⲁ]
ⲛ̄ⲧⲁϥ ⲙ̄ⲡⲓ̣[ⲙⲁ ⲉⲧⲙ̄ⲙ]ⲁ̣ⲩ·

53 the Father [brought forth from] his [bosom] / through silence (σιγή) [and] his providence (πρόνοια) / at that [place].

The description of the Doxomedon-aeon: IV 53,3 - 54,13

ⲡ[ⲓⲙⲁ]
ⲉⲧⲁϥⲣ̄ϣⲟ̣ⲣ̣[ⲡ̄] ⲛ̄[ⲟⲩ]ⲱⲛ̄ϩ ⲉ̣[ⲃⲟⲗ]
ⲙ̄ⲙⲁⲩ ⲛ̄ϭⲓ ⲇⲟⲝ̣[ⲟⲙ]ⲉ̣ⲇ̣[ⲱⲛ ⲡⲓⲉ]
ⲱⲛ ⲛ̄ⲧⲉ ⲛⲓⲉⲱⲛ [ⲙⲛ̄ ⲛⲓⲑⲣⲟⲛⲟⲥ]
ⲉⲧⲛ̄ϩⲣⲁ̈ⲓ̈ ⲛ̄ϩⲏⲧϥ̄ [ⲙⲛ̄ ⲛⲓϭⲟⲙ ⲉⲧ']
[ⲕ]ⲱ̣ⲧⲉ ⲉⲣⲟⲟⲩ ⲙ̣[ⲛ̄ ⲟⲩⲉⲟⲟⲩ]
[ⲙ]ⲛ̣ ⲟⲩⲙⲛ̄ⲧ'ⲁⲧ̣'[ϫⲱϩⲙ · ⲡⲓⲱⲧ']
[ⲛ̄ⲧ]ⲉ ⲡⲓⲛⲟϭ̣ [ⲛ̄ⲟⲩⲟⲉⲓⲛ ⲁϥⲉ͡ⲓ]
[ⲉⲃⲟⲗ] ϩ̣ⲛ̄ ⲟⲩⲙ[
[ ]. . [. . . . . ⲡⲓⲛⲟϭ ⲛ̄ⲇⲟ]
[ⲝⲟ]ⲙ̣ⲉⲇⲱⲛ [ⲛ̄ⲛⲉⲱⲛ ⲉⲧϥ̄ⲙⲟⲧⲛ̄]
[ⲙ]ⲙⲟϥ ⲛ̄ϩⲏⲧϥ̄ ⲛ̣̄[ϭⲓ ⲡⲓϣⲙⲧ̣' ϩⲟ]
[ⲟ]ⲩⲧ' ⲛ̄ⲁⲗⲟⲩ [ⲁⲩⲱ ⲁϥⲧⲁϫⲣⲟ]

53,11 Perhaps ⲟⲩⲙ[ⲛ̄ⲧⲣⲉϥⲕⲁⲣⲱϥ.

[At that place] / Doxomedon appeared, / [the] aeon (αἰών) / of the aeons (αἰών) [and the thrones (θρόνος)] / that are in him, [and the powers which] / surround them, [and glory,] / [and] in[corruption. The Father] / [of] the great [light came] / [forth] from [ ] / [the great Doxo]medon / [-aeon (αἰών)] in [which] / [the thrice-male] child [rests]. / [And the throne (θρόνος)] /

III 43,18 [ϩⲣⲁⲓ̈ ⲛ̄ϩⲏⲧ̄ϥ] ⲙ̄ⲡⲉⲑⲣⲟⲛⲟⲥ ⲙ̄ⲡⲉϥⲉ
[ⲟⲟⲩ · ⲡⲁⲓ̈ ⲉⲧ]ⲉ ⲡⲉϥⲣⲁⲛ ⲛ̄ⲁⲧⲟⲩⲱⲛϩ
20 [ⲉⲃⲟⲗ ⲥⲏϩ] ϩⲓⲱⲱϥ ϩ̄ⲛ ⲧⲡⲩⲝⲟⲥ
[ ].ⲥ ⲟⲩⲁ ⲡⲉ ⲡϣⲁϫⲉ ⲡⲉⲓ
22 [ⲱⲧ̇ ⲙ̄ⲡⲟⲩⲟ]ⲉⲓⲛ ⲙ̄ⲡⲧⲏⲣϥ· ⲡⲉⲛ
[ⲧⲁϥⲉⲓ] ⲉ̣ⲃⲟⲗ ϩ̄ⲛ ⲧⲥⲓⲅⲏ ⲉϥⲙ̄ⲧⲟⲛ
24 [ⲙ̄ⲙⲟ]ϥ ϩ̄ⲙ ⲡⲓⲕⲁⲣⲱϥ ⲡⲁⲓ̈ ⲉⲧⲉ ⲡⲉϥ

44 ⲙ̣ⲇ̣

ⲣⲁⲛ ϩ̄ⲛ ⲟⲩⲥⲩⲙⲃⲟⲗⲟⲛ ⲛ̄ⲁ[ϩⲟⲣⲁⲧⲟⲛ ⲟⲩⲙⲩ]
2 ⲥⲧⲏⲣⲓⲟⲛ ⲉϥϩⲏⲡ̄ ⲛ̄ⲁⲧ̣ⲛ̣[ⲁⲩ ⲉ]ⲣ̣[ⲟϥ ⲁϥⲡⲣⲟ]
ⲉⲗⲑⲉ ⲉⲃⲟⲗ · ⲓⲓⲓⲓⲓⲓⲓⲓⲓⲓⲓⲓⲓⲓⲓⲓⲓⲓ̣[ⲓⲓⲓ]
4 ⲏⲏⲏⲏⲏⲏⲏⲏⲏⲏⲏⲏⲏⲏⲏⲏⲏⲏⲏⲏⲏ̣[ⲏⲏ ⲟ]
ⲟⲟⲟⲟⲟⲟⲟⲟⲟⲟⲟⲟⲟⲟⲟⲟⲟⲟⲟⲟⲟⲟ ⲩⲩ[ⲩⲩⲩ]

44, 1 Superlin. stroke on ⲛ is not visible.

of his [glory] was established [in it,] / [this one] on which his unrevealable name / [is inscribed], on the tablet (*πύξος*) / [ ] one is the word, the [Father] / [of the light] of everything, he / [who came] forth from the silence (*σιγή*), while he rests / in the silence, he whose // *44* name [is] in an [invisible (*ἀόρατον*)] symbol (*σύμβολον*). [A] / hidden, [invisible] mystery (*μυστήριον*) / came forth (*προελθεῖν*) ı ı ı ı ı ı ı ı ı ı ı ı ı ı ı ı ı ı ı [ı ı ı] / ʜ [ʜ ʜ ᴏ] / ᴏ ʏ ʏ [ʏ ʏ ʏ] /

IV 53,16 [ⲛ̄ϩ]ⲣⲁⲓ̈ ⲛ̄ϩⲏⲧϥ̄ ⲛ̄ϭⲓ ⲡ̣[ⲓⲑⲣⲟⲛⲟⲥ]
[ⲛ̄]ⲧ̣ⲉ ⲡⲉϥⲉⲟⲟⲩ ⲡ̣[ⲏ ⲉⲧⲁⲩⲥϩⲁⲓ̈]
18 [ⲛ̄ϩⲣ]ⲁⲓ̈ ⲛ̄ϩⲏⲧϥ̄ [ⲙ̄ⲡⲉϥⲣⲁⲛ ⲉⲧⲉ]
[ⲙⲉ]ⲩϫⲟⲟϥ ϩ̄ⲛ ϯ[ⲡⲩⲝⲟⲥ
20 [. .].ⲱⲛ ⲉⲧⲉ ⲡ̣[ⲁⲓ̈ ⲡⲉ ⲡϣⲁϫⲉ]
[ⲛ̄ⲧ]ⲉ ⲡⲓⲱⲧ̀ ⲁⲩ̣[ⲱ ⲡⲟⲩⲟⲉⲓⲛ]
22 [ⲛ̄ⲧ]ⲉ ⲛⲁⲓ̈ ⲧⲏⲣⲟ[ⲩ ⲡⲁⲓ̈ ⲉⲧⲉⲃⲟⲗ]
[ϩ̄ⲛ] ⲟⲩⲥⲓⲅⲏ · ⲁⲩ[ⲱ ⲡⲁⲓ̈ ⲉⲧⲁϥ]
24 [ⲣ̄]ϣ̣ⲟⲣⲡ̄̀ ⲛ̄ⲉ͡ⲓ ⲉⲃ[ⲟⲗ ϩ̄ⲛ ⲟⲩⲥⲓ]
[ⲅⲏ] ⲡⲁⲓ̈ ⲉⲧ̀ⲙⲟ̣[ⲧⲛ̄ ⲙ̄ⲙⲟϥ ϩ̄ⲛ]
26 [ⲟⲩⲥ]ⲓ̣ⲅⲏ ⲡⲁⲓ̈ ⲉ[ⲧⲉ ⲡⲉϥⲣⲁⲛ]
[ϩ̄ⲛ ⲟ]ⲩⲥⲩⲙⲃ̣[ⲟⲗⲟⲛ ⲉϥⲉ ⲛ̄ⲁ]
28 [ⲧⲛ]ⲁⲩ ⲉⲣⲟϥ [
54 [ⲛ̲ⲇ̲]
[...... ⲁϥⲣ̄ϣ]ⲟⲣⲡ̄̀ ⲛ̄ⲉ͡ⲓ ⲉⲃⲟⲗ
2 [ⲛ̄ϭⲓ ⲟⲩ]ⲙⲩ[ⲥⲧⲏⲣⲓⲟ]ⲛ ⲛ̄ⲛⲁⲧ̀ϣⲁ
[ϫⲉ] ⲙ̣ⲙⲟ[ϥ · ııııı]ı̣ıııııııııı
4 [ııııı] ⲏⲏⲏ[ⲏ]ⲏ̣ⲏ[ⲏ]ⲏⲏⲏⲏⲏⲏⲏ
[ⲏⲏⲏ]ⲏⲏ̣[ⲏⲏ]ⲏ̣ ⲟⲟⲟⲟⲟⲟⲟⲟⲟ
6 [ⲟⲟⲟⲟⲟⲟⲟ]ⲟ̣ⲟⲟⲟⲟⲟ ⲩⲩⲩ̣

53,20 Perhaps [ⲡⲓ]ⲉⲱⲛ.
21 Perhaps ⲁϥ̣[instead of ⲁⲩ̣[.

of his glory [was established] in it, / [this one] on [which] / [his] ineffable [name was inscribed,] / on the [tablet (*πύξος*)] / 20 [the aeon (*αἰών*) (?)] which [is the word] / [of] the Father and [the light] / [of] everything [, he who is from] / silence (*σιγή*) and [he who] / came forth [from silence (*σιγή*),] / 25 he who rests [in] / silence (*σιγή*), he [whose name] / [is in] an [in]visible / [and hidden(?)] symbol (*σύμβολον*) // *54* [. There] came forth / [an] ineffable my- [stery (*μυστήριον*)] / [I I I I I] I I I I I I I I I I I I / [I I I I I I] H H H [H] H H [H] H H H H H H H / 5 [H H H] H H [H H] H O O O O O O O O O / [O O O O O O O] O O O O O O Y Y Y /

III 44, 6 ⲩⲩⲩⲩⲩⲩⲩⲩⲩⲩⲩⲩⲩⲩⲩⲩⲩ ⲉⲉⲉⲉⲉ̣[
ⲉⲉⲉⲉⲉⲉⲉⲉⲉⲉⲉⲉⲉⲉⲉⲉⲉ ⲁⲁⲁⲁⲁⲁⲁ[ⲁⲁⲁⲁ]
8 ⲁⲁⲁⲁⲁⲁⲁⲁⲁⲁⲁ ⲱ ⲱ ⲱ ⲱ ⲱ ⲱ ⲱ ⲱ̣[ⲱⲱⲱ]
ⲱ ⲱ ⲱ ⲱ ⲱ ⲱ ⲱ ⲱ ⲱ ⲱ ⲱ ·

44, 6 There is room for 2 more letters at the end of the line. Perhaps a diple was put here.

8 Doresse was still able to read all except the last two letters (*JA* 254, 1966, p. 344).

ⲩ ⲩ ⲩ ⲩ ⲩ ⲩ ⲩ ⲩ ⲩ ⲩ ⲩ ⲩ ⲩ ⲩ ⲩ ⲩ ⲩ ⲉ ⲉ ⲉ ⲉ ⲉ / ⲉ ⲉ ⲉ ⲉ ⲉ ⲉ ⲉ ⲉ ⲉ ⲉ ⲉ ⲉ ⲉ ⲉ ⲉ ⲉ ⲉ ⲁ ⲁ ⲁ ⲁ ⲁ ⲁ ⲁ [ⲁ ⲁ ⲁ ⲁ] / ⲁ ⲁ ⲁ ⲁ ⲁ ⲁ ⲁ ⲁ ⲁ ⲁ ⲁ ⲱ ⲱ ⲱ ⲱ ⲱ ⲱ ⲱ ⲱ ⲱ [ⲱ ⲱ] / ⲱ ⲱ ⲱ ⲱ ⲱ ⲱ ⲱ ⲱ ⲱ ⲱ ⲱ .

The presentation of praise and request of the ogdoads: III 44,9-21

ⲁⲩⲱ [ⲛ̄ⲧⲉⲉⲓ]
10 ϩⲉ ⲁⲧϣⲟⲙⲧⲉ ⲛ̄ϭⲟⲙ ϯ ⲥⲙⲟⲩ ⲉⲡ[ⲛⲟϭ]
ⲛ̄ⲁϩⲟⲣⲁⲧⲟⲛ ⲛ̄ⲡ̄ⲛ̄ⲁ̄ ⲛ̄ⲁⲧ̇ϫⲱ ⲙ̄ⲡ[ⲉϥⲣⲁⲛ]
12 ⲙ̄ⲡⲁⲣⲑⲉⲛⲓⲕⲟⲛ ⲛ̄ⲁⲕⲗⲏⲧⲟⲛ ⲙ̄ⲛ̣̄ [ⲧⲉϥ]
ⲁⲣⲥⲉⲛⲓⲕⲏ ⲛ̄ⲡⲁⲣⲑⲉⲛⲏ ⲁⲩⲁⲓⲧ[ⲓ ⲛ̄ⲟⲩ]

44,9-12 Doresse was still able to read all except the last letter in 10 and 12, and the last three letters in 9 and 11 (*JA* 254, 1966, p. 344).

13 ⲡⲁⲣⲑⲉⲛⲏ (sic!) cf. Schwyzer, *Griechische Grammatik* II, p. 32 note 4.

And [in this] / [10] way the three powers gave praise to the [great], / invisible (ἀόρατον), unnameable, / virginal (παρθενικόν), uncallable (ἄκλητον) Spirit (πνεῦμα), and [his] / male (ἀρσενική) virgin (παρθένη). They asked (αἰτεῖν) [for a] /

IV 54 [ⲩⲩⲩⲩⲩ]ⲩ̣ⲩⲩⲩⲩⲩ[ⲩ]
8 [ⲩⲩⲩⲩⲩⲩ]ⲩ ⲉⲉⲉⲉⲉ[ⲉⲉ]
[ⲉⲉⲉⲉⲉⲉⲉ]ⲉ̣ⲉⲉⲉⲉⲉ̣[ⲉⲉ]
10 [ⲁⲁⲁⲁⲁⲁⲁⲁⲁ]ⲁ̣ⲁⲁⲁ[ⲁⲁ]
[ⲁⲁⲁⲁⲁⲁⲁ ⲱ ⲱ] ⲱ̣ [ⲱ ⲱ]
12 [ⲱ ⲱ ⲱ ⲱ ⲱ ⲱ] ⲱ ⲱ ⲱ ⲱ̣[ⲱ]
[ⲱ ⲱ ⲱ ⲱ ⲱ ⲱ·]

[ⲩ ⲩ ⲩ ⲩ ⲩ] ⲩ ⲩ ⲩ ⲩ ⲩ ⲩ ⲩ [ⲩ] / [ⲩ ⲩ ⲩ ⲩ ⲩ ⲩ] ⲩ ⲉ ⲉ ⲉ ⲉ ⲉ [ⲉ ⲉ] / [ⲉ ⲉ ⲉ ⲉ ⲉ ⲉ ⲉ] ⲉ ⲉ ⲉ ⲉ ⲉ ⲉ [ⲉ ⲉ] / [10] [ⲁ ⲁ ⲁ ⲁ ⲁ ⲁ ⲁ ⲁ ⲁ] ⲁ ⲁ ⲁ ⲁ [ⲁ ⲁ] / [ⲁ ⲁ ⲁ ⲁ ⲁ ⲁ ⲁ ⲱ ⲱ] ⲱ [ⲱ ⲱ] / [ⲱ ⲱ ⲱ ⲱ ⲱ ⲱ] ⲱ ⲱ ⲱ ⲱ [ⲱ] / [ⲱ ⲱ ⲱ ⲱ ⲱ ⲱ .]

The presentation of praise and request of the ogdoads: IV 54,13 - 55,11

ⲁⲩⲱ ⲛ̄ϯϩⲉ̣
14 [ϯϣⲟⲙⲧ]ⲉ̣ ⲛ̣ϭⲟⲙ ⲁⲩⲉⲓⲛ̣[ⲉ]
[ⲉϩⲣⲁ̈ⲓ̈ ⲛ̄ⲟⲩ]ⲥ̣ⲙⲟⲩ ⲙ̄ⲡⲓⲛⲟϭ ⲛ̄
16 [ⲛⲁⲧⲛⲁⲩ ⲉⲣ]ⲟϥ ⲁⲩⲱ ⲛ̄ⲁⲧ'ϫ[ⲁϩ]
[ⲙ̄ϥ ⲛ̄ⲛⲁⲧ'ϯ ⲣⲁ]ⲛ ⲉⲣⲟϥ ⲡⲓ[ⲡⲁ]
18 [ⲣⲑⲉⲛⲓⲕⲟⲛ ⲙ̄]ⲡ̣ⲛ̄ⲁ ⲛ̄ⲧⲉ ⲡ[ⲓⲱⲧ']
[ⲁⲩⲱ ϯϩⲟⲟⲩⲧ'] ⲙ̄ⲡⲁⲣⲑⲉⲛ̣[ⲟⲥ]
20 [ϯⲃⲁⲣⲃⲏⲗⲱ] ⲁ⟨ⲩ⟩ⲣ̄ⲁⲓⲧⲓ ⲛ̄[ϣⲟ]

54,14 Imperfection in the papyrus may have caused unusual spacing.
16f. Perhaps ⲁⲧ'ϫⲁϩⲙⲉϥ (77,5), ⲁⲧ'ϫⲱϩⲙ (60,11) or ⲁⲧ'ϫⲟⲟϥ. Cf. also 65,10; 67,5; 73,8f.
20 MS. ⲁⲥⲣ̄ⲁⲓⲧⲓ.

And in this way / [the three] powers brought / [15] praise to the great, / [invisible], and [incorruptible] / [unnameable] one, the [virginal (παρθενικόν)] / Spirit (πνεῦμα) of the [Father] / [and the male] virgin (παρθένος) / [20] [Barbelo]. <They> asked (αἰτεῖν) /

54,19f. MS. reads: [And the male] virgin [Barbelo] asked etc.

III 44,14 ϭⲟⲙ · ⲁⲥⲡⲣⲟⲉⲗⲑⲉ ⲉⲃⲟⲗ ⲛ̄ϭⲓ̣ ⲟⲩⲥⲓ[ⲅⲏ ⲛ̄]
ⲟⲩⲥⲓⲅⲏ ⲉⲥⲟⲛϩ ⲛ̄ϭⲓ ϩⲉⲛ[ⲉⲟⲟⲩ] ⲙⲛ̣̄ [ϩⲉⲛⲁ]
16 ⲫⲑⲁⲣⲥⲓⲁ ϩⲛ̄ ⲛⲁⲓⲱⲛ [ⲁⲓ]
ⲱⲛ ϩⲉⲛⲧⲃⲁ ⲉⲩⲟⲩⲟϩ[ⲙ ⲡ]
18 ϣⲟⲙⲛ̄ⲧ ⲛ̄ϩⲟⲟⲩⲧ̇ ⲧ̣[ϣⲟⲙⲧⲉ ⲛ̄ϭⲓⲛ]
ⲭⲡⲟ ⲛ̄ϩⲟⲟⲩⲧ̇ ⲛ̄ⲅⲉⲛ̣[ⲉⲁ ⲛ̄ϩⲟⲟⲩⲧ̇ ⲁⲩ]
20 ⲙⲉϩ ⲡⲛⲟϭ ⲛ̄ⲇⲟⲝⲟⲙ[ⲉⲇⲱⲛ ⲛ̄ⲁⲓⲱⲛ ⲛ̄]
ⲧϭⲟⲙ ⲙ̄ⲡϣⲁϫⲉ ⲙ̄ⲡⲉⲡ[ⲗⲏⲣⲱⲙⲁ ⲧⲏⲣϥ̄]

44,15 Superlin. stroke on ⲙⲛ is not visible.
17 Corr. ⲉⲩⲟⲩⲟϩ over erased word beginning with ⲛ̄.
19 Or : ⲅⲉⲛ̣[ⲟⲥ

power. A silence (σιγή) of living silence (σιγή) / [15] came forth (προελθεῖν), namely [glories] and / incorruptions (ἀφθαρσία) in the aeons (αἰών) [aeons (αἰών)] / myriads added [on , the] / three males, [the three] / male offspring, the [male] races (γενεά) / [20] filled the great Doxomedon-[aeon (αἰών) with] / the power of the word of the [whole pleroma (πλήρωμα).] /

IV 54 [ⲣⲡ̄ ⲛ̄ⲛⲟⲩϭⲟⲙ] ⲁⲥⲣ̄ϣⲣ̄ⲡ ⲛ̣
22 [ⲟⲩⲱⲛ̄ϩ ⲉⲃⲟ]ⲗ ⲛ̄ϭⲓ ⲟⲩⲥ[ⲓⲅⲏ]
[ⲉⲥⲟⲛ̄ϩ ⲛ̄ⲥⲓ]ⲅⲏ ϩⲛ̄ ⲟⲩϭⲟⲙ
24 [ⲛⲁï ⲉⲧⲉ ϩⲉⲛⲉⲟ]ⲟⲩ ⲛⲉ ⲙⲛ̄
[ϩⲉⲛⲁⲧ'ϫⲱϩⲙ] ⲡ̣ⲓⲉⲱⲛ ⲉⲧ'
26 [ⲛ̄ⲧ]ⲉ 'ⲛ'ⲉⲱⲛ ·
55 [ⲛ̄ⲉ]
ⲡⲏ ⲉⲧⲕⲏ ⲉ[ϩⲣⲁï ⲉϫⲛ̄ ⲛⲓⲙⲩⲥⲧⲏ]
2 ⲣⲓⲟⲛ ⲛⲁï ⲉ[ⲧⲉ ϩⲉⲛⲁⲛⲧⲃⲁ ⲛⲉ]
ⲛⲓϣⲙⲧ' ϩ[ⲟⲟ]ⲩ[ⲧ'· ⲛⲓ]ϣⲙ[ⲧ' ⲅⲉ]
4 ⲛⲟⲥ · ⲛⲓϩⲟⲟ̣ⲩ[ⲧ' ⲙ̄]ⲛ ⲛⲓⲅⲉⲛ̣[ⲉⲁ]
ⲛ̄ϩⲟⲟⲩⲧ' · ⲛⲓⲉ[ⲟⲟⲩ ⲛ̄ⲧⲉ ⲡⲓⲱⲧ' ·]
6 [ⲛ]ⲓ̣ⲉⲟⲟⲩ ⲛ̄ⲧⲉ ⲡ̣[ⲓⲛ]ⲟϭ [ⲛ̄ⲭ̄ⲥ̄ ⲙⲛ̄]
[ⲛⲓ]ⲅⲉⲛⲟⲥ ⲛ̄ϩⲟⲟⲩ[ⲧ'·] ⲛⲓⲅ̣[ⲉⲛⲉⲁ ⲛ̄]
8 [ⲧⲁ]ⲩⲙⲟⲩϩ ⲙ̄ⲡⲓⲛⲟϭ̣ [ⲛ̄ⲛⲉⲱⲛ]
[ⲛ̄ⲇ]ⲟⲝⲟⲙⲉⲇⲱⲛ̣ [ⲛ̄]ϩ[ⲉⲛϭⲟⲙ ⲛ̄]
10 [ⲧⲉ ⲟ]ⲩϣⲁϫⲉ ⲛ̄ⲧⲉ ⲡ̣[ⲓⲡⲗⲏⲣⲱⲙⲁ]
[ⲛ̄ⲟ]ⲩⲟⲉⲓⲛ[·]

[for a power.] A [living], / [silent (σιγή) silence (σιγή)] / [appeared] in a power, / [these which] are [glories] and / [incorruptions,] the aeon (αἰών) which / [of] the aeons (αἰών), // *55* he who presides [over the] / [myriads of] mysteries (μυστήριον), / the three males, [the] three [offspring (γένος)], / the males [and] the male races (γενεά), / the [glories of the Father,] / [the] glories of the great [Christ and] / [the] male offspring (γένος), the [races (γενεά)] / filled the great / Doxomedon [-aeon (αἰών) with powers of] / a word of the [pleroma (πλήρωμα)] / [of] light.

The presentation of praise of the thrice-male child: III 44,22 - ?

III 44,22 ⲧⲟⲧⲉ ⲡϣⲟⲙⲛ̅ⲧ̈ ⲛ̅ϩⲟⲟⲩ[ⲧ̈ ⲛ̅ⲁⲗⲟⲩ ⲙ̅ⲡⲛⲟϭ]
ⲛ̅ⲭ̅ⲣ̅ⲥ̅ ⲛ̅ⲧⲁϥⲧⲁϩⲥϥ ⲛ̅ϭⲓ ⲡ[ⲛⲟϭ ⲛ̅ⲁϩⲟ]
24 ⲣⲁⲧⲟⲛ ⲙ̅ⲡ̅ⲛ̅ⲁ̅ ⲡⲁï ⲛ̅ⲧ[ⲁⲩϯ ⲣⲁⲛ ⲉⲧⲉϥ]
ϭⲟⲙ ϫⲉ ⲁⲓⲛⲟⲛ ⲁϥϯ [ⲛ̅ⲟ]ⲩ̣[ⲥⲙⲟⲩ ⲙ̅]
26 ⲡⲛⲟϭ ⲛ̅ⲁϩⲟⲣⲁⲧⲟⲛ ⲙ̅ⲡ̅ⲛ̅ⲁ̅ [ⲙ̅ⲛ ⲧⲉϥ]
ⲁⲣⲥⲉⲛⲓⲕⲏ ⲙ̅ⲡⲁⲣⲑⲉⲛⲟⲥ ïⲱ[ⲏⲗ ⲙ̅ⲛ]
28 ⲧⲥⲓⲅⲏ ⲛ̅ⲥⲓⲅⲏ ⲛ̅ⲥⲓⲅⲏ ⲙ̅ⲛ ⲧⲙⲛ̅ⲧ̣[ⲛⲟϭ]

44,24 Corr. ⲛ in ⲡⲛⲁ over ⲉⲓ. It seems the scribe began to write ⲡⲉⲓⲱⲧ.
45,1ff. are missing.

Then (τότε) the thrice-male [child of the great] / Christ (χριστός) whom the [great] invisible (ἀόρατον) / Spirit (πνεῦμα) had anointed — he [whose] / [25] power [was called] Ainon — gave [praise to] / the great invisible (ἀόρατον) Spirit (πνεῦμα) [and his] / male (ἀρσενική) virgin (παρθένος) Yoel, [and] / the silence (σιγή) of silent (σιγή) silence (σιγή), and the [greatness] //

The presentation of praise of the thrice-male child: IV 55,11 - 56,11

IV 55 ⲧⲟⲧⲉ ⲡⲓϣ[ⲙⲧ̀]
[ϩⲟⲟⲩ]ⲧ̀ ⲛ̄ⲁⲗ[ⲟⲩ ⲙ̄ⲡⲓ]ⲛ̣ⲟϭ̣ [ⲛ̄ⲭ̄ⲥ̄]
[ⲡ]ⲁ̣ï ⲉⲧⲁϥⲧⲁϩ[ⲥ̄ϥ ⲛ̄ϭⲓ ⲡⲓⲛⲟϭ ⲛ̄]
[ⲁⲧ]ⲛ̣ⲁⲩ ⲉⲣⲟϥ ⲙ̄[ⲡ̄ⲛ̄ⲁ̄ ⲡⲁï ⲉⲧⲁⲩ]
[ϯ ⲣ]ⲁ̣ⲛ ⲉⲧⲉϥϭⲟ[ⲙ ⲁⲓⲛⲟⲛ ⲁϥⲉⲓⲛⲉ]
[ⲉϩ]ⲣ̣ⲁï ⲛ̄ⲟⲩⲥⲙⲟⲩ ⲙ̣̄[ⲡⲓⲛⲟϭ ⲛ̄]
[ⲁⲧⲛ]ⲁⲩ ⲉⲣⲟϥ ⲙ̣̄[ⲡ̄ⲛ̄ⲁ̄ ⲙ̄ⲛ̄ ϯϩⲟ]
[ⲟⲩ]ⲧ̀ ⲙ̄ⲡⲁⲣ̣ⲑ[ⲉⲛⲟⲥ ïⲱⲏⲗ ϯ]
[ⲥⲓⲅⲏ ⲛ̄]ⲟⲩⲕⲁⲣ[ⲱϥ ⲛ̄ⲟⲩⲥⲓⲅⲏ ϯ]
[ⲙ̄ⲛ̄ⲧ̄ⲛ̄]ⲟϭ ⲉⲧⲛ̣[ⲉⲧⲉ]
[ⲙⲉ]ⲩϫ̣ⲟⲟϥ· .[ⲛ̄ⲛⲁⲧ̀]
[ϣ]ⲁϫⲉ ⲙ̄ⲙⲟ̣[ϥ . . .] . . . [
[ⲛⲁⲧ]ⲣⲟⲩⲱ ϩⲁ[ⲣⲱϥ ⲁⲩ]ⲱ ⲛ̄ⲛ[ⲁ]
[ⲧ̄ⲣ̄]ϩⲉⲣⲙⲏⲛⲉ̣[ⲩⲉ ⲙ̄]ⲙ̣ⲟϥ ⲡ[ⲓ]
[ϣⲟ]ⲣ̄ⲡ̀ ⲉⲧⲁϥ[ⲟⲩⲱ̄ⲛ̄]ϩ [ⲉ]ⲃ̣ⲟⲗ
[ⲁ]ⲩⲱ ⲛ̄ⲛⲁⲧ̀ⲧ[ⲁϣ]ⲉ ⲟⲉⲓ̣ϣ̣
[ⲙ̄]ⲙⲟϥ ⲛ̄ⲛⲁ[ⲧ̀ . .] ϭⲓⲙⲁ·

55,15 There is no room for ϫⲉ before ⲁⲓⲛⲟⲛ.

Then (τότε) the [thrice-] / [male] child [of the] great [Christ (χριστός)]/ whom [the great] / [in]visible [Spirit (πνεῦμα)] had anointed — [he] / whose power was called [Ainon — brought] / praise to [the great] / [in]visible [Spirit (πνεῦμα) and the male] / virgin (παρθένος) [Yoel, the] / [silence (σιγή) of silent (σιγή)] silence, [the] / greatness that [ ] / ineffable. [ ] / [in]effable [ ] / [un]answerable and / [un]interpretable (-ἑρμηνεύειν), the / first one who has [come forth,] / and (who is) unproclaimable /, un[ ] //

Pages 45-48 are missing.

IV 56 [Ν̄Ϛ̄]

[ ]ⲉ ⲉⲧⲉ ⲙ̄ⲙⲟⲓ̈ϩⲉ
[ⲛ̄ⲛⲁⲧ'ϣⲁ]ϫⲉ ⲙ̄ⲙⲟϥ
[. .]ⲟⲩ[ ]ϥ ⲡⲁ ⲛⲓⲙ̄ⲛ̄
[ⲧⲛ]ⲟ̣ϭ ⲧⲏ̣[ⲣⲟ]ⲩ [ⲛ̄]ⲟⲩⲙ̄ⲛ̄ⲧⲛⲟϭ
[ⲛ̄]ⲧⲉ ϯⲥⲓⲅ̣[ⲏ ⲛ̄]ⲛⲟⲩⲕⲁⲣⲱϥ ⲙ̄
[ⲡⲓⲙⲁ] ⲉ̣[ⲧⲙ̄]ⲙ̣ⲁⲩ· ⲡⲓϣⲙ̄ⲧ' ϩ̣[ⲟ]
[ⲟⲩⲧ'] ⲛ̄ⲁ[ⲗⲟ]ⲩ̣ ⲁϥⲉⲓⲛⲉ ⲉϩⲣ[ⲁⲓ̈ ⲛ̄]
[ⲟⲩⲥ]ⲙⲟⲩ̣ ⲁⲩⲱ ⲁϥⲣ̄ⲁⲓⲧ[ⲓ ⲛ̄ⲟⲩ]
[ϭⲟⲙ] ⲉⲃⲟⲗ ϩⲓ͡ⲧⲟⲟⲧϥ ⲙ̄ⲡ[ⲓⲛⲟϭ]
[ⲛ̄ⲛⲁⲧ]ⲛ[ⲁⲩ] ⲉⲣⲟϥ ⲙ̄ⲡⲛ̄ⲁ ⲙ̣̄[ⲡⲁⲣ]
[ⲑⲉⲛⲓⲕⲟ]ⲛ̣·

56 [ ] which is wonderful / [in]effable / [ ], he who has / all the greatnesses [of] greatness / [of] the silence (*σιγή*) [of] silence at / that [place]. The thrice-[male] / [child] brought / praise and asked (*αἰτεῖν*) [for a] / [power] from the [great,] / [invisible, virginal (*παρθενικόν*)] / Spirit (*πνεῦμα*).

The appearance of Youel: IV 56,11-20

ⲧⲟⲧⲉ ⲁϥⲣ̄ϣ[ⲟⲣⲡ̄]
[ⲛ̄ⲟⲩ]ϣⲛ̄ϩ ⲉⲃ̣ⲟⲗ ⲙ̄ⲡ̣ⲓⲙⲁ ⲉⲧ̣[ⲙ̄]
[ⲙⲁⲩ] ⲛ̄[ϭⲓ . . . .]ⲥ ⲉⲧ̣[
[ⲉ]ⲧⲛⲁⲩ ⲉϩⲉⲛⲉ[ⲟⲟⲩ]
[ϩⲉⲛⲁ]ϩⲱⲣ ϩⲛ̄ ⲟⲩ[

56,13 Perhaps ⲡⲓⲫⲱ]ⲥ.

Then (*τότε*) there / appeared at [that] place / [ ] who [ ] / [who] sees [glories] / [ ] treasures in a [ ] /

Pages 45-48 are missing.

IV 56,16 [ϩ]ⲉ̣ⲛⲙⲩⲥⲧⲏⲣ[ⲓⲟⲛ]
[ⲛ̄ⲛⲁⲧⲛⲁ]ⲩ ⲉⲣⲟⲟⲩ · ⲉϩⲉ[ⲛ
18 [ ]. ⲛ̣̄ⲧⲉ ϯⲥⲓⲅⲏ̣ [ⲉⲧⲉ]
[ⲧⲁï ⲧⲉ ϯϩⲟⲟ]ⲩⲧ' ⲙ̄ⲡⲁⲣ[ⲑⲉⲛ]
20 [ⲟⲥ ⲓ̈ⲟⲩⲏⲗ ·

56,18f. Or: [ⲉⲧ] / [ⲟⲛ̄ϩ ⲛ̄ϭⲓ.

[invisible] / mysteries (*μυστήριον*) to [ ] / [ ] of the silence (*σιγή*) / [who is the male] virgin (*παρθένος*) / 20 [Youel.]

The appearance of Esephech: IV 56,20-22

20 ⲧⲟ]ⲧⲉ ⲁϥⲣ̄ϣ̣[ⲟⲣⲡ̄']
[ⲛ̄ⲟⲩⲱⲛ̄ϩ ⲉ]ⲃ̣ⲟⲗ ⲛ̄ϭ[ⲓ ⲡⲁⲗ]
22 [ⲟⲩ ⲛ̄ⲧⲉ ⲡⲁ]ⲗ̣ⲟⲩ ⲏⲥⲏⲫ[ⲏⲭ]

Then (*τότε*) / [the child of the] child / Esephech [appeared.] /

The summary (?): IV 56,23 - 58,22

ⲁ̣ⲩⲱ [ⲛ̄ϯϩⲉ] ⲁϥϫⲱⲕ ⲉⲃ̣[ⲟⲗ]
24 [ⲛ̄]ϭⲓ ⲡ[ⲓⲱⲧ' ⲧ]ⲙⲁⲁⲩ ⲡϣ[ⲏ]
[ⲣ]ⲉ̣ ϯϯ[ⲉ ⲛ̄ⲥⲫⲣ]ⲁⲅⲓⲥ ϯϭⲟ̣[ⲙ ⲛ̄]
26 ⲛⲁⲧϫⲣ[ⲟ ⲉⲣ]ⲟⲥ ⲉ̣ⲧⲉ ⲡⲁ̣[ï ⲡⲉ]
ⲡⲓⲛⲟϭ [ⲛ̄ⲭ̄ⲥ̄] ⲛ̄ⲧⲉ̣ ⲛⲓⲁⲧ'ϫ̣[ⲱ]
57 [ⲛ̄ⲍ̄]
ϩ̄ⲙ ⲧⲏⲣⲟⲩ· [

And [thus] he was completed, / namely, the [Father, the] Mother, the [Son,] / 25 the [five] seals (*σφραγίς*), the / unconquerable power which [is] / the great [Christ (*χριστός*)] of all the incorruptible // *57* ones. [ ] /

Pages 45-48 are missing.

IV 57, 2 ⲉⲧⲟⲩⲁⲁ[ⲃ]ⲡⲁ[
ⲡⲓⲁⲣⲏϫ̄ϥ ϯ[ ] ⲛ̄ⲧ . . [
4 ϫⲱϩ̄ⲙ ⲙ̄ⲛ ⲛ[ ]ⲟⲩ ⲛ̄[
ϩⲉⲛϭⲟⲙ ⲛⲉ ⲙ̄[ⲛ ϩⲉⲛⲉⲟⲟⲩ]
6 [ⲙ]ⲛ̄ ϩⲉⲛⲁⲧ̓ϫⲱ̣[ϩ̄ⲙ
[. . .] ⲁⲩⲉⲓ ⲉⲃⲟ̣ⲗ[
8 [. . .]ⲛ̣̄ⲥⲃⲱ .[
[
10 [ ]. ⲉⲃⲟ̣[ⲗ
[. .]ⲉ ⲉ'ⲧ'ⲛⲁ.[
12 [.].[. . .]ⲥⲉ ⲉ[
ⲡ̣ⲁï ⲁϥⲉⲓⲛⲉ ⲉ[ϩⲣⲁï ⲛ̄ⲟⲩⲥⲙⲟⲩ]
14 ⲛ̣̄ⲡ[ⲓ]ⲁⲧⲟⲩⲱ̣[ⲛ̄ϩ ⲉⲃⲟⲗ ⲛ̄ⲙⲩⲥⲧⲏ]
[ⲣⲓⲟ]ⲛ ⲉⲧ̓ϩⲏⲡ̣̓[
16 [ⲡⲓ]ⲕⲁⲗⲩⲡⲧ̣[ⲟⲥ]ⲣ̄[
[. . .]ⲟ̣ⲛ ⲥ[
18 [. . .̄].ⲏ̄ⲛ̄· ⲉ̣[
[ ]ϯⲥ̣[
20 [ ]ⲱⲧ[
[ⲙ̄]ⲙⲟϥ ϩ̄ⲙ ⲡ[ ].
22 [ⲙ̄ⲛ] ⲛⲓⲉⲱⲛ .[ⲑ]ⲣⲟ

57, 4 Perhaps ⲛ[ⲓⲉⲟ]ⲟⲩ.
8 Trace appears to be ϥ.
14 Although ⲛ̄ before ⲡ is unprecedented in IV, *2* the trace cannot be ⲙ̄.
17f. Superlin. stroke is visible above ⲥ indicating the beginning of a name perhaps extending to ⲏⲛ in line 18.

holy [ ] / the end, [the] incorruptible [ ] / and [,] / 5 they are powers [and glories] / [and] incorruptions [ ] / [ ] they came forth [ ] / (lines 8-12) / This one brought [praise] / to the unrevealable, / 15 hidden [mystery (*μυστήριον*)] / [the] hidden (*καλυπτός*) [ ] / (lines 17-20) / him in the [ ] / [and] the aeons (*αἰών*) [ ] thrones (*θρόνος*), /

Pages 45-48 are missing

IV 57 [ⲛ]ⲟⲥ ϩⲉⲛ.[ ] ⲁ̣ⲩⲱ .[
24 [ⲡⲟ]ⲩⲁ ⲡⲟⲩⲁ [ ].[.]ⲟⲛ[
[ⲁ]ⲩⲕⲱ[ⲧ]ⲉ ⲉⲣ̣[ⲟⲟ]ⲩ ⲛ̄ϭⲓ ϩⲉ[ⲛ]
26 [ⲁ]ⲛⲧⲃⲁ ⲛ̣̄[ϭⲟⲙ ⲛ̄ⲛⲁ]ⲧ̓ϯ ⲏⲡ[ⲉ]
58 [ⲛ̄ⲏ̄]
[ⲉⲣⲟⲟⲩ· ϩⲉⲛⲉⲟ]ⲟ̣ⲩ ⲙ̄ⲛ̄ ϩⲉⲛ
2 [ⲁⲧ̓ϫ]ⲱ̣ϩⲙ [ ] ⲁⲩⲱ ⲉⲩ
[ ]ⲩⲉ[ⲛ̄ⲧ]ⲉ ⲡⲓⲱⲧ̓
4 [ⲙ̄ⲛ̄] ⲧⲙⲁ[ⲁⲩ ⲙ̄ⲛ̄] ⲡ̣ϣⲏⲣⲉ ⲙ̄ⲛ̄
[ⲡⲓⲡⲗⲏⲣⲱⲙⲁ] ⲧ̣ⲏⲣ̄ϥ ⲉⲛⲧⲁⲓ̈ⲣ̄ϣⲣ̣̄[ⲡ̄]
6 [ⲛ̄ϫⲟⲟϥ ⲙ̄ⲛ̄ ϯ]ϯⲉ ⲛ̄ⲥⲫⲣⲁ̣[ⲅⲓⲥ]
[ⲙ̄ⲛ̄ ⲡⲓⲙⲩⲥⲧⲏⲣ]ⲓⲟⲛ ⲛ̄ⲧⲉ ϩⲉ̣[ⲛ]
8 [ⲙⲩⲥⲧⲏⲣⲓⲟⲛ] · ⲁ̣ⲩⲟⲩⲱ[ⲛϩ]
[ⲉⲃⲟⲗ].[
10 [ ].ⲟⲗϭ̣ⲁ̣[
[ ]ⲟ̣ⲩⲟ̣ⲛ .[
12 [ ]. ⲛ .[. . .] . [
[ⲉⲧ̓]ⲕⲏ ⲉϩⲣⲁⲓ̈ ⲉ
14 [ϫ̣ⲛ̄] ⲙ̣̄ⲛ̄ ⲛⲓⲉⲱⲛ̣ ⲛ̄
[ϩⲛ̄ ⲟ]ⲩⲙⲛ̄ⲧⲙ[ⲉ]

57,23 Trace at the end of the line may be superlin. stroke.
24 Trace appears to be ⲉ.

[ ] and / each one [ ] / 25 myriads of [powers] / without number surround [them,] // *58* [glories] and / [in]corruptions [ ] and they / [of] the Father, / [and] the [Mother, and] the Son, and / 5 [the] whole [pleroma (πλήρωμα)] which I [mentioned] / before, [and the] five seals (σφραγίς) / [and the mystery (μυστήριον)] of / [mysteries (μυστήριον).] They [appeared] / (lines 9-12) / [who] presides [over] / [ ] and the aeons (αἰών) [of] / 15 [really] /

Pages 45-48 are missing.

IV 58,16 [ⲛⲁⲙⲉ]ⲩ ⲙ̄ⲛ ⲛⲓ̣[
ⲑ[ ]ϥⲛⲁ· ⲙ̣̄[
18 ⲣⲉ̣[ ]ϣⲁ ⲉⲛⲉϩ̣ [
ⲛ̣[ ]ⲣⲉϥ[
20 ⲉ[ ]. ⲃⲉ .[
ⲛ[ ] ⲙ̄ⲛ ⲛⲓⲉⲱ[ⲛ ⲛ̄]
22 ϣⲁ ⲉ[ⲛⲉϩ ϩ̄ⲛ ⲟ]ⲩⲙ̄ⲛ̄ⲧⲙⲉ [ⲛⲁⲙⲉ]

58,16f. Perhaps ⲛⲓ̣[ⲡⲁⲣ]ⲑ[ⲉⲛⲟⲥ.

truly[ ] and the [ ] / [ ] / [ ] eternal [ ] / (lines 19-20) / [ ] and the / [really] truly [eternal] aeons (αἰών). /

The appearance of Pronoia: IV 58,23 - 59,29

ⲧ̣ⲟⲧⲉ [ⲁⲥⲉ͡ⲓ ⲉⲃⲟ]ⲗ̣ ⲛ̄ϭⲓ ⲟⲩ[ⲡⲣⲟ]
24 [ⲛ]ⲟⲓⲁ ϩ̄[ⲛ ⲟⲩⲥⲓⲅⲏ] ⲙ̄ⲛ̣ ⲟⲩ[ⲕⲁⲣ]
ⲱϥ [ⲉ]ϥ[ⲟⲛ̄ϩ ⲛ̄ⲧ]ⲉ ⲡⲓⲡ̄ⲛ̄ⲁ̄ [ⲙ̄ⲛ̄]
26 [ⲟ]ⲩϣⲁϫⲉ̣ [ⲛ̄ⲧⲉ] ⲡⲓ̣ⲱ̣ⲧ̀ ⲙ̄ⲛ [ⲟⲩ]
[ⲟ]ⲉⲓⲛ ⲉⲁ[ⲥ]. . ⲛ̣̄[ϯϯⲉ]
59 [ⲛ̄ⲑ̄]
ⲛ̄ⲥⲫⲣⲁⲅⲓⲥ ⲛⲏ̣ ⲉⲧⲁⲡ[ⲓⲱⲧ̀ ⲛ̄ⲧⲟⲩ]
2 ⲉⲃⲟⲗ ϩ̄ⲛ ⲕⲟⲩⲛ̄ϥ· ⲉⲁⲥⲥⲓⲛ[ⲉ ⲉⲃⲟⲗ]
ϩ̄ⲛ ⲛⲓⲉⲱⲛ ⲧⲏⲣⲟⲩ ⲉⲧⲁⲓ̈ⲣ̄ϣ̣̄[ⲣ̄ⲡ̀]
4 ⲛ̄ϫⲟⲟⲩ · ⲁⲩⲱ ⲉⲁⲥⲧⲁϫⲣⲉ ϩⲉⲛ

Then (τότε) [providence (πρόνοια) came forth] / [from silence (σιγή)], and the [living silence] / [25] [of] the Spirit (πνεῦμα), [and] / the Word [of] the Father, and [a] / light. [She the five] // *59* seals (σφραγίς) which [the Father brought] / forth from his bosom, and she passed [through] / all the aeons (αἰών) which I mentioned / before. And she established /

Pages 45-48 are missing.

IV 59 ⲑⲣⲟⲛⲟⲥ ⲛ̄ⲛⲉⲟ[ⲟ]ⲩ [ⲙ]ⲛ̄ ϩⲉⲛ[ⲁⲛ]
[ⲧⲃ]ⲁ ⲛ̄ⲁⲅⲅⲉⲗⲟⲥ [ⲛ̄ⲛⲁⲧ]ϯ ⲏⲡⲉ
[ⲉⲧⲁ]ⲩⲕⲱⲧⲉ ⲉ[ⲣⲟⲟ]ⲩ ϩⲉⲛ[ϭⲟ]ⲙ
[ⲙⲛ̄ ϩⲉ]ⲛⲉⲟⲟⲩ ⲛ̄[ⲛⲁⲧϫ]ⲱ[ϩⲙ̄·] ⲉⲩ
[ϩⲱⲥ ⲁ]ⲩⲱ ⲉⲩϯ ⲉⲟⲟⲩ ⲉ[ⲩⲥ]ⲙⲟⲩ
[ⲛ̄ⲧⲟⲟⲩ] ⲧⲏ[ⲣ]ⲟⲩ ϩⲛ̄ ⲟⲩ[ⲥⲙ]ⲏ
[ⲛ̄ⲟⲩⲱ]ⲧⲉ ϩⲛ̄ [ⲟ]ⲩϩⲓⲕⲱⲛ [ϩⲛ̄]
[ⲟⲩϩⲣⲟ]ⲟⲩ ⲛ̄ⲁⲧⲕⲁⲣⲱϥ [
[.... ⲙ̄]ⲡⲓ[ⲱ]ⲧ ⲙ̄[ⲛ̄] ⲧ[ⲙⲁⲁⲩ]
[ⲙⲛ̄ ⲡϣ]ⲏⲣⲉ .[..] . [..] . [ⲙⲛ̄]
[ⲛⲓⲡⲗⲏ]ⲣⲱⲙ[ⲁ ⲧⲏⲣⲟ]ⲩ ⲉ[ⲧⲁⲓ̈ⲣ̄]
[ϣⲣⲡ̄ ⲛ̄]ϫⲟⲟ[ⲩ ⲉⲧⲉ] ⲡⲁⲓ̈ ⲡⲉ [ⲡⲓ]
[ⲛⲟϭ ⲛ̄]ⲭ︦ⲥ︦ ⲡⲓ[ⲉ]ⲃⲟⲗ ϩⲛ̄ ⲟⲩ[ⲥⲓⲅⲏ]
[ⲉⲧⲉ ⲡⲁ]ⲓ̈ ⲡⲉ ⲡⲁⲗⲟⲩ ⲛ̄ⲛⲁ[ⲧ]ϫ
[ⲱϩⲙ̄] ⲧⲉⲗⲙⲁⲏⲗ ⲧⲉⲗⲙⲁⲭ[ⲁ]ⲏⲗ
[ⲏⲗⲓ ⲏⲗ]ⲓ ⲙⲁⲭⲁⲣ ⲙⲁⲭⲁⲣ
[ⲥⲏⲑ ϯ]ϭⲟⲙ [ⲉⲧ]ⲟⲛϩ ϩⲛ̄ ⲟⲩⲙⲛ̄
[ⲧⲙⲉ ⲛⲁ]ⲙⲉ ⲙ̄[ⲛ̄ ϯϩⲟ]ⲟⲩⲧ ⲙ̄
[ⲡⲁⲣⲑⲉⲛ]ⲟⲥ ⲉⲧⲛⲙ̄[ⲙ]ⲁ[ϥ ⲓ̈]ⲟⲩⲏⲗ

59,14 Trace after ϣⲏⲣⲉ may be ⲉ, the next trace may be ⲗ.
20 Corr. ⲥ after ⲏⲗ]ⲓ crossed out.

thrones (*θρόνος*) of glory [and myriads] / of angels (*ἄγγελος*) [without] number / [who] surrounded them, [powers] / [and incorruptible] glories, who / [sing] and give glory, all giving / praise with [a single voice,] / with one accord (*εἰκών*), [with] / [one] never silent [voice] / [to] the Father, and the [Mother], / [and the] Son [and] / [all the] pleromas (*πλήρωμα*) [that I] / mentioned [before,] who is [the] / [great] Christ (*χριστός*), who is from [silence (*σιγή*),] / [who] is the [incorruptible] child / Telmael Telmachael / [Eli Eli] Machar Machar / [Seth, the] power which really truly lives, / [and the] male / [virgin (*παρθένος*)] who is with [him,] Youel, /

Pages 45-48 are missing.

IV 59,24 [ⲙⲛ̄ ⲏⲥ]ⲏ̣ⲫⲏⲭ ⲡ̣ⲓⲣⲉϥ[ⲁ]ⲙⲁϩⲧⲉ
[ⲙ̄ⲡⲉⲟⲟ]ⲩ ⲡ[ⲁⲗⲟ]ⲩ ⲛ̄ⲧⲉ ⲡⲁⲗⲟ̣[ⲩ]
26 [ⲙⲛ̄ ⲡⲓⲕⲗ]ⲟ̣ⲙ ⲛ̣̄[ⲧ]ⲉ ⲡⲉϥⲉⲟⲟⲩ
[ ].ⲛ[ ] ⲛ̄ⲧⲉ ϯϯ[ⲉ]
28 [ⲛ̄ⲥⲫⲣⲁ]ⲅ̣ⲓⲥ [ⲡⲓⲡⲗⲏ]ⲣⲱⲙⲁ ⲉ[ⲛ]
[ⲧⲁⲓ̈ⲣ̄ϣⲣ]ⲡ̄ ⲛ̄ϫ[ⲟⲟϥ]

[and] Esephech, [the] splenditenens, / 25 the [child] of the child / [and the crown of] his glory / [ ] of the five / seals (σφραγίς), [the] pleroma (πλήρωμα) [that] / [I mentioned before].

The appearance of the Logos: IV 59,29 - 60,22

ⲉⲁϥⲣ̄ϣ[ⲟⲣⲡ̄]
60 [ⲝ̅]
[ⲛ̄ⲉⲓ ⲉⲃⲟ]ⲗ̣ ⲙ̄ⲙⲁⲩ ⲛ̄ϭⲓ ⲡⲓⲛⲟϭ ⲛ̄
2 [ϣⲁϫⲉ] ⲛ̣̄ⲁⲩⲧⲟⲅⲉⲛ̣ⲏⲥ ⲉⲧⲟⲛ̄ϩ
[ⲡⲛⲟⲩ]ⲧⲉ ϩⲛ̄ ⲟⲩⲙⲛ̄ⲧⲙⲉ· ϯⲫⲩ
4 [ⲥⲓⲥ ⲛ̄]ⲛⲁⲧ̣ⲙⲓⲥⲉ ⲡⲁⲓ̈ ⲉϯⲛⲁϫⲱ
[ⲙ̄]ⲡⲉϥⲣⲁⲛ ⲉⲓ̈ϫ̣ⲱ ⲙ̄ⲙⲟⲥ ϫⲉ
6 [...]ⲁ̣ⲓ̈ⲁ[.....]ⲑⲁⲱⲑⲱⲥⲑ.[.]
[ⲉ]ⲧⲉ ⲡⲁⲓ̈ ⲡ̣[ⲉ ⲡ]ϣⲏⲣⲉ ⲙ̄ⲡ̣ⲓ[ⲛⲟϭ ⲛ̄]
8 ⲭ̣ⲥ̣ ⲉⲧⲉ [ⲡⲁⲓ̈] ⲡ̣ⲉ ⲡϣⲏⲣⲉ̣ [ⲛ̄ⲧⲉ ϯ]
ⲥⲓⲅ[ⲏ ⲛ̄]ⲛ[ⲁⲧ]ϣⲁϫⲉ ⲙ̄ⲙⲟ̣[ⲥ ⲉ]
10 ⲁϥⲉ̣[ⲓ ⲉⲃ]ⲟⲗ ϩⲙ̄ ⲡⲓⲛⲟ̣ϭ̣ ⲛ̣̄ⲁ̣[ⲧⲛⲁⲩ]
ⲉⲣ[ⲟϥ ⲁ]ⲩⲱ ⲛ̄ⲁⲧϫⲱϩ[ⲙ̄ ⲙ̄ⲡⲛ̄ⲁ]

There // *60* the great self-begotten (αὐτογενής) / living [Word came forth,] / [the] true [god], the / unborn physis (φύσις), he whose / 5 name I shall tell saying: / [ ]ⲁⲓ̈ⲁ[ ]ⲑⲁⲱⲑⲱⲥⲑ[ ], / who [is the] son of the [great] / Christ, who is the son [of] / [the in]effable silence (σιγή)[, who] / 10 came forth from the great [invisible] / and incorruptible [Spirit (πνεῦμα).] /

Pages 45-48 are missing

IV 60,12 ⲡ̣[ϣⲏ]ⲣⲉ ⲛ̄ⲧⲉ ϯⲥ̣ⲓⲅⲏ ⲙ̄ⲛ̣ [ⲟⲩⲥⲓ]
ⲅⲏ̣ [ⲁϥ]ⲟⲩⲱⲛ̄ϩ ⲉ[ⲃ]ⲟⲗ ⲛ̄[
14 [ ]. ϯ[. .] ⲧⲏ[
[. . .] . [. . . ⲁⲧⲛ]ⲁ̣ⲩ ⲉⲣ[ⲟ
16 [. . ϩ]ⲏⲡ [. . ⲡⲣⲱ]ⲙⲉ ⲉⲧ̣[
[ⲙ̄ⲛ ⲛ]ⲓⲁϩⲱⲣ̣ [ⲛ̄ⲧⲉ ⲡ]ⲉϥⲉⲟ[ⲟⲩ · ⲧⲟ]
18 [ⲧⲉ ⲁ]ϥⲟⲩⲱⲛ̄ϩ ⲉⲃ̣ⲟⲗ ϩ̄ⲙ ⲡ̣[
. [.] ⲉⲧⲟⲩⲟⲛ̄ϩ · [ⲁ]ⲩⲱ ⲁϥ[ⲧⲁϩⲟ]
20 ⲉ[ⲣ]ⲁ̣ⲧⲟⲩ ⲙ̄ⲡⲓϥ[ⲧ]ⲟⲟⲩ ⲛ̄[ⲛⲉⲱⲛ]
ϩ̄[ⲛ] ⲟⲩϣⲁϫⲉ ⲁ[ϥ]ⲧⲁϩⲟⲟ̣[ⲩ ⲉⲣⲁ]
22 ⲧⲟ̣ⲩ̣·

60,14 Trace before ϯ appears to be ⲛ.
16 Perhaps [ⲟⲩⲁⲁⲃ], see 62,11.27.

The [son] of the silence (*σιγή*) and [silence (*σιγή*)] / appeared [ ] / [ ] / [in]visible [ ] / [man] / [and the] treasures [of] his glory. [Then (*τότε*)] / he appeared in the revealed [ ]. / And he [established] / the four [aeons (*αἰών*).] / With a word [he] established / them.

The presentation of praise of the Logos: IV 60,22-30

22 ⲁϥⲉⲓⲛⲉ [ⲉϩⲣ]ⲁï ⲛ̄[ⲟⲩⲥⲙⲟⲩ]
ⲙ̄ⲡ̣ⲓⲛⲟϭ ⲛ̄ⲛ̣[ⲁⲧ]ⲛⲁⲩ [ⲉⲣⲟϥ ⲙ̄]
24 ⲡⲁⲣⲑⲉⲛ[ⲓⲕ]ⲟ̣ⲛ ⲙ̄ⲡⲛⲁ̣[· ϯⲥⲓⲅⲏ]
ⲛ̄ⲧⲉ ⲡ̣[ⲓⲱ]ⲧ̣̀ ϩ̄ⲛ ⲟⲩⲥⲓ[ⲅⲏ ⲛ̄ⲧⲉ ϯ]
26 ⲥⲓⲅⲏ ⲉ[ⲧ]ⲟⲛ̄ϩ ⲛ̄]ⲛ̣ⲟⲩⲕ[ⲁⲣⲱϥ]
[ⲡⲓ]ⲙⲁ ⲉⲧ̄ϥⲙⲟ̣[ⲧ̄ⲛ] ⲙ[ⲙⲟϥ ⲛ̄ϩⲏⲧ̄ϥ]

He brought [praise] / to the great, [in]visible, / virginal (*παρθενικόν*) Spirit (*πνεῦμα*), [the silence (*σιγή*)] / of the [Father] in a silence (*σιγή*) [of the] / living silence (*σιγή*) [of silence,] / [the] place where the man rests. /

The creation of Adamas: III 48 last line - 49,7

III 49 [ⲙⲑ]

[ⲉⲃⲟⲗ ϩⲙ̄ ⲡⲙⲁ ⲉ]ⲧ̣ⲙ̄ⲙⲁⲩ ⲛ̄ϭⲓ ⲧϭⲏ
2 [ⲡⲉ ⲙ̄ⲡ]ⲛⲟϭ ⲛ̄ⲟⲩⲟⲉⲓⲛ ⲧⲇⲩⲛⲁⲙⲓⲥ
[ⲉ]ⲧ̣ⲟⲛϩ · ⲧⲙⲁⲁⲩ ⲛ̄ⲛⲓⲁⲫⲑⲁⲣⲧⲟⲥ ⲉⲧⲟⲩ
4 [ⲁ]ⲁ̣ⲃ · ⲧⲛⲟϭ ⲛ̄ⲇⲩⲛⲁⲙⲓⲥ ⲧⲙⲓⲣⲟⲑⲟⲏ
ⲁ̣ⲩⲱ ⲁⲥϫⲡⲟ ⲙ̄ⲡⲉⲉⲓ ⲉϯⲟⲛⲟⲙⲁⲍⲉ
6 ⲙ̣̄ⲡⲉϥⲣⲁⲛ · ⲉⲉⲓϫⲱ ⲙ̄ⲙⲟⲥ ϫⲉ ⲓ̈̄ⲉ̄ⲛ̄
[ⲓ̈̄]ⲉ̣̄ⲛ̄ ⲉ̄ⲁ̄ ⲉ̄ⲁ̄ ⲉ̄ⲁ̄ ⲛ̄ϣⲟⲙ̄ⲛ̄ⲧ̄ ⲛ̄ⲥⲟⲡ̄

] // *49* [appeared at (or: from)] that [place] the cloud / [of the] great light, the living / power (δύναμις), the mother of the holy, incorruptible (ἄφθαρτος) ones, / the great power (δύναμις), the Mirothoe. / [5] And she gave birth to him whose name / I name (ὀνομάζειν) saying: ⲓⲉⲛ / ⲓⲉⲛ ⲉⲁ ⲉⲁ ⲉⲁ three times. /

IV **60,28** [ⲛ̄]ϭⲓ ⲡⲣⲱⲙ[ⲉ .]ⲉⲁϥ[
[ⲉ]ⲃⲟⲗ ϩ͡ⲓⲧⲟ[ⲟⲧ.] ⲛ̄ⲧ.[
30 [ⲉ]ⲃⲟⲗ·

60,28 Perhaps ⲉⲁϥ[ⲟⲩⲱⲛ̄ϩ].

[ ] / through [ ] / [30] [ ].

The creation of Adamas: IV 60,30 - 61,8

30 ⲧⲟ̣[ⲧⲉ ⲁⲥ]ⲉ͡ⲓ ⲉⲃⲟ̣[ⲗ ϩ̄ⲙ]
61 [ⲝ̄ⲁ̄]
ⲡⲙⲁ ⲉⲧⲙ̄ⲙⲁⲩ ⲛ̄ϭⲓ ϯⲛ̣[ⲟϭ ⲛ̄ⲕⲗⲟⲟ]
2 ⲗⲉ ⲛ̄ⲧⲉ ⲡⲟⲩⲟⲉⲓⲛ ⲛ̄ϭⲓ ⲟⲩ[ϭⲟⲙ]
ⲉⲥⲟⲛ̄ϩ ⲧⲙⲁⲁⲩ ⲛ̄ⲧⲉ ⲛⲓⲁⲧ'ϫ[ⲱϩ̄ⲙ]
4 ⲉⲧⲟⲩⲁⲁⲃ ⲛ̄ⲛⲓⲛⲟϭ ⲛ̄ϭⲟⲙ [
[ⲁ]ⲩⲱ ⲁⲥϫⲡⲟ ⲙ̄ⲡ[ⲁ̈ ⲉ]ϯⲛⲁ[ϫⲱ ⲙ̄]
6 [ⲡⲉ]ϥⲣⲁⲛ ⲉ̈ⲓϫⲱ ⲙ̄[ⲙ]ⲟ̣ⲥ ϫⲉ [ⲛ̄ⲧⲕ̄]
[ⲟⲩⲁ ⲛ̄]ⲧⲕ̄ ⲟⲩⲁ ⲛ̄ⲧ̣[ⲕ̄ ⲟ]ⲩⲁ [
8 [ⲉⲁ ⲉⲁ] ⲉⲁ̣

60,30 Superlin. stroke on ⲉⲓ is in lacuna.
61, 2 Unusual use of ⲛ̄ϭⲓ.
4 Perhaps [ⲧⲏⲣⲟⲩ]; there is room for 3 or 4 letters.
7 Perhaps ⲛ̄ⲥⲟⲡ ⲅ̄]; the scribe of IV used the numeral sign perhaps also in 65,27 and 68,2; cf. also *Koptisch-gnostische Apokalypsen* ed. Böhlig-Labib, p. 11.

Then (τότε) there came forth [at (or: from)] // *61* that place the [great cloud] / of the light, namely, a living / [power], the mother of the holy / in[corruptible] ones, of the great powers [ ]. / [5] And she gave birth to him [whose] / name I shall [tell] saying: [Thou art] / [One,] thou art One, [thou art] One [ ] / [ⲉⲁ ⲉⲁ] ⲉⲁ.

The origin of Adamas: III 49,8-16

III 49, 8 [ⲡⲁ]ⲓ̈ ⲅⲁⲣ ⲁⲇⲁⲙⲁⲥ ⲡⲟⲩⲟⲉⲓⲛ ⲉⲧⲣ̄ⲟⲩⲟ
[ⲉ]ⲓ̣ⲛ ⲡⲉⲧⲉⲃⲟⲗ ϩⲙ̄ ⲡⲣⲱⲙⲉ ⲡⲉϩⲟⲩ
10 [ⲉⲓ]ⲧ̇ ⲛ̄ⲣⲱⲙⲉ ⲡⲉⲛⲧⲁⲛ̄ⲕⲁ ⲛⲓⲙ ϣⲱ
ⲡ̣ⲉ ⲉⲃⲟⲗ ⲛ̄ϩⲏⲧϥ̄ · ⲛ̄ⲕⲁ ⲛⲓⲙ ⲉϩⲟⲩⲛ
12 ⲉⲣⲟϥ ⲉⲧⲉ ⲁϫⲛ̄ⲧϥ̄ ⲙ̄ⲡⲉⲗⲁⲁⲩ ϣⲱⲡⲉ
ⲁϥⲡⲣⲟⲉⲗⲑⲉ ⲉⲃⲟⲗ ⲛ̄ϭⲓ ⲡⲓⲱⲧ̇ ⲛ̄ⲁⲧ
14 ⲛⲟⲉⲓ ⲙ̄ⲙⲟϥ ⲛ̄ⲛⲁⲡⲉⲣⲓⲛⲟⲏⲧⲟⲥ · ⲁϥ
ⲉ͡ⲓ ⲉⲃⲟ[ⲗ] ϫⲛ̄ ⲙ̄ⲡⲥⲁϩⲣⲉ ϣⲁ ⲡⲉⲥⲏⲧ
16 ϣⲁ ⲡⲙⲟ̣ⲩⲛⲕ̣ ⲙ̄ⲡϣⲱⲱⲧ̇

49, 9 If one reads ⲡⲉ ⟨ⲉ⟩ⲧⲉⲃⲟⲗ the meaning will be similar to IV 61,8f.

For (γάρ) it is [this one], Adamas, the shining light, / who is from the Man, the first / [10] Man, he through whom / and to whom everything became, / (and) without whom nothing became. / The unknowable (-νοεῖν), / incomprehensible (ἀπερινόητος) Father came forth (προελθεῖν). He / [15] came down from above / for the annulment of the deficiency.

The union of Adamas and the Logos: III 49,16-22

16 ⲧⲟⲧⲉ
ⲡⲛⲟϭ ⲛ̄ⲗⲟⲅⲟⲥ ⲡⲁⲩⲧⲟⲅⲉⲛⲏⲥ ⲛ̄
18 ⲛⲟⲩⲧ̣ⲉ ⲙⲛ ⲡⲁⲫⲑⲁⲣⲧⲟⲥ ⲛ̄ⲣⲱⲙⲉ
ⲁⲇⲁⲙⲁⲥ ⲁⲩⲙⲟⲩϫⲧ̇ ⲙ̄ⲛ̄ ⲛⲉⲩⲉⲣⲏ
20 ⲟⲩ ⲁϥϣⲱⲡⲉ ⲛ̄ϭⲓ ⲟⲩⲗⲟⲅⲟⲥ ⲛ̄ⲧⲉ

49,20 Corr. ϥ over ⲩ. The singular is demanded by the subject.

Then (τότε) / the great Logos (λόγος), the divine Autogenes (αὐτογενής), / and the incorruptible (ἄφθαρτος) man / Adamas mingled with each other. / [20] A Logos (λόγος) of man came into being. /

The origin of Adamas : IV 61,8-18

IV 61, 8 ⲉⲡⲓⲇⲉ ⲡ̣[ⲁï] ⲁⲇ̣[ⲁⲙⲁⲥ]
[ⲟⲩⲟⲩⲟⲉⲓⲛ] ⲡⲉ ⲉⲁϥⲡⲓⲣⲉ̣ [ⲉⲃⲟⲗ]
10 [ϩ̅ⲛ ⲟⲩⲟⲉⲓ]ⲛ · ⲡⲃⲁⲗ ⲛ̅ⲧⲉ ⲡ[ⲟⲩⲟⲉⲓⲛ]
[ⲡⲉ ⲡⲁï] ⲅ̣ⲁⲣ ⲡⲓϣⲟⲣⲡ̅ ⲛ̅ⲣⲱ̣[ⲙⲉ]
12 [ⲡⲉ ⲉⲧⲉ ⲉ]ⲧ̣ⲃⲏⲏⲧϥ̅ ⲛⲁ̣ï ⲧⲏⲣ[ⲟⲩ ⲛⲉ]
[ⲉⲧⲉ ⲉⲣⲟ]ϥ ⲧⲏⲣⲟⲩ ⲛ̣[ⲉ] ⲁ̣ⲩ[ⲱ ⲁϫ̅ⲛ]
14 [ⲧ̅ϥ ⲙ̅ⲛ ⲗ]ⲁ̣ⲁⲩ· ⲡ[ⲓⲱⲧ] ⲉⲧ[ⲁϥⲉ͡ⲓ]
[ⲉⲃⲟⲗ ⲛ̅]ⲛⲁⲧ̅ⲣϫⲓⲟ[ⲟ]ⲣ̣ ⲙ̅ⲙ[ⲟϥ ⲁⲩⲱ]
16 [ⲛ̅ⲁⲧ̅ⲣ]ⲛ̣[ⲟ]ⲉⲓ̣ ⲙ̅ⲙⲟϥ ⲉⲁϥⲉ͡ⲓ ⲉ̣[ⲃⲟⲗ ⲙ̅]
[ⲡⲥⲁϩⲣ]ⲉ ⲉ[ϩ]ⲣⲁï ϣⲁ ⲡϥⲱⲧ[ⲉ] ⲉ̣[ⲃⲟⲗ]
18 [ⲛ̅ⲧⲉ ⲡⲓ]ϣⲱⲱⲧ·

For (ἐπειδή) this one, Ad[amas,] / is [a light] which radiated [from] / 10 [the light; he is] the eye of the [light]. / For (γάρ) [this is] the first man, / because of whom all things [are,] / [to] whom all things [are, and without] / [whom there is nothing,] the [Father] who [came] / 15 [forth,] (who is) inaccessable [and] / [unknowable (-νοεῖν),] and who came / [down from above] for the annulment / [of the] deficiency.

The union of Adamas and the Logos: IV 61,18-23

18 ⲧⲟⲧⲉ ⲡⲓⲛ̣[ⲟϭ]
[ⲛ̅ϣⲁϫ]ⲉ ⲛ̅ⲁⲩⲧⲟⲅⲉⲛⲏⲥ ⲛ̅ⲛⲟ[ⲩⲧⲉ]
20 [ⲙ̅ⲛ ⲡⲓⲁ]ⲧ̅ϫⲱϩ̅ⲙ ⲛ̅ⲣⲱⲙⲉ ⲁ̅[ⲇ̅ⲁ̅ⲙ̅ⲁ̅ⲥ̅]
[ⲉⲁⲩϣⲱ]ⲡⲉ ϩ̅ⲛ ⲟⲩϭⲱⲣ̅ϭ ⲉ[ⲧⲉ ⲡⲁï]
22 [ⲡⲉ ⲡⲣⲱ]ⲙ̣ⲉ· ⲁⲩⲱ ⲁϥϣⲱⲡ̣[ⲉ ⲛ̅ϭⲓ]

Then (τότε) the [great,] / self-begotten (αὐτογενής), divine [Word] / 20 [and the] incorruptible man A[damas] / [became] a mixture [which is] / [man]. And [man] came /

III 49 ⲡⲣⲱⲙⲉ ⲁⲩⲱ ⲡⲣⲱⲙⲉ ϩⲱⲱϥ
22 ⲛ̄ⲧⲁϥϣⲱⲡⲉ ϩⲓⲧⲛ̄ `ⲟⲩ´ϣⲁϫⲉ

49,22 Corr. ⲔⲈ crossed out; ⲞⲨ above the line.

However, the man / came into being through a word.

The presentation of praise of the Logos and Adamas: III 49,22 - 50,17

22 ⲁϥ
ϯ ⲛ̄ⲟⲩⲥⲙⲟⲩ ⲙ̄ⲡⲛⲟϭ ⲛⲁϩⲟⲣⲁⲧⲟⲛ
24 ⲛⲁⲧ̇ⲧⲁϩⲟϥ ⲙ̄ⲡⲁⲣⲑⲉⲛⲓⲕⲟⲛ ⲙ̄
ⲡⲛ̄ⲁ̄ ⲙⲛ̄ ⲧⲁⲣⲥⲉⲛⲓⲕⲏ ⲛ̄ⲡⲁⲣⲑⲉⲛⲟⲥ
26 ⲙⲛ̄ ⲡϣⲟⲙⲛ̄ⲧ ⲛ̄ϩⲟⲟⲩⲧ̇ ⲛ̄ⲁⲗⲟⲩ
50 [ⲛ]
ⲙⲛ̄ ⲧⲁⲣⲥⲉⲛⲓⲕ[ⲏ ⲛ̄ⲡⲁ]ⲣ̣[ⲑⲉⲛⲟⲥ]
2 ⲓ̈ⲟⲩⲏⲗ ⲙⲛ̄ ⲏⲥⲏⲫⲏⲭ ⲡⲉⲧ̣[ⲉⲙⲁϩ]
ⲧⲉ ⲙ̄ⲡⲉⲟⲟⲩ ⲡⲁⲗⲟⲩ ⲙ̄ⲡⲁⲗⲟⲩ ⲙⲛ̣̄
4 ⲡⲉⲕⲗⲟⲙ ⲙ̄ⲡⲉϥⲉⲟⲟⲩ ⲙⲛ̄ ⲡⲛⲟϭ̣
ⲛ̄ⲇⲟⲝⲟⲙⲉⲇⲱⲛ ⲛ̄ⲁⲓⲱⲛ ⲙⲛ̄
6 ⲛⲉⲑⲣⲟⲛⲟⲥ ⲉⲧⲛ̄ϩⲏⲧϥ̄ · ⲙⲛ̄ ⲛ̄
ϭⲟⲙ ⲉⲧⲕⲱⲧⲉ ⲉⲣⲟϥ ⲛⲓⲉⲟⲟⲩ ⲙ̄[ⲛ̄]
8 ⲛⲓⲁⲫⲑⲁⲣⲥⲓⲁ ⲙⲛ̄ ⲡⲉⲩⲡⲗⲏⲣ[ⲱ]

He / gave praise to the great, invisible (ἀόρατον), / incomprehensible, virginal (παρθενικόν) / Spirit (πνεῦμα), and the male (ἀρσενική) virgin (παρθένος), / and the thrice-male child, // *50* and the male (ἀρσενική) [virgin (παρθένος)] / Youel, and Esephech, the splenditenens, / the child of the child and / the crown of his glory, and the great / Doxomedon-aeon (αἰών), and / the thrones (θρόνος) which are in him, and the / powers which surround him, the glories and / the incorruptions (ἀφθαρσία), and their whole pleroma (πλήρωμα) /

IV 61 [ⲡⲣⲱⲙ]ⲉ̣ ⲉⲃⲟⲗ ϩⲓⲧⲛ ⲟⲩϣⲁ[ϫⲉ·

into being through a word.

The presentation of praise of the Logos and Adamas: IV 61,23 - 62,16

ⲁϥ]
24 [ⲉⲓⲛⲉ ⲉ]ϩⲣⲁ̈ⲓ ⲛ̄ⲟⲩⲥⲙⲟ̣ⲩ [ⲙ̄ⲡⲓⲛⲟϭ]
[ⲛ̄ⲁⲧⲛ]ⲁ̣ⲩ ⲉⲣⲟϥ ⲁⲩⲱ ⲛ̣̄[ⲁⲧ̀ⲧⲁϩⲟϥ]
26 [ⲁⲩⲱ ⲙ̄ⲡ]ⲁ̣ⲣⲑⲉⲛⲓⲕⲟ[ⲛ ⲙ̄ⲡ̄ⲛ̄ⲁ̄ ⲙⲛ̄]
[ϯϩⲟⲟⲩ]ⲧ̀ ⲙ̄ⲡⲁⲣⲑⲉ[ⲛⲟⲥ ϯⲃⲁⲣⲃⲏ]
28 [ⲗⲱ ⲙⲛ̄ ⲡⲓ]ϣⲙⲧ̀ ϩⲟⲟⲩ[ⲧ̀ ⲛ̄ⲁⲗⲟⲩ]
[ⲙⲛ̄ ϯϩⲟⲟ]ⲩⲧ̀ ⲙ̄ⲡⲁ[ⲣⲑⲉⲛⲟⲥ ⲓ̈ⲟⲩⲏⲗ]
62 [ⲝ̄ⲃ̄]
[ⲙⲛ̄ ⲡⲁⲗ]ⲟ̣ⲩ ⲏⲥⲏⲫⲏⲭ ⲡⲓⲣⲉϥⲁⲙⲁϩ
2 [ⲧⲉ ⲙ̄ⲡ]ⲉⲟⲟⲩ ⲙⲛ̄ ⟨ⲡⲁⲗⲟⲩ⟩ ⲛ̄ⲧⲉ ⲡⲓ
[ⲁⲗⲟⲩ] ⲙⲛ̄ ⲡⲓⲕⲗⲟⲙ ⲛ̄ⲧⲉ ⲡⲉϥⲉⲟⲟⲩ ·
4 [ⲙⲛ̄ ⲛ]ⲓ̣ⲛⲟϭ ⲛ̄ⲛⲉⲱⲛ ⲛ̄ⲇⲟⲝⲟⲙⲉⲇⲱⲛ
[ⲙⲛ̄ ⲛⲓ]ⲑⲣⲟⲛⲟⲥ ⲉⲧⲛ̄ϩⲏⲧⲟⲩ ⲙⲛ̄
6 [ⲛⲓϭⲟ]ⲙ̣ ⲉ[ⲧⲕ]ⲱ̣ⲧⲉ ⲉⲣⲟⲟⲩ · ϩⲉ[ⲛⲉ]
[ⲟⲟⲩ] ⲙ̣ⲛ̣̄ ϩⲉ[ⲛⲁ]ⲧ̀ϫⲱϩⲙ ⲙⲛ̄ [ⲡⲓⲡⲗⲏ]

62, 2 MS. reads ⲡⲉⲟⲟⲩ (influence of preceding ⲉⲟⲟⲩ).

[He] / [brought] praise [to the great,] / [25] [invisible,] and [incomprehensible,] / [and] virginal (*παρθενικόν*) [Spirit (*πνεῦμα*), and] / [the male] virgin (*παρθένος*) [Barbelo], / [and the] thrice-male [child,] / [and the] male [virgin (*παρθένος*) Youel,] // *62* [and the child] Esephech, the splenditenens, / and the <child> of the / [child] and the crown of his glory, / [and the] great Doxomedon-aeons (*αἰών*), / [5] [and the] thrones (*θρόνος*) that are in them, and / [the powers that] surround them, / [glories] and incorruptions, and [the whole] /

III 50 ⲙⲁ ⲧⲏⲣϥ̄ · ⲛ̄ⲧⲁⲉⲓϫⲟⲟϥ ⲛ̄ϣⲟ̣
ⲣⲡ̄ · ⲙⲛ̄ ⲡⲕⲁϩ ⲛ̄ⲁⲉⲣⲟⲇⲓⲟⲥ ⲡⲓ
ϣⲁⲡ ⲛⲟⲩⲧⲉ ⲉϩⲟⲩⲛ ⲉⲣⲟϥ ⲡⲙⲁ
ⲉϣⲁⲩϫⲓ ϩⲓⲕⲱⲛ ⲛ̄ϩⲏⲧϥ̄ ⲛ̄ϭⲓ
ⲛ̄ⲣⲱⲙⲉ ⲉⲧⲟⲩⲁⲁⲃ ⲙ̄ⲡⲛⲟϭ
ⲛ̄ⲟⲩⲟⲉⲓⲛ ⲛ̄ⲣⲱⲙⲉ ⲙ̄ⲡ̣ⲓⲱⲧ̇
ⲛ̄ⲧⲥⲓⲅⲏ ⲛ̄ⲥⲓⲅⲏ ⲉ̣[ⲧ]ⲟ̣ⲛ̄ϩ ⲡⲉⲓⲱⲧ̇
ⲙⲛ̄ ⲡⲉⲩⲡⲗⲏⲣⲱⲙⲁ ⲧⲏⲣϥ̄ · ⲛ̄
ⲑⲉ ⲛ̄ⲧⲁⲉⲓϫⲟⲟⲥ ⲛ̄ϣⲟⲣ[ⲡ̈]

which I mentioned before, / and the ethereal (ἀερόδιος) earth, the / receiver of God, where / the holy men of the / great light receive shape (εἰκών), / the men of the Father / of the silent (σιγή), living silence (σιγή), the Father / and their whole pleroma (πλήρωμα) as / I mentioned before.

The request of the Logos and Adamas: III 50,17 - 51,14

ⲁϥϯ
ⲛ̄ⲟⲩⲥⲙⲟⲩ ⲛ̄ϭⲓ ⲡⲛⲟϭ ⲛ̄ⲗⲟⲅⲟⲥ
ⲡⲁⲩⲧⲟⲅⲉⲛⲏⲥ ⲛ̄ⲛⲟⲩⲧⲉ ⲙⲛ̄
ⲡⲁⲫⲑⲁⲣⲧⲟⲥ ⲛ̄ⲣⲱⲙⲉ ⲁⲇⲁ
ⲙⲁⲥ ⲁⲩⲁⲓⲧⲓ ⲛ̄ⲟⲩⲇⲩⲛⲁⲙⲓⲥ ⲙⲛ̄
ⲟⲩⲛⲁⲙⲧⲉ ⲛ̄ϣⲁ ⲁⲛⲏϩⲉ ⲙ̄ⲡⲁⲩ
ⲧⲟⲅⲉⲛⲏⲥ ⲙ̄⟨ⲡ⟩ⲡⲗⲏⲣⲱⲙⲁ ⲙ̄ⲡⲉ

The / great Logos (λόγος), / the divine Autogenes (αὐτογενής), and / the incorruptible (ἄφθαρτος) man Adamas gave praise / (and) they asked (αἰτεῖν) for a power (δύναμις) and / eternal strength for the Autogenes (αὐτογενής) / for the completion (πλήρωμα) of the /

[ρωμα] τη̣[ρ̄ϥ] εταϊρ̄ϣρπ̄ [ν̄ϫοοϥ]
[μ̄ν πκ]α̣ϩ [μ̄π]αηρ · πι[ρ]εϥ[ϣεπ̄]
[νουτε] εροϥ πιμα [ετουϫι ϩ̂ι]
[κων ν̄]ϭ̣[ι] νιρωμε ε̣[τουααβ ν̄]
[τε π]ο̣υοειν ν̄τε πιω̣[τ ν̄τε ϯ]
[σιγη] μ̄ν ϯπηγη ετο̣ν̣[ϩ ν̄σιγη]
[πι]ωτ᾽ μ̣ν̣̄ πιπληρ[ωμα τηρ̄ϥ]
[ετν]τ̣[ωυ ν̄]θε ενταϊ[ρ̄ϣρπ̄ ν̄]
[ϫο]ος̣

62,11 ι has flaked off.
15 ετ̄ντωυ see 64,25; or ετ̄νταυ see 66,24.

[pleroma (*πλήρωμα*)] that I [mentioned] before, / [and the] earth [of the] air (*ἀήρ*), the [receiver] / [10] [of God,] where the [holy] men / [receive shape (*εἰκών*),] (those) / [of the] light of the Father [of the] / [silence (*σιγή*)] and the living [silent (*σιγή*)] spring (*πηγή*), / [the] Father and [their whole] pleroma (*πλήρωμα*) / [15] as I mentioned / [before.]

The request of the Logos and Adamas: IV 62,16 - 63,8

[αϥειν]ε εϩραϊ [ν̄ουσμου]
[ν̄ϭι π]ινοϭ̣ ν̄ϣαϫε ν̄α[υτογε]
[νη]ς̣ ν̄νουτε μ̄ν [π]ι̣[ατ᾽ϫωϩμ]
[ν̄]ρωμε αδαμας αυ[ω αυρ̄αι]
[τι] ν̄ουϭομ μ̄ν ουϫ[ρο ϣα ε]
[ν]εϩ μ̄ν ουμν̄τ᾽ατ᾽ϫ̣[ωϩμ μ̄]
[π]ιαυτογενης ευ[πληρω]

[The] great, / [self-begotten (*αὐτογενής*),] divine Word / and [the incorruptible] / man Adamas [brought praise] and [they] / [20] [asked (*αἰτεῖν*)] for a power and [eternal] / [strength] and in[corruption for] / [the] Autogenes (*αὐτογενής*), for [completion (*πλήρωμα*)] /

III 50,24 ϥⲧⲟⲟⲩ ⲛ̅ⲁⲓⲱⲛ ϫⲉⲕⲁⲁⲥ ⲉⲃⲟⲗ
ϩⲓⲧⲟⲟⲧⲟⲩ ⲉϥⲛⲁⲟⲩⲱⲛϩ ⲉⲃⲟⲗ
51 [ⲛⲁ]
[. . . . . . ⲛ̅]ϭ[ⲓ] ⲡ̣ⲉⲟⲟⲩ ⲙ̅ⲛ̅ ⲧⲁⲩ
2 [ⲛⲁⲙ]ⲓⲥ ⲙ̅ⲡⲁϩⲟⲣⲁⲧⲟⲥ ⲛ̅ⲉⲓⲱⲧ ⲛ̅
ⲛⲣⲱⲙⲉ ⲉⲧⲟⲩⲁⲁⲃ · ⲙ̅ⲡⲛⲟϭ ⲛⲟⲩ
4 ⲟⲉⲓⲛ ⲡⲁ̈ⲓ ⲉⲧⲛⲏⲟⲩ ⲉⲡⲕⲟⲥⲙⲟⲥ
ⲉϥⲟ ⲙ̅ⲡⲓⲛⲉ ⲛ̅ⲧⲉⲩϣⲏ ⲡⲁⲫⲑⲁⲣ
6 [ⲧ]ⲟⲥ ⲛ̅ⲣⲱⲙⲉ ⲁⲇⲁⲙⲁⲥ ⲁϥⲁⲓⲧⲓ ⲛⲁⲩ
ⲛ̅ⲟⲩϣⲏⲣⲉ ⲉⲃⲟⲗ ⲛ̅ϩⲏⲧϥ̅ · ϫⲉⲕⲁ
8 ⲁⲥ ⲉϥⲉϣⲱⲡⲉ ⲛ̅ⲉⲓⲱⲧ ⲛ̅ⲧⲅⲉⲛⲉⲁ
ⲉ̣ⲧⲉⲙⲉⲥⲕⲓⲙ ⲛ̅ⲁⲫⲑⲁⲣⲧⲟⲛ ϫⲉ
10 ⲕ̣ⲁⲁⲥ ⲉⲃⲟⲗ ϩⲓⲧⲟⲟⲧⲥ̅ · ⲉⲥⲛⲁⲟⲩⲱⲛϩ
ⲉⲃⲟⲗ ⲛ̅ϭⲓ ⲧⲥⲓⲅⲏ ⲙ̅ⲛ ⲧⲉⲫⲱⲛⲏ
12 ⲁⲩⲱ ⲉⲃⲟⲗ ϩⲓⲧⲟⲟⲧⲥ̅ ⲉϥⲉⲧⲟⲩⲛ̅ϥ
ⲛ̅ϭⲓ ⲡⲁⲓⲱⲛ ⲉⲧⲙⲟⲟⲩⲧ ϫⲉⲕⲁⲁⲥ
14 ⲉϥⲉⲕ[ⲁ]ⲧⲁⲗⲩ ·

51, 8 Corr. ⲱ over ⲛ ?

four aeons (αἰών), in order that, / [25] through them, there may appear // *51* [ ] the glory and the power (δύναμις) / of the invisible (ἀόρατος) Father of / the holy men of the great light / which will come to the world (κόσμος) / [5] which is the image of the night. The incorruptible (ἄφθαρτος) / man Adamas asked (αἰτεῖν) for them / a son out of himself, in order / that he (i.e. the son) may become father of the / immovable, incorruptible (ἄφθαρτον) race (γενεά), so / [10] that, through it (i.e. the race), the silence (σιγή) / and the voice (φωνή) may appear, / and, through it, / the dead aeon (αἰών) may raise itself, so that / it may dissolve (καταλύειν).

IV 62 [ⲙⲁ] ⲛ̄ⲧⲉ ⲡⲓϥⲧⲟⲟⲩ ⲛ̣[ⲛⲉⲱⲛ]
[ϩⲓⲛ]ⲁ̣ ⲉⲃⲟⲗ ϩⲓⲧⲟⲟⲧⲟ[ⲩ ⲛ̄ⲧⲉϥ]
[ⲟⲩ]ⲱⲛ̄ϩ ⲉⲃⲟⲗ ⲛ̄ϭⲓ ⲡ[ⲉⲟⲟⲩ ⲙ̄ⲛ]
[ϯϭⲟ]ⲙ̣ ⲛ̄ⲧⲉ ⲡⲓⲱⲧ̀ ⲛ̄.[... ⲛ̄ⲛ]
[ⲣⲱⲙⲉ ⲉ]ⲧⲟⲩⲁⲁⲃ ⲛ̄ⲧⲉ ⲡ̣[ⲓⲛⲟϭ ⲛ̄]
[ⲟⲩⲟⲉⲓ]ⲛ̣ ⲡⲏ ⲉⲧⲛⲁⲉ̣[ⲓ ⲉⲡⲉⲥⲏⲧ̀]
[ϣⲁ ⲡⲓⲕⲟ]ⲥⲙⲟⲥ ⲛ̄ⲉⲓ̣[ⲛⲉ ⲛ̄ⲟⲩϣⲏ]
[ⲧⲟⲧⲉ] ⲡ̣ⲓⲁⲧ̀ϫⲱϩⲙ̣ [ⲛ̄ⲛⲟϭ ⲛ̄]
[ⲣⲱⲙⲉ ⲁⲇⲁⲙ]ⲁⲥ ⲁϥⲣ̄ⲁ̣[ⲓⲧⲓ ⲛ̄]

63 [ⲝⲅ]

ⲟⲩϣⲏⲣⲉ ⲛⲁϥ ⲉⲃⲟⲗ ⲙ̄ⲙⲟ̣[ϥ ϩⲓⲛⲁ]
ⲛ̄ⲧⲟϥ ⲛ̄ⲧⲉϥϣⲱⲡⲉ ⲛ̄ⲉⲓⲱ[ⲧ̀ ⲛ̄ϯ]
ⲅⲉⲛⲉⲁ ⲛ̄ⲁⲧ̀ⲕⲓⲙ ⲁⲩⲱ ⲛ̄[ⲁⲧ̀ϫⲱ]
ϩⲙ̄ ⲁⲩⲱ ⲉⲧⲃⲏⲧⲥ̄ ⲛ̄ⲧ̣⟨ⲉ⟩ⲥⲣ̣̄[ϣⲟⲣⲡ̄]
ⲛ̄ⲟⲩⲱⲛ̄ϩ ⲉⲃⲟⲗ ⲛ̄[ϭⲓ ϯⲥ]ⲓ̣ⲅⲏ̣ [ⲙ̄ⲛ ϯ]
[ⲥ]ⲙ̣ⲏ̣ ⲁⲩⲱ ⲉⲧⲃⲏⲏⲧⲥ̄ ⲛ̄[ϥⲧⲱ]
[ⲱⲛ̄ϥ ⲛ̄]ϭⲓ ⲡⲓⲉⲱⲛ ⲉⲧⲙⲟ̣[ⲟⲩⲧ̀]
[ϫⲉⲕⲁ]ⲁⲥ̣ ⲉϥⲛⲁⲃⲱⲗ ⲉⲃ[ⲟⲗ

62,26 The remnant after ⲛ̄ is not ⲧ.
31 The line is about 3 letters shorter than the preceding ones. Perhaps the scribe did not want to split up ⲟⲩϣⲏⲣⲉ between 2 pages.
63, 4 MS. reads ⲛ̄ⲧⲁⲥ.
6 ⲛ̄[ⲧⲉϥⲧⲱ] is possible but rather long.

of the four [aeons (*αἰών*)], / [in order that (*ἵνα*)], through them, / there may appear the [glory and] / [the power] of the [ ] Father [of the] / holy [men] of the [great] / [light] that will come [down] / [to the night-like] world (*κόσμος*). / [Then (*τότε*)] the incorruptible, [great] / [man Adam]as [asked (*αἰτεῖν*)] // *63* for himself a son out of himself, [in order that (*ἵνα*)] / he (i.e. the son) may become Father [of the] / immovable and [in]corruptible race (*γενεά*), / and that because of it (i.e. the race) / [the] silence (*σιγή*) [and the] voice may appear, / and that because of it the / [dead] aeon (*αἰών*) [may raise itself,] / [so that] it may dissolve.

The creation of the four lights and Seth: III 51,14-22

III 51,14 ⲁⲩⲱ ⲛ̄ⲧⲉⲉⲓϩⲉ ⲁ
ⲥⲉⲓ ⲉⲃⲟⲗ ϫⲓⲛ ⲛ̄ⲡⲥⲁϩⲣⲉ ⲛ̄ϭⲓ ⲧⲇⲩ
16 ⲛⲁⲙⲓⲥ ⲙ̄ⲡⲛⲟϭ ⲛ̄ⲟⲩⲟⲉⲓⲛ ⲧⲉ
ⲡⲣⲟⲫⲁⲛⲓⲁ ⲁⲥϫⲡⲟ ⲙ̄ⲡⲉϥⲧⲟⲟⲩ
18 ⲙ̄ⲫⲱⲥⲧⲏⲣ ϩⲁⲣⲙⲟⲍⲏⲗ · ⲟⲣⲟⲓ̈ⲁⲏⲗ
ⲇⲁⲩⲉⲓⲑⲉ ⲏⲗⲏⲗⲏⲑ · ⲉⲧⲛⲁϣⲱϥ
20 ⲙ̄ⲛ ⲡⲛⲟϭ ⲛ̄ⲁⲫⲑⲁⲣⲧⲟⲥ ⲥⲏⲑ · ⲡϣⲏ
ⲣⲉ ⲙ̄ⲡⲁⲫⲑⲁⲣⲧⲟⲥ ⲛ̄ⲣⲱⲙⲉ ⲁⲇⲁ
22 ⲙⲁⲥ ·

And thus / [15] there came forth from above the power (δύναμις) / of the great light, the / Manifestation (προφάνεια). She gave birth to the four great / lights (φωστήρ) : Harmozel, Oroiael, / Davithe, Eleleth, / [20] and the great incorruptible (ἄφθαρτος) Seth, the son / of the incorruptible (ἄφθαρτος) man / Adamas.

The completion of the hebdomad: III 51,22 - 52,3

22 ⲁⲩⲱ ⲛ̄ⲧⲉⲉⲓϩⲉ ⲁⲥϫⲱⲕ ⲉⲃⲟⲗ
ⲛ̄ϭⲓ ⲧϩⲉⲃⲇⲟⲙⲁⲥ ⲛ̄ⲧⲉⲗⲉⲓⲁ · ⲧⲁⲓ̈
24 ⲉⲧϣⲟⲟⲡ̄ ϩ̄ⲛ ϩⲉⲛⲙⲩⲥⲧⲏⲣⲓⲟⲛ
52 [ⲛⲃ]
ⲉⲩϩⲏⲡ̄ ⲉⲥϣⲁⲛ̣ϫ̣[ⲓ ⲙ̄]ⲡ̣ⲉ̣[ⲟⲟⲩ]
2 ϣⲁⲥⲣ̄ ⲟⲩϩⲉⲛⲇⲉⲕⲁⲥ ⲛ̄ϩⲟ̣
ⲅⲇⲟⲁⲥ

And thus / the perfect (τελεία) hebdomad (ἑβδομάς) which / exists in hidden mysteries (μυστήριον) became complete. // *52* When she [receives] the [glory] / she becomes eleven (ἑνδεκάς) / ogdoads (ὀγδοάς).

The creation of the four lights and Seth: IV 63,8-17

IV 63, 8 ⲁⲩⲱ]

[ⲛ̅ϯϩⲉ ⲁⲥⲣ̅]ϣⲟⲣⲡ̅ ⲛ̅ⲉ͡ⲓ ⲉ̣[ⲃⲟⲗ ⲛ̅ⲥⲁ]

10 [ϩⲣⲁⲓ̈ ⲛ̅ϭⲓ ϯ]ϭⲟⲙ ϯⲛⲟϭ̣ [ⲛ̅ϭⲟⲙ]

[ⲛ̅ⲧⲉ ⲡ]ⲓ̣ⲛⲟϭ ⲛ̅ⲟⲩⲟⲉⲓⲛ ⟨ⲡ⟩ⲡ̅ⲣ̅[ⲉⲓⲱⲟⲩ]

12 [ⲁⲩⲱ ⲁⲥ]ϫ̣ⲡⲟ ⲙ̅ⲡⲓϥⲧⲟⲟⲩ ⲙ̅[ⲫⲱⲥ]

[ⲧⲏⲣ ⲁ̅ⲣ̅]ⲙ̅ⲟ̅ⲍ̅ⲏ̅ⲗ̅ · ⲟ̅[ⲣ̅]ⲟ̅ⲓ̈̅ⲁ̅ⲏ̅ⲗ̅

14 [ⲇ̅ⲁ̅ⲩ̅ⲉ̅ⲓ̅ⲑ̅ⲉ̅·] ⲏ̅ⲗ̅ⲏ̅ⲗ̅ⲏ̅[ⲑ̅] ⲙⲛ̅ ⲡ[ⲓⲛⲟϭ]

[ⲛ̅ⲁⲧ̓ϫⲱ]ϩⲙ ⲥ̅ⲏ̅ⲑ̅ ⲡⲓϣⲏⲣ[ⲉ ⲛ̅ⲧⲉ]

16 [ⲡⲓⲛⲟϭ ⲛ̅ⲁ]ⲧ̓ϫⲱϩⲙ ⲛ̅ⲣⲱⲙ̣ⲉ

[ⲁⲇⲁⲙⲁⲥ

[And] / [thus the] power came [forth] / [10] [from above,] the great [power] / [of the] great light, <the> [Manifestation.] / [And it] begat the four [lights (φωστήρ)] /: [Ar]mozel, Oroiael, / [Davithe,] Eleleth, and the [great,] / [15] [incorruptible] Seth, the son [of] / [the great,] incorruptible man / [Adamas.]

The completion of the hebdomad: IV 63,17-24

ⲁ]ⲩⲱ ⲛ̅ϯϩⲉ ⲁⲩϫⲱⲕ

18 [ⲉⲃⲟⲗ ⲛ̅ϯ]ϩ̣ⲉⲃⲇⲟⲙⲁⲥ ⲉⲧ̓ϫⲏⲕ

[ⲉⲃⲟⲗ ⲧⲏ ⲉⲧ̓]ϣⲟⲟⲡ̓ ϩⲛ̅ ⲟⲩⲙⲩ

20 [ⲥⲧⲏⲣⲓⲟⲛ] ⲛ̅ⲧⲉ ϩⲉⲛⲙⲩⲥⲧⲏⲣⲓⲟⲛ

[ⲉⲩϩⲏⲡ̓] ⲧⲏ ⲉⲧⲁⲥϫⲓ ⲙ̅ⲡⲉⲟ̣[ⲟⲩ]

22 [.....]ⲁ ⲉⲁⲥϣⲱⲡⲉ ⲛ̅ⲟ[ⲩϩⲉⲛ]

[ⲇⲉⲕⲁⲥ] ⲛ̅ⲟⲅⲇⲟⲁⲥ ϩ͡ⲓⲛⲁ [ⲛ̅ⲧⲉⲥ]

24 [ϫⲱⲕ ϩ]ⲛ̅ ϥⲧⲟ ⲛ̅ⲟⲅⲇⲟⲁⲥ̣

63,24 The superlin. stroke is in the lacuna.

And thus [the] / perfect hebdomad (ἑβδομάς) was completed / [which] exists in a mystery (μυστήριον) / [20] of [hidden] mysteries (μυστήριον), / she who received the [glory] / [ ] and who became [eleven (ἑνδεκάς)] / ogdoads (ὀγδοάς), in order that (ἵνα) [she may] / [be completed by] four ogdoads (ὀγδοάς).

The consorts of the lights: III 52,3-16

III 52 ⲁⲩⲱ ⲁϥⲕⲁⲧⲁⲛⲉⲩⲉ ⲛ̅ϭⲓ
4 ⲡⲉⲓⲱⲧ̇ ⲁϥⲥⲩⲛⲉⲩⲇⲟⲕⲉⲓ ⲛ̅ϭⲓ
ⲡⲉⲡⲗⲏⲣⲱⲙⲁ ⲧⲏⲣϥ̅ ⲛ̅ⲛⲉ
6 ⲫⲱⲥⲧⲏⲣ ⲁⲩⲉⲓ ⲉⲃⲟⲗ ⲛ̅ϭⲓ ⲛⲉⲩ⟨ⲥⲩ⟩
ⲍⲩⲅⲟⲥ ⲉⲡϫⲱⲕ ⲛ̅ⲧϩⲟⲅⲇⲟⲁⲥ ⲙ̅
8 ⲡⲁⲩⲧⲟⲅⲉⲛⲏⲥ ⲛ̅ⲛⲟⲩⲧⲉ ⲧⲉ
ⲭⲁⲣⲓⲥ ⲙ̅ⲡⲉϩⲟⲩⲉⲓⲧ̇ ⲛ̅ⲟⲩⲟⲉⲓⲛ ·
10 ⲁⲣⲙⲟⲍⲏⲗ ⲧⲉⲥⲑⲏⲥⲓⲥ ⲙ̅ⲡⲙⲉϩⲥ
ⲛⲁⲩ ⲛ̅ⲟⲩⲟⲉⲓⲛ ⲟⲣⲟⲓ̈ⲁⲏⲗ · ⲧⲥⲩⲛ
12 ϩⲉⲥⲓⲥ ⲙ̅ⲡⲙⲉϩϣⲟⲙⲛ̅ⲧ ⟨ⲛ̅⟩ⲟⲩⲟⲉⲓⲛ
ⲇⲁⲩⲉⲓⲑⲉ · ⲧⲉⲫⲣⲟⲛⲏⲥⲓⲥ ⲛ̅⟨ⲡ⟩ⲙⲉϩ
14 ϥⲧⲟⲟⲩ ⲛ̅ⲟⲩⲟⲉⲓⲛ ⲏⲗⲉⲗⲏⲑ . ⲧⲁⲓ̈
ⲧⲉ ⲧⲉϩⲟⲩⲉⲓⲧⲉ ⲛ̅ϩⲟⲅⲇⲟⲁⲥ ⲛ̅ⲡⲁⲩ
16 ⲧⲟⲅⲉⲛⲏⲥ ⲛ̅ⲛⲟⲩⲧⲉ ·

52, 5 Corr. ⲙ̅ crossed out before ⲛ̅ⲛⲉ.
12 MS. reads ⲙ̅ⲟⲩⲟⲉⲓⲛ.
13 MS. reads ⲛ̅ⲧⲙⲉϩ.

And the Father nodded approval (καταvεύειν); / the whole pleroma (πλήρωμα) of the / lights (φωστήρ) was well pleased (συνευδοκεῖν). / Their consorts (σύζυγος) came forth / for the completion of the ogdoad (ὀγδοάς) of / the divine Autogenes (αὐτογενής) : the / Grace (χάρις) of the first light / Harmozel, the Perception (αἴσθησις) of the second / light Oroiael, the Understanding (σύνεσις) / of the third light / Davithe, the Prudence (φρόνησις) of the / fourth light Eleleth. This / is the first ogdoad (ὀγδοάς) of the / divine Autogenes (αὐτογενής).

The consorts of the lights: IV 63,24 - 64,10

IV 63,24 [ⲁⲩⲱ]
[ⲁϥϯ ⲙⲉ]ⲧⲉ ⲛ̄ϭⲓ ⲡⲓⲱⲧ [ⲁⲩⲱ ⲁϥⲣ̄]
26 [ϣⲃⲏⲣ ⲛ̄ϯ] ⲙⲉⲧⲉ ⲛ̄ϭⲓ ⲡⲓⲡ̣[ⲗⲏⲣⲱⲙⲁ]
[ⲛ̄ⲧⲉ ⲛⲓⲫ]ⲱ̣ⲥⲧⲏⲣ ⲁⲩⲣ̄ϣ[ⲟⲣⲡ̄ ⲛ̄]
28 [ⲟⲩⲱⲛ̄ϩ] ⲉⲃⲟⲗ ⲛ̄ϭⲓ ϩⲉⲛⲥⲩ[ⲛ̄ⲍⲩⲅⲟⲥ]
[ⲉⲡⲓⲡⲗⲏⲣ]ⲱⲙⲁ ⲛ̄ⲧⲉ ϯⲟⲅⲇ̣[ⲟⲁⲥ]
64 [ⲝ̄ⲇ̄]
[ⲛ̄ⲧⲉ ⲡⲓⲁ]ⲩⲧⲟⲅ̣ⲉⲛⲏⲥ ⲛ̄ⲛⲟⲩⲧⲉ
2 [ⲡϩⲙⲟ]ⲧ ⲙ̄ⲡⲓϣⲟⲣⲡ̄ ⲙ̄ⲫⲱⲥⲧⲏⲣ
[ⲁⲣⲙⲟ]ⲍⲏⲗ · ⲧⲉⲥⲑⲏⲥⲓⲥ ⲙ̄ⲡⲓⲙⲉϩ
4 [ⲥⲛⲁⲩ] ⲙ̄ⲫⲱⲥⲧⲏⲣ · ⲟⲣⲟⲓ̈ⲁⲏⲗ ·
[ⲡⲥⲟⲟ]ⲩⲛ ⲙ̄ⲡ[ⲓ]ⲙⲉϩϣⲟⲙⲉⲧ ⲙ̄
6 [ⲫⲱⲥ]ⲧⲏⲣ ⲇ̣ⲁⲩⲉⲓⲑⲉ · ⲧⲉⲥⲃ̣[ⲱ]
[ⲙ̄ⲡⲓⲙ]ⲉϩϥⲧⲟⲟⲩ ⲙ̄ⲫⲱⲥ̣[ⲧⲏⲣ]
8 [ⲏⲗⲏⲗ]ⲏ̣ⲑ · ⲉⲧⲉ ⲧⲁⲓ̈ ⲧⲉ ϯ[ϣⲟⲣⲡ̄]
[ⲛ̄ⲟⲅⲇⲟ]ⲁⲥ ⲛ̄ⲧⲉ ⲡⲓⲁⲩⲧ̣[ⲟⲅⲉⲛⲏⲥ]
10 [ⲛ̄ⲛⲟⲩⲧⲉ]

64, 2 Superlin. stroke on ⲙ̄ⲡⲓ is in the lacuna.

[And] / [25] the Father [approved, and] / the [pleroma (πλήρωμα) of the] / lights (φωστήρ) [joined] in approval. / [Consorts (σύζυγος) appeared] / [for the] completion (πλήρωμα) of the ogdoad (ὀγδοάς) // *64* [of the] divine Autogenes (αὐτογενής) /: [the Grace] of the first light (φωστήρ) / [Armo]zel, the Perception (αἴσθησις) of the / [second] light (φωστήρ) Oroiael, / [5] [the Understanding] of the third / light (φωστήρ) Davithe, the Prudence / [of the] fourth light (φωστήρ) / [Elel]eth. This is the [first] / [ogdoad (ὀγδοάς)] of the [divine] / [10] Auto[genes (αὐτογενής).]

The ministers of the lights and their consorts: III 52,16 - 53,12

III 52,16 ⲁⲩⲱ ⲁϥⲕⲁⲧⲁ
ⲛⲉⲩⲉ ⲛ̅ϭⲓ ⲡⲉⲓⲱⲧ̇ ⲁϥⲥⲩⲛⲉⲩⲇⲟ
18 ⲕⲉⲓ ⲛ̅ϭⲓ ⲡⲉⲡⲗⲏⲣⲱⲙⲁ ⲧⲏⲣ̅ϥ̅ ⲛ̅
ⲛ̅ⲟⲩⲟⲉⲓⲛ ⲁⲩⲡⲣⲟⲉⲗⲑⲉ ⲉⲃⲟⲗ ⲛ̅
20 ϭⲓ ⲛ̅⟨ⲇⲓⲁⲕⲟⲛⲟⲥ⟩ ⲡⲉϩⲟⲩⲉⲓⲧ̇ ⲡⲛⲟϭ
ⲛ̅ⲅⲁⲙⲁⲗⲓⲏⲗ · ⲡⲉϩⲟⲩⲉⲓⲧ̇ ⲡⲛⲟϭ
22 ⲛ̅ⲟⲩⲟⲉⲓⲛ ϩⲁⲣⲙⲟⲍⲏⲗ · ⲁⲩⲱ ⲡⲛⲟϭ
ⲅ̅ⲁ̅ⲃ̅ⲣ̅ⲓ̅ⲏ̅ⲗ̅ · ⲡⲙⲉϩⲥⲛⲁⲩ ⲛ̅ⲛⲟϭ ⲛ̅
24 ⲟⲩⲟⲉⲓⲛ ⲟ̅ⲣ̅ⲟ̅ⲓ̈̅ⲁ̅ⲏ̅ⲗ̅ · ⲁⲩⲱ ⲡⲛⲟϭ
ⲥ̅ⲁ̅ⲙ̅ⲗ̅ⲱ̅ · ⲙ̅ⲡⲛⲟϭ ⲛ̅ⲟⲩⲟⲉⲓⲛ ⲇⲁⲩ
26 ⲉⲓⲑⲉ · ⲁⲩⲱ ⲡⲛⲟϭ ⲁⲃⲣⲁⲥⲁⲝ · ⲛ̅
53 [ⲛⲅ]
[ⲡⲛⲟϭ ⲛ̅ⲟⲩⲟⲉⲓⲛ] ⲏⲗⲉⲗⲏⲑ · ⲁⲩⲱ
2 [ⲁⲛⲥⲩ]ⲛⲍⲩⲅⲟⲥ ⲛ̅ⲛⲁⲓ̈ ⲡⲣⲟⲉⲗⲑⲉ ⲉ
ⲃ̣ⲟⲗ ϩ̅ⲙ̅ ⲡⲟⲩⲱϣ ⲛ̅ⲧⲉⲩⲇⲟⲕⲓⲁ
4 ⲙ̅ⲡⲉⲓⲱⲧ̇ ⲧⲉⲙⲛⲏⲙⲏ ⲙ̅ⲡⲛⲟϭ
ⲡⲉϩⲟⲩⲉⲓⲧ̇ ⲅⲁⲙⲁⲗⲓⲏⲗ · ⲧⲁⲅⲁⲡⲏ

52,20 Or emend ⲇⲓⲁⲕⲱⲛ. MS. reads ⲥⲩⲛⲍⲩⲅⲟⲥ.
21 ⲛ̅ⲛⲟϭ?

And / the Father nodded approval (*κατανεύειν*); the whole pleroma (*πλήρωμα*) / of the lights was well pleased (*συνευδοκεῖν*). / The <ministers (*διάκονος*)> came forth (*προελθεῖν*): / [20] the first one, the great / Gamaliel (of) the first great / light Harmozel, and the great / Gabriel (of) the second great / light Oroiael, and the great / [25] Samlo of the great light Davithe, / and the great Abrasax of // *53* [the great light] Eleleth. And / [the] consorts (*σύζυγος*) of these came forth (*προελθεῖν*) / by the will of the good pleasure (*εὐδοκία*) / of the Father: the Memory (*μνήμη*) of the great one, / [5] the first Gamaliel, the Love (*ἀγάπη*) /

The ministers of the lights and their consorts: IV 64,10 - 65,5

IV 64,10 ⲁ̣ⲩⲱ ⲁϥϯ ⲙ[ⲉⲧⲉ ⲛ̄ϭⲓ ⲡⲓ]
[ⲱⲧ̓ ⲁ]ⲩⲱ̣ ⲁϥⲣ̄ϣⲃⲏⲣ ⲛ̄ϯ [ⲙⲉⲧⲉ]
12 [ⲛ̄ϭⲓ] ⲡⲓⲡⲗⲏⲣⲱⲙⲁ ⲧⲏⲣ̣ϥ [ⲛ̄ⲧⲉ]
[ⲛⲓⲫ]ⲱ̣ⲥⲧⲏⲣ ⲉⲁⲩⲣ̄ϣⲟ[ⲣⲡ̓ ⲛ̄ⲉ͡ⲓ]
14 [ⲉⲃ]ⲟⲗ ⲛ̄ϭ̣ⲓ ϩⲉⲛⲇⲓⲁⲕⲱ[ⲛ ⲡⲓϣⲟ]
[ⲣⲡ̓] ⲛ̄ⲛⲟϭ ⲕⲁⲙⲁⲗⲓⲏ[ⲗ ⲛ̄ⲧⲉ ⲡⲓ]
16 [ⲛⲟϭ] ⲙ̄ⲫⲱⲥⲧⲏⲣ [ⲁⲣⲙⲟⲍⲏⲗ·]
ⲙ[ⲛ] ⲡⲓⲛⲟϭ ⲅⲁⲃⲣⲓⲏ[ⲗ ⲛ̄ⲧⲉ ⲡⲓⲛⲟϭ]
18 ⲙ̄ⲙⲉϩⲥⲛⲁⲩ ⲙ̄ⲫⲱ̣[ⲥⲧⲏⲣ ⲟⲣⲟⲓ̈ⲁⲏⲗ·]
ⲡⲓⲛⲟϭ ⲥⲁⲙⲃⲗⲱ̣ ⲛ̄[ⲧⲉ ⲡⲓⲛⲟϭ]
20 ⲙ̄ⲙⲉϩϣⲟⲙⲧ̓ ⲙ̄ⲫⲱ[ⲥⲧⲏⲣ]
ⲇⲁⲩⲉⲓⲑⲉ · ⲁⲃⲣⲁⲥⲁⲝ ⲙ̣[ⲡⲓⲛⲟϭ]
22 [ⲙ̄]ⲙⲉϩϥⲧⲟⲟⲩ ⲙ̄ⲫⲱ̣[ⲥⲧⲏⲣ]
[ⲏⲗ]ⲏ̣ⲗⲏⲑ · ⲁⲩⲱ ⲁⲩⲉ͡[ⲓ ⲉⲃⲟⲗ ⲛ̄ϭⲓ]
24 [ϩⲉⲛ]ⲥ̣ⲩⲛⲍⲩⲅⲟⲥ ϩ̄ⲛ ⲟ̣[ⲩϯ]
[ⲙⲉⲧ]ⲉ̣ ⲛ̣̄ⲧⲱⲟⲩ ⲛ̄ⲧⲉ ⲡ[ⲓⲱⲧ̓]
26 [ⲡⲓⲙⲉⲉⲩ]ⲉ ⲙ̄ⲡⲓϣⲟⲣ̣[ⲡ̓ ⲛ̄ⲛⲟϭ]
[ⲅⲁⲙⲁⲗⲓ]ⲏⲗ· ⲧⲁⲅⲁⲡ̣[ⲏ ⲙ̄ⲡⲓⲙⲉϩ]

64,16 Superlin. stroke on ⲙ̄ is in the lacuna.
18 The line must have been unusually long.
21 Superlin. stroke on ⲙ̄ is in the lacuna.
26 Superlin. stroke on ⲙ̄ is in the lacuna.

And [the Father] approved, / and the whole pleroma (πλήρωμα) / [of the] lights (φωστήρ) joined in / [approval.] Ministers (διάκων) / [came] forth: [the first] / great Gamaliel [of the] / [great] light (φωστήρ) [Armozel,] / and the great Gabriel [of the great] / second light (φωστήρ) [Oroiael,] / the great Samblo of [the great] / third light (φωστήρ) / Davithe, Abrasax of [the great] / fourth light (φωστήρ) / [El]eleth. And consorts (σύζυγος) / came [forth] through [the] / [good pleasure] (shone) to them by the [Father]: / [the Memory] of the first [great one] / [Gamali]el, the Love (ἀγάπη) [of the second] /

III 53, 6 ⲙ̄ⲡⲛⲟϭ ⲡⲙⲉϩⲥⲛⲁⲩ ⲅⲁⲃⲣⲓⲏⲗ
ϯⲣⲏⲛⲏ ⲙ̄ⲡⲙⲉϩϣⲟⲙⲛ̄ⲧ ⲡⲛⲟϭ
8 ⲛ̄ⲥⲁⲙⲃⲗⲱ · ⲡⲱⲛϩ ⲛ̄ϣⲁ ⲉⲛⲉϩ·
ⲙ̄ⲡⲛⲟϭ {ⲙ}ⲡⲙⲉϩϥⲧⲟⲟⲩ ⲁⲃⲣⲁ
10 ⲥⲁⲝ · ⲛ̄ⲧⲉⲉⲓϩⲉ ⲁⲩϫⲱⲕ ⲉⲃⲟⲗ ⲛ̄
ϭⲓ'ⲧ'ϯⲉ ⲛ̄ϩⲟⲅⲇⲟⲁⲥ ⲟⲩϩⲙ'ⲉ' ⲉⲥϫⲏⲕ ⲉ
12 ⲃⲟⲗ ⲛ̄ⲟⲩϭⲟⲙ ⲛ̄ⲁⲧⲟⲩⲁϩⲙⲉⲥ

53,11 Corr. ⲟⲩϩⲙ over erasure.
12 Corr. ϩ over ⲓ ?

of the great one, the second Gabriel, / the Peace (εἰρήνη) of the third one, the great / Samblo, the eternal Life / of the great one, the fourth, Abrasax. / [10] Thus were the five ogdoads (ὀγδοάς) completed, / a total of forty, / as an uninterpretable power.

The request of the Logos and the pleroma: III 53,12 - 54,11

12 ⲧⲟ
ⲧⲉ ⲡⲛⲟϭ ⲛ̄ⲗⲟⲅⲟⲥ ⲡⲁⲩⲧⲟⲅⲉⲛⲏⲥ
14 ⟨ⲙⲛ̄⟩ ⲡϣⲁϫⲉ ⲙ̄ⲡⲉⲡⲗⲏⲣⲱⲙⲁ
ⲙ̄ⲡⲉϥⲧⲟⲟⲩ ⲛ̄ⲟⲩⲟⲉⲓⲛ ⲁⲩϯ ⲛ̄
16 ⲟⲩⲥⲙⲟⲩ ⲛ̄ⲡⲛⲟϭ ⲛ̄ⲁϩⲟⲣⲁⲧⲟⲛ
ⲛ̄ⲡⲛ̄ⲁ ⲛ̄ⲁⲕⲗⲏⲧⲟⲛ ⲛ̄ⲡⲁⲣⲑⲉⲛⲓ
18 ⲕⲟⲛ ⲙ̄ⲛ ⲧⲁⲣⲥⲉⲛⲓⲕⲏ ⲛ̄ⲡⲁⲣⲑⲉ
ⲛⲟⲥ ⲙⲛ̄ ⲡⲛⲟϭ ⲛ̄ⲇⲟⲝⲟⲙⲉⲇⲱⲛ

53,14 MS. ⲙⲉⲛ. Cf. Crum, *Dict.* 169b.

Then (τότε) / the great Logos (λόγος), the Autogenes (αὐτογενής), / and the word of the pleroma (πλήρωμα) / [15] of the four lights gave / praise to the great, invisible (ἀόρατον), / uncallable (ἄκλητον), virginal (παρθενικόν) Spirit (πνεῦμα), / and the male (ἀρσενική) virgin (παρθένος), / and the great Doxomedon- /

IV 64,28 [ⲥⲛⲁⲩ] ⲛ̣̄ⲛⲟϭ ⲅ̅ⲁ̅ⲃ̅ⲣ̅ⲓ̅ⲏ̅[ⲗ̅· ϯⲣⲏⲛⲏ]
[ⲙ̄ⲡⲓ]ⲛ̣ⲟϭ ⲙ̄ⲙⲉϩϣ̣[ⲟⲙ̄ⲧ̀ ⲥⲁⲙⲃⲗⲱ]
65 [ⲝ̅ⲉ̅]
ⲡⲱⲛ̄ϩ ⲛ̄ϣⲁ ⲉⲛⲉϩ ⲙ̄ⲡⲛ̣ⲟ̣[ϭ ⲙ̄ⲙⲉϩ]
2 ϥⲧⲟⲟⲩ ⲁ̅ⲃ̅ⲣ̅ⲁ̅ⲥ̅ⲁ̅ⲝ̅ · ⲁⲩⲱ ⲛ̄ϯϩ[ⲉ ⲁⲩ]
ϫⲱⲕ ⲉⲃⲟⲗ ⲛ̄ϭⲓ ϯϯⲉ ⲛ̄ⲟⲅⲇ[ⲟⲁⲥ]
4 ϯⲁⲛϩⲙⲉ ⲉⲧ̀ϫⲏⲕ̣ ⲉⲃⲟⲗ · ϯ̣[ϭⲟⲙ]
ⲛ̄ⲛⲁⲧⲣ̄ϩⲉⲣⲙⲏⲛ[ⲉⲩ]ⲉ ⲙ̄ⲙ[ⲟⲥ·

great one Gabriel, [the Peace (εἰρήνη)] / [of the] great [third] one [Samblo,] // *65* the eternal Life of the [great] / fourth one Abrasax. And thus / the five ogdoads (ὀγδοάς) were completed, / a total of forty, the / [5] uninterpretable (-ἑρμηνεύειν) [power.]

The request of the Logos and the pleroma: IV 65,5-30

ⲧⲟ]
6 [ⲧ]ⲉ̣ ⲡⲓⲛⲟϭ ⲛ̄ϣⲁϫⲉ ⲛ̄ⲁⲩⲧ[ⲟⲅⲉⲛⲏⲥ]
[ⲙ̄]ⲛ̣ ⲡⲓⲡⲗⲏⲣⲱⲙⲁ ⲧⲏⲣ̄ϥ ⲛ̄[ⲧⲉ ⲡⲓ]
8 [ϥⲧⲟⲟ]ⲩ ⲙ̄ⲫⲱⲥⲧⲏⲣ · ⲁⲩ[ⲉⲓⲛⲉ]
[ⲉϩⲣ]ⲁï ⲛ̄ⲟ̣ⲩⲥⲙⲟⲩ ⲙ̄ⲡⲓⲛ[ⲟϭ ⲛ̄]
10 [ⲁⲧⲛⲁⲩ] ⲉ̣ⲣ̣[ⲟϥ] ⲁⲩⲱ ⲛ̄ⲁⲧ̣̀[ϫⲁϩⲙ̄ϥ]
[ⲛ̄ⲁⲧ̀ϯ] ⲣⲁ̣[ⲛ] ⲉⲣⲟϥ ⲙ̄ⲡⲁⲣ[ⲑⲉⲛⲓⲕⲟⲛ]
12 [ⲙ̄ⲡⲛ̄]ⲁ ⲙⲛ̄ ϯϩⲟⲟⲩⲧ̀ ⲙ̄ⲡ[ⲁⲣⲑⲉ]
[ⲛⲟⲥ] ⲙ̣ⲛ̣̄ ⲛ̣ⲓⲛⲟϭ ⲛ̄ⲛⲉⲱⲛ ⲛ̄ⲁ̣[ⲟⲝⲟ]

65, 6 Superlin. stroke on ⲛ̄ⲁⲩⲧ is in the lacuna.
7 Superlin. stroke on ⲛ̄ is in the lacuna.
10 For [ϫⲁϩⲙ̄ϥ] or [ϫⲱϩ̄ⲙ] see *supra* 54,16f. note.

[Then (τότε)] / the great, self-[begotten (αὐτογενής)] Word / [and] the whole pleroma (πλήρωμα) [of the] / [four] lights (φωστήρ) [brought] / praise to the [great,] / [10] [invisible,] and in[corruptible,] / [unnameable,] virginal (παρθενικόν) / [Spirit (πνεῦμα),] and the male [virgin (παρθένος),] / and the great [Doxomedon] -/

III 53,20 ⲛ̄ⲁⲓⲱⲛ ⲙⲛ̄ ⲛⲉⲑⲣⲟⲛⲟⲥ ⲉⲧⲛ̄ϩⲏ
ⲧⲟⲩ ⲙⲛ̄ ⲛ̄ϭⲟⲙ ⲉⲧⲕⲱⲧⲉ ⲉⲣⲟⲟⲩ
ⲙⲛ̄ ϩⲉⲛⲉⲟⲟⲩ ⲙⲛ̄ ϩⲉⲛⲉⳓⲟⲩⲥⲓⲁ
ⲙⲛ̄ ⲛ̄ϭⲟⲙ ⲙ̄⟨ⲛ⟩ ⲡϣⲟⲙⲛ̄ⲧ̇ ⲛ̄ϩⲟⲟⲩⲧ̇
ⲛ̄ⲁⲗⲟⲩ ⲙⲛ̄ ⲧⲁⲣⲥⲉⲛⲓⲕⲏ ⲛ̄ⲡⲁⲣ
ⲑⲉⲛⲟⲥ ⲓ̈ⲟ̄ⲩ̄ⲏ̄ⲗ̄ ⲙⲛ ⲏ̄ⲥ̄ⲏ̄ⲫ̄ⲏ̄ⲭ̄

54 ⲛⲇ

ⲡⲉⲧⲉⲙⲁϩⲧⲉ ⲙ̄ⲡ̣ⲉ̣[ⲟ]ⲟ̣[ⲩ ⲡⲁⲗⲟⲩ]
ⲙ̄ⲡⲁⲗⲟⲩ ⲙⲛ̄ ⲡⲉⲕⲗⲟⲙ ⲙ̄ⲡ̣ⲉ̣[ϥⲉ]
ⲟⲟⲩ ⲡⲉⲡⲗⲏⲣⲱⲙⲁ ⲧⲏⲣ̄ϥ · ⲙⲛ̄ ⲛⲓ
ⲉⲟⲟⲩ ⲧⲏⲣⲟⲩ ⲉⲧⲙ̄ⲙⲁⲩ ⲛⲓⲡⲗⲏ
ⲣⲱⲙⲁ ⲉⲧⲉ ⲙⲛ̄ ⲁⲣⲏϫⲟⲩ ⲙ̄⟨ⲛ⟩ ⲛⲓⲁⲓ
ⲱⲛ ⲛ̄ⲁⲧⲟⲛⲟⲙⲁⲍⲉ ⲙ̄ⲙⲟⲟⲩ ϫⲉ
ⲕⲁⲁⲥ ⲉⲩⲛⲁϯ ⲣⲁⲛ ⲉⲡⲉⲓⲱⲧ̇ ϫⲉ
ⲡⲙⲁϩ`ϥⲧⲟⲟⲩ' ⲡⲉ ⲙⲛ ⲧⲅⲉⲛ⟨ⲉ⟩ⲁ ⲛ̄
ⲁⲫⲑⲁⲣⲧⲟⲥ ⲉⲩⲉⲙⲟⲩⲧⲉ ⲉⲧⲉⲥⲡⲟ
ⲣⲁ ⲛ̄ⲡⲓⲱⲧ̇ ϫⲉ ⲧⲉⲥⲡⲟⲣⲁ ⲛ̄ⲡⲛⲟϭ
ⲛ̄ⲥ̄ⲏ̄ⲑ̄ ·

53,23 Corr. ⲧ in ⲙⲛⲧ over ⲛ.
54, 8 Corr. ϣϥⲉⲧⲁϥ crossed out. ϥⲧⲟⲟⲩ written above the line. ⲧⲉ changed to ⲡⲉ, but probably to be deleted.

aeon (αἰών), and the thrones (θρόνος) which are in / them, and the powers which surround them, / glories, authorities (ἐξουσία), / and the powers, <and> the thrice-male / child, and the male (ἀρσενική) virgin (παρθένος) / Youel, and Esephech, // *54* the splenditenens, [the child] / of the child and the crown of [his] / glory, the whole pleroma (πλήρωμα), and / all the glories which are there, the / infinite pleromas (πλήρωμα) <and> the / unnameable (-ὀνομάζειν) aeons (αἰών), in / order that they may name the Father / the fourth with the incorruptible (ἄφθαρτος) / race (γενεά), (and) that they may call the seed (σπορά) / of the Father the seed (σπορά) of the great / Seth.

IV 65,14 [ⲙⲉⲁⲱⲛ] ⲙ̅ⲛ̅ ⲛⲓⲑⲣⲟⲛⲟⲥ ⲉⲧ̅[ⲛ̅]
[ϩⲣⲁ̈ⲓ̈ ⲛ̅ϩⲏⲧ]ⲟ̣ⲩ ⲙ̅ⲛ̅ ⲛⲓϭⲟⲙ ⲉⲧⲕ[ⲱ]
16 [ⲧⲉ ⲉⲣⲟⲟ]ⲩ ⲙ̅ⲛ̅ ϩⲉⲛⲉⲟⲟⲩ ⲙ̅[ⲛ̅ ϩⲉⲛ]
[ϭⲟⲙ ⲙ̅]ⲛ̣̅ ϩ[ⲉⲛ]ⲉⲝⲟⲩⲥⲓⲁ ⲙ̅ⲛ̅ ⲡ̣̅ϣ̅ⲙ̅[ⲧ̅]
18 [ϩⲟⲟⲩⲧ ⲛ̅ⲁⲗ]ⲟ̣ⲩ ⲙ̅ⲛ̅ ϯϩⲟⲟⲩⲧ ⲙ̅
[ⲡⲁⲣⲑⲉⲛⲟⲥ] ⲓ̈ⲟⲩⲏ̣ⲗ ⲙ̅ⲛ̅ ⲏⲥⲏⲫⲏⲭ
20 [ⲡⲓⲣⲉϥⲁⲙⲁϩ]ⲧ̣ⲉ ⲙ̅ⲡⲉⲟⲟⲩ ⲙ̅ⲛ̅
[ⲡⲓⲕⲗⲟⲙ ⲛ̅ⲧⲉ] ⲡⲉϥⲉⲟⲟⲩ ⲙ̅ⲛ̅
22 [ⲡⲓⲡⲗⲏⲣ]ⲱⲙⲁ ⲧⲏⲣϥ̅ ⲙ̅ⲛ̅ ⲛⲓⲉⲟⲟ̣[ⲩ]
[ⲧⲏⲣⲟⲩ] ⲉⲧⲛ̅ϩⲣⲁ̈ⲓ̈ ϩ̅ⲛ̅ ⲛⲓⲡⲗⲏⲣ̣ⲱ[ⲙⲁ]
24 [ⲛ̅ⲛⲁⲧϫⲓ]ⲟⲟⲣ ⲙ̅ⲙⲟ[ⲟⲩ] ⲙ̣̅[ⲛ̅ ⲛⲓ]
[ⲉⲱⲛ ⲛ̅ⲛ]ⲁ̣ⲧϯ ⲣⲁⲛ ⲉⲣ[ⲟⲟⲩ ϩⲓⲛⲁ]
26 [ⲛ̅ⲧⲟⲟⲩ] ⲛ̅ⲥⲉⲙⲟⲩⲧⲉ̣ [ⲉⲡⲓⲱⲧ ϫⲉ]
[ⲡⲓⲙⲉϩⲇ̅] ⲙ̣̅ⲛ̅ ϯⲅⲉⲛⲉⲁ̣ [ⲛ̅ⲁⲧⲕⲓⲙ]
28 [ⲛ̅ⲁⲧϫⲱϩ]ⲙ ⲛ̅ⲧⲉ ⲡ[ⲓ]ⲱ[ⲧ ⲁⲩⲱ]
[ⲛ̅ⲧⲟ]ⲟⲩ ⲛ̅ⲥⲉⲙⲟⲩⲧⲉ̣ [ⲉⲣⲟⲥ ϫⲉ]
30 [ϯⲥ]ⲡ̣ⲟ̣ⲣⲁ ⲛ̅ⲧⲉ ⲡⲓⲛⲟϭ ⲥ̣[ⲏⲑ·

65,20 ⲡⲁⲗⲟⲩ ⲙ̅ⲡⲁⲗⲟⲩ is omitted.
24 Or ϩ̣[ⲛ̅ ⲛⲓ].
27 For [ⲡⲓⲙⲉϩⲇ̅] see *supra* 61,7 note.
29 Superlin. stroke on ⲛ̅ is in the lacuna.

aeons (*αἰών*), and the thrones (*θρόνος*) that [are] / 15 [in] them, and the powers which [surround] / [them], glories, / [powers, and] authorities (*ἐξουσία*), and the thrice-/[male child,] and the male / [virgin (*παρθένος*)] Youel, and Esephech, / 20 [the] splendi[tenens,] and / [the crown of] his glory, and / [the] whole [pleroma (*πλήρωμα*),] and [all] the / glories that are in the [in]accessable / pleromas (*πλήρωμα*), [and the] / 25 unnameable [aeons (*αἰών*), in order that (*ἵνα*)] / [they] may name [the Father] / [the fourth] with the [immovable, incorruptible] / race (*γενεά*) of the [Father, and] / [that they] may call [it] / 30 [the] seed (*σπορά*) of the great [Seth.]

The response to the request: III 54,11 - 55,2

III 54 ⲧⲟⲧⲉ ⲁⲩⲕⲓⲙ ⲛ̄ϭⲓ ⲛ̄ⲕⲁ
ⲛⲓⲙ · ⲁⲩⲱ ⲁⲡⲉⲥⲧⲱⲧ̀ ϫⲓ ⲛ̄ⲛⲓⲁ
ⲫⲑⲁⲣⲧⲟⲥ · ⲧⲟⲧⲉ ⲡϣⲟⲙⲛⲧ ⲛ̄ϩⲟ
ⲟⲩⲧ̀ ⲛ̄ⲁⲗⲟⲩ ⲁⲩⲡⲣⲟⲉⲗⲑⲉ ⲉⲃⲟⲗ
ϫⲓⲛ ⲛ̄ⲡⲥⲁϩⲣⲉ ϣⲁ ⲡⲉⲥⲏⲧⲉ ⲛ̄
ϩⲣⲁⲓ̈ ϩⲛ̄ ⲛⲁⲅⲉⲛⲛⲏⲧⲟⲥ ⲙⲛ̄ ⲛⲁⲩ
ⲧⲟⲅⲉⲛⲓⲟⲥ ⲙⲛ̄ ⲛⲉⲛⲧⲁⲩϫⲡⲟⲟⲩ
ϩⲙ̄ ⲡⲅⲉⲛⲛⲏⲧⲟⲥ · ⲁⲥⲡⲣⲟⲉⲗⲑⲉ
ⲉⲃⲟⲗ ⲛ̄ϭⲓ ϯⲙⲛ̄ⲧⲛⲟϭ ϯⲙⲛ̄ⲧ
ⲛⲟϭ ⲧⲏⲣⲥ ⲙ̄ⲡⲛⲟϭ ⲛ̄ⲭⲣ̄ⲥ̄ ⲁϥ
ⲧⲁϫⲣⲟ ⲛ̄ϩⲉⲛⲑⲣⲟⲛⲟⲥ ϩⲛ̄ ⲟⲩⲉⲟⲟⲩ
ϩⲉⲛⲧⲃⲁ ⲉⲙⲛ̄ⲧⲟⲩ ⲏⲡⲉ ⲛ̄ϩⲣⲁⲓ̈
ϩⲙ̄ ⲡⲉϥⲧⲟⲟⲩ ⲛ̄ⲁⲓⲱⲛ ⲙ̄ⲡⲉⲩ
ⲕⲱⲧⲉ ϩⲉⲛⲧⲃⲁ ⲉⲙⲛ̄ⲧⲟⲩ ⲏⲡⲉ
ϩⲉⲛⲇⲩⲛⲁⲙⲓⲥ ⲙⲛ̄ ϩⲉⲛⲉⲟⲟⲩ

55 ⲛ̣ⲉ̣

ⲙⲛ̄ ϩⲉⲛⲁⲫⲑⲁⲣⲥ̣ⲓⲁ · ⲁⲩⲱ ⲁⲩⲡⲣⲟⲉⲗ
ⲑⲉ ⲉⲃⲟⲗ ⲛ̄ⲧⲉⲓϩⲉ ·

Then (τότε) everything shook, / and trembling took hold of the incorruptible (ἄφθαρτος) / ones. Then (τότε) the three male / children came forth (προελθεῖν) / [15] from above down / into the unborn (ἀγέννητος) ones, and the self- / begotten (αὐτογένιος) ones, and those who were begotten / in what is begotten (γεννητός). / The greatness came forth (προελθεῖν), the / [20] whole greatness of the great Christ (χριστός). He / established thrones (θρόνος) in glory, / myriads without number, / in the four aeons (αἰών) around them, / myriads without number, / [25] powers (δύναμις) and glories // *55* and incorruptions (ἀφθαρσία). And they came / forth (προελθεῖν) in this way.

54,18 Or: in the begotten one.

The response to the request: IV 65,30 - 66,14

IV 65,30 ⲧⲟ]
[ⲧⲉ ⲁⲩⲕⲓ]ⲙ ⲛ̄ϭⲓ ⲛⲁⲓ̈ ⲧⲏⲣ̣[ⲟⲩ·]
66 [ⲝ̅ⲋ̅]
[ⲁⲩⲱ ⲟⲩϣ]ⲧⲣ̣̄ⲧⲣ̄ ⲁϥⲧⲁϩⲟ ⲛ̄ⲛⲓⲁⲧ'
2 [ϫⲱϩ̄]ⲙ ϩⲟⲧⲁⲛ ⲉⲧⲁⲡⲓϣⲙ̄ⲧ' ϩⲟⲟⲩⲧ'
[ⲛ̄ⲁⲗⲟ]ⲩ ⲉ͡ⲓ ⲉⲃⲟⲗ ⲛ̄ⲥⲁϩⲣⲁⲓ̈ ϣⲁϩⲣⲁⲓ̈
4 [ⲉⲛⲓⲁⲧ']ⲙⲓⲥⲉ ⲙ̣ⲛ̣̄ ⲛⲓϫⲡⲟ ⲉⲃⲟⲗ ⲙ̄ⲙⲟ̣
[ⲟⲩ ⲙ]ⲁ̣ⲩⲁ̣[ⲁⲩ] ⲙ̣ⲛ̄ ⲉϩⲣⲁⲓ̈ ⲉⲛⲏ ⲉⲧ[ⲁⲩ]
6 [ϫⲡⲟⲟ]ⲩ ⲉϩⲣⲁⲓ̈ ⲉⲡⲓϫⲡⲟ · ⲁϥⲉ͡ⲓ ⲉ̣[ⲃⲟⲗ]
[ⲛ̄ϭⲓ ⲡⲓ]ⲛⲟϭ ⲡⲁ ⲛⲓⲙⲛ̄ⲧⲛⲟ[ϭ ⲧⲏⲣⲟⲩ]
8 [ⲛ̄ⲧⲉ] ⲡ̣ⲓⲛⲟϭ ⲛ̄ⲭ̄ⲥ̄ · ⲁⲩⲱ ⲁϥⲧⲁϫ̣[ⲣⲟ]
[ⲛ̄ϩⲉⲛ]ⲑⲣⲟⲛⲟⲥ ⲛ̄ⲧⲉ ⲡⲉ̣ⲟⲟⲩ [ϩⲙ̄]
10 [ⲡⲓϥⲧⲟⲟⲩ] ⲛ̄ⲛⲉⲱⲛ̣ [ⲁⲩⲱ ⲛ̄ⲧⲁⲩ]
[ⲕⲱⲧ]ⲉ [ⲉ]ⲣⲟⲟⲩ ⲛ̄ϭⲓ ϩⲉⲛⲁⲛ[ⲧⲃⲁ ⲛ̄]
12 [ϭⲟⲙ] ⲛ̄ⲁⲧ'ϯ ⲏⲡⲉ ⲉⲣⲟⲟⲩ · [ϩⲉⲛ]
[ⲉⲟ]ⲟⲩ ⲙⲛ̄ ϩ[ⲉ]ⲛⲁⲧ'ϫⲱϩⲙ̄ [ⲁⲩⲱ ⲛ̄ϯ]
14 [ϩⲉ] ⲁϥⲉ͡ⲓ ⲉⲃⲟ̣ⲗ

Then (τότε)] / all of them [shook,] // *66* [and a] disturbance seized the in[corruptible] / ones. When (ὅταν) the thrice-male / [child] came forth from above down to / [the un]born ones, and the self-begotten / [5] ones, and to those who [were] / [begotten] into what is begotten, there came [forth] / [the] great one who possesses [all] greatnesses / [of] the great Christ (χριστός). And he established / thrones (θρόνος) of the glory [in] / [10] [the four] aeons (αἰών), [and] / [myriads of powers] / without number [surround] them, / [glories] and incorruptions. [And thus] / he came forth.

66, 6 Or: into the begotten one.

The emergence of the heavenly church: III 55,2-16

III 55, 2 ⲁⲩⲱ ⲁⲥⲁϣⲁⲉⲓ ⲛ̄
ϭⲓ ϯⲁ⟨ⲫⲑ⟩ⲁⲣⲧⲟⲥ ⲛ̄ⲡⲛⲉⲩⲙⲁⲧⲓⲕⲏ
4 ⲛ̄ⲉⲕⲕⲗⲏⲥⲓⲁ ⲛ̄ϩⲣⲁï ϩⲙ̄ ⲡⲉϥⲧⲟⲟⲩ ⲛ̄
ⲟⲩⲟⲉⲓⲛ ⲙ̄ⲡⲛⲟϭ ⲛ̄ⲁⲩⲧⲟⲅⲉⲛⲏⲥ ⲉ
6 ⲧⲟⲛϩ ⲡⲛⲟⲩⲧⲉ ⲛ̄ⲧⲙⲏⲉ ⲉⲩⲥⲙⲟⲩ
ⲉⲩϩⲱⲥ ⲉⲩϯ ⲉⲟⲟⲩ ϩⲛ̄ ⲟⲩⲥⲙⲏ ⲛ̄
8 ⲟⲩⲱⲧ̇ ϩⲛ̄ ⲟⲩϩⲓⲕⲱⲛ ϩⲛ̄ ⲟⲩⲧⲁⲡⲣⲟ
ⲉⲙⲉⲥⲙ̄ⲧⲟⲛ ⲙ̄ⲙⲟⲥ ⲉⲡⲉⲓⲱⲧ̇ ⲙⲛ̄
10 ⲧⲙⲁⲁⲩ ⲙⲛ̄ ⲡϣⲏⲣⲉ ⲙⲛ̄ ⲡⲉⲩⲡⲗⲏ
ⲣⲱⲙⲁ ⲧⲏⲣϥ̄ · ⲛ̄ⲑⲉ ⲛ̄ⲧⲁⲉⲓϫⲟⲟⲥ ⲛ̄
12 ⲧϯⲉ ⲛ̄ⲥⲫⲣⲁⲅⲓⲥ ⲉⲧⲉ ⲛⲁ ⲛⲓⲧⲃⲁ ⲙⲛ̄
ⲛⲉⲧⲁⲣⲭⲓ ⲉϫⲛ̄ ⲛⲓⲁⲓⲱⲛ ⲙⲛ̄ ⲛⲉⲧ
14 ⲫⲟⲣⲉⲓ ⲙ̄ⲡⲉⲟⲟⲩ ⲛ̄ⲛⲓⲥⲧⲣⲁ⟨ⲧ⟩ⲏ⟨ⲅ⟩ⲟⲥ

55, 3 MS. reads ⲁⲡⲫⲁⲣⲧⲟⲥ. See also ApocryJn III 11,16.
6 Corr. ⲡ over ⲉⲓ ?
11 ϣⲟⲣⲡ̄ dropped out after ⲛ̄. It is unclear what else is missing (see IV 66,25).
13 Corr. ⲛ in ⲛⲉⲧ over ⲧ.
14 MS. reads ⲥⲧⲣⲁⲅⲏⲧⲟⲥ.

And / the incorruptible (ἄφθαρτος), spiritual (πνευματική) / church (ἐκκλησία) increased in the four / [5] lights of the great, living Autogenes (αὐτογενής), / the god of truth, praising, / singing (and) giving glory with one voice, / with one accord (εἰκών), with a mouth / which does not rest, to the Father, and / [10] the Mother, and the Son, and their whole / pleroma (πλήρωμα), just as I mentioned <before>. / The five seals (σφραγίς) which possess the myriads, and / they who rule (ἄρχειν) over the aeons (αἰών) and they who / bear (φορεῖν) the glory of the leaders (στρατηγός) /

The emergence of the heavenly church: IV 66,14 - 67,1

IV 66,14 ⲁⲩⲱ ⲁⲥϫ[ⲓⲥⲉ ⲛ̄ϭⲓ ϯ]
[ⲁⲧ']ϫⲱϩ̄ⲙ· ϯⲡ̄ⲛ̄ⲁⲧ[ⲓⲕⲏ ⲛ̄ⲉⲕ]
16 [ⲕⲗⲏ]ⲥ̣ⲓ̣ⲁ ⲛ̄ϩⲣⲁⲓ̈ ϩ̄ⲙ ⲡⲓϥⲧ̣[ⲟⲟⲩ ⲙ̄]
ⲫⲱ̣ⲥ̣ⲧⲏⲣ ⲛ̄ⲧⲉ ⲡⲓ̣[ⲛⲟϭ ⲛ̄ϣⲁϫⲉ]
18 ⲛ̄ⲁⲩⲧⲟⲅⲉⲛⲏⲥ ⲉⲧ[ⲟⲛ̄ϩ ⲡⲓⲛⲟⲩⲧⲉ]
ⲛ̄ⲧⲉ ⲧ̣ⲙ̄ⲛ̄ⲧ̣ⲙⲉ· ⲉⲩ[ⲥⲙⲟⲩ ⲁⲩⲱ]
20 ⲉⲩϩⲱ̣ⲥ ⲉⲩϯ ⲉⲟ̣[ⲟⲩ ϩ̄ⲛ ⲟⲩⲥⲙⲏ]
ⲧⲏⲣ̣ⲟⲩ ϩ̄ⲛ ⲟⲩϩⲓ︦ⲕ̣ⲱ̣[ⲛ ⲛ̄ⲟⲩⲱⲧⲉ]
22 ϩ̄ⲛ ⲟⲩϩⲣⲟⲟⲩ ⲛ̄ⲁⲧ'ⲕⲁⲣⲱ̣[ϥ ⲙ̄ⲡⲓⲱⲧ']
ⲙ̄ⲛ̣ ⲧⲙⲁⲁⲩ ⲙ̄ⲛ ⲡϣⲏⲣ[ⲉ ⲙ̄ⲛ ⲡⲓ]
24 [ϫⲱ]ⲕ [ⲉⲃⲟ]ⲗ̣ ⲉⲧⲛ̄ⲧⲁⲩ· [ⲛ̄ⲑⲉ ⲉⲛ]
[ⲧⲁⲓ̈ⲣ̄ϣⲟⲣⲡ̄'] ⲛ̄ϫⲟⲟϥ ⲉ . . [. ϯϯⲉ ⲛ̄]
26 [ⲥⲫⲣⲁⲅⲓⲥ] ⲉⲧ'ⲕⲏ ⲉϩⲣⲁⲓ̈ [ⲉϫ̄ⲛ ⲛⲓ]
[ⲁⲛⲧⲃⲁ] ⲙ̣̄ⲛ̣ ⲛⲏ ⲉⲧ'[ⲣ̄ⲁⲣⲭⲓ ⲉϩⲣⲁⲓ̈]
28 [ⲉϫ̄ⲛ ⲛⲓⲉ]ⲱⲛ ⲙ̄ⲛ ⲛⲓⲥ̣[ⲁ]ϯⲅⲟ[ⲥ ⲛⲏ]
[ⲉⲧⲣ̄ⲫⲟ]ⲣⲓ ⲙ̄ⲡⲉⲟⲟⲩ ⲉⲁⲩϯ

66,14 Reconstruction ϫ[ⲓⲥⲉ corresponds to ⲁϣⲁⲓ in III 55,2 = αὐξάνεσθαι; cf. Crum, *Dict.* 788b.
25 Perhaps ⲉⲃ̣.[
27 ⲙ̣̄ⲛ̣ very uncertain.

And [the] / 15 [in]corruptible, spiritual (πνευματική) / [church (ἐκκλησία) increased] in the [four] / lights (φωστήρ) of the [great] / self-begotten (αὐτογενής), [living Word, the god] / of truth, all [praising and] / 20 singing, giving [glory with one voice,] / with [one] accord (εἰκών), / with a never silent voice, [to the Father,] / and the Mother, and the Son, [and] / their [pleroma, just as] / 25 [I] mentioned [before. . . . the five] / [seals (σφραγίς)] which preside [over the] / [myriads, and] they who [rule (ἄρχειν)] / [over the] aeons (αἰών), and the leaders (στρατηγός) / [who bear (φορεῖν)] the glory were given /

III 55 ⲁⲩϯ ⟨ⲛⲁⲩ⟩ ⲛ̅ⲧⲉⲡⲓⲧⲣⲟⲡⲏ ⲉⲩⲱⲛϩ ⲉⲃⲟⲗ
16 ⲛ̅ⲛⲉⲧⲙ̅ⲡϣⲁ ϩⲁⲙⲏⲛ ·

15 were given the command (ἐπιτροπή) to reveal / to those who are worthy. Amen (ἀμήν).

The presentation of praise of Seth and the request for his seed: III 55,16 - 56,3

16 ⲧⲟⲧⲉ ⲡⲛⲟϭ
ⲛ̅ⲥⲏⲑ · ⲡϣⲏⲣⲉ ⲙ̅ⲡⲁⲫⲑⲁⲣⲧⲟⲥ ⲛ̅
18 ⲣⲱⲙⲉ ⲁⲇⲁⲙⲁⲥ ⲁϥϯ ⲛ̅ⲟⲩⲥⲙⲟⲩ
ⲙ̅ⲡⲛⲟϭ ⲛ̅ⲁϩⲟⲣⲁⲧⲟⲥ ⲛ̅ⲛⲁⲕⲗⲏⲧⲟⲥ
20 ⲛ̅ⲁⲧⲟⲛⲟⲙⲁⲍⲉ ⲙ̅ⲙⲟϥ ⲙ̅ⲡⲁⲣⲑⲉ
ⲛⲓⲕⲟⲛ ⲙ̅ⲡ̅ⲛ̅ⲁ̅ ⲙ̅ⲛ̅ ⲧ⟨ⲁⲣⲥ⟩ⲉⲛⲓⲕⲏ
⟨ⲛ̅ⲡⲁⲣⲑⲉⲛⲟⲥ ⲙ̅ⲛ̅ ⲡϣⲟⲙ̅ⲛ̅ⲧ̅ ⲛ̅
ϩⲟⲟⲩⲧ ⲛ̅ⲁⲗⲟⲩ ⲙ̅ⲛ̅ ⲧⲁⲣⲥⲉⲛⲓⲕⲏ⟩
22 ⲛ̅ⲡⲁⲣⲑⲉⲛⲟⲥ ⲓ̈ⲟⲩⲏⲗ ⲙ̅ⲛ̅ ⲏⲥⲏⲫⲏⲭ
ⲡⲉⲧⲉⲙⲁϩⲧⲉ ⲙ̅ⲡⲉⲟⲟⲩ ⲙ̅ⲛ̅ ⲡⲉ
24 ⲕⲗⲟⲙ ⲙ̅ⲡⲉϥⲉⲟⲟⲩ ⲡⲁⲗⲟⲩ ⲙ̅ⲡⲁⲗⲟⲩ
56 ⲛⲋ
ⲙ̅ⲛ̅ ⲛ̅ⲛⲟϭ ⲛ̅ⲇⲟⲝⲟⲙⲉⲇⲱⲛ ⲛ̅ⲁⲓⲱ[ⲛ]

55,21 MS. reads ⲡⲁⲣⲑⲉⲛⲓⲕⲏ. The scribe skipped almost 2 lines due to homoioteleuton.
24 Corr. ⲁ over ⲓ. The scribe began to write ⲡⲓⲁⲗⲟⲩ.

Then (τότε) the great / Seth, the son of the incorruptible (ἄφθαρτος) / man Adamas, gave praise / to the great, invisible (ἀόρατος), uncallable (ἄκλητος), / 20 unnameable (-ὀνομάζειν), virginal (παρθενικόν) / Spirit (πνεῦμα), and the <male (ἀρσενική)> <virgin (παρθένος), and the thrice-male child, and the male (ἀρσενική)> / virgin (παρθένος) Youel, and Esephech, / the splenditenens, and the / crown of his glory, the child of the child, // *56* and the great Doxomedon-aeons (αἰών), /

IV 66,30 [ⲛⲁⲩ ⲙ̄]ⲡⲟⲩⲁϩ ⲥⲁϩⲛⲉ [ⲉⲟⲩⲱⲛ̄ϩ̄]
67 [ⲝ̄ⲍ̄]
ⲉⲃⲟⲗ ⲛ̄ⲛⲏ ⲉⲧⲙ̄ⲡϣ[ⲁ] ϩ[ⲁⲙⲏⲛ:]

[30] the command [to reveal] // *67* to those who are worthy. [Amen (ἀμήν).] /

The presentation of praise of Seth and the request for his seed: IV 67,2 - ?

2 ⲧⲟⲧⲉ ⲡⲓⲛⲟϭ ⲥ̄ⲏ̄ⲑ̄ ⲡϣⲏⲣⲉ [ⲛ̄ⲧⲉ ⲡⲓ]
ⲁⲧ̓ϫⲱϩⲙ̄ ⲛ̄ⲣⲱⲙⲉ ⲁ[ⲇ]ⲁⲙ[ⲁⲥ ⲁϥⲉⲓ]
4 ⲛⲉ ⲉϩⲣⲁ̈ⲓ ⲛ̄ⲟⲩⲥ̣[ⲙⲟⲩ] ⲙ̄ⲡ[ⲓⲛⲟϭ ⲛ̄]
ⲛ̣ⲁⲧⲛⲁⲩ ⲉⲣⲟ[ϥ ⲁⲩⲱ ⲛ̄ⲁⲧ̓ϫⲁϩⲙ̄ϥ]
6 [ⲁⲩ]ⲱ ⲛ̄[ⲁ]ⲧ̓ϯ ⲣⲁⲛ ⲉⲣⲟϥ [ⲙ̄ⲡⲁⲣⲑⲉⲛⲓ]
[ⲕⲟⲛ ⲙ̄]ⲡ̄ⲛ̄ⲁ̄ ⲙⲛ̄ ϯϩⲟⲟⲩ[ⲧ̓ ⲙ̄ⲡⲁⲣ]
8 [ⲑⲉⲛⲟ]ⲥ ⲙⲛ̄ ⲡⲓϣⲙⲧ̓ ϩⲟⲟ̣[ⲩⲧ̓ ⲛ̄ⲁⲗⲟⲩ]
[ⲙ̄ⲛ ϯ]ϩⲟⲟⲩⲧ̓ ⲙ̣̄ⲡ̣ⲁⲣⲑ[ⲉⲛⲟⲥ ⲓ̈ⲟⲩⲏⲗ]
10 [ ]..[

11 ff. are lost.

67, 5 For [ϫⲁϩⲙϥ] or [ϫⲱϩⲙ] see *supra* 54,16f. note.

Then (τότε) the great Seth, the son [of the] / incorruptible man Adamas, brought / [praise] to the [great], / [5] invisible, [and incorruptible,] / [and] unnameable, [virginal (παρθενικόν)] / Spirit (πνεῦμα), and the male [virgin (παρθένος),] / and the thrice-male [child,] / [and the] male virgin (παρθένος) [Youel,] / (lines 10 - ?)

III 56, 2 ⲙⲛ̄ ⲡⲉⲡⲗⲏⲣⲱⲙⲁ ⲛ̄ⲧⲁⲉⲓϫⲟⲟϥ ⲛ̣̄
ϣⲟⲣⲡ̄ ⲙⲛ̄ ⲧⲉϥⲥⲡⲟⲣⲁ ⲁϥⲁⲓ̓ⲧⲓ̓ ⲙ̄ⲙⲟⲥ

and the pleroma (πλήρωμα) which I mentioned / before; and he asked (αἰτεῖν) for his seed (σπορά). /

Plesithea and her work: III 56, 4-13

4 ⲧⲟⲧⲉ ⲁⲥⲉⲓ ⲉⲃⲟⲗ ϩⲙ̄ ⲡⲙⲁ ⲉⲧⲙ̄ⲙⲁⲩ
ⲛ̄ϭⲓ ⲧⲛⲟϭ ⲛ̄ⲇⲩⲛⲁⲙⲓⲥ ⲙ̄ⲡⲛⲟϭ ⲛ̄
6 ⲟⲩⲟⲉⲓⲛ ⲡⲗⲏⲥⲓⲑⲉⲁ ⲧⲙⲉⲉⲩ ⲛ̄ⲛⲁⲅ̄
ⲅⲉⲗⲟⲥ ⲧⲙⲉⲉⲩⲉ ⲛ̄ⲛⲟⲩⲟⲉⲓⲛ ⲧⲙⲉ
8 ⲉⲩⲉ ⲉⲑⲁⲉⲟⲟⲩ · ⲧⲡⲁⲣⲑⲉⲛⲟⲥ ⲧⲁ ⲧⲉ
ϥⲧⲟ ⲛ̄ⲕⲓⲃⲉ ⲉⲥⲉⲓⲛⲉ ⲛ̄ⲡⲕⲁⲣⲡⲟⲥ ⲉ
10 ⲃⲟⲗ ϩⲛ̄ ⲅⲟⲙⲟⲣⲣⲁ ⲛ̄ⲡⲏⲅⲏ ⲙⲛ̄ ⲥⲟ
ⲇⲟⲙⲁ ⲉⲧⲉ ⲡⲕⲁⲣⲡⲟⲥ ⲛ̄ⲧⲡⲏⲅⲏ ⲛ̄
12 ⲅⲟⲙⲟⲣⲣⲁ ⲉⲧⲛ̄ϩⲏⲧⲥ̄ · ⲁⲥⲉⲓ ⲉⲃⲟⲗ
ϩⲓⲧⲟⲟⲧϥ̄ ⲙ̄ⲡⲛⲟϭ ⲛ̄ⲥⲏⲑ·

56, 9 Corr. ⲃ over erasure, perhaps ⲙ.

Then (τότε) there came forth from that place / [5] the great power (δύναμις) of the great / light Plesithea, the mother of the angels (ἄγγελος), / the mother of the lights, the / glorious mother, the virgin (παρθένος) with the / four breasts, bringing the fruit (καρπός) / [10] from Gomorrah as spring (πηγή) and Sodom, / which is the fruit (καρπός) of the spring (πηγή) of / Gomorrah which is in her. She came forth / through the great Seth.

Plesithea and her work: IV 67,?-27

11-23 are lost.

IV **67,24** [ ]ⲛ̣[
[ ]ⲧⲉ ⲙ̄ⲡ[
26 [ ]ⲙ̣ⲉ ϩⲏⲧ .[ⲉⲃⲟⲗ]
[ϩⲓⲧⲟⲟⲧ̄ϥ] ⲙ̄ⲡⲓⲛⲟ[ϭ ⲛ̄ⲥⲏⲑ·

67,24ff. The line numbers are based on an estimate.

(lines ?-24) / [25] [ ] the [ ] / [
through] / the great [Seth.]

The rejoicing of Seth: III 56,13-22

III 56 ⲧⲟⲧⲉ
14 ⲡⲛⲟϭ ⲛ̄ⲥⲏⲑ · ⲁϥⲧⲉⲗⲏⲗ ⲉϩⲣⲁ̈ⲓ̈ ⲉϫⲙ̄
ⲡⲉϩⲙⲟⲧ ⲛ̄ⲧⲁⲩⲭⲁⲣⲓⲍⲉ ⲙ̄ⲙⲟϥ ⲛⲁϥ
16 ⲉⲃⲟⲗ ϩⲓⲧⲟⲟⲧϥ̄ ⲙ̄ⲡⲁⲫⲑⲁⲣⲧⲟⲥ ⲛ̄
ⲁⲗⲟⲩ ⲁϥϫⲓ ⲛ̄ⲧⲉϥⲥⲡⲟⲣⲁ ⲉⲃⲟⲗ
18 ϩⲓⲧⲟⲟⲧⲥ̄ ⲛ̄ⲧⲁ ⲧⲉϥⲧⲟ ⲛ̄ⲕⲓⲃⲉ ⲧⲡⲁⲣ
ⲑⲉⲛⲟⲥ ⲁϥⲧⲁϩⲟ ⲙ̄ⲙⲟⲥ ⲉⲣⲁⲧ⟨ⲥ⟩ ⲛ̄ⲙ
20 ⲙⲁϥ ⲛ̄ϩⲣⲁ̈ⲓ̈ ϩⲛ̄ ⲡⲙⲉϩϥⲧⲟⲟⲩ ⲛ̄ⲁⲓ
ⲱⲛ ϩⲙ̄ ⲡⲙⲉϩϣⲟⲙⲛⲧ ⲛ̄ⲛⲟϭ ⲛ̄
22 ⲟⲩⲟⲉⲓⲛ ⲇⲁⲩⲉⲓⲑⲉ

56,19 MS. reads ⲉⲣⲁⲧϥ̄.

Then (τότε) / the great Seth rejoiced about / the gift which was granted (χαρίζεσθαι) him / by the incorruptible (ἄφθαρτος) / child. He took his seed (σπορά) / from her with the four breasts, the virgin (παρθένος), / and he placed it with / him in the fourth aeon (αἰών), / in the third great / light Davithe.

The creation of the rulers of the world: III 56,22 - 58,22

22 ⲙⲛ̄ⲛ̄ⲥⲁ ϯⲟⲩ
ⲛ̄ϣⲟ ⲛ̄ⲣⲟⲙⲡⲉ ⲡⲉϫⲁϥ ⲛ̄ϭⲓ ⲡⲛⲟϭ
24 ⲛ̄ⲟⲩⲟⲉⲓⲛ ⲏⲗⲉⲗⲏⲑ · ϫⲉ ⲙⲁⲣⲉⲟⲩⲁ ⲣ̄
ⲣ̄ⲣⲟ ⲉϫⲙ̄ ⲡⲉⲭⲁⲟⲥ ⲙⲛ̄ ⲁⲙⲛ̄ⲧⲉ ·

56,22 Corr. ⲟ crossed out before ⲟⲩ (dittography).

After five / thousand years the great / light Eleleth spoke, "Let someone / reign over the chaos (χάος) and Hades". /

The rejoicing of Seth: IV 67,27 - 68,5

IV 67 ⲁϥ]
28 [ⲧⲉⲗⲏⲗ ⲉϩⲣ]ⲁⲓ̈ [ⲉ]ϫ̅ⲛ̅ ⲡⲓϩ̣[ⲙⲟⲧ̀ ⲉⲧ]
[ⲁⲩ. . . .]ⲧ̀ ⲙ̅ⲙⲟϥ ⲛ[ⲁϥ ⲉⲃⲟⲗ ϩ͡ⲓ]
30 [ⲧⲟⲟⲧ̅ϥ] ⲙ̣̅ⲡ̣[ⲓⲁ]ⲧ̀ϫⲱϩ[ⲙ ⲛ̅ⲁⲗⲟⲩ]
[ⲉϫⲓ ⲧⲉϥ]ⲥⲡ[ⲟⲣⲁ] ϩ̅ⲛ [
68 [ⲝ̅ⲏ̅]
[ ]ϯⲡⲁⲣⲑⲉⲛⲟⲥ ⲧⲁ
2 [ⲛ̅ⲕⲓⲃⲉ ⲇ̅] ⲉⲧ̣ⲁϥⲧⲁϩⲟⲥ ⲉⲣⲁⲧ̅ⲥ̅ ⲛ̅ⲙ̅
[ⲙⲁϥ ϩ̅ⲙ] ⲡ̣ⲓϥⲧⲟⲟⲩ ⲛ̅ⲛⲉⲱⲛ ϩ̅ⲙ ⲡⲓ
4 [ⲛⲟϭ ⲙ̅]ⲙ̣ⲉ[ϩ]ϣ[ⲟ]ⲙⲉⲧ̀ ⲙ̅ⲫⲱⲥⲧⲏⲣ
[ⲇ̅ⲁ̅ⲩ̅ⲉ̅ⲓ̅]ⲑ̅ⲉ̣̅

67,27-31 The line numbers are based on an estimate.
68, 2 See *supra* 61,7 note.

[He] / [rejoiced] about the [gift which] / [ ] him [by] / [30] [the in]corruptible [child] / [to take his seed (σπορά)] from [ ] // *68* [ ] the virgin (παρθένος) with / [the four breasts,] which he placed with / [him in] the four aeons (αἰών) in the / [great] third light (φωστήρ) / [5] [Davi]the.

The creation of the rulers of the world: IV 68,5 - 70,?

[ⲁⲗⲗⲁ] ⲙ̅ⲛ̅ⲛ̅ⲥⲁ ϯⲟⲩ ⲛ̅
6 [ϣⲟ ⲛ̅ⲣⲟⲙⲡⲉ ⲡⲉϫ]ⲁϥ ⲛ̅ϭ̣ⲓ ⲡⲓⲛⲟ̣[ϭ]
[ⲙ̅ⲫⲱⲥⲧⲏ]ⲣ̣ ⲏ̅ⲗ̅ⲏ̅ⲗ̅ⲏ̣̅ⲑ̅ ϫⲉ ⲙ[ⲁ]ⲣⲉ̣[ⲟⲩ]
8 [ⲟⲛ ⲣ̅ ⲣ̅ⲣⲟ] ⲉϩⲣⲁⲓ̈ ⲉϫⲛ̅ ⲡⲭⲁⲟ̣[ⲥ ⲙ̅ⲛ̅]

[But (ἀλλά)] after five / [thousand years] the great / [light (φωστήρ)] Eleleth [spoke] "Let [someone] / [reign] over the chaos (χάος) [and] /

III 56,26 ⲁⲩⲱ ⲁⲥⲟⲩⲱⲛϩ ⲉⲃⲟⲗ ⲛ̄ϭⲓ ⲟⲩϭⲏⲡⲉ
57 [ⲛⲍ]
[ⲉⲧⲉⲡⲉⲥⲣⲁⲛ ⲡ]ⲉ ϩⲩⲗⲓⲕⲏ ⲥⲟⲫⲓⲁ
2 [ⲁⲥ]ϭⲱϣⲧ̇ ⲉⲃⲟⲗ ⲉⲛⲙⲉ
[ⲣⲟⲥ ⲙ̄ⲡⲉⲭⲁⲟⲥ] ⲉⲣⲉⲡⲉⲥϩⲟ ⲟ ⲛ̄ⲑⲉ ⲛ̄
4 [ϩ]ⲙ ⲡⲉⲥⲥⲙⲟⲧ ⲛⲉϥ
[ ]ⲥ̣ⲛⲟϥ · ⲁⲩⲱ ⲡⲉϫⲁϥ
6 [ⲛ̄ϭⲓ ⲡⲛⲟϭ ⲛ̄ⲁ]ⲅ̣ⲅⲉ̣ⲗⲟⲥ ⲅⲁⲙⲁⲗⲓⲏⲗ ·
[ⲙ̄ⲡⲛⲟϭ ⲅⲁⲃⲣⲓⲏ]ⲗ̣ · ⲡⲇⲓⲁⲕⲱⲛ ⲙ̄
8 [ⲡⲛⲟϭ ⲙ̄ⲫⲱⲥⲧ]ⲏⲣ · ⲟ̄ⲣ̄ⲟ̄ⲓ̈̄ⲁ̄ⲏ̄ⲗ̄ · ⲡⲉ
[ϫⲁϥ ϫⲉ ⲙⲁⲣⲉⲩ]ⲁⲅⲅⲉⲗⲟⲥ ⲉⲓ ⲉⲃⲟⲗ
10 [ϫⲉⲕⲁⲁⲥ ⲉϥⲉⲣ̄ ⲣ̄]ⲣⲟ ⲉϫ̄ⲙ ⲡⲉⲭⲁⲟⲥ
[ⲙⲛ̄ ⲁⲙⲛ̄ⲧⲉ · ⲧ]ⲟ̣ⲧⲉ ⲧϭⲏⲡ'ⲉ' ⲉⲥⲙⲁ
12 [ⲧⲱⲟⲩ ⲁⲥⲉⲓ ⲉⲃⲟ]ⲗ̣ ϩⲛ̄ ⲧⲙⲟⲛⲁⲥ ⲥ̄ⲛⲧⲉ
[ⲉⲩⲛ̄ⲧⲉ ⲧⲟⲩⲉⲓ ⲧ]ⲟⲩⲉⲓ ⲛ̄ⲟⲩⲟⲉⲓⲛ · ⲛ̄
14 [ⲑⲣⲟⲛ]ⲟⲥ ⲡⲉⲛⲧⲁⲥⲧⲁϩⲟϥ
[ⲉⲣⲁⲧ̄ϥ ⲛ̄ϩⲣⲁⲓ̈] ϩⲛ̄ ⲧϭⲏⲡⲉ ⲙ̄ⲡⲥⲁ⟨ϩ⟩
16 [ⲣⲉ · ⲧⲟⲧⲉ ⲁϥⲛ]ⲁ̣ⲩ ⲛ̄ϭⲓ ⲥⲁⲕⲗⲁ ⲡⲛⲟϭ

57, 2 Perhaps ⲁⲥⲡⲣⲟⲉⲗⲑⲉ in the lacuna.
11 Corr. ⲉ above the line is partly blotted (haplography).
14 Perhaps in the lacuna: [ⲧⲟⲥ ⲙⲛ̄ ⲡⲉⲑⲣⲟⲛ]ⲟⲥ or ...... ⲁⲅⲅⲉⲗ]ⲟⲥ.
15f. Perhaps ⲙ̄ⲡⲥⲁⲣ[ϩⲉ is a misspelling of ⲙ̄ⲡⲥⲁϩⲣⲉ.

And there appeared a cloud // *57* [whose name is] hylic (ὑλική) Sophia / [She] looked out on the parts (μέρος) / [of the chaos (χάος)], her face being like / [in] her form ... / 5 [ ] blood. And / [the great] angel (ἄγγελος) Gamaliel spoke / [to the great Gabriel], the minister (διάκων) of / [the great light (φωστήρ)] Oroiael; / [he said, "Let an] angel (ἄγγελος) come forth / 10 [in order that he may] reign over the chaos (χάος) / [and Hades".] Then (τότε) the cloud being / [agreeable came forth] in the two monads (μονάς), / each one [of which had] light. / [the throne (θρόνος)], which she had placed / 15 in the cloud [above.] / [Then (τότε)] Sakla, the great /

IV 68 [ⲁⲙ̅ⲛ̅ⲧⲉ· ⲁ]ⲩⲱ ⲁⲥ̣ⲉ͡ⲓ ⲉⲃⲟ̣ⲗ ⲛ̅ϭⲓ ⲟ[ⲩ]
[ⲕⲗⲟⲟⲗⲉ . . .]ⲧ[
11-25 are lost.

[ ]ϭ̅ ⲁⲥ̣ⲭ̣.[
[ⲥ̅]ⲛ̅ⲧⲉ ⲛ̅ⲧ[
[ ] ⲙ̣̅ⲡⲓⲕⲟⲩ[
[ ]ⲛ ⲡⲏ [ⲉ]ⲧⲁ[ⲥⲧⲁϩⲟϥ ⲉ]
[ⲣⲁⲧ̅ϥ̅]ⲉ͡ⲓ ⲉⲃⲟⲗ [ⲉ]ⲃⲟⲗ̣ [ϩ̅ⲛ̅
[ ]ⲉⲡⲓ [. . . .] . . [
69 [ⲝ̅ⲑ̅]
ⲛ̅ϭⲓ ⲥ̅ⲁ̅ⲕ̅ⲗ̅ⲁ̅ ⲡⲓⲛⲟϭ [ⲛ̅ⲁⲅⲅⲉⲗⲟⲥ ⲉ]

68,26-31 The line numbers are based on an estimate.

[Hades".] And [a cloud] came forth / (lines 10 - 25) / [ ] she [ ] / [ ] two [ ] / [ ] the ... [ ] / [ ] the one which [she had placed] / [ ] came forth from [ ] / [ ] the [ ] // *69* Sakla, the great [angel (ἄγγελος), saw] /

III 57 [ⲛ̄ⲁⲅ̄ⲅⲉⲗⲟⲥ ⲉ]ⲡ̣ⲛⲟϭ ⲛ̄ⲇⲁⲓⲙⲱⲛ ⲉ

18 [ⲧⲛ̄ⲙ̄ⲙⲁϥ ⲛⲉⲃⲣ]ⲟ̣ⲩⲏⲗ· ⲁⲩⲱ ⲁⲩϣⲱⲡⲉ

[ⲛ̄ⲙ̄ⲙⲁⲩ ⲛ̄ⲟⲩ]ⲡ̣ⲛ̄ⲁ̄ ⲛ̄ϫⲡⲟ ⲛ̄ⲧⲉ ⲡⲕⲁϩ

20 [ⲁⲩϫⲡⲟ ⲛ̄ϩⲉⲛ]ⲁⲅ̄ⲅⲉⲗⲟⲥ ⲉⲩⲡⲁⲣⲁⲥ

[ⲧⲁⲧⲉⲓ· ⲡⲉϫⲁϥ] ⲛ̄ϭⲓ ⲥⲁⲕⲗⲁ ⲙ̄ⲡⲛⲟϭ

22 [ⲛ̄ⲇⲁⲓⲙⲱⲛ ⲛⲉⲃ]ⲣⲟⲩⲏⲗ · ϫⲉ ⲙⲁⲣⲟⲩϣⲱ

[ⲡⲉ ⲛ̄ϭⲓ ⲡⲙ̄ⲛ̄ⲧ̄ⲥ̄]ⲛ̣ⲟⲟⲩⲥ ⲛ̄ⲁⲓⲱⲛ ϩ̄ⲙ

24 [ⲡ]ⲁⲓⲱⲛ ϩ̄ⲛ̄ⲕⲟⲥⲙⲟⲥ ⲛ̄

[ⲡⲉ]ϫ̣ⲁϥ ⲛ̄ϭⲓ ⲡⲛⲟϭ ⲛ̄ⲁⲅ

26 [ⲅⲉⲗⲟⲥ ⲥⲁⲕⲗⲁ] ϩ̄ⲙ ⲡⲟⲩⲱϣ ⲙ̄ⲡⲁⲩⲧⲟ

58 [ⲛⲏ]

ⲅⲉⲛⲏⲥ ϫⲉ ⲉⲣⲉⲡⲉ[

2 ⲛ̄ⲧⲏⲡⲉ ⲛ̄ⲥⲁϣϥ[

ⲁⲩⲱ ⲡⲉϫⲁϥ ⲛ̄ⲛ[ⲓⲛⲟϭ ⲛ̄ⲁⲅ̄ⲅⲉⲗⲟⲥ]

4 ϫⲉ ⲙⲁϣⲉ ⲛⲏⲧ̄ⲛ̄ ⲛ̄[ⲧⲉⲡⲟⲩⲁ ⲡⲟⲩⲁ]

ⲙ̄ⲙⲱⲧ̄ⲛ̄ ⟨ⲣ̄⟩ⲣ̄ⲣⲟ ⲉⲡⲉϥ[ⲕⲟⲥⲙⲟⲥ · ⲁⲩ]

6 ϣⲉ ⲛ̄ϭⲓ ⲡⲟⲩⲁ ⲡⲟⲩ[ⲁ ⲉⲃⲟⲗ ϩ̄ⲛ̄ ⲡⲉⲉⲓ]

ⲙ̄ⲛ̄ⲧ̄ⲥ̄ⲛⲟⲟⲩⲥ ⲛ̄[ⲁⲅ̄ⲅⲉⲗⲟⲥ · ⲡϣⲟⲣⲡ̄]

8 ⲛ̄ⲁⲅ̄ⲅⲉⲗⲟⲥ ⲡⲉ ⲁⲑ̣[ⲱⲑ ⲡⲁ̈ ϩⲱⲱϥ]

57,25 Corr. ϭ in ⲛ̄ϭⲓ over ⲛ (dittography).
58, 8 ⲡⲁ̈ ϩⲱⲱϥ uncertain.

[angel (ἄγγελος), saw] the great demon (δαίμων) / [who is with him, Nebr]uel. And they became / [together a] begetting spirit (πνεῦμα) of the earth. / [20] [They begot] assisting (παραστατεῖν) angels (ἄγγελος). / Sakla [said] to the great / [demon (δαίμων) Neb]ruel, "Let / [the] twelve aeons (αἰών) come into being in / [the] aeon (αἰών), worlds (κόσμος) / [25] ["] the great angel (ἄγγελος) / [Sakla] said by the will of the Autogenes (αὐτογενής), // *58* "There shall [be] the [ ] / of the number of seven [ ]". / And he said to the [great angels (ἄγγελος)], / "Go and [let each] / [5] of you reign over his [world (κόσμος)".] / Each one [of these] / twelve [angels (ἄγγελος)] went [forth. The first] / angel (ἄγγελος) is Ath[oth. He is the one] /

IV 69, 2 ⲡⲏ ⲉⲧⲛ̄ⲙ̄ⲙⲁϥ ⲛ̄ⲉ̄ⲃ̄ⲣ̣̄[ⲟ̄ⲩ̄ⲏ̄ⲗ̄ ⲡⲓⲛⲟϭ ⲛ̄]
ⲇⲉⲙⲱⲛ· ⲁⲩⲱ ⲁ̣[ⲩϣⲱⲡⲉ ⲛ̄ⲙ̄ⲙⲁⲩ ⲛ̄]
4 ⲟⲩⲡ̄ⲛ̄ⲁ̄ ⲛ̄ϫⲡⲟ̣ [ⲛ̄ⲧⲉ ⲡⲕⲁϩ· ⲡⲓⲙ̄ⲛ̄ⲧ̄ⲥ̄ⲛⲟ]
ⲟⲩⲥ̣ ⲛ̄ⲁ̣[ⲅ]ⲅ[ⲉⲗⲟⲥ
6 ff. are lost.

him who is with him, Nebr[uel, the great] / demon (δαίμων). And [they became together] / a begetting spirit (πνεῦμα) [of the earth. The twelve] / [5] [angels (ἄγγελος)] /

III **58** ⲡⲉⲧⲟⲩⲙⲟⲩⲧⲉ ⲉⲣ[ⲟϥ ⲛ̅ϭⲓ ⲛ̅ⲛⲟϭ ⲛ̅ⲅⲉ]
ⲛⲉⲁ ⲛ̅ⲛ̅ⲣⲱⲙⲉ ϫⲉ [· ⲡⲙⲉϩ]
ⲥⲛⲁⲩ ⲡⲉ ϩⲁⲣⲙⲁⲥ [ⲉⲧⲉ ⲡⲃⲁⲗ ⲙ̅ⲡⲕⲱϩⲧ̇]
ⲡⲉ ⲡⲙⲉϩϣⲟⲙⲛ̅[ⲧ̅ ⲡⲉ ⲅⲁⲗⲓⲗⲁ ⲡⲙⲉϩ]
ϥⲧⲟⲟⲩ ⲡⲉ ϊⲱⲃⲏⲗ [ⲡⲙⲉϩϯⲟⲩ ⲡⲉ ⲁ]
ⲁⲱⲛⲁⲓⲟⲥ ⲡⲉⲧⲟⲩⲙ[ⲟⲩⲧⲉ ⲉⲣⲟϥ ϫⲉ ⲥⲁ]
ⲃⲁⲱⲑ· ⲡⲙⲉϩⲥⲟⲟⲩ [ⲡⲉ ⲕⲁϊⲛ ⲡⲉⲧⲟⲩ]
ⲙⲟⲩⲧⲉ ⲉⲣⲟϥ ⲛ̅ϭⲓ ⲛ̅[ⲛⲟϭ ⲛ̅ⲅⲉⲛⲉⲁ ⲛ̅]
ⲣ̅ⲣⲱⲙⲉ ϫⲉ ⲡⲣⲏ ⲡ[ⲙⲉϩⲥⲁϣϥ̅ ⲡⲉ ⲁⲃⲉⲗ ·]
ⲡⲙⲉϩϣⲏ̅ ⲁⲕⲓⲣⲉⲥⲥⲓⲛⲁ ⲡ̣[ⲙⲉϩⲯⲓⲥ ϊⲟⲩⲃⲏⲗ ·]
ⲡⲙⲉϩⲙⲏⲧ̇ ⲡⲉ ϩⲁⲣⲙ̣[ⲟⲩⲡⲓⲁⲏⲗ · ⲡⲙⲉϩ]
ⲙ̅ⲛ̅ⲧⲟⲩⲏⲉ ⲡⲉ ⲁⲣⲭ[ⲉⲓⲣ ⲁⲁⲱⲛⲉⲓⲛ]
ⲡⲙⲉϩⲙ̅ⲛ̅ⲧ̅ⲥⲛⲟⲟⲩ[ⲥ ⲡⲉ ⲃⲉⲗⲓⲁⲥ ⲛⲉ]
ⲉⲓ ⲛⲉⲧϩⲓϫ̅ⲛ̅ ⲁⲙⲛ̅ⲧ̅[ⲉ ⲙⲛ ⲡⲉⲭⲁⲟⲥ ·]

58,11 Or ⲙ̅ⲡⲕⲱϩ, see ApocryJn II 10,31.
14 Corr. ⲱ over ⲁ.
20 Corr. ⲭ over ⲙ.

whom [the great] generations (*γενεά*) / 10 of men call [. The] / second is Harmas, [who] is [the eye of the fire.] / The third [is Galila. The] / fourth is Yobel. [The fifth is] / Adonaios, who is [called] / 15 Sabaoth. The sixth [is Cain, whom] / the [great generations (*γενεά*) of] / men call the sun. The [seventh is Abel;] / the eighth Akiressina; the [ninth Yubel.] / The tenth is Harm[upiael. The] / 20 eleventh is Arch[ir-Adonin.] / The twelfth [is Belias. These] / [are] the ones who preside over Hades [and the chaos (*χάος*).] /

IV **70** [ⲟ̄]

[.. ⲡⲉⲧⲟⲩⲙ]ⲟⲩⲧⲉ ⲉⲣⲟϥ ⲛ̄ϭⲓ ⲛ̄ⲅⲉ

2 [ⲛⲉⲁ ⲧⲏⲣⲟⲩ] ⲛ̄ⲧⲉ ⲛⲓⲣⲱⲙⲉ ϫⲉ ⲡⲣⲏ·

[ⲡⲙⲉϩⲥⲁϣϥ ⲁⲃⲉⲗ]· ⲡⲙⲉϩϣⲙⲟⲩⲛ

4 [ⲁⲕⲓⲣⲉⲥⲥⲓⲛⲁ· ⲡⲙⲉϩ]ⲯⲉⲓⲧ ⲓ̈ⲟⲩⲃⲏⲗ

[ⲡⲙⲉϩⲙⲏⲧ ϩⲁⲣⲙⲟ]ⲩⲡ̣[ⲓⲁⲏⲗ·] ⲡⲙ[ⲉϩ]

6 ff. are lost.

70, 3 Part of the stroke over ⲁⲃⲉⲗ is visible.

// *70* [whom all] the generations (*γενεά*) / of men call the sun; / [the seventh Abel]; the eighth / [Akiressina; the] ninth Yubel; / [5] [the tenth Harmupiael;] the / (lines 6- ?)

The arrogance of Sakla: III 58,23 - 59,1

III 58 ⲁⲩⲱ ⲙ̄ⲛ̄ⲛ̄ⲥⲁ ⲡⲥⲁⲃⲧ̣[ⲉ ⲙ̄ⲡⲕⲟⲥⲙⲟⲥ]
24 ⲡⲉϫⲉ ⲥⲁⲕⲗⲁ ⲛ̄ⲛⲉϥⲁ̣[ⲅ̇ⲅⲉⲗⲟⲥ ϫⲉ ⲁ]
ⲛⲟⲕ ⲁⲛⲟⲕ ⲟⲩⲛⲟⲩ[ⲧⲉ ⲛ̄ⲣⲉϥⲕⲱϩ]
26 ⲁⲩⲱ ⲁϫⲛ̄ⲧ̇ ⲙ̄ⲡⲉⲗⲁⲁ[ⲩ ϣⲱⲡⲉ ⲉϥⲡⲓ]
59 [ⲛⲑ]
ⲑⲉ ⲉⲧⲉϥϩⲩⲡⲟⲥⲧⲁⲥⲓⲥ

And after the founding [of the world (κόσμος)] / Sakla said to his [angels (ἄγγελος),] / [25] "I, I am a [jealous] god, / and apart from me nothing has [come into being", since he] // *59* trusted (πείθεσθαι) in his nature (ὑπόστασις).

The rebuke of Sakla and the creation of man: III 59,1-9

ⲧⲟⲧⲉ ⲟⲩⲥⲙⲏ
2 ⲁⲥⲉⲓ̣ ϩⲓ ⲡϫⲓⲥⲉ ⲉⲥϫⲱ ⲙ̄ⲙⲟⲥ ϫⲉ ϥϣⲟ
ⲟⲡ̇ ⲛ̄ϭⲓ ⲡⲣⲱⲙⲉ ⲙ̄ⲛ ⲡϣⲏⲣⲉ ⲛ̄ⲡⲣⲱ
4 ⲙⲉ ⲉⲧⲃⲉ ⲧⲕⲁⲧⲁⲃⲁⲥⲓⲥ ⲛ̄ⲧϩⲓⲕⲱⲛ ⲙ̄
ⲡⲥⲁϩⲣⲉ ⲉϯⲛⲉ ⲛ̄ⲧⲉⲥⲥⲙⲏ ϩ̄ⲙ ⲡϫⲓⲥⲉ
6 ⲛ̄ⲧϩⲓⲕⲱⲛ ⲛ̄ⲧⲁⲥϭⲱϣⲧ̇ ⲉⲃⲟⲗ ⲉ
ⲃⲟⲗ ϩⲓⲧ̄ⲙ̄ ⲡϭⲱϣⲧ̇ ⲛ̄ⲧϩⲓⲕⲱⲛ ⲙ̄
8 ⲡⲥⲁϩⲣⲉ ⲁⲩⲡⲗⲁⲥⲥⲁ ⲙ̄ⲡⲉϩⲟⲩⲉⲓⲧ̇ ⲛ̄
ⲡⲗⲁⲥⲙⲁ

59, 6 Corr. ⲉⲃ over ⲡⲉ.
9 Corr. ⲣⲱⲙⲉ crossed out at the beginning of the line.

Then (τότε) a voice / came from on high saying, / "The Man exists, and the Son of the Man". / Because of the descent (κατάβασις) of the image (εἰκών) / [5] above, which is like its voice in the height / of the image (εἰκών) which has looked out, / through the looking out of the image (εἰκών) / above, the first creature (πλάσμα) was / formed (πλάσσειν).

IV 70, 6 — end is lost.

The redeeming activity of Metanoia: III 59,9 - 60,2

III 59 ⲡⲁï ⲉⲧⲃⲏⲏⲧ̄ϥ̄ ⲁ
ⲧⲙⲉⲧⲁⲛⲟⲓⲁ ϣⲱⲡⲉ · ⲁⲥϫⲓ ⲙ̄ⲡⲉⲥ
ϫⲱⲕ ⲙ̄ⲛ̄ ⲧⲉⲥϭⲟⲙ ϩ̄ⲙ ⲡⲟⲩⲱϣⲉ
ⲙ̄ⲡⲉⲓⲱⲧ̇ ⲙ̄ⲛ̄ ⲧⲉϥⲉⲩⲇⲟⲕⲓⲁ ⲉⲧⲁϥ
ⲉⲩⲇⲟⲕⲓ ⲉϫ̄ⲛ̄ ⲧⲛⲟϭ ⲛ̄ⲅⲉⲛⲉⲁ ⲛ̄ⲁ
ⲫⲑⲁⲣⲧⲟⲛ ⲉⲧⲉ ⲙⲉⲥⲕⲓⲙ ⲛ̄ⲛⲓⲛⲟϭ
ⲛ̄ⲣⲱⲙⲉ ⲛ̄ϫⲱⲱⲣⲉ ⲙ̄ⲡⲛⲟϭ ⲛ̄ⲥⲏⲑ·
ⲉⲧⲣⲉϥϫⲱ ⲙ̄ⲙⲟⲥ ⲉⲛⲁⲓⲱⲛ ⲛ̄ⲧⲁⲩ
ϫ⟨ⲡ⟩ⲟⲟⲩ ϫⲉⲕⲁⲁⲥ ⲉⲃⲟⲗ ϩⲓⲧⲟⲟⲧ̄ⲥ̄ ⲉⲩⲉ
ϫⲱⲕ ⲉⲃⲟⲗ ⲙ̄ⲡⲓϩⲩⲥⲧⲉⲣⲏⲙⲁ ⲛⲉ
ⲁⲥⲉⲓ ⲅⲁⲣ ⲉⲃⲟⲗ ϩⲓ ⲡⲥⲁϩⲣⲉ ⲉⲡⲉⲥⲏⲧ̇
ⲉⲡⲕⲟⲥⲙⲟⲥ ⲉⲧⲟ ⲙ̄ⲡⲓⲛⲉ ⲛ̄ⲧⲉⲩϣⲏ
ⲛ̄ⲧⲉⲣⲉⲥⲉⲓ ⲁⲥⲧⲱⲃϩ ⲙ̄ⲛ̄ ⲛ̄ⲥⲁ ⲧⲉⲥⲡⲟⲣⲁ
ⲙ̄ⲡⲁⲣⲭⲱⲛ ⲙ̄ⲡⲉⲉⲓⲁⲓⲱⲛ ⲙ̄ⲛ̄ ⟨ⲛ⟩ⲉⲝⲟⲩ
ⲥⲓⲁ ⲛ̄ⲧⲁⲩϣⲱⲡⲉ ⲉⲃⲟⲗ ⲛ̄ϩⲏⲧ̄ϥ̄ ⲧⲏ
ⲉⲧⲥⲟⲟϥ ⲉⲧⲛⲁⲧⲁⲕⲟ ⲛ̄ⲧⲉ ⲡⲛⲟⲩⲧⲉ
ⲛ̄ⲣⲉϥϫⲡⲉ ⲇⲁⲓⲙⲱⲛ ⲙ̄ⲛ̄ ⲛ̄ⲥⲁ ⲧⲉⲥⲡⲟ

59,17 For the emendation see 60,11.

Because of this / Metanoia came to be. She received her / completion and her power by the will / of the Father and his approval (*εὐδοκία*) with which he / approved (*εὐδοκεῖν*) of the great incorruptible (*ἄφθαρτον*), / immovable race (*γενεά*) of the great, / mighty men of the great Seth, / in order that he may sow it in the aeons (*αἰών*) which / had been brought forth, so that, through her (i.e. Metanoia), / the deficiency (*ὑστέρημα*) may be filled up. / For (*γάρ*) she had come forth from above down / to the world (*κόσμος*) which is the image of the night. / When she had come, she prayed for (the repentance of) both the seed (*σπορά*) / of the archon (*ἄρχων*) of this aeon (*αἰών*) and <the> authorities (*ἐξουσία*) / who had come forth from him, that / defiled (seed) of the demon (*δαίμων*)-begetting god / which will be destroyed, and the seed (*σπορά*) //

The redeeming activity of Metanoia: IV 70,? - 71,11

IV **71** ⲟ̅ⲁ̅

ⲡⲏ ⲉⲧⲁϥⲥⲟⲧ̅ⲥ̅ ⲉϩⲣⲁ̈ⲓ ⲉⲛⲓⲉⲱⲛ ⲛ̅ϫⲡⲟ
ⲛ̅ⲕⲁϩ ϩⲓⲛⲁ ⲉⲧⲃⲏⲏⲧ̅ⲥ̅ ⲛ̅ⲥⲉϫⲱⲕ ⲛ̅ϭ[ⲓ]
ⲛⲓϩⲁⲉⲟⲩ· ⲧⲏ [ⲅⲁ]ⲣ ⲉⲧⲁⲥⲉⲓ ⲉⲡⲉⲥⲏⲧ̀
ⲉⲃⲟⲗ ϩ̅ⲙ̅ ⲡϫⲓⲥⲉ ⲉϩⲣⲁ̈ⲓ ⲉⲡⲕⲟⲥⲙ[ⲟⲥ]
ⲛ̅ⲉⲓⲛⲉ ⲛ̅ⲟⲩϣⲏ ⲉⲁ..[.]ⲁⲥ ⲁⲥⲉ[ⲓ ⲉⲉ]
[ⲣ]ⲏⲧ̀· ⲁⲩⲱ ⲙ̅ⲛ̅ ⲛ̅ⲥⲁ ⲧⲥ̣ⲡⲟⲣⲁ ⲛ̅[ⲧⲉ]
[ⲡ]ⲁ̣ⲣⲭⲱⲛ ⲛ̅ⲧⲉ ⲡⲉ̈ⲓⲁⲓⲱⲛ [ⲁ]ⲩⲱ ⲛⲓ[ⲉⲃⲟⲗ]
[ⲙ̅ⲙ]ⲟϥ [ⲧ]ⲏ ⲉⲧ̀ⲥⲟⲟϥ ⲁⲩⲱ [ⲉ]ⲧ̣̀[ⲧⲁⲕ]
[ⲏⲩ]ⲧ̣̀ ⲛ̅ⲧⲉ ⲡⲓⲛⲟⲩⲧⲉ ⲛ̅ϭ.[

71, 5 Perhaps ⲉⲁⲩⲕ̣[ⲁ]ⲁⲥ.
7 The line is unusually long.

(lines 70, ?-end) // *71* who sowed it in the earth-born aeons (*αἰών*), / so that (*ἵνα*), because of her, the deficiencies / may be filled up. For (*γάρ*) she who came down / from the height to the night-like / world (*κόσμος*), [having been appointed (?) came to] / [pray] for (the repentance of) both the seed (*σπορά*) [of] / [the] archon (*ἄρχων*) of this aeon (*αἰών*) and those [who] / [are from] him, [which (i.e. the seed)] is defiled and [perishable] / of the [ ] god, /

III 60 ⲝ

ⲣⲁ ⲛ̄ⲁⲇⲁⲙ ⲧⲉϯⲛⲉ ⲛ̄ⲡⲣⲏ ⲙ̄ⲛ ⲡ
ⲛⲟϭ ⲛ̄ⲥⲏⲑ ·

60, 1 Corr. ⲁ in ⲣⲁ over ⲟ.

60 of Adam and the great Seth, / which is like the sun.

The work of Hormos: III 60,2-8

ⲧⲟⲧⲉ ⲁϥⲉⲓ ⲛ̄ϭⲓ ⲡⲛⲟϭ
ⲛ̄ⲁⲅⲅⲉⲗⲟⲥ ϩⲟⲣⲙⲟⲥ ⲉⲥⲁⲃⲧⲉ ⲉⲃⲟⲗ
ϩⲓⲧⲟⲟⲧⲟⲩ ⲛ̄ⲙ̄ⲡⲁⲣⲑⲉⲛⲟⲥ ⲙ̄ⲡⲉ
ⲧϫⲟ ⲉⲧϫⲁϩⲙ̄ · ⲛ̄ⲧⲉ ⲡⲉⲉⲓⲁⲓⲱⲛ ϩ̄ⲛ
ⲟⲩⲥⲕⲉⲩⲟⲥ ⲛ̄ⲗⲟⲅⲟⲅⲉⲛⲏⲥ ⲉ⟨ϥ⟩ⲟⲩⲁ
ⲁⲃ · ⲉⲃⲟⲗ ϩⲓⲧⲟⲟⲧϥ̄ ⲙ̄ⲡⲉⲡⲛ̄ⲁ̄ ⲛ̄ϩⲁ
ⲅⲓⲟⲛ ⟨ⲛ̄⟩ⲧⲉⲥⲡⲟⲣⲁ ⲙ̄ⲡⲛⲟϭ ⲛ̄ⲥⲏⲑ ·

60, 6 MS. reads ⲉⲩⲟⲩⲁ.

Then (τότε) the great / angel (ἄγγελος) Hormos came to prepare, / through the virgins (παρθένος) of the / [5] corrupted sowing of this aeon (αἰών), in / a Logos-begotten (λογογενής), holy vessel (σκεῦος), / through the holy (ἅγιον) Spirit (πνεῦμα), / the seed (σπορά) of the great Seth. /

The placing of the seed of Seth: III 60,9-18

ⲧⲟⲧⲉ ⲡⲛⲟϭ ⲥ̄ⲏ̄ⲑ̄ · ⲁϥⲉⲓ ⲁϥⲉⲓⲛⲉ ⲛ̄ⲧⲉϥ
ⲥⲡⲟⲣⲁ ⲁⲩⲱ ⲁⲩϫⲟ ⲙ̄ⲙⲟⲥ ⲉⲛⲁⲓⲱⲛ
ⲛ̄ⲧⲁⲩϫⲡⲟⲟⲩ ⲉⲧⲉⲩⲏⲡⲉ ⲡⲉ ⲡϣⲓ ⲛ̄
ⲥⲟⲇⲟⲙⲏⲛ ϩⲟⲉⲓⲛ ⲉⲩϫⲱ ⲙ̄ⲙⲟⲥ

Then (τότε) the great Seth came and brought his / [10] seed (σπορά). And it was sown in the aeons (αἰών) / which had been brought forth, their number being the amount of / Sodom. Some say /

IV 71,10 [ⲁⲩⲱ ⲙ̅ⲛ̅ ⲛ̅ⲥⲁ] ⲧⲥⲡⲟⲣⲁ ⲛ̅ⲁ[ⲇⲁⲙ ⲡⲣⲏ]
[ⲙ̅ⲛ̅ ⲥ̅ⲏ̅ⲑ̅ ⲡⲓⲛ]ⲟ̣ϭ·

[10] [and] the seed (σπορά) of [Adam, the sun,] / [and Seth the] great.

The Work of Hormos: IV 71,11-18

ⲧⲟⲧⲉ ⲁϥⲉ[ⲓ ⲉⲃⲟⲗ] ⲛ̣̅ϭⲓ
12 [ⲡⲓⲛⲟϭ ⲛ̅]ⲁⲅⲅⲉ̣ⲗⲟⲥ ϩⲟⲣⲙⲟⲥ ⲉⲥ̣[ⲟ]ⲃⲧⲉ
[ⲉⲃⲟⲗ ϩⲓⲧⲟⲟⲧ]ⲟⲩ ⲛ̅ⲛⲓⲡⲁⲣⲑⲉⲛⲟⲥ
14 [ⲛ̅ⲧⲉ ⲧⲥⲡⲟⲣ]ⲁ ⲉⲧϫⲁϩⲙ̅ ⲛ̅ⲧⲉ ⲡⲉⲓ̈ⲁⲓⲱ̣[ⲛ]
[ϩ̅ⲛ ⲟⲩⲥⲕⲉ]ⲩⲟⲥ ⲛ̅ϫⲡⲟ ⲛ̅ϣⲁϫⲉ ⲉϥ
16 [ⲟⲩⲁⲁⲃ ⲉⲃⲟⲗ ϩ]ⲓ̣ⲧⲟⲟⲧϥ̅ ⲙ̅ⲡ̣[ⲡ]ⲛ̅ⲁ̅ ⲉ
[ⲧⲟⲩⲁⲁⲃ ⲛ̅ⲧⲥ]ⲡⲟⲣⲁ ⲛ̅ⲧⲉ̣ [ⲡ]ⲓ̣ⲛⲟϭ
18 [ⲛ̅ⲥ̅ⲏ̅ⲑ̅·

Then (τότε) [the great] / angel (ἄγγελος) Hormos [came forth] to prepare, / [through] the virgins (παρθένος) / [of the] corrupt [seed (σπορά)] of this aeon (αἰών), / [15] [in a] Logos-begotten, [holy] vessel (σκεῦος), / through the [holy] Spirit (πνεῦμα), / [the] seed (σπορά) of [the] great / [Seth.]

The placing of the seed of Seth: IV 71,18-30

18 ⲧⲟⲧ]ⲉ ⲡⲓⲛⲟϭ ⲥ̅ⲏ̅[ⲑ ⲁϥ]ⲉ̂ⲓ
[ⲁϥⲉⲓⲛⲉ ⲛ̅ⲧⲉ]ϥⲥⲡⲟⲣⲁ ⲁ[ⲩⲱ ⲁ]ϥⲥⲁ
20 [ⲧ̅ⲥ̅ ⲉϩⲣⲁї ⲉⲛⲓ]ⲉⲱⲛ ⲛ̅ϫ[ⲡⲟ ⲛ̅]ⲕⲁϩ
[ⲉⲧⲉ ⲡⲉⲩϣⲓ ⲡⲉ] ⲟⲩⲁⲧⲧ̀ⲓ̀ [ⲏⲡⲉ ⲉ]ⲣⲟ
22 [ϥ ⲛ̅ⲧⲉ] ⲥⲟⲇⲟⲙⲏ · ⲛ̅ⲧ[ⲟⲟⲩ ⲇ]ⲉ ⲁⲩ

[Then (τότε)] the great Seth came / [and brought] his seed (σπορά), [and] he sowed / [20] [it in the] earth- [born] aeons (αἰών) / [of which the amount is] an uncountable (number) / [of] Sodom. [But (δέ) they] /

III 60 ϫⲉ ⲥⲟⲇⲟⲙⲏⲛ ⲡⲉ ⲡⲙⲁ ⲛ̄ⲙⲟⲛⲉ
14 ⲙ̄ⲡⲛⲟϭ ⲛ̄ⲥⲏⲑ · ⲉⲧⲉ ⲅⲟⲙⲟϩⲣⲁ ⲡⲉ
ϩⲟⲉⲓⲛ ⲇⲉ ϫⲉ ⲁⲡⲛⲟϭ ⲛ̄ⲥⲏⲑ ϥⲓ ⲙ̄
16 ⲡⲉϥⲧⲱϭⲉ ⲉⲃⲟⲗ ϩ̄ⲛ ⲅⲟⲙⲟϩⲣⲁ ⲁⲩⲱ
ⲁϥⲧⲱϭⲉ ⲙ̄ⲙⲟⲥ ϩ̄ⲙ ⲡⲙⲉϩ ⲧⲟⲡⲟⲥ
18 ⲥⲛⲁⲩ ⲡⲁї ⲛ̄ⲧⲁϥϯ ⲣⲛ̄ϥ ϫⲉ ⲥⲟⲇⲟⲙⲁ

60,13 Corr. ⲚⲈ over ϩ and ?
16 Corr. ϩ in ⲅⲟⲙⲟϩⲣⲁ over ⲣ.

that Sodom is the place of pasture / of the great Seth, which is Gomorrah. / 15 But (δέ) others (say) that the great Seth took / his plant out of Gomorrah and / planted it in the second place (τόπος) / which he gave the name Sodom. /

The race of Edokla: III 60,19 - 61,1

ⲧⲁї ⲧⲉ ⲧⲅⲉⲛⲉⲁ ⲛ̄ⲧⲁⲥⲉⲓ ⲉⲃⲟⲗ ϩⲓⲧⲟ
20 ⲟⲧⲥ̄ ⲛ̄ⲉⲇⲱⲕⲗⲁ · ⲁⲥϫⲡⲟ ⲅⲁⲣ ϩ̄ⲙ ⲡϣⲁ
ϫⲉ ⲛ̄ⲧⲁⲗⲏⲑⲉⲓⲁ ⟨ⲙ⟩ⲛ̄ ⲑⲉ{ⲛ}ⲙⲓⲥⲥⲁ ⲧⲁⲣ
22 ⲭⲏ ⲛ̄ⲧⲉⲥⲡⲟⲣⲁ ⲙ̄ⲡⲱⲛϩ̄· ⲛ̄ϣⲁ ⲁ
ⲛⲏϩⲉ ⲉⲧϣⲟⲟⲡ̄ ⲙⲛ̄ ⲛⲉⲧⲛⲁϩⲩⲡⲟ

60,21 MS. reads ⲛ̄ⲑⲉ ⲛ̄ⲙⲓⲥⲥⲁ; see 62,20.

This is the race (γενεά) which came forth through / 20 Edokla. For (γάρ) she gave birth through the word / to Truth (ἀλήθεια) and Justice (θέμισσα), the origin (ἀρχή) / of the seed (σπορά) of the eternal life / which is with those who will persevere (ὑπομένειν) /

IV 71 [ⲙⲟⲩⲧⲉ] ⲉ̣ⲣⲟⲟⲩ ϫⲉ ⲥ[ⲟⲇⲟⲙ]ⲏ ⲛ̅
[ⲧⲉ ⲡⲓⲛⲟ]ϭ̣ ⲥ̅ⲏ̅ⲑ̅· ⲉⲧⲉ̣ [ⲧⲁⲓ̈ ⲧⲉ] ⲅⲟⲙⲟ
[ϩⲣⲁ ⲁϥⲧⲱⲟⲩ]ⲛ̅ ⲛ̅ϭⲓ ⲡⲓ̣[ⲛⲟϭ ⲥ̅ⲏ̅]ⲑ̣̅
[ⲉⲃⲟⲗ ϩⲛ̅ ϯ]ⲡⲏⲅⲏ ⲛ̅ⲧⲉ̣ [ⲅⲟⲙⲟϩ]
[ⲣⲁ ⲛ̅ⲧⲥⲡⲟⲣⲁ] ⲁⲩⲱ ⲁϥ̣[ⲧⲟϭ̅ⲥ̅]
[ϩⲙ̅ ⲡⲓⲙⲉϩⲙⲁ] ⲥⲛⲁⲩ ϩⲛ̅ ⲟ̣[ⲩⲙⲁ]
[ⲙ̅ⲙⲟⲟⲛⲉ] ϩⲱⲱϥ ⲁⲩⲙ[ⲟⲩⲧⲉ]
[ⲉⲣⲟϥ ϫⲉ ⲥ]ⲟ̣[ⲇ]ⲟⲙⲁ·

[called] them [Sodom] of / [the great] Seth, which [is] Gomorrah. / [25] The [great Seth carried] / [the seed (σπορά) from the] spring (πηγή) of / [Gomorrah] and [planted it] / [in the] second [place], even in [a place] / [of pasture;] they [called] / [30] [it] Sodom.

The race of Edokla: IV 71,30 - 72,10

ⲧⲁ̣ⲓ̈ [ⲧⲉ]
[ϯⲅⲉⲛⲉⲁ ⲛ̅ⲧⲁⲥⲟ]ⲩⲱⲛ̅ϩ ⲉ̣[ⲃⲟⲗ]
72 ⲟ̅ⲃ̅
ϩⲓⲧⲟⲟⲧⲥ̅ ⲛ̅ⲛⲉⲇⲱⲕⲗⲁ·
ⲁⲥϫⲡⲟ ⲅⲁⲣ ϩⲛ̅ ⲟⲩϣⲁϫⲉ ⲛ̅ⲁⲗ⟨ⲏ⟩ⲑⲉⲁ
ⲙ̅ⲛ ⲑⲉⲙⲓⲥⲥⲁ· ⲉ̣ⲧⲉ ⲧⲁⲣⲭⲏ ⲧⲉ ⲛ̅ⲧⲉ
ⲟ̣ⲩⲥⲡⲟⲣⲁ ⲛ̅ⲧⲉ ⲡⲓⲱⲛ̅ϩ ϣⲁ ⲉⲛⲉϩ
ⲙ̣̅ⲛ ⲟⲩⲟ̣[ⲛ] ⲛ̣[ⲓ]ⲙ ⲉⲧⲛⲁⲣ̅ϩⲩⲡⲟⲙⲓⲛ̣[ⲉ]

72, 1 The line is extra short due to some large cursive writing in the top right corner of the page.
2 MS. omits ⲏ. ⲉⲁ for ⲓⲁ.

This [is] / [the race (γενεά) that] appeared // *72* through Edokla. / For (γάρ) she gave birth through a word to Truth (ἀλήθεια) / and Justice (θέμισσα), which is the origin (ἀρχή) of / the seed (σπορά) of the eternal life, / [5] and everyone who will persevere (ὑπομένειν) /

III 60,24 ⲙⲓⲛⲉ ⲉⲧⲃⲉ ⲡⲥⲟⲟⲩⲛ ⲛ̄ⲧⲉⲩⲁⲡⲟ
ϩⲣⲟⲓⲁ ⲧⲁï ⲧⲉ ⲧⲛⲟϭ ⲛ̄ⲅⲉⲛⲉⲁ ⲛ̄ⲁ
26 ⲫⲑⲁⲣⲧⲟⲥ ⲉⲣⲉⲓ ⲉⲃⲟⲗ ϩⲓⲧⲛ̄ ϣⲟⲙⲛ̄ⲧ
61 ⲝ̣ⲁ̣
ⲛ̄ⲕⲟⲥⲙⲟⲥ ⲉⲡⲕⲟⲥⲙⲟⲥ

because of the knowledge of their emanation (ἀπόρροια). / 25 This is the great, incorruptible (ἄφθαρτος) / race (γενεά) which has come forth through three // *61* worlds (κόσμος) to the world (κόσμος).

The perils facing the seed of Seth: III 61,1-15

ⲁⲩⲱ ⲁⲡⲕⲁ
2 ⲧⲁⲕⲗⲩⲥⲙⲟⲥ ϣⲱⲡⲉ ⲛ̄ⲟⲩⲧⲩⲡⲟⲥ
ϣⲁ ⲧⲥⲩⲛⲧⲉⲗⲓⲁ ⲙ̄ⲡⲁⲓⲱⲛ ⲡⲁï ⲇⲉ
4 ⲥⲉⲛⲁϫⲟⲟⲩϥ ⲉϩⲣⲁï ⲉⲡⲕⲟⲥⲙⲟⲥ ⲉ
ⲧⲃⲉ ⲧⲉⲉⲓⲅⲉⲛⲉⲁ ⲟⲩⲛ̄ ⲟⲩⲣⲱⲭϩ ⲛⲁ
6 ϣⲱⲡⲉ ϩⲓϫⲙ̄ ⲡⲕⲁϩ· ⲁⲩⲱ ⲉⲣⲉⲡⲉϩ
ⲙⲟⲧ̄ ϣⲱⲡⲉ ⲙⲛ̄ ⲛⲉⲧⲏⲡ̈ ⲉⲧⲅⲉ
8 ⲛⲉⲁ ⲉⲃⲟⲗ ϩⲓⲧⲟⲟⲧⲟⲩ ⲛ̄ⲛⲉⲡⲣⲟⲫⲏ
ⲧⲏⲥ ⲙⲛ̄ ⲛ̄ϩⲟⲩⲣⲓⲧ̄ ⲉⲧϩⲁⲣⲏϩ ⲉⲡⲱⲛϩ
10 ⲛ̄ⲧⲅⲉⲛⲉⲁ · ⲉⲧⲃⲉ ⲧⲉⲉⲓⲅⲉⲛⲉⲁ ⲉⲣⲉ
ϩⲉⲛϩⲉⲃⲱⲱⲛ ϣⲱⲡⲉ ⲙⲛ̄ ϩⲉⲛⲗⲟⲓ

And the / flood (κατακλυσμός) came as an example (τύπος) / for the consummation (συντέλεια) of the aeon (αἰών). But (δέ) it / will be sent into the world (κόσμος) / 5 because of this race (γενεά). A conflagration will / come upon the earth. And grace / will be with those who belong to the race (γενεά) / through the prophets (προφήτης) / and the guardians who guard the life / 10 of the race (γενεά). Because of this race (γενεά) / famines will occur and plagues (λοιμός). /

IV 72, 6 [ⲉ]ⲃⲟⲗ ϩⲓⲧⲟⲟⲧⲥ̄ ⲛ̄ϯⲅⲛⲱⲥ[ⲓⲥ] ⲛ̄ⲧ[ⲉ]
ⲧ̣ⲟⲩⲁⲡ̣[ⲟ]ⲣⲟⲓⲁ · ⲧⲁï ⲧⲉ ϯⲛⲟ̣ϭ ⲛ̄[ⲅⲉ]
8 [ⲛⲉ]ⲁ ⲁ[ⲩ]ⲱ ⲛ̄ⲁⲧϫⲱϩⲙ̄· ⲧⲏ̣ ⲉⲧ̣[ⲁⲥ]
[ⲟⲩⲱⲛ]ϩ̣ ⲉⲃⲟⲗ ϩⲛ̄ ϣⲟⲙⲧ̄ ⲛ̄ⲕ̣[ⲟⲥ]
10 [ⲙⲟⲥ·]

72, 9 Trace appears to be ⲙ rather than ϩ.

because of the knowledge (γνῶσις) of / their emanation (ἀπόρροια). This is the great / and incorruptible [race (γενεά)] that [has] / [appeared] in three / [worlds (κόσμος).]

The perils facing the seed of Seth: IV 72,10-27

10 ⲁ̣ⲩⲱ ϥⲛⲁϣ[ⲱⲡⲉ ⲛ̄ϭⲓ ⲡⲓ]
ⲕ̣[ⲁⲧⲁ]ⲕⲗⲩⲥⲙⲟⲥ ⲉⲩ[ⲧⲩⲡⲟⲥ ϣⲁ]
12 [ⲧⲥ]ⲩ̣ⲛⲧⲉⲗⲓⲁ ⲛ̄ⲧⲉ ⲡ̣ⲓⲉϣ[ⲛ ⲛ̄ϥⲉⲓ]
ⲉϩⲣⲁï ⲉⲡⲕⲟⲥⲙⲟⲥ [ⲉⲧⲃⲉ ⲧⲉï]
14 ⲅⲉⲛⲉⲁ ⲥⲉⲛⲁϣⲱⲡ[ⲉ ⲛ̄ϭⲓ ϩⲉⲛ]
ⲣⲱⲕϩ̄ ϩⲓϫ̣ⲛ̄ ⲡⲕⲁϩ [
16 .ⲛ[..]ⲛ̣ⲏ ⲛ̄ⲧⲉ ϯⲙ[ϥⲛⲁϣⲱ]
ⲡⲉ ⲛ̄[ϭⲓ] ⲡⲓϩⲙⲟⲧ ⲉ̣[ⲃⲟⲗ ϩⲓⲧⲟⲟⲧⲟⲩ]
18 ⲛ̄[ⲛⲓⲡⲣ]ⲟⲫⲏⲧⲏⲥ ⲙ̄[ⲛ ⲛⲓϩⲟⲩⲣⲓⲧ]
ⲛ̄ⲧ[ⲉ ϯⲅ]ⲉⲛⲉⲁ ⲉⲧ[ⲟⲛ̄ϩ · ⲉⲧⲃⲉ]
20 ⲧⲉ[ïⲅⲉⲛⲉ]ⲁ ⲥⲉⲛⲁϣ[ⲱⲡⲉ ⲛ̄ϭⲓ]
ϩⲉ[ⲛⲙⲟ]ⲩ̣ ⲙ̄ⲛ̄ ϩⲉⲛϩ̣ⲉⲃⲱ[ⲱⲛ·]

72,16 The first letter is ⲥ or ϭ.
18 Or ⲙ̄[ⲛ ⲛⲓⲣⲉϥⲁⲣⲉϩ].

And [the] flood (κατακλυσμός) will / [come] as an [example (τύπος) for] / [the] consummation (συντέλεια) of the aeon (αἰών), [and it will come] / into the world (κόσμος) [because of this] / race (γενεά). Conflagrations will come / upon the earth [ ] / [ ] of the [ ] / grace [will come to be through] / [the] prophets (προφήτης) [and the guardians] / of [the living] race (γενεά). [Because of]/ [this race (γενεά) plagues] / will [occur] and famines. /

III 61,12 ⲙⲟⲥ ⲛⲁï ⲇⲉ ⲉⲩⲛⲁϣⲱⲡⲉ ⲉⲧⲃⲉ ϯ
ⲛⲟϭ ⲛ̄ⲅⲉⲛⲉⲁ ⲛ̄ⲁⲫⲑⲁⲣⲧⲟⲥ · ⲉⲧⲃⲉ
ⲧⲉⲉⲓⲅⲉⲛⲉⲁ ⲉⲣⲉϩⲛ̄ⲡⲓⲣⲁⲥⲙⲟⲥ ϣⲱ
ⲡⲉ ⲟⲩⲡⲗⲁⲛⲏ ⲛ̄ⲡⲣⲟⲫⲏⲧⲏⲥ ⲛ̄ⲛⲟⲩϫ

61,15 Corr. ⲛ in ⲡⲗⲁⲛⲏ over ?

But (δέ) these things will happen because of the / great, incorruptible (ἄφθαρτος) race (γενεά). Because of / this race (γενεά) temptations (πειρασμός) will come, / a falsehood (πλάνη) of false prophets (προφήτης). /

Seth recognizes the devil's schemes: III 61,16-23

ⲧⲟⲧⲉ ⲡⲛⲟϭ ⲛ̄ⲥⲏⲑ · ⲁϥⲛⲁⲩ ⲉⲧⲉⲛⲉⲣ
ⲅⲓⲁ ⲙ̄ⲡⲇⲓⲁⲃⲟⲗⲟⲥ ⲙⲛ̄ ⲡⲉϥⲁⲧⲟ ⲛ̄
ⲥⲙⲟⲧ ⲙⲛ̄ ⲛⲉϥⲙⲉⲉⲩⲉ ⲉⲧⲛⲁϣⲱⲡⲉ
ⲉϫⲛ̄ ⲧⲉϥⲅⲉⲛⲉⲁ ⲛ̄ⲁⲫⲑⲁⲣⲧⲟⲛ ⲉⲧⲉ
ⲙⲉⲥⲕⲓⲙ ⲙⲛ̄ ⲛ̄ⲇⲓⲱⲅⲙⲟⲥ ⲛ̄ⲛⲉϥ
ϭⲟⲙ ⲙⲛ̄ ⲛⲉϥⲁⲅⲅⲉⲗⲟⲥ ⲙⲛ̄ ⲧⲉⲩ
ⲡⲗⲁⲛⲏ ϫⲉ ⲁⲩⲧⲟⲗⲙⲁ ⲉⲣⲟⲟⲩ ⲙ̄ⲙⲓⲛ
ⲙ̄ⲙⲟⲟⲩ ·

61,20 Corr. ⲛⲟϭ crossed out at end of line.

Then (τότε) the great Seth saw the activity (ἐνέργεια) / of the devil (διάβολος), and his many / guises, and his schemes which will come / upon his incorruptible (ἄφθαρτον), immovable race (γενεά), / and the persecutions (διωγμός) of his / powers and his angels (ἄγγελος), and their / error (πλάνη), that they acted (τολμᾶν) against them/selves.

IV 72,22 ⲛⲁ[ï ⲧⲏⲣ]ⲟⲩ ⲥⲉⲛⲁϣⲱⲡ[ⲉ ⲉⲧⲃⲉ]
ⲧⲉï[ⲛⲟϭ ⲛ̄ⲅ]ⲉⲛⲉⲁ ⲁⲩⲱ̣ [ⲛ̄ⲁⲧ']
24 ϫⲱ[ϩ̄ⲙ ·] ⲉ̣ⲧⲃⲉ ⲧⲉï[ⲅⲉⲛⲉⲁ]
ⲥ̣[ⲉⲛⲁϣ]ⲱⲡⲉ ⲛ̄ϭ[ⲓ ϩⲉⲛⲡⲉⲓⲣⲁ]
26 [ⲥⲙⲟⲥ ⲙ̄]ⲛ ϩⲉⲛⲡⲗⲁ[ⲛⲏ ⲛ̄ⲧⲉ]
[ⲛⲓⲡⲣⲟ]ⲫⲏⲧⲏⲥ ⲛ̄[ⲛⲟⲩϫ ·

All [these] things will happen [because of] / this [great] and [incorruptible] race (*γενεά*). / Because of this [race (*γενεά*)] / [25] [temptations (*πειρασμός*) will] come / and falsehoods (*πλάνη*) [of] / [the false] prophets (*προφήτης*).

Seth recognizes the devil's schemes: IV 72,27 - 73,6

ⲧⲟ]
28 [ⲧⲉ ⲡⲓⲛ]ⲟϭ ⲥ̄ⲏ̄ⲑ̄ ⲛ̄ⲧ[ⲁϥⲛⲁⲩ]
[ⲉϯⲉ]ⲛ̣ⲉⲣⲅⲓⲁ ⲙ̣̄[ⲡⲓ]ⲇ̣[ⲓⲁⲃⲟⲗⲟⲥ]
73 ⲟ̣̄[ⲅ̄]
ⲙ̄ⲛ ⲛⲉϥⲕⲟⲧ̄ⲥ ⲉⲧⲛ̄ⲧⲁϥ· ⲁⲩⲱ ⲙ̄ⲛ
2 ⲡⲓⲙⲉⲉⲩⲉ ⲉ[ⲧ]ⲛ̣̄ⲧⲁϥ ⲉⲧ̄ϥⲛⲁ̣
ⲛ̄ⲧ̄ϥ ⲉϩⲣⲁï ⲉϫ̄ⲛ ϯⲅⲉⲛⲉⲁ [ⲛ̄ⲁⲧ']
4 ⲕⲓⲙ ⲙ̄ⲛ ⲡⲓⲇⲓⲱⲅⲙ[ⲟⲥ ⲛ̄ⲧⲉ ⲛⲉϥ]
[ϭ]ⲟ̣ⲙ ⲙ̄ⲛ ⲛⲉϥⲁⲅⲅⲉⲗⲟⲥ̣ [ⲙ̄ⲛ ⲧⲉϥ]
6 [ⲡⲗ]ⲁⲛⲏ ϫⲉ ϥⲛⲁⲣ̄ⲧⲟⲗⲙⲁ [ⲉⲣⲟϥ]

[Then (*τότε*)] / [the] great Seth [saw] / [the] work (*ἐνέργεια*) of [the devil (*διάβολος*),] // *73* and his crooked tricks, and / his scheme which he will / bring upon the [im]movable race (*γενεά*), / and the persecution (*διωγμός*) [of his] / [5] [powers] and his angels (*ἄγγελος*), [and his] / error (*πλάνη*), that he will act (*τολμᾶν*) [against himself.] /

Seth requests guardians for his race: III 61,23 - 62,13

III 61 ⲧⲟⲧⲉ ⲡⲛⲟϭ ⲛ̄ⲥⲏⲑ · ⲁϥϯ
24 ⲛ̄ⲟⲩⲥⲙⲟⲩ ⲙ̄ⲡⲛⲟϭ ⲛ̄ⲁⲕⲁⲗⲏⲧⲟⲛ
ⲙ̄ⲡⲁⲣⲑⲉⲛⲓⲕⲟⲛ ⲙ̄ⲡⲛ̄ⲁ̄ ⲙⲛ̄ ⲧⲁⲣ
62 ⲝ̄[ⲃ̄]
ⲥⲉⲛⲓⲕⲏ ⲙ̄ⲡⲁⲣⲑⲉⲛⲟⲥ ⲧⲃⲁⲣⲃⲏⲗⲟⲛ
2 ⲙⲛ̄ ⲡϣⲟⲙⲛⲧ̇ ⲛ̄ϩⲟⲟⲩⲧ̇ ⲛ̄ⲁⲗⲟⲩ ⲧⲉⲗ
ⲙⲁⲏⲗ · ⲧⲉⲗⲙⲁⲏⲗ · ϩⲏⲗⲓ ϩⲏⲗⲓ · ⲙⲁⲭⲁⲣ
4 ⲙⲁⲭⲁⲣ · ⲥⲏⲑ ⲧϭⲟⲙ ⲉⲧⲟⲛϩ ⲁⲗⲏⲑⲉⲥ
ⲁⲗⲏⲑⲱⲥ ⲙⲛ̄ ⲧⲁⲣⲥⲉⲛⲓⲕⲏ ⲛ̄ⲡⲁⲣⲑⲉ
6 ⲛⲟⲥ ⲓ̈ⲟⲩⲏⲗ · ⲙⲛ̄ ⲏⲥⲏⲫⲏⲭ ⲡⲉⲧⲙⲁϩ
ⲧⲉ ⲙ̄ⲡⲉⲟⲟⲩ ⲙⲛ̄ ⲡⲉⲕⲗⲟⲙ ⲙ̄ⲡⲉϥⲉⲟ
8 ⲟⲩ ⲙⲛ̄ ⲡⲛⲟϭ ⲛ̄ⲇⲟⲝⲟⲙⲉⲇⲱⲛ ⲛ̄ⲁⲓ
ⲱⲛ ⲙⲛ̄ ⲛⲉⲑⲣⲟⲛⲟⲥ ⲉⲧⲛ̄ϩⲏⲧϥ · ⲙⲛ̄
10 ⲛ̄ϭⲟⲙ ⲉⲧⲕⲱⲧⲉ ⲉⲣⲟⲟⲩ ⲙⲛ̄ ⲡⲉⲡⲗⲏ
ⲣⲱⲙⲁ ⲧⲏⲣϥ ⲛ̄ⲑⲉ ⲛ̄ⲧⲁⲉⲓϣⲣ⟨ⲡ⟩ ⲛ̄ϫⲟ

62, 6 Corr. ⲛ in ⲙⲛ̄ over ⲏ.

Then (τότε) the great Seth gave / praise to the great, uncallable (ἄκλητον), / virginal (παρθενικόν) Spirit (πνεῦμα), and the male (ἀρσενική) // *62* virgin (παρθένος) Barbelon, / and the thrice-male child Telmael / Telmael Heli Heli Machar / Machar Seth, the power which really truly (ἀληθὲς ἀληθῶς) / lives, and the male (ἀρσενική) virgin (παρθένος) / Youel, and Esephech, the / splenditenens, and the crown of his / glory, and the great Doxomedon-aeon (αἰών), / and the thrones (θρόνος) which are in him, and / the powers which surround them, and the whole / pleroma (πλήρωμα), as I mentioned before. /

Seth requests guardians for his race: IV 73,7-26

IV 73 [ⲧⲟ]ⲧⲉ ⲡⲓⲛⲟϭ ⲥⲏⲑ ⲁϥⲉⲓⲛ[ⲉ ⲉϩⲣⲁï]
8 [ⲛ̄ⲟⲩ]ⲥ̣ⲙⲟⲩ ⲙ̄ⲡⲓⲛⲟϭ ⲛ̣̄[ⲛⲁⲧ'ϫⲁ]
[ϩⲙ̄ϥ] ⲛ̄ⲛⲁⲧⲛⲁⲩ ⲉⲣⲟϥ ⲛ̣̄[ⲁⲧ'ϯ ⲣⲁⲛ]
10 [ⲉⲣⲟϥ] ⲙ̄ⲡⲁ[ⲣ]ⲑⲉⲛⲓⲕⲟⲛ ⲙ̄[ⲡⲛ̄ⲁ] ⲛ̣̄
[ⲧⲉ ⲡⲓⲱ]ⲧ' ⲛⲙ ϯϩⲟⲟⲩⲧ' ⲙ̄ⲡⲁⲣⲑⲉ
12 [ⲛⲟⲥ ϯⲃ]ⲁⲣⲃⲏⲗⲱ ⲙ̄ⲛ ⲡⲓϩⲟⲟⲩⲧ'
[ⲛ̄]ⲁⲗⲟⲩ ⲧⲉⲗⲙⲁⲏⲗ ⲧⲉⲗⲙⲁⲭⲁⲏⲗ
14 [ⲏ]ⲗⲓ ⲏⲗⲓ ⲙⲁⲭⲁⲣ ⲙⲁⲭⲁⲣ ⲥⲏⲑ
[ϯ]ϭⲟⲙ ⲉⲧⲟⲛ̄ϩ · ϩⲛ̄ ⲟⲩⲙⲛ̄[ⲧ]ⲙⲉ ⲛⲁ
16 [ⲙ]ⲉ ϯϩⲟⲟⲩⲧ' ⲙ̄ⲡⲁⲣⲑⲉⲛⲟ[ⲥ] ïⲟ̣ⲩ[ⲏⲗ]
[ⲙ̄ⲛ ⲏ]ⲥ̣ⲏⲫⲏⲭ ⲡⲓⲣⲉϥⲁⲙⲁϩⲧⲉ ⲙ̄
18 [ⲡⲉⲟⲟ]ⲩ ⲙ̄ⲛ ⲡⲕⲗⲟⲙ ⲛ̄ⲧⲉ ⲡⲉϥⲉⲟ
[ⲟⲩ] ⲙ̄ⲛ ⲡⲓⲛⲟϭ ⲛ̄ⲛⲉⲱⲛ ⲛ̄ⲣⲉϥ
20 [ϯ ⲉ]ⲟ̣ⲟⲩ ⲙ̄ⲛ ⲛⲓⲑⲣⲟⲛⲟⲥ ⲉⲧⲛ̄ϩⲣⲁï
[ⲛ̄ϩ]ⲏⲧϥ ⲙ̄ⲛ ⲛⲓⲛⲟϭ ⲉⲧ'ⲕⲱⲧⲉ
22 [ⲉⲣ]ⲟⲟⲩ ⲙ̄ⲛ ϩⲉⲛⲉⲟ̣[ⲟ]ⲩ ⲙ̄ⲛ
[ϩⲉ]ⲛ̣ⲁⲧ'ϫⲱϩⲙ ⲙ̄ⲛ [ⲡⲓ]ⲡⲗⲏⲣⲱ
24 [ⲙⲁ] ⲧⲏ̣ⲣϥ ⲉ̣ⲧⲁïⲣ̄ϣⲣⲡ' ⲛ̄ϫⲟⲟϥ

73, 8f. For [ϫⲁϩⲙ̄ϥ] or [ϫⲱϩ̄ⲙ] see *supra* 54,16f. note.
9 Superlin. stroke on ⲛ̄ⲛ is in the lacuna.

[Then (τότε)] the great Seth brought / praise to the great, [incorruptible,] / invisible, [unnameable,] / 10 virginal (παρθενικόν) [Spirit (πνεῦμα)] / [of the Father,] and the male virgin (παρθένος) / Barbelo, and the male / child Telmael Telmachael / Eli Eli Machar Machar Seth, / 15 [the] power which really truly / lives, the male virgin (παρθένος) Youel, / [and] Esephech, the [splendi]tenens, / and the crown of his glory, / and the great glory-[giving] / 20 aeon (αἰών), and the thrones (θρόνος) that are / in him, and the great ones who surround / them, glories and / incorruptions, and [the] whole / pleroma (πλήρωμα) which I mentioned before. /

III 62,12 ⲟⲥ ⲁⲩⲱ ⲁϥⲁⲓⲧⲓ ⲛ̅ϩⲉⲛⲣⲉϥⲁⲣⲉϩ ⲉⲧⲉϥ
ⲥⲡⲟⲣⲁ

And he asked (*αἰτεῖν*) for guards over his / seed (*σπορά*).

The arrival of the guardians: III 62,13-24

ⲧⲟⲧⲉ ⲁⲩⲉⲓ ⲉⲃⲟⲗ ϩⲛ̅ ⲛ̅ⲛⲟϭ ⲛ̅
14 ⲁⲓⲱⲛ ⲛ̅ϭⲓ ϥⲧⲟⲩϣⲉ ⲛ̅ⲛⲁⲉⲣⲟⲥⲓⲟⲥ ⲛ̅
ⲁⲅ̅ⲅⲉⲗⲟⲥ ⲉϥⲛ̅ⲙ̅ⲙⲁⲩ ⲛ̅ϭⲓ ⲡⲛⲟϭ ⲛ̅
16 ⲁⲉⲣⲟⲥⲓⲏⲗ ⲙⲛ̅ ⲡⲛⲟϭ ⲥⲉⲗⲙⲉⲭⲉⲗ ⲉ
ϩⲁⲣⲉϩ ⲉⲧⲛⲟϭ ⲛ̅ⲅⲉⲛⲉⲁ ⲛ̅ⲁⲫⲑⲁⲣⲧⲟⲥ
18 ⲡⲉⲥⲕⲁⲣⲡⲟⲥ ⲙⲛ̅ ⲛ̅ⲛⲟϭ ⲛ̅ⲣⲱⲙⲉ
ⲙ̅ⲡⲛⲟϭ ⲥⲏⲑ ϫⲓⲛ ⲙ̅ⲡⲉⲟⲩⲟⲉⲓϣ ⲙⲛ̅
20 ⲡⲕⲉⲣⲟⲥ ⲛ̅ⲧⲁⲗⲏⲑⲉⲓⲁ ⲙⲛ̅ ⲑⲉⲙⲓⲥⲥⲁ
ϣⲁ ⲧⲥⲩⲛⲧⲉⲗⲓ̈ⲁ ⲙ̅ⲡⲁⲓⲱⲛ ⲙⲛ̅ ⲛⲉϥ
22 ⲁⲣⲭⲱⲛ · ⲛⲁⲓ̈ ⲛ̅ⲧⲁⲩⲕⲣⲓⲛⲉ ⲙ̅ⲙⲟⲟⲩ
ⲛ̅ϭⲓ ⲛ̅ⲛⲟϭ ⲛ̅ⲕⲣⲓⲧⲏⲥ ϣⲁϩⲣⲁⲓ̈ ⲉ
24 ⲡⲙⲟⲩ ·

62,13 Corr. ⲩ over ϥ.
14 ⲥ for ⲇ in ⲁⲉⲣⲟⲥⲓⲟⲥ, see SCHWYZER, *Griechische Grammatik* I, p. 208.
15 Corr. ⲉϥⲛ̅ⲙ over erasure.
23 Corr. ⲧ over ⲛ in ⲕⲣⲓⲧⲏⲥ.

Then (*τότε*) there came forth from the great / aeons (*αἰών*) four hundred ethereal (*ἀερόδιος*) / [15] angels (*ἄγγελος*), accompanied by the great / Aerosiel and the great Selmechel, to / guard the great, incorruptible (*ἄφθαρτος*) race (*γενεά*), / its fruit (*καρπός*), and the great men / of the great Seth, from the time and / [20] the moment (*καιρός*) of Truth (*ἀλήθεια*) and Justice (*θέμισσα*) / until the consummation (*συντέλεια*) of the aeon (*αἰών*) and its / archons (*ἄρχων*), those whom the great judges (*κριτής*) / have condemned (*κρίνειν*) to / death.

IV 73 [ⲁⲩⲱ] ⲁϥⲣ̄ⲁⲓⲧⲓ ⲛ̄ϣⲟⲣ̣ⲡ̄' ⲛ̄ϩⲉⲛ
26 [ⲣⲉϥ]ⲁⲣⲉϩ ⲛ̄ⲧⲉ ⲧⲉϥⲥⲡⲟⲣⲁ·

25 [And] he asked (αἰτεῖν) for / guards of his seed (σπορά). /

The arrival of the guardians: IV 73,27 - 74,9

[ⲧⲟ]ⲧⲉ ⲁⲩⲉ̣͡ⲓ̣ ⲉⲃⲟⲗ ϩⲛ̄ ⲛⲓⲛⲟ̣[ϭ] ⲛ̄
28 [ⲛⲉ]ⲱⲛ ⲛ̣̄ϭⲓ ϥⲧⲟⲩϣⲉ ⲛ̣̄[ⲁⲅⲅⲉ]
[ⲗⲟⲥ ⲙ̄ⲡⲁⲏ]ⲣ ⲉϥ̣ⲛ̄ⲙ̄ⲙⲁ[ⲩ ⲛ̄ϭⲓ]
74 [ⲟ̄]ⲗ̄
ⲁ̄ⲉ̄ⲣ̄ⲟ̄ⲥ̄ⲓ̄ⲏ̄ⲗ̄ ⲙⲛ̄ ⲡⲓⲛⲟϭ ⲥ̄ⲉ̄ⲗ̄ⲙ̄ⲉ̄ⲗ̄ⲭ̄ⲉ̄ⲗ̄
2 ⲛ̣ⲓⲣ[ⲉ]ϥⲁⲣⲉϩ ⲛ̄ⲧⲉ ϯⲛⲟϭ ⲛ̄ⲁⲧ'ϫⲱϩⲙ̄
ⲛ̄ⲅ[ⲉ]ⲛⲉⲁ ⲙⲛ̄ ⲡⲉ̣[ⲥⲕ]ⲁⲣⲡⲟⲥ ⲙⲛ̄ ⲛⲓⲣⲱ
4 [ⲙⲉ ⲉⲧ]ⲛⲉⲁⲩ ⲛ̄ⲧⲉ ⲡⲓⲛⲟϭ ⲥ̄ⲏ̄ⲑ̄· ⲉϣ
[... ⲡ]ⲓ̣ⲭ̣ⲣⲟ[ⲛ]ⲟⲥ ⲙⲛ̄ ⲡⲓⲟⲩⲟⲉⲓϣ ⲛ̄
6 [ⲁ̄ⲗ̄ⲏ̄ⲑ̄ⲉ̄ⲓ̄]ⲁ̄ ⲙ̄ⲛ̄ ⲑ̄ⲉ̄ⲙ̄ⲓ̄ⲥ̄ⲥ̄ⲁ̄ ϣⲁ ⲧⲥⲩ̣[ⲛ]
[ⲧⲉⲗⲓⲁ ⲛ̄ⲧⲉ] ⲛⲉϊⲁⲓⲱⲛ ⲙⲛ̄ ⲛⲉ̣ⲩⲁⲣⲭ[ⲱⲛ]
8 [ⲙⲛ̄ ⲛⲏ ⲉⲧ]ⲁⲩϯ ϩⲁⲡ' ⲛ̄ϭⲓ ⲛⲓⲛⲟϭ ⲛ̄[ⲕⲣⲓ]
[ⲧⲏⲥ ϣⲁϩ]ⲣⲁϊ ⲉⲡⲙⲟⲩ·

74, 4f. Perhaps ⲉϣ[ϫⲉⲛ as form of ⲓⲥϫⲉⲛ (B).
8f. MS. omits ⲉⲣⲟⲟⲩ. One could also emend ⟨ⲛⲁⲩ⟩.

Then (τότε)] there came forth from the great / aeons (αἰών) four [undred [angels (ἄγγελος)] / [of the air (ἀήρ)] accompanied by // h*4* Aerosiel and the great Selmelchel, / the guardians of the great, 7ncorruptible / race (γενεά), and [its] fruit (καρπός), and the / great imen of the great Seth, / 5 [from (?) the] time (χρόνος) and the moment of / [Truth (ἀλήθεια)] and Justice (θέμισσα) until the / [consummation (συντέλεια) of] these aeons (αἰών) and their archons (ἄρχων), / [and those whom] the great [judges (κριτής)] have / condemned to death.

The mission of Seth: III 62,24 - 63,4

III 62,24 ⲧⲟⲧⲉ ⲡⲛⲟϭ ⲛ̄ⲥⲏⲑ · ⲁϥⲧⲛ̄

ⲛⲟⲟⲩ ⲉⲃⲟⲗ ϩⲓⲧⲟⲟⲧⲟⲩ ⲙ̄ⲡⲉϥⲧⲟⲟⲩ

26 ⲛ̄ⲟⲩⲟⲉⲓⲛ ϩⲙ̄ ⲡⲉⲑⲉⲗⲏⲙⲁ ⲙ̄ⲡⲁⲩⲧⲟ

63 ⲝⲅ

ⲅⲉⲛⲏⲥ ⲙⲛ̄ ⲡⲉⲡⲗⲏⲣⲱⲙⲁ ⲧⲏⲣϥ̄ ϩⲓⲧⲙ̄

2 ⟨ⲡϯ⟩ ⲙⲛ̄ ⲧⲉⲩⲇⲟⲕⲓⲁ ⲙ̄ⲡⲛⲟϭ ⲛ̄ⲁ

ϩⲟⲣⲁⲧⲟⲛ ⲙ̄ⲡⲛ̄ⲁ̄ ⲙⲛ̄ ⲧϯⲉ ⲛ̄ⲥⲫⲣⲁⲅⲓⲥ

4 ⲙⲛ̄ ⲡⲉⲡⲗⲏⲣⲱⲙⲁ ⲧⲏⲣϥ̄ ·

62,24f. Perhaps ⲁ⟨ⲩ⟩ⲧⲛⲛⲟⲟⲩ⟨ϥ⟩.
63, 2 MS. reads ⲡⲛⲟⲩⲧⲉ; see *infra* p. 191.

Then (τότε) the great Seth was / 25 sent by the four / lights, by the will (θέλημα) of the Autogenes (αὐτογενής) // *63* and the whole pleroma (πλήρωμα), through / <the gift> and the good pleasure (εὐδοκία) of the great invisible (ἀόρατον) / Spirit (πνεῦμα), and the five seals (σφραγίς), / and the whole pleroma (πλήρωμα).

The work of Seth: III 63,4 - 64,9

4 ⲁϥⲟⲩⲱⲧⲃ̄

ⲛ̄ⲧϣⲟⲙⲧⲉ ⲛ̄ⲡⲁⲣⲟⲩⲥⲓⲁ ⲛ̄ⲧⲁⲉⲓϫⲟⲟⲩ

6 ⲛ̄ϣⲟⲣⲡ̄ ⲙⲛ̄ ⲡⲕⲁⲧⲁⲕⲗⲩⲥⲙⲟⲥ ⲙⲛ̄ ⲡⲣⲱ

ⲕϩ̄ ⲙⲛ̄ ⲡϩⲉⲡ̄ ⲛ̄ⲛⲁⲣⲭⲱⲛ ⲙⲛ̄ ⲛ̄ⲇⲩⲛⲁ

8 ⲙⲓⲥ ⲙⲛ̄ ⲛ̄ⲉⲝⲟⲩⲥⲓⲁ ⲉⲛⲟⲩϩⲙ̄ ⲧⲏ ⲉⲧⲡⲗⲁ

63, 7 Corr. ϩ over ⲛ.
8 ⲛⲟⲩϩⲙ̄ normally construct form used here as if absolute.

He passed through / 5 the three parousias (παρουσία) which I mentioned / before: the flood (κατακλυσμός), and the conflagration, / and the judgement of the archons (ἄρχων) and the powers (δύναμις) / and the authorities (ἐξουσία), to save her (i.e. the race) who went astray (πλανᾶσθαι), /

The mission of Seth: IV 74,9-17

IV 74 ⲧⲟⲧⲉ ⲡ[ⲓⲛⲟϭ] [ⲥⲏⲑ ⲁⲩⲧ]ⲁⲩⲟϥ ⲉⲃⲟⲗ ϩⲓⲧ̣[ⲟⲟⲧⲟⲩ] [ⲙ̅ⲡⲓϥⲧⲟ]ⲟⲩ ⲛ̅ⲛⲟϭ ⲙ̅ⲫⲱⲥⲧ̣[ⲏⲣ ϩ̅ⲙ] ⲡ[ⲟⲩ]ⲱϣⲉ ⲛ̅ⲧⲉ ⲡⲓⲁⲩⲧⲟⲅⲉⲛ[ⲏⲥ ⲙ̅ⲛ] ⲡⲓ̣ⲡⲗⲏⲣⲱⲙⲁ ⲧⲏⲣϥ̅ ⲉⲧ[ⲛ̅ⲧⲁⲩ ϩ̅ⲛ] ⲟⲩϯ ⲛ̅ⲧⲁϥ ⲙ̅ⲛ ⲟⲩϯ ⲙⲉⲧ̣ⲉ [ⲛ̅ⲧⲉ] ⲡⲓⲛⲟϭ ⲛ̅ⲛⲁⲧⲛⲁⲩ ⲉⲣⲟϥ ⲙ̅ⲡⲛ̅[ⲁ] ⲙ̅ⲛ ϯϯⲉ ⲛ̅ⲥⲫⲣⲁⲅⲓⲥ ⲙ̅ⲛ ⲡⲓⲡⲗ[ⲏ]ⲣⲱⲙⲁ̣ ⲧⲏⲣϥ̅·

Then (τότε) the [great] / [Seth] was sent by / [the four] great lights (φωστήρ), [by] / the will of the Autogenes (αὐτογενής) [and] / [their] whole pleroma (πλήρωμα), [by] / a gift and good pleasure [of] / the great invisible Spirit (πνεῦμα), / and the five seals (σφραγίς), and the / whole pleroma (πλήρωμα).

The work of Seth: IV 74,17 - 75,24

ⲉ⟨ϥ⟩ⲥ̣ⲓ̣[ⲛ]ⲉ ⲉⲃⲟⲗ ϩ̅ⲛ̣ ϯ[ϣ]ⲟⲙⲧⲉ ⲙ̅ⲡⲁⲣⲟⲩⲥⲓⲁ ⲉ̣[ⲧⲁⲓ̈ⲣ̅] ϣⲣⲡ̅ ⲛ̅ϫⲟⲟⲩ· ⲉⲃⲟⲗ ⲇⲉ [ϩ̅ⲙ ⲡⲓ] ⲕⲁⲧⲁⲕⲗⲩⲥⲙⲟⲥ ⲙ̅ⲛ ⲡⲓⲣⲱ[ⲕ̅ϩ] ⲙ̅ⲛ ⲡⲓϩⲁⲡ̅ ⲛ̅ⲧⲉ ⲛⲓⲁⲣⲭⲱⲛ ⲙ̣̅[ⲛ] ⲛⲓⲉⲝⲟⲩⲥⲓⲁ ⲙ̅ⲛ ⲛⲓϭⲟⲙ ⲉⲛⲟ[ⲩ]

74,17 MS. reads ⲉⲥⲥⲓ[ⲛ]ⲉ.

<He> passes through / the three parousias (παρουσία) [which I] / mentioned before, through (+ δέ) [the] / flood (κατακλυσμός), and the conflagration, / and the judgement of the archons (ἄρχων) [and] / the authorities (ἐξουσία) and the powers, to save /

III 63

ⲛⲁ ϩⲓⲧⲙ̅ ⲡϩⲱⲧⲡ̈ ⲙ̅ⲡⲕⲟⲥⲙⲟⲥ ⲙⲛ̅
ⲡⲃⲁⲡⲧⲓⲥⲙⲁ ϩⲓⲧⲛ̅ ⲟⲩⲗⲟⲅⲟⲅⲉⲛⲏⲥ ⲛ̅
ⲥⲱⲙⲁ ⲛ̅ⲧⲁϥⲥⲃⲧⲱⲧϥ̅ ⲛⲁϥ ⲛ̅ϭⲓ ⲡⲛⲟϭ
ⲛ̅ⲥⲏⲑ · ϩⲛ̅ ⲟⲩⲙⲩⲥⲧⲏⲣⲓⲟⲛ ⲉⲃⲟⲗ ϩⲓⲧⲟ
ⲟⲧⲥ̅ ⲛ̅ⲧⲡⲁⲣⲑⲉⲛⲟⲥ ⲉⲧⲣⲟⲩϫⲡⲟ ⲛ̅ⲛⲉ
ⲧⲟⲩⲁⲁⲃ ϩⲓⲧⲛ̅ ⲡⲉⲡⲛ̅ⲁ ⲉⲧⲟⲩⲁⲁⲃ · ϩⲓⲧⲛ̅
ϩⲉⲛⲥⲩⲙⲃⲟⲗⲟⲛ ⲛ̅ⲁϩⲟⲣⲁⲧⲟⲛ ⲉⲩϩⲏⲡ
ϩⲛ̅ ⲟⲩϩⲱⲧⲡ ⲙ̅ⲡⲕⲟⲥⲙⲟⲥ ⲉⲡⲕⲟⲥ
ⲙⲟⲥ ϩⲓⲧⲛ̅ ⲡⲁⲡⲟⲧⲁⲥⲥⲉ ⲙ̅ⲡⲕⲟⲥⲙⲟⲥ
ⲙⲛ̅ ⲡⲛⲟⲩⲧⲉ ⲙ̅ⲡⲙⲛ̅ⲧϣⲟⲙⲧⲉ ⲛ̅ⲁⲓⲱⲛ
ⲙⲛ̅ ⲛⲉⲡⲓⲕⲗⲏⲧⲟⲥ ⲛ̅ⲛⲉⲧⲟⲩⲁⲁⲃ ⲙⲛ̅
ⲛⲓⲁϩⲣⲏⲧⲟⲥ ⲙⲛ̅ ⲛⲓⲁⲫⲑⲁⲣⲧⲟⲥ ⲛ̅ⲕⲟⲗ
ⲡⲟⲥ ⲙⲛ̅ ⲡⲛⲟϭ ⲛⲟⲩⲟⲉⲓⲛ ⲙ̅ⲡⲉⲓⲱⲧ̇

63,16 Corr. final ⲥ over ?
19 Corr. ⲧ over ⲣ.
20 Corr. ϩ over ⲣ.

through the reconciliation of the world (*κόσμος*), and / [10] the baptism (*βάπτισμα*) through a Logos-begotten (*λογογενής*) / body (*σῶμα*) which the great Seth / prepared for himself, / secretly (*μυστήριον*) through the virgin (*παρθένος*), in order that the / saints may be begotten by the holy Spirit (*πνεῦμα*), through / [15] invisible (*ἀόρατον*), secret symbols (*σύμβολον*), / through a reconciliation of the world (*κόσμος*) with the world (*κόσμος*), / through the renouncing (*ἀποτάσσεσθαι*) of the world (*κόσμος*) / and the god of the thirteen aeons (*αἰών*), / and (through) the convocations (*ἐπίκλητος*) of the saints, and / [20] the ineffable ones (*ἄρρητος*), and the incorruptible (*ἄφθαρτος*) bosom (*κόλπος*), / and (through) the great light of the Father /

IV 74 ϩⲙ̄ ⲛ̄ⲧⲏ ⲉⲧⲁⲥⲥⲱⲣⲙ̄ ⲉⲃⲟⲗ ϩⲓⲧ̣[ⲛ̄] ⲟⲩϩⲱⲧ̣[ⲡ̄] ⲛ̄ⲕⲟⲥⲙⲟⲥ· ⲙⲛ̄ ⲡ[ⲓϫⲱ] ⲕⲙ̄ ⲛ̄ⲟ[ⲩⲥ]ⲱⲙⲁ· ⲉⲃⲟ[ⲗ] ϩ[ⲓ]ⲧⲙ̣̄ [ⲡⲓ] ϫⲡⲟ ⲛ̄ϣⲁϫⲉ ⲡⲏ ⲉ̣[ⲧ]ⲁϥⲥⲃⲧ[ⲱⲧϥ̄] ⲛ̄ϭⲓ ⲡⲓ[ⲛ]ⲟ̣ϭ ⲥⲏⲑ̄ ϩⲛ̄ ⲟ̣ⲩⲙ[ⲩⲥⲧⲏ]ⲣⲓⲟⲛ ⲉⲃⲟⲗ ϩⲓⲧⲟⲟⲧⲥ̄ [ⲛ̄]ϯⲡⲁⲣⲑ̣[ⲉ]ⲛ̣[ⲟ]ⲥ ⲉⲟⲩⲉϩⲙ̄ ϫⲡⲟ ⲛ̄ⲛⲉⲧⲟ̣[ⲩ][ⲁⲁⲃ· ⲉ]ⲃⲟⲗ ϩⲓⲧⲟ̣ⲟⲧϥ̄ ⲙ̄[ⲡⲡ̄ⲛ̄ⲁ̄ ⲉⲧ']

75 ⲟ[ⲉ]ⲟⲩⲁⲁⲃ ⲙⲛ̄ ϩⲉⲛⲥⲩⲙⲃⲟⲗⲟⲛ ⲛ̄ⲛⲁⲧⲛⲁⲩ ⲉⲣⲟⲟⲩ ⲁ̣ⲩⲱ̣ ⲉⲩϩⲏⲡ' ⲉⲃⲟⲗ ϩⲓⲧⲛ̄ ⲟⲩϩⲱⲧⲃ ⲛ̄[ⲧ]ⲉ̣ ⲟⲩⲕⲟⲥⲙⲟⲥ ⲉⲩⲕⲟⲥⲙⲟⲥ· ⲉⲃⲟⲗ ϩ̣ⲓⲧⲛ̄ ⲟⲩⲁⲡⲟⲧⲁⲅⲏ ⲛ̄ⲧⲉ ⲟⲩⲕⲟⲥⲙⲟⲥ ⲙⲛ̄ ⲡⲛⲟⲩⲧ̣ⲉ ⲛ̄ⲧⲉ ⲡⲓⲙⲛ̄ⲧϣⲟⲙⲧⲉ ⲛ̄ⲛⲉⲱⲛ· ⲉⲃⲟⲗ ϩⲓⲧⲛ̄ ⲟⲩⲧⲱϩⲙ̄ ⲉⲃⲟⲗ ϩⲓⲧⲛ̄ ⲛ[ⲉ]ⲧⲟ̣ⲩⲁⲁⲃ ⲙⲛ̄ ⲛⲓⲁⲧ'ϣⲁϫⲉ ⲙ̄ⲙⲟⲟⲩ̣ ⲙⲛ̄ ⲛⲓⲁⲧ'ϫⲱϩⲙ̄ ⲛ̄ⲕⲟⲩⲟ̣ⲩⲛ̄ϥ ⲛ̄[ⲧⲉ] ⲡⲟⲩⲟⲉⲓⲛ ⲉⲧⲛⲉⲁϥ· ⲡⲏ̣ ⲉⲧ̣[ⲣϣⲣⲡ']

74,24 Or ϩⲱⲧ̄[ⲃ]; see *infra* 75,3.

75, 3 ϩⲱⲧⲃ sound spelling for ϩⲱⲧⲡ'; see also *infra* p. 192. Superlin. stroke on ⲛ̄[ⲧ]ⲉ̣ is in the lacuna.

her (i.e. the race) who went astray, through / cosmic (κόσμος) reconciliation, and the [baptism] / of the body (σῶμα), through [the] / Logos-begotten one, which the great / Seth secretly (μυστήριον) prepared / through the virgin (παρθένος), / to beget again the [saints] / through the holy [Spirit (πνεῦμα),] // *75* and invisible / and secret symbols (σύμβολον), / through the reconciliation of world (κόσμος) / with world (κόσμος), through the / renunciation (ἀποταγή) of the world (κόσμος) and the god / of the thirteen aeons (αἰών), / through convocation by the / saints, the ineffable ones / and the incorruptible bosom [of] / the great light which [pre-]exists /

III 63,22 ⲉⲧⲁϥⲣ̄ϣⲣ̄ⲡ ⲛ̄ϣⲱⲡⲉ ⲙⲛ̄ ⲧⲉϥⲡⲣⲟ
ⲛⲟⲓ̈ⲁ ⲁⲩⲱ ⲁϥⲕⲩⲣⲟⲩ ⲉⲃⲟⲗ ϩⲓⲧⲟⲟⲧⲥ̄
24 ⲛ̄ⲡⲃⲁⲡⲧⲓⲥⲙⲁ ⲉⲧⲟⲩⲁⲁⲃ · ⲉⲧⲟⲩⲁⲧⲃ·
ⲉⲧⲡⲉ ⲉⲃⲟⲗ ϩⲓⲧⲟⲟⲧϥ̄ ⲙ̄ⲡⲓⲁϥⲑⲁⲣⲧⲟⲥ
64 ⲝ̄ⲇ̄
ⲛ̄ⲗⲟⲅⲟⲅⲉⲛⲏⲥ ⲙⲛ̄ ⲓ̄ⲏ̄ⲥ̄ ⲡⲉⲧⲟⲛϩ ⲙⲛ̄
2 ⲡⲉⲛⲧⲁϥϯ ⲙ̄ⲙⲟϥ ϩⲓⲱⲱϥ ⲛ̄ϭⲓ ⲡⲛⲟϭ
ⲛ̄ⲥⲏⲑ · ⲁⲩⲱ ⲁϥⲱϥⲧ̇ ⲛ̄ⲛ̄ⲇⲩⲛⲁⲙⲓⲥ
4 ⲙ̄ⲡⲙⲛ̄ⲧ̇ϣⲟⲙⲧⲉ ⲛ̄ⲁⲓⲱⲛ ⲁⲩⲱ ⲁϥ
ⲕⲩⲣⲟⲩ ⲉⲃⲟⲗ ϩⲓⲧⲟⲟⲧϥ̄ · ⲛ̄ⲛⲉⲧⲁⲅⲉ ⲙⲛ̄
6 ⲛⲉⲧⲁⲡⲁⲅⲉ ⲁϥϩⲟⲡⲗⲓⳅⲉ ⲙ̄ⲙⲟⲟⲩ
ϩⲛ̄ ⲟⲩϩⲟⲡⲗⲟⲛ ⲛ̄ⲥⲟⲟⲩⲛ ⲛ̄ⲧⲉⲓ̈ⲁⲗⲏ
8 ⲑⲉⲓⲁ ϩⲛ̄ ⲟⲩⲇⲩⲛⲁⲙⲓⲥ ⲛ̄ⲁⲧ̇ϫⲣⲟ ⲉⲣⲟⲥ
ⲛ̄ⲧⲉ ⲧⲁϥⲑⲁⲣⲥⲓⲁ

63,22 Corr. ϥ in ⲉⲧⲁϥ over ⲣ.
24 Corr. ⲧ in ⲟⲩⲁⲧⲃ over ⲁ (dittography).
64, 3 Corr. ⲩ in ⲁⲩⲱ over ?, ⲙ over ⲧ.

who pre-existed with his Providence (πρόνοια) / and established (κυροῦν) through her / the holy baptism (βάπτισμα) that surpasses / [25] the heaven, through the incorruptible (ἄφθαρτος), // *64* Logos-begotten (λογογενής) one, even Jesus the living one, even / he whom the great Seth has / put on. And through him he nailed the powers (δύναμις) / of the thirteen aeons (αἰών), and / [5] established (κυροῦν) those who are brought forth (ἄγειν) and / taken away (ἀπάγειν). He armed (ὁπλίζειν) them / with an armor (ὅπλον) of knowledge of this truth (ἀλήθεια), / with an unconquerable power (δύναμις) / of incorruptibility (ἀφθαρσία).

IV 75 ⲛ̣̄ϣ[ⲟ]ⲟⲡ' ϩⲛ̄ ⲟⲩⲡⲣⲟⲛⲟⲓⲁ ⲁⲩⲱ̣ ⲁϥ
12 ⲧⲁϫⲣⲟ ⲙ̄ⲡⲉⲧ'ⲟⲩⲁⲁⲃ ⲉⲃⲟⲗ ϩⲓⲧⲟⲟⲧⲥ̄
ⲙⲛ̄ ⲡⲓⲱⲙⲥ ⲉⲧ'ⲥⲁϩⲣⲁï ⲛ̄ⲛⲓⲡⲏⲩⲉ
14 ⲉⲃⲟⲗ ϩⲓⲧⲟⲟⲧϥ̄ ⲙ̄ⲡⲉⲧ'ⲟⲩⲁⲁⲃ ⲙⲛ̄
ⲡ[ⲓ]ⲁⲧ'ϫⲱϩⲙ· ⲙⲛ̄ ⲓ̅ⲥ̅ ⲡⲏ ⲉⲧⲁⲩϫⲡⲟϥ
16 ϩⲛ̄ ⲟⲩϣⲁϫⲉ [ⲉ]ϥⲟⲛ̄ϩ· ⲡⲏ ⲉⲧⲁϥⲧⲁ
ⲁϥ ϩⲓⲱⲱϥ ⲛ̄ϭⲓ ⲡⲓⲛⲟϭ ⲥⲏⲑ ⲁ[ⲩ]ⲱ̣
18 ⲁϥϯ ⲉⲓϥⲧ' ⲛ̄ⲛⲓϭⲟⲙ ⲛ̄ⲧⲉ ⲡⲓⲙⲛ̄ⲧ'
ϣⲟⲙⲧⲉ ⲛ̄ⲛⲉⲱⲛ ⲁⲩⲱ ⲁϥⲟⲩⲟⲥϥⲟⲩ
20 ⲉⲃⲟⲗ ϩⲓⲧⲟⲟⲧϥ̄· ϣⲁⲩⲛ̄ⲧⲟⲩ ⲁⲩ[ⲱ]
ϣⲁⲩϫⲓⲧⲟⲩ· ⲁⲩⲱ ϣⲁⲩϩⲟⲕⲟⲩ
22 ϩⲛ̄ ⲟⲩϩⲟⲡⲗⲟⲛ ⲛ̄ⲧⲉ ⲡⲥⲟⲟⲩⲛ ⲛ̄ⲧ̣ⲙⲉ
ϩⲛ̄ ⲟⲩϭⲟⲙ ⲛ̄ⲁⲧ'ϫ[ⲱ]ϩⲙ ⲛ̣̄ⲁⲧ'ϫⲣⲟ
24 ⲉⲣⲟⲥ·

in Providence (πρόνοια) and established / through her the holy one / and the baptism that surpasses the heavens, / through the holy one, and / 15 the incorruptible one, even Jesus who has been begotten / by a living word, he whom / the great Seth has put on. And / through him he nailed down the powers of the / thirteen aeons (αἰών), and rendered them / 20 motionless. They are brought (forth) and / taken back, and are armed / with an armor (ὅπλον) of the knowledge of the truth, / with an incorruptible, unconquerable / power.

The list of the bringers of salvation: III 64,9 - 65,26

III 64 ⲁϥⲟⲩⲱⲛϩ ⲛⲁⲩ ⲉ
ⲃⲟⲗ ⲛ̄ϭⲓ ⲡⲛⲟϭ ⲛ̄ⲡⲁⲣⲉⲥⲧⲁⲧⲏⲥ ⲓ̈ⲉⲥⲥⲉⲁ
ⲙⲁⲍⲁⲣⲉⲁ ⲓ̈ⲉⲥⲥⲉⲇⲉⲕⲉⲁ · ⲡⲙⲟⲟⲩ
ⲉⲧⲟⲛϩ · ⲙⲛ̄ ⲛⲓⲛⲟϭ ⲛ̄ⲥⲧⲣⲁⲧⲏⲅⲟⲥ
ⲓ̈ⲁⲕⲱⲃⲟⲥ ⲡⲛⲟϭ ⲙⲛ̄ ⲑⲉⲟⲡⲉⲙ
ⲡⲧⲟⲥ ⲙⲛ̄ ⲓ̈ⲥⲁⲟⲩⲏⲗ ⲙⲛ̄ ⲛⲉⲧϩⲓϫⲛ̄
ⲧⲡⲏⲅⲏ ⲙ̄ⲙⲏⲉ ⲙⲓⲭⲉⲁ ⲙⲛ̄ ⲙⲓⲭⲁⲣ
ⲙⲛ̄ ⲙⲛⲏⲥⲓⲛⲟⲩⲥ ⲙⲛ̄ ⲡⲉⲧϩⲓϫⲙ̄
ⲡϫⲱⲕⲙ̄ ⲛ̄ⲛⲉⲧⲟⲛϩ · ⲙⲛ̄ ⲛⲓⲣⲉϥ
ⲧⲟⲩⲃⲟ ⲙⲛ̄ ⲥⲉⲥⲉⲅ̈ⲅⲉⲛⲫⲁⲣⲁⲅ̈ⲅⲏⲛ
ⲙⲛ̄ ⲛⲉⲧϩⲓϫⲛ̄ ⲙ̄ⲡⲩⲗⲏ ⲛ̄ⲙⲙⲟⲩⲉⲓⲟ
ⲟⲩⲉ ⲙⲓⲭⲉⲩⲥ ⲙⲛ̄ ⲙⲓⲭⲁⲣ ⲙⲛ̄ ⲛⲉⲧ
ϩⲓϫⲙ̄ ⲡⲧⲟⲟⲩ ⲛ̄ⲥⲉⲗⲇⲁⲱ ⲙⲛ̄ ⲛⲉⲗⲁⲓ̈
ⲛⲟⲥ ⲙⲛ̄ ⲛⲉⲛⲡⲁⲣⲁⲗⲏⲙⲡⲧⲱⲣ ⲛ̄

There appeared to them / the great attendant (*παραστάτης*) Yesseus / Mazareus Yessedekeus, the living / water, and the great leaders (*στρατηγός*), / *'Ιάκωβος* the great and Theopemptos / and Isavel, and they who preside over / the spring (*πηγή*) of truth, Micheus and Michar / and Mnesinous, and he who presides over / the baptism of the living, and the / purifiers, and Sesengenpharanges, / and they who preside over the gates (*πύλη*) of the waters, / Micheus and Michar, and they who / preside over the mountain Seldao and Elainos, / and the receivers (*παραλήμπτωρ*) of /

The list of the bringers of salvation: IV 75,24 - 77,?

IV 75,24 ⲁⲩ[ⲱ ⲁⲩ]ⲟⲩⲱⲛϩ ⲛⲁï ⲉⲃⲟⲗ
ⲛⲛⲓⲛ̣ⲟϭ ⲉⲧⲁϩⲉⲣⲁⲧⲟⲩ ïⲉⲥⲉⲁ
26 ⲙⲁⲥⲁⲣⲉⲁ · ïⲉⲥⲥⲉⲇⲉⲕⲉⲁ · ⲡⲓⲙⲟ
ⲟⲩ ⲉⲧⲟⲛϩ ⲙⲛ ⲛⲓⲛⲟϭ ⲛⲥⲁϯ[ⲅⲟⲥ]
28 ⲡⲓⲛⲟϭ ïⲁⲕⲱⲃ ⲙⲛ ⲑⲉⲟⲡ[ⲉⲙⲡⲧⲟⲥ]
76 ⲟⲥ
ⲙⲛ ïⲥ̣ⲁⲟⲩⲏⲗ ⲙⲛ ⲡⲏ ⲉⲧⲕⲏ ⲉϩⲣⲁï
2 ⲉϫⲙ̣ ⲡⲛⲁ ⲙⲏ̣ⲡ̣[..]ⲏ̣ⲗ · ⲙⲛ ⲛⲏ ⲉⲧ
ⲕⲏ ⲉϩⲣⲁï ⲉϫⲛ ⲛⲓⲡⲏⲅⲏ ⲛⲧⲉ ⲧⲙⲉ
4 ⲙⲓⲭⲉⲁ ⲙ[ⲛ] ⲙⲓⲭⲁⲣ ⲙⲛ ⲙⲛⲏⲥⲓⲛⲟⲩ
ⲙⲛ ⲡⲏ ⲉⲧⲕⲏ ⲉϩⲣⲁï ⲉϫⲛ̣ ⲡⲓϫⲱ
6 ⲕⲙ ⲛⲧⲉ ⲛⲉⲧⲟ̣ⲛϩ ⲡⲓⲣⲉϥⲧⲃⲃⲟ
ⲥⲉⲥⲉⲅ̣ⲅⲉⲛⲃⲁⲣⲫⲁⲣⲁⲅⲅⲏⲥ ⲙⲛ
8 [ⲛ]ⲏ ⲉⲧⲕ̣ⲏ ⲉϩⲣⲁï ⲉϫⲛ ⲛⲓⲡⲩⲗⲏ ⲛ
[ⲧⲉ ⲛⲓ]ⲙⲟ̣ⲟⲩ ⲛⲧⲉ ⲡⲓⲱⲛϩ ⲙⲓ̣ⲥⲉⲩⲥ
10 [ⲙⲛ] ⲙⲓⲭⲁⲣ ⲙⲛ ⲛⲏ ⲉⲧⲕⲏ ⲉϩⲣ̣[ⲁ]ï ⲉ
ϫⲛ ⲡⲧⲱⲱⲛϥ ⲥⲉⲗⲇⲁⲱ ⲙⲛ ⲉⲗⲉ
12 ⲛⲟⲥ ⲙⲛ ⲛⲓⲡⲁⲣⲁⲗⲏⲙⲡⲧⲱⲣⲟⲥ

75,27 Superlin. stroke on ⲛϩ is in the lacuna.
76, 2 Or ⲙⲏ̣ⲧ̣[
9 ⲙⲓⲥⲉⲩⲥ for ⲙⲓⲭⲉⲩⲥ; cf. SCHWYZER, *Griechische Grammatik* I, p. 210.

And they revealed / 25 the great attendants to me: Yesseus / Mazareus Yessedekeus, the / living water, and the great leaders (στρατηγός), / the great Ἰακώβ and Theop[emptos] // *76* and Isavel, and he who presides / over the grace, Mep[. .]el, and they who / preside over the springs (πηγή) of the truth, / Micheus and Michar and Mnesinous, / 5 and he who presides over the baptism / of the living, the purifier / Sesengenbarpharanges, and / they who preside over the gates (πύλη) / [of the] waters of life, Micheus / 10 [and] Michar, and they who preside over / the rising, Seldao and Elenos, / and the receivers (παραλήμπτωρ) /

III 64 ⲧⲛⲟϭ ⲛ̄ⲅⲉⲛⲉⲁ ⲛⲁⲫⲑⲁⲣⲧⲟⲛ ⲛ̄{ⲓ}ⲣⲱ
24 ⲙⲉ ⲛ̄ϫⲱⲱⲣⲉ ⟨ⲙ̄⟩ⲡⲛⲟϭ ⲛ̄ⲥⲏⲑ · ⲛ̄ⲇⲓⲁ
ⲕⲟⲛⲟⲥ ⲙ̄ⲡⲉϥⲧⲟⲟⲩ ⲛ̄ⲟⲩⲟⲉⲓⲛ
26 ⲡⲛⲟϭ ⲛ̄ⲅⲁⲙⲁⲗⲓⲏⲗ · ⲡⲛⲟϭ ⲛ̄ⲅⲁⲃⲣⲓ
ⲏⲗ· ⲡⲛⲟϭ ⲥⲁⲙⲃⲗⲱ ⲙ̄ⲛ ⲡⲛⲟϭ

65 ⲝ̣[ⲉ]

ⲛⲁⲃⲣⲁⲥⲁⲝ · ⲙ̄ⲛ ⲛⲉⲧϩⲓϫⲙ̄ ⲡⲣⲏ ⲧⲉϥϩⲓ
2 ⲏ ⲛ̄ⲉⲓ ⲉⲃⲟⲗ ⲟ̄ⲗ̄ⲥ̄ⲏ̄ⲥ̄ ⲙ̄ⲛ ϩⲩⲡⲛⲉⲩⲥ ⲙ̄ⲛ
ϩⲉⲩⲣⲩⲙⲁⲓⲟⲩⲥ ⲙ̄ⲛ ⲛⲉⲧϩⲓϫⲛ̄ ⲧⲉϩⲓⲏ
4 ⲛ̄ϣⲉ ⲉϩⲟⲩⲛ ⲉⲧⲁⲛⲁ{ⲩ}ⲡⲁⲩⲥⲓⲥ ⲙ̄ⲡⲱⲛϩ
ⲛ̄ϣⲁ ⲉⲛⲉϩ · ⲛⲓⲡⲣⲩⲧⲁⲛⲓⲥ ⲙⲓⲝⲁⲛⲑⲏⲣ
6 ⲙ̄ⲛ ⲙⲓⲭⲁⲛⲟⲣⲁ ⲙ̄ⲛ ⲛⲉⲧ̇ϩⲁⲣⲉϩ ⲉⲛⲉ
ⲯⲩⲭⲟⲟⲩⲉ ⲛ̄ⲛ̄ⲥⲱⲧⲡ̄ ⲁⲕⲣⲁⲙⲁⲛ ⲙ̄ⲛ
8 ⲥⲧⲣⲉⲙⲯⲟⲩⲭⲟⲥ ⲙ̄ⲛ ⲧⲛⲟϭ ⲛ̄ⲇⲩⲛⲁⲙⲓⲥ

64,23 MS. has ⲓ squeezed between ⲛ̄ and ⲣ, probably a correction.
65, 5 Corr. ⲛ in ⲛⲓ over ⲡ.
8 Between lines 8 and 9 ⲧⲉⲗⲙⲁⲏⲗ (bis) has inadvertently been left out.

the great race (γενεά), the incorruptible (ἄφθαρτον), / mighty men <of> the great Seth, the / [25] ministers (διάκονος) of the four lights, / the great Gamaliel, the great Gabriel, / the great Samblo, and the great // *65* Abrasax, and they who preside over the sun, its / rising, Olses and Hypneus and / Heurumaious, and they who preside over the / entrance into the rest (ἀνάπαυσις) of eternal / [5] life, the rulers (πρύτανις) Mixanther / and Michanor, and they who guard the / souls (ψυχή) of the elect, Akramas and / Strempsouchos, and the great power (δύναμις) /

IV 76 ⲛ̄ⲧⲉ ϯⲅⲉⲛⲉⲁ ⲉⲧⲟⲩⲁⲁⲃ ⲙ̄ⲛ̄ ⲛⲓ
14 ⲁⲧϫⲱϩⲙ ⲛ̄ⲣⲱⲙⲉ ⲁⲩⲱ ⲉⲧϫⲟ
ⲟⲣ ⲛ̄ⲧⲉ ⲡⲓⲛⲟϭ ⲥⲏⲑ· ⲛⲓⲇ[ⲓ]ⲁ̣ⲕⲱⲛ
16 [ⲛ̄ⲧ]ⲉ ⲡⲓϥⲧⲟⲟⲩ ⲙ̄ⲫⲱⲥⲧⲏⲣ ⲡⲓ
ⲛⲟϭ ⲛ̄ⲅⲁⲙⲁⲗⲓⲏⲗ ⲙ̄ⲛ̄ ⲡⲓⲛⲟϭ ⲛ̄
18 ⲅⲁⲃⲣ[ⲓ]ⲏⲗ ⲙ̄ⲛ̄ ⲡⲓⲛⲟϭ ⲥⲁⲙⲃ̣ⲗⲱ
ⲙ̄ⲛ̄ ⲡⲓⲛⲟϭ ⲁⲃⲣⲁⲥⲁⲝ ⲙ̄ⲛ̄ ⲛⲏ ⲉⲧ
20 ⲕ̣ⲏ ⲉϩⲣⲁï ⲉϫⲛ̄ ϯϩⲓⲏ ⲛ̄ⲉⲓ ⲉⲃⲟⲗ
ⲛ̣̄ⲧⲉ ⲡⲣⲏ̣ ⲟⲗⲥⲏⲥ ⲙ̄ⲛ̄ ⲩ̈ⲙⲛⲉⲟⲥ
22 ⲙ̄ⲛ̄ ⲉⲩ̣[ⲣ]ⲩⲙⲉ̣[ⲟ]ⲩ̣[ⲥ] ⲙ̄ⲛ̄ ⲛⲏ ⲉⲧ
ⲕⲏ ⲉϩⲣⲁï ⲉϫⲛ̄ ⲡⲓ̣[ⲙⲟ]ⲉⲓⲧ ⲛ̄ⲉⲓ ⲉ
24 ϩⲟⲩⲛ ⲉⲡⲙ̄ⲧⲟⲛ ⲛ̄ⲧⲉ ⲡⲓ̣ⲱⲛ̄ϩ
ϣⲁ ⲉⲛⲉ̣ϩ ⲫⲣⲓⲧⲁⲛ̣ⲓ̣ⲥ̣ ⲙ̄ⲛ̣̄ ⲙⲓⲕⲝⲁⲛ
26 [ⲑⲏ]ⲣⲁ̣ ⲙ̄ⲛ̄ ⲙⲓⲭⲁ̣ⲛⲟⲣⲁ ⲙ̄ⲛ̄ ⲛⲓ
[ⲣⲉϥⲁ]ⲣ[ⲉ]ϩ ⲛ̄ⲧⲉ ⲛⲓⲯⲩⲭⲏ ⲉⲧϩⲟⲧⲃ
77 [ⲟⲍ]
ⲁⲕⲣⲁⲙⲁⲛ ⲙ̄ⲛ̄ ⲥⲧ'ⲣ'ⲉⲙⲯⲟⲩⲭ[ⲟⲥ]
2 ⲙ̄ⲛ̄ ϯⲛⲟϭ ⲛ̄ϭⲟⲙ [ⲧⲉⲗⲙ]ⲁⲭⲁⲏ[ⲗ]

76,15 ⲓ has flaked off.
18 ⲓ has flaked off.

of the holy race (*γενεά*) and the / incorruptible and mighty men / of the great Seth, the ministers (*διάκων*) / [of] the four lights (*φωστήρ*), the / great Gamaliel, and the great / Gabriel, and the great Samblo, / and the great Abrasax, and they who / preside over the rising / of the sun, Olses and Umneos / and Eurumaious, and they who / preside over the entrance / into the rest of eternal / life, Phritanis and Mixanther / and Michanor, and the / [guardians] of the slain souls (*ψυχή*), // 77 Akramas and Strempsouchos, / and the great power [Telm]achael /

III 65 ϩⲏⲗⲓ ϩⲏⲗⲓ ⲙⲁⲭⲁⲣ ⲙⲁⲭⲁⲣ ⲥⲏⲑ ⲙⲛ̄
ⲡⲛⲟϭ ⲛ̄ⲁϩⲟⲣⲁⲧⲟⲥ ⲛ̄ⲁⲕⲁⲗⲏⲧⲟⲛ ⲛ̄ⲁⲧⲟ
ⲛⲟⲙⲁⲍⲉ ⲙ̄ⲙⲟϥ ⲙ̄ⲡⲁⲣⲑⲉⲛⲓⲕⲟⲛ ⲙ̄
ⲡⲛ̄ⲁ̄ ⲙⲛ̄ ⲧⲥⲓⲅⲏ ⲙⲛ̄ ⲡⲛⲟϭ ⲛ̄ⲟⲩⲟⲉⲓⲛ
ϩⲁⲣⲙⲟⲍⲏⲗ · ⲡⲙⲁ ⲙ̄ⲡⲁⲩⲧⲟⲅⲉⲛⲏⲥ ⲉ
ⲧⲟⲛϩ ⲡⲛⲟⲩⲧⲉ ⲛ̄ⲧⲙⲏⲉ ⲙⲛ̄ ⟨ⲡ⟩ⲉⲧ{ⲛ}ⲛ̄ⲙ
ⲙⲁϥ ⲡⲁⲫⲑⲁⲣⲧⲟⲥ ⲛ̄ⲣⲱⲙⲉ ⲁⲇⲁⲙⲁⲥ ·
ⲡⲙⲉϩⲥⲛⲁⲩ ⲟⲣⲟⲓ̈ⲁⲏⲗ ⲡⲙⲁ ⲙ̄ⲡⲛⲟϭ
ⲛ̄ⲥⲏⲑ· ⲙⲛ̄ ⲓ̄ⲥ̄ ⲡⲁ ⲡⲱⲛϩ· ⲙⲛ̄ ⲡⲉⲛⲧⲁϥ
ⲉ̄ⲓ̄ ⲁϥⲥⲧⲁⲩⲣⲟⲩ ⲙ̄ⲡⲉⲧϩⲙ̄ ⲡⲛⲟⲙⲟⲥ
ⲡⲙⲉϩϣⲟⲙⲛ̄ⲧ ⲇⲁⲩⲉⲓⲑⲉ ⲡⲙⲁ ⲛ̄ⲛ̄
ϣⲏⲣⲉ ⲙ̄ⲡⲛⲟϭ ⲛ̄ⲥⲏⲑ · ⲡⲙⲉϩϥⲧⲟⲟⲩ
ⲏⲗⲉⲗⲏⲑ· ⲡⲙⲁ ⲉⲧⲉⲣⲉⲛ̄ⲯⲩⲭⲟⲟⲩⲉ
ⲛ̄ⲛ̄ϣⲏⲣⲉ ⲙ̄ⲧⲟⲛ ⲙ̄ⲙⲟⲟⲩ ⲛ̄ϩⲏⲧϥ ·
ⲡⲙⲉϩϯⲟⲩ ⲓ̈ⲱⲏⲗ ⲡⲉⲧϩⲓϫⲙ̄ ⲡⲣⲁⲛ
ⲙ̄ⲡⲉⲧⲟⲩⲛⲁⲧⲁⲁⲥ ⲛⲁϥ ⲉϫⲱⲕⲙ̄ ϩⲙ̄
ⲡⲃⲁⲡⲧⲓⲥⲙⲁ ⲉⲧⲟⲩⲁⲁⲃ ⲉⲧⲟⲩⲁⲧⲃ̄ ⲉⲧⲡⲉ
ⲡⲓⲁⲫⲑⲁⲣⲧⲟⲥ

65, 14 MS. reads ⲛ.
26 Corr. ⲟ over ⲓ.

Heli Heli Machar Machar Seth, and / the great, invisible (ἀόρατος), uncallable (ἄκλητον), / unnameable (-ὀνομάζειν), virginal (παρθενικόν) / Spirit (πνεῦμα), and the silence (σιγή), and the great light / Harmozel, the place of the living Autogenes (αὐτογενής), / the God of the truth, and ⟨he⟩ who is with / him, the incorruptible (ἄφθαρτος) man Adamas, / the second, Oroiael, the place of the great / Seth, and Jesus, who possesses the life and who came / and crucified (σταυροῦν) that which is in the law (νόμος), / the third, Davithe, the place of the / sons of the great Seth, the fourth, / Eleleth, the place where the souls (ψυχή) / of the sons are resting, / the fifth, Yoel, who presides over the name / of him to whom it will be granted to baptize with / the holy baptism (βάπτισμα) that surpasses the heaven, / the incorruptible (ἄφθαρτος) one.

IV 77 ⲧⲉⲗⲙⲁⲭⲁⲏⲗ ⲏⲗⲓ ⲏ̣ⲗⲓ ⲙⲁⲭⲁⲣ
4 ⲙⲁⲭⲁⲣ ⲥⲏⲑ ⲙⲛ̣ ⲡⲓⲛⲟϭ ⲛⲛⲁ̣[ⲧ]
ⲛ̣ⲁⲩ ⲉⲣ[ⲟ]ϥ ⲁⲩⲱ ⲛⲁⲧϫⲁϩⲙ[ⲉϥ ⲛ]
6 ⲁⲧϯ ⲣⲁⲛ̣ ⲉⲣⲟϥ· ⲉⲧⲉ ⲡⲁϊ ϩⲛ ⲟⲩ
ⲡ[ⲛ]ⲁ ⲙⲛ ⲟⲩⲥⲓⲅⲏ ⲙⲛ ⲡⲓⲛⲟ̣ϭ [ⲛ]
8 ⲫⲱⲥⲧⲏⲣ ⲁⲣⲙⲟⲍⲏⲗ ⲡ[ⲓⲙⲁ] ⲉⲧ̣[ϥⲙ]
ⲙⲟϥ ⲛϭⲓ ⲡⲓⲁⲩⲧⲟⲅ̣[ⲉ]ⲛ̣[ⲏⲥ ⲉ]ⲧⲟⲛ[ϩ]
10 ⲡⲛ[ⲟ]ⲩⲧⲉ ϩⲛ ⲟⲩⲙⲛⲧⲙⲉ ⲉϥ[ⲛ]ⲙ̣
ⲙⲁϥ ⲛϭⲓ ⲡⲓⲁⲧϫⲱϩⲙ ⲛⲣⲱⲙⲉ̣
12 ⲁⲇⲁⲙⲁⲥ ⲙⲛ ⲟⲣⲟϊⲁⲏⲗ ⲡⲓⲙⲁ [ⲉⲧϥ]
ⲙⲙⲁⲩ ⲛϭⲓ ⲡⲓⲛⲟϭ ⲥⲏⲑ ⲙⲛ ⲓ̣[ⲥ]
14 ⲛⲧⲉ ⲡⲱⲛϩ· ⲡⲏ ⲉⲧⲁϥⲉ͡ⲓ ⲁⲩⲱ ⲁ[ϥ]
ⲉⲓϣⲉ̣ ⲙ̣ⲡⲏ ⲉⲧϩⲁ ⲡ̣[ⲛ]ⲟ̣ⲙⲟⲥ
16 ⲡⲓⲙⲉϩϣⲟⲙⲉⲧ ⲁ̣[ⲩⲉⲓⲑⲉ ⲡⲓⲙⲁ]
ⲉⲧⲟⲩⲙⲟⲧⲛ ⲙⲙⲟⲟ̣[ⲩ] ⲛϩⲏⲧ[ϥ ⲛϭⲓ]
18 ⲛϣⲏ̣ⲣⲉ ⲙⲡⲓⲛⲟ[ϭ] ⲥⲏⲑ· ⲡ̣ⲓ̣ⲙ̣[ⲉϩ]
ϥⲧⲟⲟⲩ ⲏⲗⲏⲗⲏⲑ [ⲡⲓ]ⲙⲁ ⲉ̣[
20 ..[..]...ⲩ[
21 ff. are lost.

Telmachael Eli Eli Machar / Machar Seth, and the great, / 5 invisible and incorruptible, / unnameable one, who is in / spirit (πνεῦμα) and silence (σιγή), and the great / light (φωστήρ) Armozel, the [place] where / the living Autogenes (αὐτογενής) is, / 10 the God in truth, with whom is / the incorruptible man / Adamas, and Oroiael, the place [where] / the great Seth is, and [Jesus] / of the life, he who came and / 15 crucified that which is under the law (νόμος), / the third, [Davithe, the place] / where the sons of the / great Seth rest, the / fourth, Eleleth, [the] place [where] / (lines 20-?)

The certainty of salvation in the present: III 65,26 - 66,8

III 65,26 ⲁⲗⲗⲁ ϫⲛ̄ ⲛ̄ϯⲛⲟⲩ

66 ⲝⲋ

ϩⲓⲧⲙ̄ ⲡⲓⲣⲱⲙⲉ ⲛ̄ⲁⲫⲑⲁⲣⲧⲟⲥ ⲡⲟⲓ

2 ⲙⲁⲏⲗ · ⲙⲛ̄ ⲛⲉⲧⲙ̄ⲡϣⲁ ⲛ̄ⲉⲡⲓⲕⲗⲏⲥⲓⲥ

ⲛⲁⲡⲟⲧⲁⲝⲓⲥ ⲛ̄ⲧϯⲉ ⲛ̄ⲥⲫⲣⲁⲅⲓⲥ ϩⲙ̄

4 ⲡⲓⲃⲁⲡⲧⲓⲥⲙⲁ ⲙ̄ⲡⲏⲅⲏ ⲛⲉⲉⲓ ⲉⲩⲛⲁ

ⲥⲟⲩⲛ̄ ⲛⲉⲩⲡⲁⲣⲁⲗⲏⲙⲡⲧⲱⲣ · ⲛ̄ⲑⲉ

6 ⲉⲧ̄ⲥ̄ⲧⲥⲁⲃⲟ ⲙ̄ⲙⲟⲟⲩ ⲉⲣⲟⲟⲩ ⲛ̄ⲥⲉ

ⲥⲟⲩⲱⲛⲟⲩ ⲉⲃⲟⲗ ϩⲓⲧⲟⲟⲧⲟⲩ ⲛⲁϊ

8 ⲛ̄ⲛⲉⲩϫⲓ ϯⲡⲉ ⲙ̄ⲡⲙⲟⲩ

66, 2 Corr. ⲙ̄ⲛ̄ⲛⲉ over erased word beginning with ⲛ̄ⲛ. ⲧⲙ̄ written above the line. ⲡϣⲁ over ϣⲉⲉ.

3 Corr. ⲁⲡⲟ over ⲉⲡⲓⲕ (dittography).

7 Corr. ⲧⲟⲩ over ⲧϥ̄.

But (ἀλλά) from now on // *66* through the incorruptible (ἄφθαρτος) man Poimael, / and they who are worthy of (the) invocation (ἐπίκλησις), / the renunciations (ἀπόταξις) of the five seals (σφραγίς) in / the spring (πηγή)–baptism (βάπτισμα), these will / [5] know their receivers (παραλήμπτωρ) as / they are instructed about them, and they will / know them (or: be known) by them. These / will by no means taste death.

Hymnic section (part I): III 66,8-22

8 ⲓⲏ ⲓⲉⲩⲥ

ⲏⲱ ⲟⲩ ⲏⲱ ⲱⲩⲁ · ⲁⲗⲏⲑⲱⲥ ⲁⲗⲏⲑⲱⲥ

10 ⲓⲉⲥⲥⲉⲩ ⲙⲁⲍⲁⲣⲉⲩ ⲓⲉⲥⲥⲉⲇⲉⲕⲉⲩ

ⲡⲙⲟⲟⲩ ⲉⲧⲟⲛϩ ⲡⲁⲗⲟⲩ ⲙ̄ⲡⲁⲗⲟⲩ

66, 9 Corr. first ⲑ over ⲗ (dittography).

ⲓⲏ ⲓⲉⲩⲥ / ⲏⲱ ⲟⲩ ⲏⲱ ⲱⲩⲁ! Really truly (ἀληθῶς ἀληθῶς), / [10] O Yesseus Mazareus Yessedekeus, / O living water, O child of the child, /

The certainty of salvation in the present: IV 77,? - 78,10

IV 78 [ⲟ̅]ⲏ
[. . .]ⲛ ⲉⲃⲟⲗ ϩⲓⲧⲟⲟⲧϥ̅ ⲙ̅ⲡⲏ ⲉⲧ'
[ⲟⲩ]ⲁ̣ⲁ̣ⲃ̣ ⲁ[ⲩⲱ ⲛ̅ⲁ]ⲧ̣'ϫⲱϩⲙ ⲡⲓⲙⲁⲏⲗ
[ⲙ̅ⲛ̅] ⲛ̣ⲏ ⲉⲧⲛ̅ⲡ̣ϣⲁ ⲛ̅ⲛⲓϫⲱⲕ̅ⲙ̅
[ⲛ̅ⲧ]ⲉ ϯⲁⲡⲟⲧⲁⲅⲏ ⲙ̅ⲛ̅ ⲛ̣ⲓⲥⲫⲣⲁ̣
[ⲅⲓⲥ ⲛ̅]ⲛ̣ⲁⲧ'ϣⲁϫⲉ ⲙ̅ⲙⲟ[ⲟ]ⲩ ⲛ̅ⲧⲉ
[ⲡⲉ]ⲩ̣ϫⲱⲕ̅ⲙ̅· [ⲛ]ⲁ̈ⲓ ⲁⲩⲥⲟⲩⲱⲛ
[ⲛⲉ]ⲩⲡ̣ⲁⲣⲁⲗⲏⲙⲁⲱⲣⲟⲥ ϩⲱ̣ⲥ
[ⲁⲩ]ⲧ̣ⲥ̣[ⲃⲟⲟ]ⲩ ⲉ̣ⲣⲟⲟⲩ ⲉⲁⲩⲉⲓⲙⲉ
[ⲉⲃⲟⲗ ϩⲓⲧ]ⲟ̣ⲟ̣ⲧⲟⲩ ⲁⲩⲱ ⲛ̅ⲛ[ⲉ]ⲩ
[ϫⲓ] ϯ̣ⲡ̣ⲉ ⲙ̅ⲡⲙⲟⲩ :

78,1-10 Part of the text has become illegible due to flaking.

[ ] // *78* [ ] through him who / [is holy and in]corruptible, Poimael, / [and] those who are worthy of the baptisms / [of] the renunciation (ἀποταγή) and the / [5] ineffable seals (σφραγίς) of / [their] baptism, these have known / [their] receivers (παραλήμπτωρ) as (ὡς) / they [have learned] about them, having known / [through] them, and they shall not / [10] taste death.

Hymnic section (part I): IV 78,10 - 79,3

ⲓ̈ⲉⲥ̣ⲥ̣ⲉⲟⲥ
[ⲟⲏ]ⲱ ⲏⲟⲩⲱ ⲱⲩⲁ ϩ̅ⲛ ⲟⲩⲙ̅ⲛ̅
[ⲧⲙ]ⲉ ⲛⲁⲙⲉ ⲓ̈ⲉⲥⲥⲉⲟⲥ ⲙⲁⲍⲁⲣⲉⲟⲥ
[ⲓ̈ⲉⲥⲥ]ⲉ̣ⲇⲉⲕⲉⲟⲥ ⲡⲓⲙⲟⲟ̣ⲩ ⲉⲧⲟⲛϩ̅
[ⲡ]ⲁ̣ⲗ̣[ⲟ]ⲩ ⲛ̅ⲧⲉ ⲡⲁⲗⲟ̣ⲩ· ⲡ̣[ⲓⲣ]ⲁⲛ

Yesseus / [. ⲏ]ⲱ ⲏⲟⲩⲱ ⲱⲩⲁ, really / truly, O Yesseus Mazareus / [Yess]edekeus, O living water, / [O child] of the child, [O] name /

III 66,12 ⲡⲣⲁⲛ ⲉⲑⲁⲉⲟⲟⲩ ⲁⲗⲏⲑⲱⲥ ⲁⲗⲏⲑⲱⲥ
ⲁⲓⲱⲛⲟⲱⲛ ⲓⲓⲓⲓ ⲏⲏⲏⲏ ⲉⲉⲉⲉ ⲟⲟ
14 ⲟⲟ ⲩⲩⲩⲩ ⲱⲱⲱⲱ ⲁⲁⲁⲁ{ⲁ} ⲁ
ⲗⲏⲑⲉⲥ ⲁⲗⲏⲑⲱⲥ ⲏⲓ ⲁⲁⲁⲁ ⲱⲱ
16 ⲱⲱ ⲡⲉⲧϣⲟⲟⲡ̄ ⲉⲧⲛⲁⲩ ⲉⲛⲁⲓⲱⲛ
ⲁⲗⲏⲑⲉⲥ ⲁⲗⲏⲑⲱⲥ ⲁⲉⲉ ⲏⲏⲏ ⲓⲓⲓⲓ
18 ⲩⲩⲩⲩⲩⲩ ⲱ ⲱ ⲱ ⲱ ⲱ ⲱ ⲱ ⲱ
ⲡⲉⲧϣⲟⲟⲡ̄ ⲛ̄ϣⲁ ⲁⲛⲏϩⲉ ⲛ̄ⲉⲛⲉϩ
20 ⲁⲗⲏⲑⲉⲥ ⲁⲗⲏⲑⲱⲥ ⲓⲏⲁ ⲁⲓⲱ ϩⲙ̄
ⲫⲏⲧ ⲡⲉⲧϣⲟⲟⲡ̄ ⲩⲁⲉⲓ ⲉⲓⲥⲁⲉⲓ
22 ⲉⲓⲟⲉⲓ ⲉⲓⲟⲥⲉⲓ

66,14 The scribe probably wrote one ⲁ too many.

O glorious name, really truly (*ἀληθῶς ἀληθῶς*), / *αἰὼν ὁ ὤν*, ⲓⲓⲓⲓ ⲏⲏ ⲏⲏ ⲉⲉⲉⲉ ⲟⲟ/ⲟⲟ ⲩⲩⲩⲩ ⲱⲱⲱⲱ ⲁⲁⲁⲁ{ⲁ}, really (*ἀληθές*) / truly (*ἀληθῶς*), ⲏⲓ ⲁⲁⲁⲁ ⲱⲱ/ⲱⲱ, O existing one who sees the aeons (*αἰών*)! / Really truly (*ἀληθὲς ἀληθῶς*), ⲁⲉⲉ ⲏⲏⲏ ⲓⲓⲓⲓ / ⲩⲩⲩⲩⲩⲩ ⲱⲱⲱⲱⲱⲱⲱⲱ, / who is eternally eternal, / really truly (*ἀληθὲς ἀληθῶς*), ⲓⲏⲁ ⲁⲓⲱ in / the heart, who exists, ⲩ *ἀεὶ εἰς ἀεί, εἶ ὃ εἶ, εἶ ὅς εἶ*!

Hymnic section (part II): III 66,22 - 68,1

22 ⲡⲉⲉⲓⲛⲁϭ ⲛ̄ⲣⲁⲛ
ⲉⲧⲛ̄ⲧⲁⲕ ϩⲓϫⲱⲉⲓ ⲡⲓⲁⲧϣⲱⲱⲧ̄
24 ⲛ̄ⲁⲩⲧⲟⲅⲉⲛⲏⲥ ⲡⲁï ⲉⲧⲙ̄ⲡⲁⲃⲟⲗ ⲁⲛ
ⲉⲉⲓⲛⲁⲩ ⲉⲣⲟⲕ ⲡⲓⲁⲧ̄ⲛⲁⲩ ⲉⲣⲟϥ ⲛ̄

66,23 Corr. first ⲱ written above crossed out ⲟ.
24 Corr. ⲉ in ⲉⲧⲙ̄ over ⲛ.

This great name / of thine is upon me, O self-begotten (*αὐτογενής*) Perfect one, who art not outside me. / I see thee, O thou who art invisible /

66,24f. Or: Thou who art not outside me, I see thee.

IV 78 [ⲛ̄ⲧⲉ ⲛⲓ]ⲉ̣[ⲟⲟⲩ] ⲧ̣ⲏⲣⲟⲩ ϩⲛ̄ ⲟⲩⲙ̄ⲛ

16 [ⲧⲙ]ⲉ ⲛ̣ⲁ̣[ⲙⲉ] ⲡ̣ⲉⲧϣⲟⲟ̣ⲡ̄ ϣⲁ ⲉ

[ⲛ]ⲉ̣ϩ ⲓⲓⲓⲓ [ⲏ]ⲏ̣ⲏⲏ ⲉⲉⲉⲉ̣ ⲟ̣ⲟⲟⲟ

18 [ⲩⲩ]ⲩ̣[ⲩ] ⲱⲱⲱⲱ ⲁⲁⲁⲁ ϩ̣[ⲛ]

[ⲟⲩⲙ̄ⲛⲧⲙⲉ ⲛⲁ]ⲙ[ⲉ] ⲟ̣ⲏ̣[ⲓ ⲁⲁⲁⲁ]

20 ff. are lost.

79 [ⲟⲑ]

ⲉⲛⲉϩ ⲉⲧϣⲟⲟⲡ̄ ϩⲛ̄ [ⲡⲓϩⲏⲧ]

2 ⲡⲓϣⲁ ⲉⲛⲉϩ · ⲩ[ⲁⲉⲓ ⲉⲓⲥⲁⲉⲓ]

ⲉ[ⲓⲟ] ⲉⲓ̣ⲉⲓ ⲟⲥⲉ[ⲓ·

79, 1 ⲡⲓϩⲏⲧ is too short. ⲧⲕⲁⲣⲇⲓⲁ fits well but is not attested in Coptic.

15 [of] all [the glories], really / [truly], who exists eternally, / [ⲓⲓⲓⲓ ⲏⲏⲏ]ⲏ ⲉⲉⲉⲉ ⲟⲟⲟⲟ / [ⲩⲩⲩⲩ] ⲱⲱⲱⲱ ⲁⲁⲁⲁ, / [really truly, ⲟⲏⲓ ⲁⲁⲁⲁ,] / (lines 20-end) // *79* eternal who is in [the heart,] / O Eternal one, ⲩ [ἀεὶ εἰς ἀεί,] / εἶ [ὃ] εἶ, εἶ ὃς εἶ.

Hymnic section (part II): IV 79,3 - 80,15

ⲡⲉⲓ̈ⲛⲟϭ ⲛ̄ⲣⲁⲛ]

4 ⲟⲩ[.. ⲟ]ⲩⲙⲉⲣⲟ̣[ⲥ

ⲧⲙⲏ[...] ⲁⲓ̈ⲟⲩ[ⲡⲓⲁ]

6 ⲧ̣ⲣϩⲁⲉ· ⲉⲩⲭⲡⲟ ⲉ̣[ⲃⲟⲗ ⲙ̄ⲙⲟϥ ⲙⲁⲩ]

ⲁⲁϥ ⲡⲉ̣ ⲉⲩⲉⳅ[ⲟⲩⲥⲓⲁ ⲉⲃⲟⲗ ⲙ̄]

8 ⲙⲟϥ ⲙⲁⲩⲁⲁϥ ⲡⲉ ⲡ̣[ⲏ ⲉⲧⲉ ⲛ̄ⲛⲁⲧ]

ⲛⲁⲩ ⲉ̣[ⲣ]ⲟ̣ϥ ⲥⲁⲃⲟⲗ ⲙ̄ⲙ̣[ⲟⲓ̈ ⲡⲏ ⲉⲧⲉ]

[This great name] / [ ] a part (μέρος) [ ] / 5 the [, O] / Perfect one who art [self-] begotten / (and) autonomous (ἐξουσία), / [who art in]visible / except to [me, who art] /

III 66,26 ⲛⲁϩⲣ̄ⲛ ⲟⲩⲟⲛ ⟨ⲛ⟩ⲓⲙ ⲛⲓⲙ ⲅⲁⲣ ⲡⲉⲧⲛⲁϣ
ⲭⲱⲣⲓ ⲙ̄ⲙⲟⲕ ϩ̄ⲛ ⲕⲉⲥⲙⲏ ⲧⲉⲛⲟⲩ
67 ⲝⲍ
ϫⲉ ⲁⲉⲓⲥⲟⲩⲱⲛⲕ ⲁⲉⲓⲙⲟⲩϫⲧ̇ ⲙ̄ⲙⲟ
2 ⲉⲓ ⲉⲡⲉⲧⲉ ⲙⲉϥϣⲓⲃⲉ ⲁⲉⲓϩⲟⲡⲗⲓⲍⲉ
ⲙ̄ⲙⲟⲉⲓ ϩ̄ⲛ ⲟⲩϩⲟⲡⲗⲟⲛ ⲛ̄ⲟⲩⲟⲉⲓⲛ
4 ⲁⲉⲓⲣ̄ⲟⲩⲟⲉⲓⲛ ⲛⲉⲣⲉⲧⲙⲁⲁⲩ ⲅⲁⲣ ⲙ̄
ⲡⲙⲁ ⲉⲧⲙ̄ⲙⲁⲩ ⲉⲧⲃⲉ ϯⲙⲛ̄ⲧⲥⲁⲉⲓ
6 ⲉ ⲉⲧⲛⲉⲥⲱⲥ ⲛ̄ⲧⲉ ⲡⲉϩⲙⲟⲧ̇ ⲉⲧⲃⲉ
ⲡⲉⲓ̈ ⲁⲉⲓⲡⲱⲣϣ ⲛ̄ⲛⲁϭⲓϫ ⲉⲃⲟⲗ ⲉⲩ
8 ⲕⲏⲃ · ⲁⲉⲓϫⲓ ⲙⲟⲣⲫⲏ ϩ̄ⲙ ⲡⲕⲩⲕⲗⲟⲥ
ⲛ̄ⲧⲙⲛ̄ⲧⲣ̄ⲙⲙⲁⲟ ⲙ̄ⲡⲟⲩⲟⲉⲓⲛ ⲉϥϩ̄ⲛ
10 ⲕⲟⲩⲟⲩⲛⲧ̇ ⲉϥϯ ⲙⲟⲣⲫⲏ ⲙ̄ⲡⲓⲁⲧⲟ
ⲛ̄ϫⲡⲟ ϩ̄ⲙ ⲡⲟⲩⲟⲉⲓⲛ ⲉⲧⲉ ⲙⲛ̄ ⲉⲛⲕⲗⲏ
12 ⲙⲁ ϫⲓ ⲉϩⲟⲩⲛ ⲉⲣⲟϥ ϯⲛⲁϫⲱ ⲙ̄ⲡⲉ
ⲕⲉⲟⲟⲩ ⲁⲗⲏⲑⲱⲥ ϫⲉ ⲁⲉⲓⲣ̄ⲭⲱⲣⲓ ⲙ̄
14 ⲙⲟⲕ ⲥ̣ⲟⲩ ⲓ̄ⲏ̄ⲥ̄ ⲓ̄ⲇ̄ⲉ̄ ⲁ̄ⲉ̄ⲓ̄ⲱ̄ ⲁ̄ⲉ̄ⲓ̄ⲉ̄ ⲟ̄ⲓ̄ⲥ̄ ⲱ̄

66,26 Corr. ⲉ over ϩ?
67, 1 Corr. first ⲓ over ⲥ.
14 Corr. ⲥⲟⲩ over erasure. ⲛ̄ faintly written above the ⲩ.

to everyone. For (γάρ) who will be able / to comprehend (χωρεῖν) thee in another tongue? Now // *67* that I have known thee, I have mixed / myself with the immutable. I have armed (ὁπλίζειν) / myself with an armor (ὅπλον) of light; / I have become light. For (γάρ) the Mother was at / that place because of the / splendid beauty of grace. Therefore / I have stretched out my hands while they were / folded. I was shaped (μορφή) in the circle (κύκλος) / of the riches of the light which is in / my bosom, which gives shape (μορφή) to the many / begotten ones in the light into which no complaint (ἔγκλημα) / reaches. I shall declare thy / glory truly (ἀληθῶς), for I have comprehended (χωρεῖν) / thee, ⲥⲟⲩ ⲓⲏⲥ ⲓⲇⲉ ⲁⲉⲓⲱ ⲁⲉⲓⲉ ⲟⲓⲥ ⲱ̑ /

67, 7 Or: spread out my hands which were folded.

IV 79,10 ⲛ̄ⲛⲁⲧⲛⲁ̣ⲩ ⲉⲣⲟϥ ⲛ̄ⲛ[ⲟⲩⲟⲛ ⲛⲓⲙ·]
ⲟⲩ ⲅⲁⲣ ⲡⲉⲧ'ϣ⟨ⲱ⟩ⲡ̣' [ⲙ̄ⲙⲟⲕ ϩ̄ⲛ ⲟⲩ]
12 ⲥⲙⲏ ⲙ̄ⲛ ⲟⲩⲥⲙⲟⲩ [ⲉⲁⲓ̈ⲥⲟⲩⲱⲛ̄ⲕ]
ⲁⲛⲟⲕ ϯⲛⲟⲩ ⲁⲓ̈ⲙⲟⲩ[ϫ̄ⲧ̄' ⲙ̄ⲛ ⲡⲉⲕ]
14 ⲧⲱϭⲉ· ⲁⲩⲱ [ⲁ]ⲓ̈[ϩⲱⲱⲕ ⲙ̄ⲙⲟⲓ̈]
ⲁⲓ̈ϣⲱⲡ̣ⲉ̣ [ϩ̄]ⲛ ⲟ[ⲩϩⲟⲡⲗⲟⲛ ⲛ̄ⲧⲉ ⲡⲓ]
16 ϩⲙⲟⲧ' ⲙ̄ⲛ ⲡⲓⲟⲩ[ⲟⲉⲓⲛ ⲁⲓ̈ⲣ̄ⲟⲩⲟⲉⲓⲛ]
ⲁⲩⲱ ⲉⲃ̣ⲟⲗ ϩ̄ⲓ̄ⲧⲟⲟ̣[ⲧϥ̄ ⲁⲓ̈ⲡⲱⲣ̄ϣ ⲛ̄]
18 ⲛⲁϭⲓϫ [ⲉⲃ]ⲟⲗ ⲉ̣[ⲩⲕⲏⲃ· ⲁⲩⲱ ⲁⲓ̈ϫⲓ]
ⲙⲟⲣⲫⲏ̣[. .]. ⲛ[
20 ⲛ̣̄ⲛⲟⲩⲕ̣ⲁⲗⲩ[ⲙⲙⲁ ⲛ̄ⲧⲉ ϯⲙ̄ⲛⲧⲣ̄ⲙ]
ⲙⲁⲟ ⲉⲥⲕⲱⲧ̣[ⲉ
22 ⲛ̄ⲟⲩⲙⲏ[ⲧⲣⲁ
ϩ̣̄ⲛ ⲟⲩⲉⲓⲛ[ⲉ
24 [
ϩ̄ⲛ ⲟⲩⲙ̄ⲛⲧ[ⲙⲉ ϫⲉ ⲁⲓ̈ⲣ̄ⲭⲱⲣⲓ ⲙ̄]
26 ⲙⲟⲕ ⲓ̄ⲥ̄ ⲛ̄ⲧⲉ ⲡⲏ ⲉⲧ̣'[
ⲏ̄ⲉ̄ⲉ̄ ⲁ̄ⲓ̄ⲉ̄ⲉ̄ ⲟ̄ⲓ̄ⲥ̄ [ⲱ

79,11 MS. reads ϣⲟⲟⲡ.
25 Superlin. stroke on ⲙ̄ⲛ is in the lacuna.

[10] invisible to [everyone]. / For (γάρ) who comprehends [thee in] / voice and praise? [Having known thee] / I now have mixed [with thy] / steadfastness, and [I have armed myself;] / [15] I have come to be in [an armor (ὅπλον) of] / grace and the [light; I have become light.] / And because of [it I have stretched] / out my hands [while they were folded. And I was] / shaped (μορφή) [ ] / [20] a veil (κάλυμμα) [of the] richness / which surround [ ] / a [womb (μήτρα)] / in a likeness [ ] / [ ] / [25] truly, [because I have comprehended (χωρεῖν)] / thee, Jesus of the one who [ ] / ⲏⲉⲉ ⲁⲓⲉⲉ ⲟⲓⲥ [ⲱ]//

79,17f. Or: spread out my hands which were folded.

III 67 ⲁ̅ⲓ̅ⲱ̅ⲛ̅ ⲁ̅ⲓ̅ⲱ̅ⲛ̅ ⲡⲛⲟⲩⲧⲉ ⲛ̅ⲧⲥⲓⲅⲏ ϯ
ⲁⲝⲓⲟⲩ ⲙ̅ⲙⲟⲕ ⲧⲏⲣⲕ ⲛ̅ⲧⲟⲕ ⲡⲉ ⲡⲁ
ⲙⲁ ⲛ̅ⲙ̅ⲧⲟⲛ ⲡϣⲏⲣⲉ ⲏ̅ⲥ̅ ⲏ̅ⲥ̅ ⲟ̅ ⲉ̅ ⲡⲓ
ⲁⲧⲥ̅ⲙⲟⲧ̇ ⲉⲧϣⲟⲟⲡ ϩ̅ⲛ̅ ⲛⲓⲁⲧⲥ̅ⲙⲟⲧ̇
ⲉϥϣⲟⲟⲡ ⲉϥⲧⲟⲩⲛⲟⲥ ⲙ̅ⲡⲣⲱⲙⲉ
ⲉⲧⲕⲛⲁⲧⲟⲩⲃⲟⲉⲓ ⲛ̅ϩⲏⲧ̅ϥ̅ ⲉϩⲟⲩⲛ
ⲉⲡⲉⲕⲱⲛϩ · ⲕⲁⲧⲁ ⲡⲉⲕⲣⲁⲛ ⲉⲧⲉ ⲙⲉϥ
ⲱϫ̅ⲛ̅ ⲉⲧⲃⲉ ⲡⲁϊ ⲡⲉⲥⲧⲟⲉⲓ ⲙ̅ⲡⲱⲛϩ
ⲛ̅ϩⲏⲧ̇ ⲁⲉⲓⲕⲉⲣⲁ ⲙ̅ⲙⲟϥ ϩ̅ⲛ̅ ⲟⲩⲙⲟ
[ⲟ]ⲩ ⲉⲡⲧⲩⲡⲟⲥ ⲛ̅ⲛ̅ⲁⲣⲭⲱⲛ ⲧⲏⲣⲟⲩ
ϫⲉ ⲉⲉⲓⲛⲁⲱⲛϩ ϩⲁⲧⲏⲕ ϩ̅ⲛ̅ ϯⲣⲏⲛⲏ
ⲛ̅ⲛⲉⲧⲟⲩⲁⲁⲃ ⲡⲉⲧϣⲟⲟⲡ ⲛ̅ϣⲁ ⲉⲛⲉϩ

68 ⲝ̅ⲏ̅

ⲁⲗⲏⲑⲱⲥ ⲁⲗⲏⲑⲱⲥ

67,15 Corr. ⲛ̅ over ⲥ ?
68, 1 ⲁⲗⲏⲑⲱⲥ ⲁⲗⲏⲑⲱⲥ could also belong with the following paragraph. The several possible translations are discussed in the commentary.

αἰών, αἰών, O God of silence (*σιγή*) ! I / honor (*ἀξιοῦν*) thee completely. Thou art my / place of rest, O son ⲏⲥ ⲏⲥ ⲟ ⲉ, the / formless one who exists in the formless ones, / who exists, raising up the man / in whom thou wilt purify me into / thy life, according to (*κατά*) thine imperishable name. / Therefore the incense of life / is in me. I mixed (*κερᾶν*) it with water / after the model (*τύπος*) of all archons (*ἄρχων*), / in order that I may live with thee in the peace (*εἰρήνη*) / of the saints, thou who existeth really truly (*ἀληθῶς ἀληθῶς*) // *68* for ever.

IV 80 [π]

[ε]τογααβ πνογτε

2 [ντε †ϲιγη ...]... [ντ]οκ πε

[ ]νμτον ντ[ε π]ϣη

4 [ρε]ετϣο[οπ] ϩν

[ ] πιμα[ει]ν πιμα

6 [ ] νογρωμε ακτ[β]

[βο μμοϊ νϩητϥ] ϩμ πεκωνϩ

8 [κατα πεκραν ν]νατϥωτε εβολ

[ετβε παϊ ϥϣο]οπ νϩητϥ νϭι ογ

10 [ϲτοει ντε πω]νϩ · εαϥϭωρϭ ϩν

[ογμοογ νϫ]ωκμ ν[τε] νιαρχων

12 [τηρογ ετραω]νϩ ϩατοοτκ ϩν ογ

[ιρηνη ντε νετογ]ααβ [πι]ϣα ενεϩ

14 [πη ετϣοοπ] ϩ[ν] ογμντμε να

[με·

80,14 See III 68,1 note.

80 [O] holy [ ], O God / [of silence (σιγή) .] Thou art / [ ] of rest of [the] son / [ ] who exists in / 5 [ ] the [mark], the place(?) / [ ] a man, thou hast / [purified me in him] in thy life, / [according to (κατά) thine] imperishable [name.] / [Therefore, there is] in him / 10 [incense of life] that has mixed with / baptismal [water] of [all] the / archons (ἄρχων), [in order that I may] live with thee in the / [peace (εἰρήνη) of the saints. O] eternal one / [who exists] really / 15 truly.

The first conclusion: III 68,1-9

III 68 ⲧⲁⲓ̈ ⲧⲉ ⲧⲃⲓⲃⲗⲟⲥ
2 ⲛ̄ⲧⲁϥⲥⲁϩⲥ ⲛ̄ϭⲓ ⲡⲛⲟϭ ⲛ̄ⲥⲏⲑ ⲁϥⲕⲱ
ⲙ̄ⲙⲟⲥ ϩⲛ̄ ϩⲉⲛⲧⲟⲟⲩ ⲉⲩϫⲟⲥⲉ ⲉⲙ̄
4 ⲡⲉⲡⲣⲏ ϣⲁ ⲉϫⲱⲟⲩ ⲟⲩⲇⲉ ⲉⲙⲛ̄
ϭⲟⲙ · ⲁⲩⲱ ϫⲓⲛ ⲛⲉϩⲟⲟⲩ ⲛ̄ⲛⲉⲡⲣⲟ
6 ⲫⲏⲧⲏⲥ ⲙⲛ̄ ⲛⲁⲡⲟⲥⲧⲟⲗⲟⲥ ⲙⲛ̄ ⲛ̄
ⲕⲏⲣⲩⲝ ⲙ̄ⲡⲉⲡⲣⲉ'ⲛ' ϩⲟⲗⲱⲥ ⲧⲁⲗⲟ
8 ⲉϫⲛ̄ ⲛⲉⲩϩⲏⲧ̀ ⲟⲩⲧⲉ ⲙⲛ̄ ϣϭⲟⲙ
ⲁⲩⲱ ⲙ̄ⲡⲉⲡⲉⲩⲙⲁϫⲉ ⲥⲱⲧⲙ ⲉⲣⲟϥ

68, 4 Corr. ϫⲱⲟ over ⲉⲱϥ.
7 Corr. ⲉ in ⲣⲉ over ⲏ ? See 68,4.

This is the book (*βίβλος*) / which the great Seth wrote, and placed / in high mountains on which / the sun has not risen, nor (*οὐδέ*) is it / [5] possible. And since the days of the prophets (*προφήτης*), / and the apostles (*ἀπόστολος*), and the / preachers (*κῆρυξ*), the name has not at all (*ὅλως*) risen / upon their hearts, nor (*οὔτε*) is it possible. / And their ear has not heard it. /

The second conclusion: III 68,10-69,5

10 ⲧⲉⲉⲓⲃⲓⲃⲗⲟⲥ ⲁϥⲥⲁϩⲥ ⲛ̄ϭⲓ ⲡⲛⲟϭ
ⲛ̄ⲥⲏⲑ · ϩⲛ̄ ϩⲉⲛⲥϩⲁⲓ̈ ⲛ̄ϣⲉⲙⲁⲁⲃ
12 ⲛ̄ⲣⲟⲙⲡⲉ ⲁϥⲕⲱ ⲙ̄ⲙⲟⲥ ϩⲙ̄ ⲡⲧⲟ
{ⲟ}ⲟⲩ ⲉϣⲁⲩⲙⲟⲩⲧⲉ ⲉⲣⲟϥ ϫⲉ ⲭⲁ
14 ⲣⲁⲝⲓⲱ ϫⲉⲕⲁⲁⲥ ϩⲛ̄ ⲛ̄ϩⲁⲉ ⲛ̄ⲛⲉ

[10] The great Seth wrote this book (*βίβλος*) / with letters in one hundred and thirty / years. He placed it in the mountain / that is called Charaxio, / in order that, at the end of the /

The first conclusion: IV 80,15-25

IV 80 ⲡⲉⲓ̈ϫⲱⲱ]ⲙⲉ̣ [ⲁ]ϥⲥ̣ⲁϩϥ ⲛ̄ϭⲓ
16 [ⲡⲓⲛⲟϭ ⲥⲏⲑ ⲁⲩⲱ] ⲁϥⲕⲁⲁϥ ⲛ̄ϩⲣⲁⲓ̈ ϩ͡ⲓ
[ϫ̄ⲛ ⲟⲩⲧⲟⲟⲩ ⲉϥ]ϫⲟⲥⲉ ⲡⲏ ⲉⲧⲉ ⲙⲁ
18 [ⲣⲉⲡⲣⲏ ϣⲁ ⲉϩⲣⲁⲓ̈ ⲉϫⲱϥ] ⲟⲩⲧⲉ
[ ]ⲉ[...] ⲁⲩⲱ ⲛ̄
20 [ϫⲓⲛ ⲛⲉϩⲟⲟⲩ ⲛ̄ⲛⲓⲡⲣ]ⲟⲫⲏⲧⲏⲥ ⲙ̣̄[ⲛ]
[ⲙ̄ⲛ ⲛⲓ]ⲁ̣ⲡⲟⲥⲧⲟⲗⲟⲥ
22 [ ]ⲙ̄ⲛⲥ̣ⲱ[
[ ]ⲉ͡ⲓ ⲉⲃ̣[ⲟⲗ
24 [ⲁⲩⲱ ⲡⲉⲩ]ⲙⲁ
[ϫⲉ ⲙ̄ⲡϥ̄ⲥⲱⲧ̄ⲙ ⲉ]ⲣ̣ⲟⲥ :

[The great Seth] wrote / [this book, and] he placed it on / [a] high [mountain] on which / [the sun] does not [rise] nor (οὔτε) / [.] And / [20] [from the days of the] prophets (προφήτης), [and] / [and the] apostles (ἀπόστολος), / [ ] ... / [ ] come forth / [, and their] ear / [25] [has not heard] it. /

The second conclusion: IV 80,26 - 81,?

26 [ⲡⲉⲓ̈ϫⲱⲱⲙⲉ ⲁϥ]ⲥⲁϩ̄ϥ ⲛ̄ϭⲓ ⲡⲓⲛⲟϭ
81 [ⲡⲁ̄]
ⲥⲏⲑ ϩⲛ̄ ϩⲉⲛⲥϩⲁⲓ̈ [
2 ⲁϥⲕⲁ̣ⲁ̣ϥ ϩ̄.[...].[
3 ff. are lost.

The great Seth wrote [this] / *81* [book] with letters [ ]. / He placed [it

III 68 ⲭⲣⲟⲛⲟⲥ ⲙ̅ⲛ̅ ⲛ̅ⲕⲉⲣⲟⲥ ϩ̅ⲙ̅ ⲡⲉⲑⲉ
16 ⲗⲏⲙⲁ ⲙ̅ⲡⲁⲩⲧⲟⲅⲉⲛⲏⲥ ⲛ̅ⲛⲟⲩⲧⲉ
ⲙ̅ⲛ̅ ⲡⲉⲡⲗⲏⲣⲱⲙⲁ ⲧⲏⲣϥ ϩⲓⲧ̅ⲙ̅ ⲡϯ
18 ⲛ̅ⲡⲟⲩⲱϣⲉ ⲛ̅ⲁⲧⲛ̅ ⲣⲁⲧϥ · ⲛ̅ⲁⲧ̇
ⲙⲉⲟⲩⲉ ⲉⲣⲟϥ ⲛ̅ⲉⲓⲱⲧ̇ ⲉϥ⟨ⲉ⟩ⲡⲣⲟ
20 ⲉⲗⲑⲉ ⲉⲃⲟⲗ · ⲛ̅ϥⲟⲩⲱⲛ̅ϩ̅ ⲛ̅ⲧⲉⲉⲓ
ⲅⲉⲛⲉⲁ ⲛ̅ⲁⲫⲑⲁⲣⲧⲟⲥ ⲉⲧⲟⲩⲁⲁⲃ ·
22 ⲛ̅ⲧⲉ ⲡⲛⲟϭ ⲛ̅ⲥⲱⲧⲏⲣ ⲙ̅ⲛ̅ ⲛⲉⲧ̇
ϭⲁⲗⲏⲟⲩ ⲉⲣⲟⲟⲩ ϩ̅ⲛ̅ ⲟⲩⲁⲅⲁⲡⲏ ⲙ̅ⲛ̅
24 ⲡⲛⲟϭ ⲛ̅ⲁϩⲟⲣⲁⲧⲟⲥ ⲛ̅ϣⲁ ⲁⲛⲏϩⲉ̣
ⲙ̅ⲡ̅ⲛ̅ⲁ ⲙⲛ ⲡⲉϥⲙⲟⲛⲟⲅⲉⲛⲏⲥ
26 ⲛ̅ϣⲏⲣⲉ ⲙ̅ⲛ̅ ⲡⲟⲩⲟⲉⲓⲛ ⲛ̅ϣⲁ ⲉ

69 ⲝ̅ⲑ̅

ⲛⲉϩ ⲙ̅ⲛ̅ ⲧⲉϥⲛⲟϭ ⲛ̅ⲥⲩⲛⲍⲩⲅⲟⲥ
2 ⲛ̅ⲁⲫⲑⲁⲣⲧⲟⲥ ⲙ̅ⲛ̅ ⲧⲁⲫⲑⲁⲣⲧⲟⲥ ⲛ̅
ⲥⲟⲫⲓⲁ ⲙ̅ⲛ̅ ⲧⲃⲁⲣⲃⲏⲗⲟⲛ ⲙ̅ⲛ̅ ⲟⲩⲡⲗⲏ
4 ⲣⲱⲙⲁ ⲧⲏⲣϥ ϩ̅ⲛ̅ ⲟⲩⲙⲛ̅ⲧϣⲁ ⲉⲛⲉϩ·
ϩⲁⲙⲏⲛ

15 times (*χρόνος*) and the eras (*καιρός*), by the / will (*θέλημα*) of the divine Autogenes (*αὐτογενής*) / and the whole pleroma (*πλήρωμα*), through the gift / of the untraceable, unthinkable, / fatherly love, it may / 20 come forth (*προελθεῖν*) and reveal this / incorruptible (*ἄφθαρτος*), holy race (*γενεά*) / of the great savior (*σωτήρ*), and those who / dwell with them in love (*ἀγάπη*), and / the great, invisible (*ἀόρατος*), eternal / 25 Spirit (*πνεῦμα*), and his only begotten (*μονογενής*) / Son, and the eternal light, // *69* and his great, incorruptible (*ἄφθαρτος*) / consort (*σύζυγος*), and the incorruptible (*ἄφθαρτος*) / Sophia, and the Barbelon, and the / whole pleroma (*πλήρωμα*) in eternity. / 5 Amen (*ἀμήν*). /

IV 81, 3 — end is lost.

The colophon: III 69,6-17

ⲡⲉⲩⲁⲅ̀ⲅⲉⲗⲓⲟⲛ ⟨ⲛ̅⟩ⲛ̅ⲣⲙ̅ⲛ̅ⲕⲏⲙⲉ
ⲧⲃⲓⲃⲗⲟⲥ ⲛ̅ⲥϩⲁⲓ̈ ⲛ̅ⲛⲟⲩⲧⲉ ⲧϩⲓⲉ
ⲣⲁ ⲉⲧϩⲏⲡ̈ ⲧⲉⲭⲁⲣⲓⲥ ⲧⲥⲩⲛϩⲉⲥⲓⲥ
ⲧⲉⲥⲑⲏⲥⲓⲥ ⲧⲉⲫⲣⲟⲛⲏⲥⲓⲥ ⲙⲛ̅ ⲡⲉ
ⲣ̅ⲥϩⲏⲧⲥ̅ · ⲉⲩⲅⲛⲱⲥⲧⲟⲥ ⲡⲁⲅⲁⲡⲏ
ⲧⲓⲕⲟⲥ ϩⲙ̅ ⲡⲉⲡ̅ⲛ̅ⲁ̅ ϩⲛ̅ ⲧⲥⲁⲣⲝ ·
ⲡⲁⲣⲉⲛ ⲡⲉ ⲅⲟⲅ̀ⲅⲉⲥ'ⲥ'ⲟⲥ ⲙ̅ⲛ̅ ⲛⲁ
ϣⲃ̅ⲣⲟⲩⲟⲉⲓⲛ ϩ̅ⲛ̅ ⲟⲩⲁⲫⲑⲁⲣⲥⲓⲁ
ⲓ̅ⲥ̅ ⲡⲉⲭ̅ⲥ̅ ⲡϣⲏⲣⲉ ⲙⲡⲛⲟⲩⲧⲉ
ⲡⲥⲱⲧⲏⲣ · ⲓ̅ⲭ̅ⲑ̅ⲩ̅ⲥ̅ ⲑⲉⲟⲅⲣⲁⲫⲟⲥ
ⲧⲃⲓⲃⲗⲟⲥ ⲧϩⲓⲉⲣⲁ ⲙ̅ⲡⲛⲟϭ ⲛ̅ⲁϩⲟ
ⲣⲁⲧⲟⲛ ⲙ̅ⲡ̅ⲛ̅ⲁ̅ ϩⲁⲙⲏⲛ

9,6 See *supra*, p. 18.

The gospel (*εὐαγγέλιον*) of <the> Egyptians. / The God-written, holy (*ἱερά*), secret / book (*βίβλος*). Grace (*χάρις*), understanding (*σύνεσις*), / perception (*αἴσθησις*), prudence (*φρόνησις*) (be) with him / [10] who has written it, Eugnostos the beloved (*ἀγαπητικός*) / in the Spirit (*πνεῦμα*) — in the flesh (*σάρξ*) / my name is Gongessos — and my / fellow lights in incorruptibility (*ἀφθαρσία*), / Jesus Christ (*χριστός*), Son of God, / [15] Savior (*σωτήρ*), ⲓⲭⲑⲩⲥ. God-written (*θεόγραφος*) (is) / the holy (*ἱερά*) book (*βίβλος*) of the great, invisible (*ἀόρατον*) / Spirit (*πνεῦμα*). Amen (*ἀμήν*).

The title : III 69, 18-20

ⲧ̅ⲃ̅ⲓ̅ⲃ̅ⲗ̅ⲟ̅ⲥ̅ ⲧ̅ϩ̅ⲓ̅ⲉ̅ⲣ̅ⲁ̅ ⲙ̅ⲡ̅ⲛ̅ⲟ̅ϭ̅
ⲛ̅ⲁ̅ϩ̅ⲟ̅ⲣ̅ⲁ̅ⲧ̅ⲟ̅ⲛ̅ ⲙ̅ⲡ̅ⲛ̅ⲉ̅ⲩ̅
ⲙ̅ⲁ̅ ϩ̅ⲁ̅ⲙ̅ⲏ̅ⲛ̅

The holy (*ἱερά*) book (*βίβλος*) of the great, / invisible (*ἀόρατον*) Spirit (*πνεῦμα*). / [20] Amen (*ἀμήν*).

Only a blank top fragment of IV 82 survives.
The colophon was probably absent (see pp. 8f.).

COMMENTARY

The Introduction: III 40,12 - 41,7 = IV 50,1-23.

III 40,12f.: See the chapter on the title, *supra*, pp. 20ff. The holy book is linked with the Spirit, which is at first characterized in three ways expressing its nature and origin. Then follow a series of seven more appositives which describe the Spirit as light. After these come three other appositives: the Father, the Aeon of the aeons, and the uninterpretable Power. To each of the first two of these appositives, three attributes are added. The third attribute is different in the two versions. Since some of the differences between III, *2* and IV, *2* can be explained in terms of mistranslations from the Greek, the *Vorlage* has been reconstructed as follows:

ἡ βίβλος ἡ ἱερὰ τῶν Αἰγυπτίων
  τοῦ μεγάλου ἀοράτου πνεύματος,
  τοῦ πατρὸς ἀκλήτου,
  τοῦ προελθόντος ἐκ τῶν ὑψίστων,
  τοῦ τελείου τοῦ φωτός,
  τοῦ φωτὸς εἰς αἰῶνα τῶν αἰώνων,
  τοῦ φωτὸς (ἐκ) σιγῆς προνοίας καὶ σιγῆς τοῦ πατρός,
  τοῦ φωτὸς (ἐκ) λόγου καὶ ἀληθείας,
  τοῦ φωτὸς ἀφθαρσιῶν,
  τοῦ φωτὸς ἀπεράντου,
  τοῦ φωτὸς τοῦ προελθόντος εἰς αἰῶνα τῶν αἰώνων,
  τοῦ πατρὸς
    τοῦ ἀδήλου
    τοῦ ἀσημάντου
    (τοῦ ἀγηράτου)
    τοῦ ἀνευαγγελιζομένου,
  τοῦ αἰῶος τῶν αἰώνων,
  (τοῦ αὐτογενοῦς)
    τοῦ αὐτογενίου
    τοῦ ἐπιγενίου
    τοῦ ἀλλογενίου
  τῆς ἀνερμηνεύτου δυνάμεως τοῦ ἀρρήτου πατρός.

III 40,15f.: III mistakenly read *τοῦ τελείου* "perfection" (LAMPE, p. 1381a) with the preceding rather than the following noun. This led to the merging of the first two "light clauses". III 40,16f.: it is not clear why III translated εἰς αἰῶνα τῶν αἰώνων by ΝΙΑΙΩΝ ΝΟΥΟΕΙΝ (cf. 41,2). 40,17f.: III usually supplied a definite article where the Greek must have been indefinite. The varying translations, ΠΕΙΩΤ ΝΤϹΙΓΗ in III 40,18 over against ΟΥϹΙΓΗ ΝΤΕ ΠΕΙΩΤ in IV 50,9, presuppose the same Greek Vorlage, σιγῆς τοῦ πατρός. Since σιγή lacked an article in Greek, III mistakenly assumed that it depended on τοῦ πατρός. Thus the intended parallel between Pronoia and the Father was lost (cf. III 42,1f.; 43,5f.; 63,21f.). The genitive constructions in III 40,17.19 correspond to the phrases with ϨΝ- in IV 50,8.10. It is likely that both the genitive constructions in III 40,17.19 and the phrases with ϨΝ- in IV 50,8.10 go back to the same text. The intention of the text is to qualify the term "light" by specifying its origin. Therefore the genitive in III can be seen as the translation of the original Greek text (genitive of origin). On the other hand, IV perhaps interpreted the Greek genitive as ἐκ plus the genitive (ϨΝ- often equals ΕΒΟΛ ϨΝ-; cf. CRUM, *Dict.* p. 684a). Here the genitive of origin comes very close to a partitive genitive. The striking rendering of (ἐκ) σιγῆς προνοίας as ϨΝ ΟΥϹΙΓΗ ϨΝ ΟΥΠΡΟΝΟΙΑ shows that IV interpreted σιγῆς and προνοίας as coordinate nouns. On the other hand, ἐκ could have occurred before the first genitive as IV suggests and III has simplified it. The same applies to the subsequent expression in III 40,18f. = IV 50,9f. III 41,1: The same conflict between III and IV is found in III 41,22f. par.; 42,8 par.; 64,9 par.; IV 59,8. In III 41,2 ΠΕΙΡΕ ΕΒΟΛ "come forth" includes the concept "light" (cf. CRUM, *Dict.* p. 267a). III 41,3f.: Most likely both III and IV mistakenly connected this clause to the preceding with ΝΤΕ, forgetting that it stands in apposition to the great invisible Spirit. IV normally connects a series of adjectives with ΑΥΩ. The ΑΤϮ ϢΩΛϨ (ΑϹΗΜΑΝΤΟϹ) may mean that the supreme God cannot be expressed in writing. ΝΑΤϨΛΛΟ (τοῦ ἀγηράτου) is missing in IV 50,16. "The aeon of aeons" expresses primacy of origin. One could consider ΝΑΥΤΟΓΕΝΗϹ in III 41,5 as a comment in the margin, that was included in the text by a later scribe, or that ΝΑΥΤΟΓΕΝΗϹ needs to be emended to ΠΑΥΤΟΓΕΝΗϹ. In the latter case the translator of III, *2* did not recognize that τοῦ αὐτογενοῦς in the Greek Vorlage stands in apposition to the great invisible Spirit. Then IV translated τοῦ αὐτογενοῦς τοῦ αὐτογενίου by means of a single expression, since otherwise it would become an overly redundant construction in Coptic translation. IV turned the attributive adjectives τοῦ ἐπιγενίου and τοῦ ἀλλογενίου into substantives parallel to τοῦ αὐτογενοῦς. The forms ending in -ιος are unattested and must have been designed for stylistic effect (cf. Zost VIII 18,14 ΝΙⲀⲨⲦⲞⲄⲈⲚⲒⲞⲚ [Ⲛ̄Ⲛ]ⲈⲰⲚ). The difference between αὐτογένιος and ἐπιγένιος may lie in that the former indicates that the Spirit had his origin in himself while the latter stresses that he appeared out of himself (cf. III 41,2 = IV 50,13). III 41,7 differs greatly from IV 50,21f. Perhaps IV is closest to the original while III restates 41,5. Ending with the ineffable Father would appropriately round off this section which spoke of the metaphysical and mysterious domain of the great invisible Spirit.

The appearance of the three powers: III 41,7-12 = IV 50,23 - 51,2. The trinity of Father, Mother and Son does not originate through emanation, as in ApocryJn, but through evolution, a self-unfolding of the supreme God. ⲠⲒⲢⲈ is a typical expression for the coming forth of light (*supra*, p. 169). In IV ⲚⲒⲠⲒⲢⲈ is an appositive to Father, Mother, Son (in 50,26f.). The *Vorlage* may have been ἐπιγένιοι ἐκ σιγῆς ζώσης τοῦ πατρὸς ἀφθάρτου. III, however, saw τοῦ πατρός as an appositive to σιγῆς ζώσης, and thus introduced both with ⲈⲂⲞⲖ ϩⲚ̄-. If one considers III to be correct, then ⲠⲠⲒⲢⲈ would be either an appositive to ⲤⲒⲄⲎ or to Father, Mother, Son seen collectively as the offspring of the primal Father. In the former case, the Greek may have been ἐκ σιγῆς ζώσης τοῦ ἐπιγενίου (ἐκ) τοῦ πατρὸς ἀφθάρτου. For the latter possibility, ὁ ἐπιγένιος may have been in the *Vorlage* instead of τοῦ ἐπιγενίου. This last reconstruction could habe led to the translations of both III and IV. The δέ in III 41,12 is no longer postpositive, perhaps due to a transposition of the verb by the Coptic translator.

The composition of the realm of Light: III 41,13-23 = IV 51,2-15. (Cf. *supra*, pp. 41ff.) IV cannot be reconstructed with certainty. Apparently the sentence in Greek began with ἐξ αὐτοῦ Δοξομέδων which III interpreted to refer to a place (cf. III 41,23 par., III 43,8 par.). The designation "aeon of the aeons" has also been attributed to the great invisible Spirit. However, here it appears not to refer to primacy of origin but to the all-comprehensive character of his being, in which the light, i.e. the supreme God, presents himself. Some text has dropped out in III 41,16 (cf. IV 51,4-6). "Their powers" refers to the Doxomedon as a collective entity. According to this section he contains a trinity (41,22f.; cf. 41,1 comm.), which is supplemented by a second trinity.

The three ogdoads: III 41,23 - 43,8 = IV 51,15 - 53,3.

a) Their appearance: III 41,23 - 42,4 = IV 51,15-22.

The ogdoads come forth from the Doxomedon (see 41,13 comm.). This is a speculative description of the trinity. The "from him" in IV could refer both to Doxomedon and the great invisible Spirit. In IV ⲡⲣⲟⲛⲟⲓⲁ is parallel to ⲥⲓⲅⲏ and a characteristic of the Father. In III ⲡⲣⲟⲛⲟⲓⲁ appears to be a mythological figure as is suggested by 40,17f. and par., 43,6 and par. Thus III has "his Pronoia", i.e. his female complement. This is in agreement with the origin of the ogdoads pictured as a birth. In Gnosticism "ogdoad" refers first of all to the firmament of fixed stars which stands above the hebdomad of the planets. Secondly, and probably originally, it was a numerical grouping, a unit of eight, which was, especially in Valentinianism, used as a description of the intelligible world. For the Egyptian ogdoad concept see KURT SETHE, *Amun und die acht Urgötter von Hermopolis* (*Abh. Preuss. Akademie d. Wiss.*, Berlin 1929, No. 4). GEgypt employs the ogdoads as a stylistic device for the arrangement of the heavenly world. Thus the heavenly lights form together with their consorts one such ogdoad (*infra*, p. 179f.), as do their ministers with their consorts (*infra*, p. 180). Together with the three ogdoads of the trinity they form five ogdoads, a total of forty heavenly beings referred to in Coptic idiom as "a forty" (III 53,11 = IV 65,3f.). The trinity and five seals also add up to eight.

b) The first ogdoad: III 42,5-11 = IV 51,22 - 52,2.

The first ogdoad belongs to the Father. Since the ogdoad contains the person which brought it into being, the ogdoad remains a part of the trinity. The Father's unity and originality is attested by the fact that he is androgenous. See *supra*, pp. 43ff. on the thrice-male child. III and IV differ in the list of the parts of the first ogdoad. Surprising is the translation of ἀφθαρσία by ⲛ̄ⲁⲧϫⲱϩⲙ in IV 50,11; 51,26; 59,8; and 75,23 (see III 41,1 comm.). Thus IV collapsed "incorruption and eternal life" into "eternal, incorruptible life". III is supported by ApocryJn BG 28,15 - 29,4, where ἔννοια, πρόγνωσις, ἀφθαρσία and αἰωνία ζωή come forth at the request of the Barbelo, while νοῦς, θέλημα and λόγος come forth through Christ, i.e. the Son (BG 31,6-16). Since Father, Mother and Son are identified with the three ogdoads (IV 51,16ff.), the question arises whether the naming of the androgenous Father indicates that he alone is equated with the entire ogdoad or that he, together with seven other beings, forms the ogdoad. The latter corresponds fully with gnostic thought patterns.

c) The second ogdoad: III 42,11-21 = IV 52,2-14.

For Barbelo and her role in this writing, see *supra*, pp. 40f. The lacunae in both versions preclude the possibility of knowing the secret names used in this section. The text in the lacuna in IV 52,10f. is missing in III unless it was in the lacuna in 42,18. The ⲡⲉⲓⲣⲉ in 42,17f. must here too mean "originate" (cf. *supra*, p. 169). The *εὐδοκεῖν* in III 42,19 par. testifies to the legitimacy of Barbelo.

d) The third ogdoad: III 42,21 - 43,4 = IV 52,15-24.

The Son is described in terms of his origin. He is the offspring of the primal Power and as such he is the "Son of silence". III 42,23 is missing in IV. He is called the *δόξα* of the Father and *ἀρετή* of the Mother which recalls the use of both attributes in 2 Pet 1: 3, although here they are distributed between two divine beings. ⲤⲞⲞⲨⲚ in IV 52,17 is a misinterpretation of *δόξα*. The Son completes himself. Most likely the planets are meant, and the voices would refer to the harmony of spheres which is based on Pythagorean number mysticism. For the use of the plural *κόλποι* see Lampe, p. 766a. IV 52,22f. should be preferred. The Logos is the product of the hebdomad. III has simply placed hebdomad and Logos beside each other without explaining their relationship.

e) The summary: III 43,4-8 = IV 52,24 - 53,3.

The relative particle in IV 52,24 and in other places probably corresponds to a relative construction in the Greek. (For the relationship between the Father and Pronoia cf. III 42,1 f. comm.) The section on the trinity of ogdoads ends as it started with a reference to the place where they came into being. This is the same place where the Doxomedon-aeon originated and thus it must refer to the all-encompassing realm of light.

The description of the Doxomedon-aeon: III 43,8 - 44,9 = IV 53,3 - 54,13.

In IV 53,3f., in contrast to III 43,8f., the coming of the Doxomedon is closely linked to the preceding event. The reconstruction ⲡⲏ or ⲡⲁï in IV 53,3 is too short. ⲡⲁï ⲡⲉ or ⲡⲁï ⲡ (cleft sentence) is possible although this construction is not used elsewhere in IV. The ⲙ̄ⲙⲁⲩ in IV 53,5 leaves no doubt that the ⲡⲓⲙⲁ in the preceding section is meant. The transition to this section is made by means of the relative clause (ⲡⲓⲙⲁ = ὅπου) the antecedent of which is ⲡⲓⲙⲁ ⲉⲧ̄ⲙ̄ⲙⲁⲩ. (For the Doxomedon-aeon cf. *supra*, pp. 41ff.). The plural with ⲑⲣⲟⲛⲟⲥ in IV 53,6 is supported by the ⲉⲣⲟⲟⲩ in IV 53,8 and shows that IV consistently understood the Doxomedon-aeon to be a collective being. The singular ⲡⲉⲑⲣⲟⲛⲟⲥ in III 43,10f. may go back to a variant in the Greek text but more likely, since all the parallel occurrences are plural, III made the change to fit the throne in 43,18 and par. ⲛⲓⲉⲟⲟⲩ ⲙ̄ⲛ ⲛⲓⲁⲫⲑⲁⲣⲥⲓⲁ (III 43,12) stands in apposition to ⲛ̄ⲇⲩⲛⲁⲙⲓⲥ just as in IV 53,8f., where ⲙ̄ⲛ ... ⲙ̄ⲛ = καὶ ... καί, "both ... and", occurs. The alien God made his appearance in the Doxomedon-aeon. The lacuna in IV 53,11f. has no corresponding text in III. III 43,15ff. and par. gives a further description of the Doxomedon-aeon. Whether the throne belongs to the thrice-male child (*supra*, p. 42) or the Doxomedon is not clear. The name of the one who possesses the throne is written on a tablet made of boxwood (cf. LIDDELL-SCOTT, p. 1554b, and Zost VIII 130,2) which is attached to the throne. III 43,21ff. differs from IV. The text in IV 53,22 second half and 23 is missing in III. There is also no equivalent in III for the unreconstructed text in IV 54,1. The ineffable name is made up of the Greek vowels written twenty two times each — the number of letters in the Semitic alphabet. The order is ⲓⲏⲟⲩⲉⲁⲱ which might possibly mean Ἰήου ἐ(στὶν) Α (καὶ) Ω. In that case the personified Doxomedon could be identified with Yeou since he is a kind of second god (cf. *supra*, p. 43).

The presentation of praise and request of the ogdoads: III 44,9-21 = IV 54,13 - 55,11.

(For the form of the presentations of praise cf. *supra*, pp. 39f.) IV 54,18 ⲛ̄ⲧⲉ ⲡ[ⲓⲱⲧ] (cf. IV 73,10f.) is lacking in III. Some text must be missing before the ⲛ̄ϭⲓ in III 44,15, the equivalent of ϩ̄ⲛ ⲟⲩϭⲟⲙ in IV 54,23 (ⲛ̄ϭⲓ is unusual here). The parallel to IV 54,25-55,2 must have been different and shorter. IV 55,4b-7a are missing in III due to homoioteleuton. The reconstruction ⲛ̄ⲭ̄ⲥ̄ in 55,6 is suggested by the occurrence in III 44,23 and par. The reconstruction ⲥⲏⲑ is also possible since there is a close connection between the thrice-male child and Seth (cf. *supra*, p. 45), but it is very unlikely since Seth has not yet appeared. The scene describes the filling of the Doxomedon-aeon with light-beings. The three males described in IV 55,3-7 are most likely the same as the thrice-male child. The reference to the word (= λόγος) of the pleroma of light means that the powers build a realm of light through the rational ordering power of the Logos (cf. *TDNT* IV, pp. 84ff. [76 ff.]).

The presentation of praise of the thrice-male child: III 44,22-? = IV 55,11 - 56,11.

This section is largely missing in III and poorly preserved in IV. The first part, IV 55,11 - 56,6, contains an expanded presentation of praise. Then the presentation of praise is repeated and a request is uttered. (For the relationship between the child and Christ cf. *supra*, p. 46. For ϊωηλ cf. *supra*, p. 47). The presentation of praise is addressed to the great invisible Spirit and his female counterpart. The name Ainon may be the accusative of *αἶνος* which means praise — in the sense of *δόξα*. Also *αἶνος* = *δεινός* is possible as a description of the alien God.

The appearance of Youel and Esephech: IV 56,11-22.

(For Youel cf. *supra*, pp. 46ff.). Since in the preceding section the appearance of the thrice-male child is reported, and the appearance of Esephech comes in IV 56,20-22, it is to be expected that in IV 56,11-20 the appearance of Youel is mentioned. Unfortunately the lacunae make an unambiguous interpretation of this section exceedingly difficult. Nevertheless, the restoration of Youel in line 20 is made certain by line 19. The difficulty with this interpretation is that the being in 56,11ff. is masculine. Perhaps we can read [πιφω]c here. This radiant figure appears to be identified with Youel in lines 19f. In Allog XI 50, 52, 55 and 59 she is called τⲁ ⲛⲓⲉⲟⲟⲩ ⲧⲏⲣⲟⲩ, "she who has all the glories". For Esephech see *supra*, pp. 48f.

The summary (?): IV 56,23 - 58,22.

This section is so poorly preserved that it is difficult to decide whether it forms a unit. An ogdoad has now been completed made up of the Father, the Mother, the Son, and the five seals which must be the three male virgins, Youel and Esephech. (For the five seals cf. *supra*, p. 50). They are the seal imprint of the first trinity. These seals are not the five sacraments as one might assume from GPh (cf. H.-G. Gaffron, *Studien zum koptischen Philippusevangelium unter besonderer Berücksichtigung der Sakramente*, Bonn 1969). The references to the five seals in III 55,12 and 66,3 appear to be secondary since they are lacking in IV. In both cases the sacraments are meant, and the number five must come from a cultic situation similar to GPh. The poor state of pages 57-58 obscure the argument until 58,23.

The appearance of Pronoia: IV 58,23 - 59,29.

IV 58,23f.: Various reconstructions are possible here: [ⲡⲣⲟⲛ]ⲟⲓⲁ, [ⲁⲡⲟⲣⲣ]ⲟⲓⲁ, "emanation", or [ⲉⲛⲛ]ⲟⲓⲁ. By introducing Pronoia the author reaches back to the beginning. This fits well in light of the derivation of the Logos from the Father which follows. If this interpretation is correct, the reconstruction of Pronoia is better than ⲁⲡⲟⲣⲣⲟⲓⲁ, since ⲁⲡⲟⲣⲣⲟⲓⲁ lacks a definite character. Pronoia and the Logos come forth directly out of the supreme God. Pronoia creates an entourage for the light-being mentioned at the end of the section. The mentioning of Christ is surprising and, perhaps, secondary. He is associated with the thrice-male child. The close connection between them is also evident in III 44,22f. = IV 55,11f. and III 54,13-20 = IV 66,2-8.

The appearance of the Logos: IV 59,29 - 60,22.

The Logos does not appear as a response to the usual presentation of praise and request. The partially preserved name in 60,6 is typical for Gnostic literature, and similar to the unintelligible secret names of magical literature. The reading ⲭ̄ⲥ̄ in 60,8 is as good as certain. « The son of silence » in 60,8 and 12 refers to the Logos. The reference to him as the son of the great Christ is best understood as an interpolation. That Christ is connected with the coming of the Logos is known from other Gnostic sources, but to refer to the Logos as the Son of Christ is unprecedented. The relative clauses in 60,7 and 8 are parallel. The descent from the primal Father nicely explains the missing request. Thus the passage attests to the direct emanation of the Logos from the primal Father. 60,17-22 may be a different unit of tradition (*τότε* !) which presents the Logos as the creator of the heavenly world.

The presentation of praise of the Logos: IV 60,22-30.

The fact that the presentation of praise of the Logos is addressed only to the great invisible Spirit could be due to an especially close relationship between the Father and the Logos. This section does not belong to the presentations of praise addressed to the pantheon.

The creation of Adamas: III 48 end-49,7 = IV 60,30-61,8.

In contrast to the Logos, the being next in order is not an *αὐτογενής*. The Adamas, the heavenly prototype of the earthly man, is created. This is indicated by ϫⲡⲟ, the typical word for such an act (cf. III 51,17; 54,17; 60,11.20; 63,13; 67,11. IV 63,12; 66,6; 72,2; 75,15). To accomplish this a creator-deity is needed. In III 49,4 ⲙⲓⲣⲟⲑⲟⲏ plays this role. The end of the parallel line in IV 61,4 is lost. There is not enough room for the name although it could have been crowded in and have extended into the margin. The name refers to a mother deity also known from Zost VIII 6,30; 30,14 where the name is spelled ⲙⲓⲣⲟⲑⲉⲁ. The meaning would be "the goddess *μοῖρα*". In GEgypt the name has the Ionic feminine ending. Due to stress on the ultima the vowels of the penult and antepenult have been assimilated. The reference to *μοῖρα* as creator of the primal Adam appears to come from ancient mythology, since Zeus made the *Μοῖραι*, the goddesses of fate, especially significant for man (cf. Hes. *Theog.* 903ff.). Yet her mythological role can vary. The most basic is her general character as "mother of the holy, incorruptible ones". This special role as mother can also be transferred to a male deity. For that reason the ⲅⲉⲣⲁⲇⲁⲙⲁⲥ, the primal Adam, in the 3StSeth is praised by Seth as the ⲙⲓⲣⲱⲑⲉⲁⲥ (VII 119,12). (For Greek name ending in -*ᾶς* cf. Blass-Debrunner § 125). Finally, this form is changed to ⲙⲓⲣⲱⲑⲉⲟⲥ (VII 119,12f.; 120,15). The name given to Adamas in III 49,6f. is made up of groups of letters, while in IV 61,6f. a meaning is given. Unfortunately the passage in IV is obscured by lacunae. It reads at first (IV 61,6f.) three times "thou art one". The same is said in Zost VIII 53,24f. of the Splenditenens and again in 54,6 where the context is lost. In the hymn to the supreme God in 3StSeth we find the phrase "thou art one" twice in a row (VII 125,23). Thus ϊⲉⲛ in III may be *εἶ ἕν*, which the author of III mistook for nonsense syllables but which in IV are correctly translated. (Cf. III 66,13 and IV 78,16f. for a similar situation). IV 61,8 has [ⲉⲁ ⲉⲁ] ⲉⲁ. What was at the end of the preceding line, however, remains a question. To take ⲉⲁ as an abbreviation for *εἶ ἕν* is problematic when one considers that previously *εἶ* was rendered by ϊ. If one sees in ϊⲉⲛ and ⲉⲁ the same meaning, then one must take ϊⲉⲛ as a Greek phrase that was not understood, and ⲉⲁ as a cryptogram consisting of the first letter of the written word *εἶ* and the alpha as the number 1. The chief problem remains, however, whether in the Greek *Vorlage* ϊⲉⲛ or ⲉⲓⲉⲛ occurred. If ⲉⲓⲉⲛ were not there, one could hypothecize that IV interpreted the text capriciously. Perhaps one could see these letters as the initial letters of the following words: Ἰ(ήου) ἐ(στὶ) ν(έος), ἐ(στὶν) Ἄ(δαμας). The meaning would then be that Ἰήου renews himself and appears in the Light-Adam. (Cf. ιηουεαω *supra*, p. 173). Of course, this remains only a purely hypothetical possibility.

The origin of Adamas: III 49,8-16 = IV 61,8-18.

ⲉⲡⲓⲇⲉ in IV 61,8 corresponds to ⲅⲁⲣ in III 49,8. For the spelling ἐπειδέ see E. Schwyzer, *Griechische Grammatik* II, pp. 658f. One could also read ἐπεὶ δέ, see ThCont II 138,7. IV 61,8-11 and III 49,8-10 differ considerably. The shorter text in III as well as the version in IV have Adamas originate from "Man" (meaning God). The longer text in IV is obscured by lacunae, but Adamas is called "the eye". Whose eye he is can be reconstructed from SJC (BG) 100,12ff. and 108,8-11 where Adamas is called "the eye of the light". From IV 61,11ff. it is clear that the light is identical with the first Man, while in III 49,8 the light is connected with Adamas (cf. φῶς "light" and φώς "man" in Clem. *Paed.* I 6). The quotation from the New Testament (Col 1:16; John 1:3) and the identification of the Father with the first man in IV make it clear that the "Man" from whom Adamas originates is God. God has come down in Adamas to remove the ὑστέρημα. In ApocryJn the statement about the God-man is part of a presentation of praise to the invisible Spirit by Adamas after his creation (BG 35,13ff. = III 13,11ff. = II 9,5ff.).

The union of Adamas and the Logos: III 49, 16-22 = IV 61,18-23.

In III the Greek word λόγος appears twice (49,17.20) and ϣⲁϫⲉ once (49,22) in this section. This may mean that the Coptic translator attempted to make a distinction between Logos as a mythological figure and the normal meaning "word" (cf. A. Böhlig, *Die griechischen Lehnwörter*, pp. 24f.). IV uses only ϣⲁϫⲉ. Just as in Gnosticism the earthly man does not have life simply by virtue of his creation, so also Adamas must be joined with the Logos. The Logos and Adamas mingle with each other (III, 49,19f.) or become a "synthesis" or "mixture" (cf. Crum, *Dict.* p. 831a σύνθεσις, κρᾶμα) "which is man" (IV 61,21f.). κρᾶμα refers to the union of soul and body in patristic texts (cf. Lampe, p. 774b). III 49,20-22 is somewhat more detailed than IV and points out two aspects. On the one hand man possesses a logos, on the other hand he is created by a word. It appears that III or his Greek *Vorlage* added an interpretive comment at this point.

The presentation of praise of the Logos and Adamas: III 49,22-50,17 = IV 61,23 - 62,16.

Cf. *supra*, p. 49 for this section. The mixing of the Logos and Adamas leads to joint action. For Esephech as "the child of the child" see Zost VIII 45,11; 58,25. For the plural with Doxomedon in IV 62,4 see *supra*, p. 42. For the ethereal earth see U 361,35, and ⲕⲁϩ ⲛ̄ⲛⲁⲏⲣ in Zost VIII 8,11; 9,2ff. It forms the lowest part of the heavenly world. According to Zost it came into being through a word. As such it is the counterpart of the cosmic earth. "It reveals the created and corruptible ones in incorruptibility" (Zost VIII 9,4ff.). Thus it is a place of transformation. The description "the receiver of God" (III 50,10f. = IV 62,9f.) must mean that the deification takes place there (cf. U 361,35ff). The ⲛ̄ⲣⲱⲙⲉ in III 50,14 appears to be a secondary addition. III 50,15 leaves out ⲡⲏⲅⲏ. IV has the better text as the parallelism suggests:

"[the] light of the Father [of the] silence
and the living spring [of silence,]
[the] Father and [their whole] pleroma".

The request of the Logos and Adamas: III 50,17-51,14 = IV 62,16 - 63,8.

After this presentation of praise has been completed, the text resumes with a summarizing reference to it, perhaps to place the emphasis on the ones who present the praise. Once again the Greek term λόγος is used in III. The petition is divided into two parts. In the first one the Logos and Adamas together ask for the creation of the lights. In the second part Adamas requests a son, i.e. Seth, to be the father of a new race. III probably left out inadvertently the ⲙⲛ̄ⲧⲁⲧϫⲱϩ̄ⲙ present in IV 62,21. III 50,23 = IV 62,22 indicates that the requested power (the lights) will complete the four aeons. It will shine into the cosmos which exists in the darkness of night. In IV 62,31 - 63,1 in contrast to III 51,6, Adamas asks for a son "for himself", which shows that we are dealing with an independent tradition. This supports the reconstruction ⲧⲟⲧⲉ in IV 62,30. III has harmonized it with the preceding part by translating "for them". III 51,7-14 = IV 63,1-8 presents the task of the race of Seth. Its appearance serves as the judgment of the dead aeon. The voice precedes the raising of the aeon and is indeed the prerequisite for the judgement (cf. 1 Cor 15:52). If IV 63,4 ⲚⲦⲀⲤ is left unemended, it would have to be II Perfect. The gnostic reader then viewed the requested events not from the perspective of those who make the request (the Logos and Adamas), but from his own perspective since the creation of Seth and the race of Seth have already brought about the possibility of salvation. The race of Seth has the same function as the light elements or light spirits in Gnosticism (cf. Böhlig-Labib II, *5*, p. 101).

The creation of the four lights and Seth: III 51,14-22 = IV 63,8-17. In III 51,19 ⲉⲧⲛⲁϣⲱϥ meaning "great" has been added as an attribute of the four lights. ⲛⲟϭ is missing in III 51,21 in contrast to IV 63,16. As in the case of Adamas (*supra*, p. 176), an auxiliary power comes into being to create the four lights, Harmozel, Oroiael, Davithe and Eleleth, and Seth. III 51,17 takes *προφάνεια* to be the name of this power. *προφάνεια* is represented in IV 63,11 by ⲡ̄ⲣⲣⲓⲱⲟⲩ. Other examples of the Qualitative functioning as a noun are ⲁⲥⲱⲟⲩ "hastiness", ⲓⲏⲥ "speed", and ⲙⲟⲧ̄ⲛ "ease". A detailed description of the creation of the four lights can be found in ApocryJn (BG 32,19ff. = III 11,15ff. = II 7,30ff.). For its place in the myth see *supra*, p. 33. The inhabitants of the four lights are mentioned in III 65,12ff. = IV 77,7ff. ApocryJn deals with this immediately following the creation of the lights. (BG 35,5ff. = III 13,3ff. = II 8,35ff.).

The completion of the Hebdomad: III 51,22 - 52,3 = IV 63,17-24. The omission of ⲟⲩⲙⲩⲥⲧⲏⲣⲓⲟⲛ in III 51,24 may be due to homoioteleuton in the Greek text. IV 63,23f. ⲛ̄ⲟⲅⲇⲟⲁⲥ ϩⲓⲛⲁ ⲛ̄ⲧⲉⲥϫⲱⲕ ϩⲛ̄ ϥⲧⲟ may also be missing in III due to homoioteleuton. This piece of traditional material is an arithmological speculation typical for Gnostic literature. The unit of seven — its content is not specified — becomes through the addition of the four a group of eleven. These eleven are themselves ogdoads. A different arithmological scheme lies behind III 53,10ff. = IV 65,2ff. which speaks of five ogdoads.

The consorts of the lights: III 52,3-16 = IV 63,24 - 64,10. In this section GEgypt differs from ApocryJn where each light receives three aeons: Harmozel receives *χάρις, ἀλήθεια* and *μορφή*; Oroiael receives *πρόνοια, αἴσθησις* and *μνήμη*; Davithe receives *σύνεσις, ἀγάπη* and *ἰδέα*; Eleleth receives *τελειότης, εἰρήνη* and *σοφία* (BG 33,10ff. = III 12,2ff. = II 8,7ff.). However ApocryJn also knows the tradition that only four consorts, *χάρις, αἴσθησις, σύνεσις* and *φρόνησις* belong to the light (BG 33,6f. = III 11,22f. = II 8,3f.).

The ministers of the lights and their consorts: III 52,16 - 53,12 = IV 64,10 - 65,5.

The ogdoad formed by the four lights and their consorts is complemented by a second ogdoad which has a typical auxiliary function. Three of the ministers are also known from ApocAd V 75,22ff. where they rescue the people of Seth. The two ogdoads of the Autogenes are now added to the three of the Father, Mother and Son and so form together a total of forty beings. The designation "uninterpretable power" heightens their mysterious character. For forty as an unmixed "four" see fragment 16 of Heracleon (Origen, *in Jo* 2:20 = ed. Preuschen, pp. 214,30-215,1).

The request of the Logos and the pleroma: III 53,12-54,11 = IV 65,5 - 30.

The ⲡϣⲁϫⲉ ⲙ̄- in III 53,14 is a secondary addition under the influence of the preceding expression. IV 65,13 has Doxomedon-aeon in the plural. It should be noted that "which are in them" in III 53,20f. also assumes a plural in spite of the singular article in 53,19. The expected ⲡⲁⲗⲟⲩ ⲛ̄ⲧⲉ ⲡⲁⲗⲟⲩ is missing in IV 65,20. ⲡⲗⲏⲣⲱⲙⲁ in III 54,3 stands in apposition. Perhaps the ⲙ̄ⲛ-ⲙ̄ⲛ in IV 65,21f. means "both - and". ⲉⲧⲛ̄ϩⲣⲁï ϩ̄ⲛ- in IV 65,23 should be preferred over ⲉⲧⲙ̄ⲙⲁⲩ in III. For the presentation of praise see *supra*, pp. 39f. The content of the petition presents difficulties due to the differences between III 54,6ff. and IV 65,25ff. The first request is that the Father may be called the fourth, the second that the race of the Father may be called the seed of Seth. This second request establishes the connection between the children of Seth on earth and the supreme God. Only because the great invisible Spirit is the father of the Gnostics can they be certain that they are a "divine race". That is why the Sethians as the seed of Seth need a mythological explanation for their relationship to the Father. The response to the request satisfies this need. The meaning of the first part of the petition is obscure (cf. *infra*, p. 181). Together with the incorruptible race the Father forms a unit of four. Four is a basic number. However, it is unclear who the three are who, together with the Father, make a group of four. The following section, which speaks of the thrice-male child and Christ, may be involved here. One should also note III 42,5ff. = IV 51,22ff., which shows that the thrice-male child originated from the Father. In contrast with III, the version in IV mentions *σπορά* only once.

The response to the request: III 54,11 - 55,2 = IV 65,30 - 66,14. The two-fold ϩⲉⲛⲧⲃⲁ ⲉⲙ̄ⲛ̄ⲧⲟⲩ ⲏⲡⲉ in III appears to be secondary. The shaking of heaven and earth here (cf. OnOrWld, II 102 (150),26ff.) is not a sign of insurrection but the work of heavenly beings. This agrees with the general character of the tractate, for the opposition of the evil powers is only briefly mentioned and the initiative lies essentially with the heavenly beings. The incorruptible ones who make up the heavenly world consist of several groups of differing quality. Some are unborn, some self-begotten, and the third group is begotten in the created part of the heavenly world. For ϫⲡⲟ ⲉ- with the meaning "created into" cf. Crum, *Dict.* p. 779a. For ϩⲛ̄ with the meaning "into" cf. Crum, *Dict.* pp. 683a and 684b. Into this world a unit of four descends which could be the heavenly model of Seth and his children. It affects the heavenly world and consists of the thrice-male child and Christ. For this combination see *supra*, p. 46. The plural form of the verbal prefix (III 54,14) stresses the number three. Both the child and Christ are beings which are not created but have come into being (*προελθεῖν*). Perhaps in the second part of the tractate Seth and his children correspond to this unit of four in the sense that the threefold creation through Plesithea, Hormos and Edokla together with the earthly Seth form such a group of four. The combination of three and one reminds one of the then widely known story of the three young men in the fiery furnace and the angel who joins them (Dan 3:24-25 MT = 3:91-92 LXX). Christ surrounds himself with a court, an act which already points to the following section, but undoubtedly belongs here as can be seen from the concluding sentence (III 55,1f. = IV 66,13f.). In III the unit of four is the subject of this sentence; in IV it seems to be Christ. The founding of the four aeons was described in IV 60,19ff.

The emergence of the heavenly church: III 55,2-16 = IV 66,14 - 67,1. *Λόγος* or ϣⲁϫⲉ dropped out in III 55,5. The development of the heavenly world, which has occurred as a response to the petitions of the Logos and the pleroma of the lights, finally leads to the formation of a heavenly church (πνευματικὴ ἐκκλησία), whose task it is to praise the trinity of Father, Mother and Son. The first main section ends with "Amen" (III 55,16 = IV 67,1). For the structure of the tractate as a whole see *supra*, pp. 26ff.

The presentation of praise of Seth and the request for his seed: III 55,16 - 56,3 = IV 67,2- ?

For the presentation of praise see *supra*, pp. 39f.

Plesithea and her work: III 56,4-13 = IV 67, ? -27.

As with the creation of Adamas, a female creation-deity must appear in order to fulfill Seth's request. Earlier it was Moirothea (III 49,4), this time it is Πλησιθεά which means "full goddess". She is called mother three times. The name seems to suggest extraordinary fertility such as is reported of the Ephesian goddess Artemis. But in contrast to her she does not have many breasts but only four. Perhaps this indicates her ability to give birth as a virgin (cf. Böhlig-Labib, II, *5*, pp. 74f.; Thund VI 13,19ff.). This conception is combined with a positive view of Sodom and Gomorrah (see *supra*, pp. 28f.). Each place is given a special function (cf. III 60,9-18 = IV 71,18-30). Gomorrah is the spring and Sodom the fruit. ⲉⲧⲛ̄ϩⲏⲧⲥ̄ in III 56,12 could refer back to either Sodom or Plesithea. In the latter case Sodom and Gomorrah are seen as spring and fruit within the mother Plesithea.

The rejoicing of Seth: III 56,13-22 = IV 67,27 - 68,5.

This section forms an independent piece of traditional material along with the preceding section. This is evident from the reference to the child without mentioning its threefold nature. ϩⲙⲟⲧ (= χάρις) in III 56,15 means "gift". The place where the creation takes place is, as in all previous cases, the heavenly world (III 56,4 ϩⲙ ⲡⲙⲁ ⲉⲧⲙ̄ⲙⲁⲩ). III 56,20 presents a typical misinterpretation. According to III Seth placed the seed "in the *fourth* aeon in the third great light Davithe". IV 68,3ff., on the other hand, reads correctly "in the *four* aeons in the third great light Davithe". These aeons were mentioned already in IV 60,19ff. The children of Seth are in them "with him" (Seth). III pictures Seth as dwelling in Davithe. This contradicts III 65,16ff. = IV 77,12f. which states that he lives in Oroiael. For the dwelling of the children of Seth "in the third aeon in the third great light Davithe" see ApocryJn BG 36,2ff. = III 13,19ff. = II 9,14ff.

The creation of the rulers of the world: III 56,22 - 58,22 = IV 68,5- ?
In GEgypt the absolute rule of the heavenly world can be seen in the creation of the world ruler, who comes into being by its expressed wish rather than through a fall as in ApocryJn and in Valentinianism. The light Eleleth is closest to Chaos and Hades. That is why he utters the command. Why he does this "after 5000 years" remains unclear. Again GEgypt employs the now familiar creation scheme. The hylic Sophia comes forth in the form of a cloud. After this the minister of Harmozel communicates the creation order to the minister of Oroiael. Next the cloud appears in two monads of light. The two monads are possibly Sophia herself and her throne. Then ⲛ̄[ⲧⲟⲥ ⲙ̄ⲛ ⲡⲑⲣⲟⲛ]ⲟⲥ is to be read. Perhaps the throne represents the Demiurge. ApocryJn also speaks about a throne for the ruler of the world in a cloud of light (BG 38,6ff. = III 15,16ff. = II 10,14ff.). In this abbreviated form the Sophia-demiurge myth has been incorporated into the tractate. The ruler of the world is called Sakla, not Ialdabaoth. Nebruel is connected with him as in the Manichaean cosmogony, see F. Cumont. *La cosmogonie manichéenne* (Recherches sur le Manchéisme I) Bruxelles 1908, p. 42 n. 3. Perhaps Nebruel is derived from *Νεβρώδ*, in Hebrew נִמְרֹד. He is indeed a primeval ruler according to Gen 10:8-12 = 1 Chron 1:10: "And Cush begot Nimrod; he was the first mighty one on the earth". If Nimrod in Mic 5:6 is a ruler of the Assyrians this would give the name a pejorative meaning. Names ending in -ⲏⲗ are common in the tractate, e.g. ⲓ̈ⲱⲏⲗ III 65,23 and ⲡⲟⲓⲙⲁⲏⲗ III 66,1 = IV 78,2. The archangel Sakla and the great or chief demon join together to become a creator-spirit of the earth. Their products are the twelve assisting angels and the twelve aeons. Sakla gives each angel authority over an aeon. These twelve angels, who are listed by name, are also present in ApocryJn (BG 40,5ff. = III 16,20ff. = II 10,28ff.):

	GEgypt	BG	III, *1*	II, *1*
1	ⲁⲑ[ⲱⲑ]	ⲓⲁⲱⲑ	ϩⲁⲱⲑ	ⲁⲑⲱⲑ
2	ϩⲁⲣⲙⲁⲥ	ϩⲉⲣⲙⲁⲥ	ϩⲁⲣⲙⲁⲥ	ϩⲁⲣⲙⲁⲥ
3	[ⲅⲁⲗⲓⲗⲁ]	ⲅⲁⲗⲓⲗⲁ	ⲅⲁⲗⲓⲗⲁ	ⲕⲁⲗⲓⲗⲁ ⲟⲩⲙⲃⲣⲓ
4	ⲓ̈ⲱⲃⲏⲗ	ⲓ̈ⲱⲃⲏⲗ	ⲓ̈ⲱⲃⲏⲗ	ⲓ̈ⲁⲃⲏⲗ
5	[ⲁ]ⲇⲱⲛⲁⲓⲟⲥ	ⲁⲇⲱⲛⲁⲓⲟⲥ	ⲁⲇⲱⲛⲁⲓⲟⲥ	ⲁⲇⲱⲛⲁⲓ̈ⲟⲩ
6	[ⲕⲁⲓ̈ⲛ]	ⲥⲁⲃⲁⲱⲑ	ⲥⲁⲃⲁⲱⲑ	ⲕⲁⲓ̈ⲛ
7	[ⲁⲃⲉⲗ]	ⲕⲁⲓ̈ⲛⲁⲛ and ⲕⲁⲏ	ⲕⲁⲓ̈ⲛⲁⲛ ⲕⲁⲥⲓⲛ	ⲁⲃⲉⲗ

8	ⲁⲕⲓⲣⲉⲥⲥⲓⲛⲁ	ⲁⲃⲓⲣⲉⲥⲥⲓⲛⲉ	ⲁⲃⲓⲣⲉⲥⲥⲓⲁ	ⲁⲃⲣⲓⲥⲉⲛⲉ
9	ⲓ̈ⲟⲩⲃⲏⲗ	ⲓ̈ⲱⲃⲏⲗ	ⲓ̈ⲱⲃⲏⲗ	ⲓ̈ⲱⲃⲏⲗ
10	ϩⲁⲣⲙ̣[ⲟⲩⲡⲓⲁⲏⲗ]	ϩⲁⲣⲙⲟⲩⲡⲓⲁⲏⲗ	ⲁⲣⲙⲟⲩⲡⲓⲁⲏⲗ	ⲁⲣⲙⲟⲩⲡⲓⲉⲏⲗ
11	ⲁⲣⲭ[ⲉⲓⲣ ⲁⲇⲱⲛⲉⲓⲛ]	ⲁⲇⲱⲛⲓⲛ	ⲁⲇⲱⲛⲓⲛ	ⲙⲉⲗⲭⲉⲓⲣ ⲁⲇⲱⲛⲉⲓⲛ
12	[ⲃⲉⲗⲓⲁⲥ]	ⲃⲉⲗⲓⲁⲥ	ⲃⲉⲗⲓⲁⲥ	ⲃⲉⲗⲓⲁⲥ

GEgypt in agreement with ApocryJn gives several of the angels a second name or defines them with a predicate. BG and III, *1* call ϩⲁⲣⲙⲁⲥ "the eye of the fire", II, *1* "the eye of jealousy". All versions call ⲕⲁⲓ̈ⲛ "the sun". ApocryJn II calls ⲁⲇⲱⲛⲁⲓ̈ⲟⲩ also ⲥⲁⲃⲁⲱⲑ. GEgypt agrees in each case with the Codex II version against BG and III, *1*. The ⲕ in ⲁⲕⲓⲣⲉⲥⲥⲓⲛⲁ must be a mistake for ⲃ. Such errors, which are common in the spelling of unfamiliar names, as well as the other orthographical variants are insignificant.

The arrogance of Sakla: III 58,23-59,1. IV is lost.

GEgypt gives the words of Sakla a somewhat different form from NatArch II 86(134),30f.; 94(142),21f.; OnOrWld II 103(151),11ff. and GrSeth VII 53,30f.,which quote Is 46:9 (LXX). With ApocryJn (BG 44,14 = II 13,8f.) and Irenaeus, *Adv. Haer.* I, 29.4 it adds the adjective "jealous" probably on the basis of Ex 20:5. Further GEgypt reads "and apart from (or: without) me nothing has come into being". The first meaning would have gradually changed into the second. The reconstruction ϣⲱⲡⲉ is necessary because of the preceding Perfect negative. Sakla's hybris is seen in that he relies on his nature which does not have the quality he assumes. The parallel in ApocryJn at this point (BG 43,4f. = III 18,20ff.) states that he became disobedient to the nature (*ὑπόστασις*) from which he originated. However there is not enough room to negate ⲡⲓⲑⲉ in III 58,26.

The rebuke of Sakla and the creation of man: III 59,1-9. IV is lost.

Sakla is rebuked by an unidentified voice from on high. In contrast to OnOrWld II 103(151), 15ff. where Pistis addresses a lengthy rebuke to the chief archon, GEgypt and ApocryJn (BG 47,15f. = III 21,17f. = II 14,14f.) have simply the statement about the existence of Man and the Son of Man. The difference in ApocryJn is that the words are spoken to Sophia though heard by Ialdabaoth. The identity of the Man and the Son of Man is not clear. The different systems do not interpret these beings in the same way. Thus the Man can be the supreme God (Irenaeus, *Adv. Haer.* I, 30.6) as well as his first manifestation in his female complement (BG 27,19 = III 7,23 = II 5,7), or another secondary manifestation of the supreme God. Son of Man need not be Christ, as it appears to be in GPh where Christ plays an important role. It is used as the description of the savior in III 85,11f. (Eug), who is the consort of Pistis Sophia (III 81,23ff.; 82,7f.). Yet above him stands not the supreme God but an emanation, "the immortal man" (III 85,10f.). In OnOrWld II 103(151),19; 107(155),26 the "true man" could perhaps refer to the supreme God. In that case he should be distinguished from his manifestation in the world since it became contaminated by a deficiency during its stay on earth (II 111(159),29ff.). This manifestation can be compared to the primal Man of the Manichaeans. For further material on the Man and the Son of Man in Gnosticism see H.-M. Schenke, *Der Gott "Mensch" in der Gnosis* (Berlin 1962). In GEgypt "Man" and "Son of Man" are part of traditional material and are not further integrated into the cosmogony of the tractate. Only in the section on the creation of Adamas can a possible reference to the god "Man" be discerned. As was mentioned before, the rebuke is followed by a voice from on high, the light-image, which, in Gnostic myths is seen by the archons and so becomes the occasion for the creation of man (cf. II 112(160),32ff. and Böhlig-Labib II, *5*, pp. 70f.). This is the Gnostic interpretation of the creation of man in the image of God in Gen 1 : 26. Since the story of creation is only of peripheral interest to the author it is summarized in one phrase. He states that the first creature (*πλάσμα*) was formed on account of the looking out of the image above. ϭⲱϣⲧ (ⲉⲃⲟⲗ) in III 59,6.7 can not be passive since it is used only intransitively (cf. Crum, *Dict.* p. 837f.).

The redeeming activity of Metanoia: III 59,9 - 60,2 = IV 70, ? - 71,11.

Metanoia also appears quite unexpectedly. As a soteriological auxiliary being she follows upon the creation. ⲡⲁϊ ⲉⲧⲃⲏⲏⲧ̄ϥ could mean simply "therefore". However, it is more likely that the ⲡⲁϊ resumes ⲡⲗⲁⲥⲙⲁ. Just as Sophia needed Metanoia to return to the realm of light after the fall, so too the earthly creature stands in need of her. As a mythological entity she appears wholly within the framework of the divine economy. In GEgypt mankind as such is not the object of the saving activity, but rather the people of Seth, the chosen race, which also needs to be rescued from *ὑστέρημα*, "the deficiency", due to its stay on earth (cf. IV 71,1f. ⲛⲓⲉⲱⲛ ⲛ̄ϫⲡⲟ ⲛ̄ⲕⲁϩ; III 59,16 lacks ⲛ̄ⲕⲁϩ). It is this deficiency that Metanoia is to "fill up" (the ⲉⲃⲟⲗ ϩⲓⲧⲟⲟⲧ̄ⲥ in III 59,17 could also refer to the race of Seth). ὑστέρημα in III 59,18 corresponds to ϩⲁⲉⲟⲩ in IV 71,3. For the attribute "night-like" see III 51,5 = IV 62,29. ἐξουσίαι in III 59,22 could be an explanatory addition. For ἄρχων τοῦ αἰῶνος τούτου see IGN. *Eph.* 17,1; 19,1; *Magn.* 1,3 etc. (see W. BAUER, *Lexicon* s.v.). III 59,25 "demon-begetting" is hard to fit in the lacuna in IV 71,9. The ⲙⲛ̄ - ⲙⲛ̄ in III 59,21 and 25 corresponds to ⲁⲩⲱ ⲙⲛ̄ - ⲁⲩⲱ ⲙⲛ̄ (= καὶ-καί) in IV 71,6. [10].

As in St. Augustine's *Civitas Dei*, (cf. A. BÖHLIG, "Zu gnostischen Grundlagen der Civitas-Dei-Vorstellung bei Augustin" ZNW 60 (1969), 291-295) the world is divided into two groups, the seed of the demon-begetting God and the seed of Adam and Seth. The pristine element in Adam has, after his fall, been transferred to Seth (cf. ApocAd V 64,24ff.). The identification of Adam with the sun (IV 71,10), since it is more concrete, appears to have greater claim to being original than the identification of the seed of Adam with the sun. The most difficult to understand is the work of Metanoia. ⲧⲱⲃϩ (III 50,21) corresponds to ⲉⲣⲏⲧ (IV 71,5f.). In both cases the verb is linked to the object by ⲛ̄ⲥⲁ. It probably means that Metanoia prayed for the repentance of both groups. The concern of the heavenly world for the children of the world rulers becomes understandable when one reads in ApocAd that repentance also occurs among the seed of Ham and Japheth (V 74,10f.; 76,11ff.).

The work of Hormos: III 60,2-8 = IV 71,11-18.

Hormos is also present in a list of angels in Zost where it is said that he is "over the [holy] seed" (VIII 47,9ff.). In this passage the birth of Seth in the world (III 63,10ff. = IV 74,25ff.) seems to have been transferred to the seed of Seth and projected back into prehistory. Just as Plesithea (see *supra*, p. 36) had created the seed of Seth in the realm of light, so Hormos gives the race its relationship with the perishable world. That is why the Hormos episode, in contrast with the Plesithea episode, comes after the story of creation. Yet the light elements of the children of Seth are dominant. Just as Seth prepared himself a "Logos-begotten body" through a virgin (III 63,10ff. = IV 74,25ff.), so Hormos creates the seed of Seth through mortal virgins — the plural is necessary because of the plurality of the children of Seth — in a "Logos-begotten vessel". The use of σκεῦος instead of σῶμα is explained by the frequent use of σκεῦος for "body" (cf. W. BAUER, *Lexicon s.v.*).

The placing of the seed of Seth: III 60,9-18 = IV 71,18-30.

The basic difference between III and IV regarding the work of Seth is that in contrast to IV, III has divided the content of IV 71,22-30 into two alternative views each introduced by the phrase, "some say ..." IV is probably based on an earlier form of the text, from which the text underlying III was derived. This follows from the lack of "source" (πηγή) in III. For πηγή as Gomorrah, cf. III 56,10-11 (IV is lost.). The view proposed by the first group in III, that Sodom is the pasture of the great Seth, can also be found in IV. However, here it is set forth in the context of the view attributed to the second group in III. The main difference between III and IV lies in the introduction to the views concerning Sodom and Gomorrah. Both manuscripts report that Seth sowed his seed in the created aeons. Concerning the aeons III says that the number of the seed is the amount of Sodom, while IV, the text of which is considerably damaged, may permit the following reconstruction: [ⲉⲧⲉ ⲡⲉⲩϣⲓ ⲡⲉ] ⲟⲩⲁⲧϯ [ⲏⲡⲉ ⲉ]ⲣⲟ[ϥ ⲛ̄ⲧⲉ] ⲥⲟⲇⲟⲙⲏ ["of which the amount is] an un-[countable (amount) of] Sodom". III has simplified the extravagant expression presented in IV. The decisive difference is found in IV 71,22f. over against III 60,12f. What is the antecedent of ⲛ̄ⲧⲟⲟⲩ and ⲉⲣⲟⲟⲩ in IV 71,22f. ? Grammatically it must refer to the created aeons, since they are the place in which the seed of Seth is placed; cf. IV 68,2f. = III 56,19ff. On the other hand, as a result of the identification of Sodom and Gomorrah, Sodom can also be seen as the collective of the seed of Seth. Then the plural in IV 71,22f. must be taken as a *constructio ad sensum* referring to the seed (σπορά). The first meaning appears to be more probable in this case, although III 56,10f. designates the fruit as Sodom. Furthermore, this passage, which has not survived in IV, gives the impression of being textually less certain. The difference between the placing of the seed of Seth produced by Plesithea and the placing of the seed of Seth brought forth by Hormos is that the former are placed in aeons of the light-world while the latter are put in earth-produced aeons (IV 71,20 ϫⲡⲟ ⲛ̄ⲕⲁϩ in contrast to III 60,10f. ⲛ̄ⲧⲁⲩϫⲡⲟⲟⲩ). The Greek word γηγενής may be involved here. "Earth" here perhaps expresses the incompleteness which is also mentioned in the section concerning the work of Hormos.

The race of Edokla: III 60,19 - 61,1 = IV 71,30 - 72,10.

The name ⲉⲇⲟⲕⲗⲁ is not attested elsewhere. Perhaps the ending is related to proper names ending in -*κλης* (m.) and -*κλα* (f.), e.g. Heracles and Thecla. If the first part of the name is related to *ἕδ-* "seat" then the meaning would be something like "goddess of origin", since *ἕδος* also means "base". Edokla gives birth to *ἀλήθεια* and *θέμισσα* through the word. The absence of the articles before *ἀλήθεια* and *θέμισσα* in IV 72,2f. could indicate that they are proper names. The usual supralinear strokes (see *supra*, pp. 3f.) are absent here but present in the parallel occurrence in IV 74,6. III did not understand the passage at all, as the scribal mistake indicates. The passage is of great interest for the history of religions since the expected connection between the two beings had not been attested before (cf. H. Hommel, "Wahrheit und Gerechtigkeit", *Antike und Abendland* 15 [1969], 174). So apparently two goddesses, who are personifications of ethical concepts, form "the beginning" (*ἀρχή*) of the seed of eternal life. For *ἀρχή* "beginner" see Col 1:18 and Gen 49:3. This seed is further identified as Gnostics who know their emanation (*ἀπόρροια*). The ⲉⲧϣⲟⲟⲡ ⲙ̄ⲛ- in III 60,23 appears to be a secondary interpretation. It must refer back to eternal life with the meaning that the Gnostics who know their origin possess eternal life. III 60,25ff. = IV 72,8ff. completes the myths about the creation of the seed of Seth. The meaning of "in" or "through three worlds" is puzzling. IV may have in mind the three "worlds" in which the children of Seth are situated, the heavenly world, the world of angels, and the earthly world. III may have changed the meaning. Keeping in mind that *κόσμος* can also mean "mankind" (see W. Bauer, *Lexicon s.v.*) III could perhaps have meant with "through three *κόσμοι*" that the race of Seth has come into the world through three groups of beings who make up the children of Seth. This would also do some justice to the ⲉⲡⲕⲟⲥⲙⲟⲥ in III 61,1.

The perils facing the seed of Seth: III 61,1-15 = IV 72,10-27.

The section consists of four parts, one dealing with the flood, the second with the conflagration, the third with famines and plagues, and the fourth with temptations by false prophets. IV projects all these events into the future. This must be the correct reading over against III which speaks of the flood in the past. Keeping in mind that Seth is the mythological author of the book and that he lived *before* the flood, it is apparent that III altered the text to fit the viewpoint of the *reader*. To understand the flood as a type of the end of the world is similar to Celsus' idea that the flood in the course of history is followed by burning — he means the final conflagration. (Orig. *c. Cels.* IV, 11). ϣⲁ- in III 61,3 and ⲉ- in IV 72,11 with τύπος go back to the Greek εἰς meaning "with reference to" (cf. W. Bauer, *Lexicon s.v.*). This meaning is not attested in Coptic for ϣⲁ-. The conflagration at the end must be distinguished from the fire from which the children of Seth are protected by the prophets and guardians (cf. ApocAd V 75,9ff.). The III Fut. here stresses certainty (cf. Stern, *Kopt. Gramm.* § 381). λιμός and λοιμός (III 61,11 = IV 72,21) are typical signs of the end time in the N.T. (cf. W. Bauer, *Lexicon s.v.*). Here they belong to the perils which especially the children of Seth must face. The same is true for the πειρασμός and πλάνη of false prophets. For ⲙⲟⲩ with the meaning λοιμός see Crum, *Dict.* p. 159b. It seems that something was left out after ⲡⲕⲁϩ in III 61,6. The parallel in IV 72,15f. is obscured by lacunae.

Seth recognizes the devil's schemes: III 61,16-23 = IV 72,27 - 73,6. This section supplements the preceding one. Where earlier the perils were described which threaten the children of Seth, now it is made clear that the activity of the devil stands behind all of them. ἐνέργεια means "mode of operation"; it is also found in other Gnostic texts (cf. II 107(155),2.15). ⲛⲉϥⲕⲟⲧ̄ⲥ (IV 73,1) means "his tricks" (cf. Crum, *Dict.* p. 127b and Eph 6:11 τὰς μεθοδείας τοῦ διαβόλου), while ⲡⲉϥⲁⲧⲟ ⲛ̄ⲥⲙⲟⲧ (III 61,17f.) translates "his many guises". The difference may be due to divergent interpretations of ἀμφιβολία. For ⲕⲟⲧ̄ⲥ = ἀμφίβολος see Crum, *Dict.* p. 127b. ⲙⲉⲉⲩⲉ must be plans or schemes. III 61,20ff. = IV 73,4ff. speaks about the devil's entourage. As in the case of the ruler of the world, the devil is an angel and a ruler of angels (see *supra*, p. 183; also "the devil and his angels" in Mt 25:41). It is a special trait of the demonic world, and of the devil himself, to act against itself. Again the Fut. in IV is the original reading against the Perf. in III (see *supra*, pp. 188f.). For internal strife as a typical characteristic of the demonic world see GTr I 29,15f. In the *Kephalaia* of Mani this trait is developed in terms of Mt 12:25 (Kephalaion 52). ⲁⲩⲧⲟⲗⲙⲁ in III corresponds to ϥⲛⲁⲧⲟⲗⲙⲁ in IV. In III the subject is the demonic powers; in IV the devil himself is the subject. Probably III is a simplification.

Seth requests guardians for his race: III 61,23 - 62,13 = IV 73,7-26.

For the presentation of praise see *supra*, pp. 39f. III has left out two attributes of the great invisible Spirit (cf. IV 73,9). ⲧⲉⲗⲙⲁⲏⲗ along side ⲧⲉⲗⲙⲁⲭⲁⲏⲗ in IV 73,13 is not a scribal error but an accepted variant of the name, as 59,19 shows. Also III 62, 2f. has ⲧⲉⲗⲙⲁⲏⲗ. For the absence of ⲡⲁⲗⲟⲩ ⲙ̄ⲡⲁⲗⲟⲩ see *supra*, p. 48. Only here has IV translated ⲇⲟⲝⲟⲙⲉⲇⲱⲛ as ⲣⲉϥϯ ⲉⲟⲟⲩ. The "great ones" (IV 73,21) who surround the throne suggest the picture of a royal court. III 62,10 has the expected ⲛ̄ϭⲟⲙ. III has left out "and glories and incorruptions" found in IV 73,22f. These and the earlier omissions in the presentation of praise in III give the impression of imprecision. Since ⲣ̄ⲁⲓⲧⲓ ⲛ̄ϣⲟⲣ̄ⲡ equals προαιτεῖν in IV 73,25 and means "to ask beforehand", the omission of ⲛ̄ϣⲟⲣⲡ in III 62,12 is easily explained as another instance of simplification in which the refinement of meaning indicated by προ- has been ignored (cf. *supra*, p. 12).

The arrival of the guardians: III 62,13-24 = IV 73,27 - 74,9.

The number of guards is given as 400. This number is often used in the Bible for groups of people, e.g. Gen 32:7; 1 Sam 22:2; 25:13; 30:10.17; 1 Kgs 18:19; 22:6; Acts 5:36. They are called ἀερόδιοι; cf. U 361,39; 362,11. For the spelling of the word in III see 62,14note. U 362,13 also mentions Selmelche, who in III is called "Selmechel" and in IV "Selmelchel". ⲁⲉⲣⲟⲥⲓⲏⲗ may be a transformation of the evil ἄρχων τῆς ἐξουσίας τοῦ ἀέρος of Eph 2:2 into a good assistant. The ⲉϩⲁⲣⲉϩ ⲉ- in III 62,16f. must be a free rendering of ⲛⲓⲣⲉϥⲁⲣⲉϩ which in IV 74,2 stands in apposition. The guarding lasts for the duration of the stay on earth of the children of Seth. It is specified as beginning with the creation of Aletheia and Themissa, and lasts until the end of this world. The condemnation of the archons is being treated here because of their mistreatment of the race of Seth mentioned earlier.

The mission of Seth: III 62,24 - 63,4 = IV 74,9-17.

After the long segment which spoke about the creation, the abode and the guarding of the children of Seth, a specifically soteriological part follows. It deals with the sending of Seth into the world and his saving work. He is sent by the lights — in one of which he lives — according to the will of the Autogenes, i.e. the Logos, and the whole pleroma. But approval is also granted by the highest authority.

The statement is a good example of the Gnostic concept of the divine economy. The great invisible Spirit himself participates, through his approval, in this soteriological event together with his pantheon, the five seals and the pleroma. The pleroma in general and the pleroma of the lights probably should be distinguished (cf. III 52,5f. = IV 63,26f.). The ⲡⲛⲟⲩⲧⲉ in III 63,2 is incorrect. IV 74,14 has correctly translated ⲟⲩϯ ⲛ̄ⲧⲁϥ, "his (gracious) giving" (cf. ⲡϯ in III 68,17). Since III in contrast to IV often supplies the definite article the Coptic *Vorlage* of III must have read ⲡϯ. The version of ApocryJn in Codex III does not mistake ⲡϯ for ⲡⲛⲟⲩⲧⲉ, but it is found in BG 32,21 (= III 11,16); 34,12f. (= III 12,21); 34,20f. (= III 12,25). It may come from the abbreviation ⲛ̄ϯ for ⲛⲟⲩⲧⲉ which is used in BG while III, *1* and II, *1* use the regular ⲛⲟⲩⲧⲉ (BG 31,19; 34,9; III 10,23; 12,17f.; II 7,11; 8,21; as well as in SJC in BG 112,13; cf. Eug III 87,15). The abbreviation reminds one of the BF ⲫϯ (see Till/Schenke, *BG 8502*, pp. 323ff. and 341). Crum has found the form ⲛ̄ϯ in a fragment of the letter to the Romans (see *JEA* 13 [1927] 19-26). The question raised by Till how this Fayyumic spelling could have intruded into Sahidic MSS is hard to answer. It should be remembered that such Fayyumic forms are by no means unique in the Nag Hammadi texts (cf. ⲛⲉ- for ⲛⲁ- in Fut.). In agreement with Till's observation concerning Codex III this passage proves that we are not dealing with the first Coptic copy of this version of GEgypt.

The work of Seth: III 63,4 - 64,9 = IV 74,17 - 75,24.

This section appears to be grammatically linked to the preceding one. III starts with a new main verb in 63,4, but IV 74,17 is connected with the preceding section whether emended to ⲉϥⲥⲓⲛⲉ or to ⲉⲥⲓⲛⲉ. Also Seth passes through the three *παρουσίαι* experienced by his children; first the flood, secondly the conflagration, and thirdly the judgment of the archons. One can also interpret the structure of ApocAd in terms of this passage. The appositive to *παρουσία* in III 63,6f. is divided by ⲙ̄ⲛ ... ⲙ̄ⲛ ... ⲙ̄ⲛ = *καὶ ... καὶ ... καί*, while in IV 74,19f. it is introduced by repeating the ⲉⲃⲟⲗ ϩ̄ⲛ-. For *κατακλυσμός*, conflagration and the judgment of the archons see III 61,1f. = IV 72,11; III 61,5 = IV 72,15; III 62,22 = IV 74,7f. In III 63,8 = IV 74,22 Seth's task is more narrowly defined through a further infinitive ⲉⲛⲟⲩϩ̄ⲙ: "to save (the race) which goes astray" (cf. H.-M. Schenke in *NTS* 16 [1970] 205).

What follows are the means of salvation: 1) The reconciliation of the world, i.e. the re-establishment of peace between God and man (for ϩⲱⲧⲡ see III 63,16f. = IV 75,3). 2) The physical baptism. Both are administrated by a *λογογενής*, which is brought forth mysteriously by a virgin. The birth of Seth in Jesus seems to be intended here (cf. III 64,1 = IV 75,15). The object of baptism is rebirth through the Holy Spirit. IV 74,29 in contrast to III 63,13 has translated literally "beget again". It is not certain whether the *σύμβολα* refer to esoteric rites during baptism. 3) The reconciliation of the world with the world. ϩⲱⲧ̄ⲃ in IV 75,3 is best taken as a phonetic spelling of ϩⲱⲧ̄ⲡ. It translates *καταλλάσσειν* (cf. 2 Cor 5:19; Col 1:20). This reconciliation puts an end to the state of unrest in the world. 4) The *ἀποταγή*. Just as 2) presented a personal happening after a cosmic happening in 1), so 4) could be a personal act following upon a cosmic one in 3). The special encratic character of the tractate becomes clear here, which is not unexpected in view of the separation of the children of Seth and their dissimilarity from the world. The renunciation is also in respect to a mythological being, the god of the thirteen aeons. For the negative character of the thirteen aeons see ApocAd V 77,27ff., where the thirteen kingdoms are valued less than the domain without a king. Over against this, in PS the thirteenth aeon is an aeon of righteousness. The difference between III 63,19 = IV 75,7 is due to varying interpretations of *ἐπίκλητος τῶν ἁγίων*. ⲚⲈⲠⲒⲔⲖⲎⲦⲞⲤ Ⲛ̄ⲚⲈⲦⲞⲨⲀⲀⲂ (III 63,19) can be translated as "the called ones among the saints", or as "the convocations of the saints". IV took the genitive not as possession but as indicating the personal agent: "through a calling by the saints". Probably "calling" or "convocation" is correct. The plural suggests that III took it to be "called ones". Those who call, to be sure, are members of the heavenly world, especially the pre-existent Father — the word Father is missing in IV — and his Pronoia. As mentioned *supra*, p. 191 the divine economy is pictured as having its root in the great invisible Spirit. For the difference between ⲘⲚ̄ ⲦⲈϤⲠⲢⲞⲚⲞⲒⲀ (III) and ϩⲚ̄ ⲞⲨⲠⲢⲞⲚⲞⲒⲀ (IV) see *supra*, p. 171. If one takes the ⲀϤⲔⲨⲢⲞⲨ = ⲀϤⲦⲀϪⲢⲞ, "he established", to refer to the Father, then the sentence receives its meaning *sub specie aeternitatis*. Then in IV, the supreme Light established "the holy one", i.e. Seth-Jesus, through Pronoia, and through him baptism. It seems something is missing in III, for only baptism is mentioned. In Ⲣ̄ϢⲢⲠ Ⲛ̄ϢⲰⲠⲈ (III 63,22 = IV 75,10) the Ⲣ̄ϢⲢⲠ has only the character of a structural element corresponding to *προ-*. The actual infinitive is ϢⲰⲠⲈ. Therefore in I Perfect ⲣ̄ϣⲣ̄ⲡ ⲛ̄ϣⲱⲡⲉ is used while in the Present and its satellites the qualitative ϣⲟⲟⲡ occurs. ⲣ̄ϣⲣ̄ⲡ ⲛ̄ϣⲟⲟⲡ is thus the qualitative of ⲣ̄ϣⲣ̄ⲡ ⲛ̄ϣⲱⲡⲉ. This would solve the problem raised by H. Quecke in "Eine missbräuchliche Verwendung des Qualitativs im Koptischen", *Le Muséon* 75 (1962) 291-300, and P. Nagel, "Die Einwirkung des Griechischen auf die Entstehung der Koptischen Literatursprache", *Christentum am Roten Meer* I, ed. Altheim/Stiehl, p. 353. III 63,25ff. = IV 75,14ff. reports that Seth appeared in the form of Jesus (cf. III 63,10ff. = IV 74,25ff.). On this matter see Epiphanius, *Pan.* 39,1.2-3 (p. 72 ed. Holl) who reports of the Sethians, whom he may have come to know personally in Egypt: *ἀλλὰ καὶ Χριστὸν αὐτὸν* (i.e. Seth) *ὀνομάζουσι καὶ αὐτὸν εἶναι τὸν Ἰησοῦν διαβεβαιοῦντα* (39,1.3 = p. 72,11-12 ed. Holl); cf. also *ὅ ἐστιν αὐτὸς ὁ Σὴθ ὁ τότε καὶ Χριστὸς νῦν ἐπιφοιτήσας τῷ γένει τῶν ἀνθρώπων* (39,3.5 = p. 74,19f. ed. Holl); cf. further Ps.-Tertull. *Adv. Omn. Haer.* 2. Keeping in mind the differences between III and IV, the following text could have been the *Vorlage* of both versions: "through the holy, incorruptible *λογογενής* Jesus, the living one, whom the great Seth has put on". The Greek can be reconstructed as follows: *διὰ τοῦ ἁγίου καὶ ἀφθάρτου καὶ λογογενοῦς Ἰησοῦ τοῦ ζῶντος καὶ ἐνδεδυμένου ὑπὸ Σήθ*. III forgot *ἁγίου*. Probably the Coptic translators followed the Gnostic trend of developing more and more separate mythological beings, which led in the course of the Coptic transmission to a growing misunderstanding of this passage. For example, III could simply have transposed *λογογενής* and *καί*. IV can perhaps also be interpreted in the following way: "through the holy one (i.e. the whole person), as well as through the incorruptible one (i.e. Seth), as also through the living *λογογενής* Jesus (i.e. the bodily appearance)". Then ⲙ̄ⲛ̄ ... ⲙ̄ⲛ̄ again has the meaning "both ... and" (cf. *supra*, p. 180). The close connection between Seth and Jesus is also brought out by the fact that both dwell in the light Oroiael (see III 65,16f. = IV 77,12f.). If the subject of the verbs in III 64,3 (ⲁϥⲱϥⲧ) = IV 75,18 (ⲁϥϯ ⲉⲓϥⲧ) is Seth, then the ⲉⲃⲟⲗ ϩⲓⲧⲟⲟⲧϥ refers to Jesus; if the pre-existent Father is the subject, then he works through Seth-Jesus. The question is whether this is a separate sentence or a continuation of the relative clause in III 63,22ff. = IV 75,10ff. The topic is the elimination of the powers of the aeons and the establishment of the firmament of fixed stars through the fastening of the thirteen aeons and the fixing in place of heavenly bodies. ⲁϥⲟⲩⲟⲥϥⲟⲩ in IV 75,19 corresponds to ⲁϥⲕⲩⲣⲟⲩ in III 63,23. Here IV has a literal translation meaning "to be idle, motionless", while III has retained the Greek word. The arming of the stars with knowledge could have been derived from astrology. They are in this case not evil powers. This may presuppose the redemption of the cosmos.

The list of the bringers of salvation: III 64,9 - 65,26 = IV 75,24 - 77,?.

The two versions differ considerably in the beginning of the section. The list of the bringers of salvation gives the impression that it is only superficially related to the preceding context. It is probably an independent piece of traditional material or a summary of several pieces. This is especially evident from the "me" in IV 75,24. Seth as author normally does not refer to himself in the first person. In IV the section begins with "And they revealed to me the great attendants, Yesseus, Mazareus, Yessedekeus". The Greek *Vorlage* must also have had the third person plural to express the indefinite subject as is evident from the accusative forms of the names in both versions. It is not impossible that this plural was interpreted in terms of the preceding plural (the stars) which then made a revelation based on their knowledge of the truth. III, or its Greek *Vorlage*, made "the attendant" — here in the singular — the subject, and changed the "me" in IV to "them". Here it is more obvious that the "them" refers to the stars. For the acc. ⲓ̈ⲉⲥⲥⲉⲁ ⲙⲁⲍⲁⲣⲉⲁ ⲓ̈ⲉⲥⲥⲉⲇⲉⲕⲉⲁ see ApocAd V 85,30f. which has the nom. ⲓ̈ⲉⲥⲥⲉⲩⲥ ⲙⲁⲍⲁⲣⲉⲩⲥ ⲓ̈ⲉⲥⲥⲉⲇⲉⲕⲉⲩⲥ. The nom. does not occur in GEgypt except in the abbreviated form ⲓⲉⲩⲥ in III 66,8 for which IV 78,10 has ⲓ̈ⲉⲥⲥⲉⲟⲥ. This shift from the third to the second declension can also be observed in IV 78,12ff. where III 66,10 has the vocative ending -ⲉⲩ. The threefold name is further defined by the appositive "the living water" (cf. ApocAd V 85,31). In Zost VIII 47,5f. he is one of the guardians of the immortal soul. For the title στρατηγοί with reference to heavenly beings see III 55,14 = IV 66,28; see also στρατηλάτης in U 353,41. Three such commanders are mentioned: 1) James the great ("the great Jacob" in IV, cf. *supra*, p. 16). In view of the great regard the Gnostics have for James it is no surprise that he is counted amoung the heavenly beings. 2) Theopemptos, according to Zost VIII 47,16f., belongs to "the guardians of the glories". 3) ⲓ̈ⲥⲁⲟⲩⲏⲗ is perhaps related to ⲥⲁⲩⲏⲗ in ApocAd V 79,2 who is an evil commander. The name could have been derived from Ἰεζάβελ„ the wife of Ahab, which was re-interpreted to refer to a good person. The next figure whose name is partially in a lacuna in the text (IV 76,1f.) is missing in III. He is followed by Micheus, Michar and Mnesinous (III 64,15f. = IV 76,4). This group of three presents a tradition different from the pair Micheus and Michar in III 64,20 = IV 76,9f., although their role is the same. For the trio in the context of the spring of truth — but as unfaithful guardians who baptize with water instead of *gnosis* — see ApocAd V 84,5f. For the pair with apparently positive meaning see U 362,7 and Zost VIII 6,10 (in connection with baptism). The form ⲙⲓⲭⲉⲁ in III 64,15 = IV 76,4 is acc.; ⲙⲓⲭⲉⲩ in ApocAd V 84,5 is voc.; ⲙⲛⲏⲥⲓⲛⲟⲩⲥ in III 64,16 is nom. (cf. ApocAd V 84,6); ⲙⲛⲏⲥⲓⲛⲟⲩ in IV 76,4 is perhaps acc. like the preceding ⲙⲓⲭⲉⲁ, if it is assumed that the line over the last letter to indicate a final ⲛ dropped out due to the long superlinear stroke over the proper name. Sesengenbarpharanges is known from other Gnostic literature and from Greek and Coptic magical texts. For the meaning see A. Kropp, *Ausgewählte koptische Zaubertexte* III, § 211 and G. G. Scholem, *Jewish Gnosticism, Merkabah Mysticism, and Talmudic Tradition*, Appendix B, pp. 94ff. One would expect the name to be a phrase, especially since the first part is not always present. "Barpharanges" is either a hybrid meaning "son of the ravine" or, what is more likely, "the one from the Baara-ravine". For his function as purifier see U 362,8 and Zost VIII 6,11f. The ⲥⲉⲥⲉⲅⲅⲉⲛ is obscure. III misunderstood this passage. He separated the function from the name and placed it in the plural with the result that they become separate beings. Furthermore a misunderstanding can be seen in III 64,12f. IV reads correctly "they who preside over the rising, Seldao and Elenos". That these are names is confirmed by U 362,13 where Seldao and Elainos exist in the place of Pistis Sophia. They follow also in Zost VIII 6,16 upon Micheus and Michar. For ⲛⲉⲛ- in III 64,22 see *supra*, p. 3. That the παραλήμπτορες, the receivers of the race of Seth, are the ministers of the four lights is also evident from ApocAd V 75,21ff., where Abrasax, Samblo and Gamaliel (Gabriel is missing) rescue the people of Seth from the fire. Gamaliel is in the list of the "guardians of the immortal soul" in Zost VIII 47,2. ⲟⲗⲥⲏⲥ and ⲉⲩⲣⲩⲙⲁⲓⲟⲩⲥ are found together also in Zost VIII 47,17f., where they belong to the guardians of the glories without a further description of their function. ϩⲩⲡⲛⲉⲩⲥ (III 65,2) or ϋⲙⲛⲉⲟⲥ (IV 76,21) is not attested elsewhere. The form of the name in III seems improbable if it is taken to be derived from ὕπνος since these beings preside over the rising rather than the setting of the sun. It is also a question whether ϓⲘⲚⲈⲞⲤ is related to ὑμνέω. Since three beings preside over the rising of the sun the same number is expected in connection with the setting. Therefore, it is probable that ⲚⲒⲠⲢⲨⲦⲀⲚⲒⲤ in III 65,5 is a secondary interpretation which has changed the name to the function of the two following beings. For ⲀⲔⲢⲀⲘⲀⲤ and ⲤⲦⲢⲈⲘⲮⲞⲨⲬⲞⲤ as guardians of souls in III 65,7f. = IV 77,1 see Zost VIII 47,3. The difference between "slain souls" (IV) and "souls of the elects" may be due to an attempt by III to improve on a difficult reading. The difference could also be explained as variant understandings of ἐξαιρεθεῖσαι (ψυχαί) (cf. *supra*, p. 17). This participle can be both the passive form of ἐξαιρέω "destroy" and ἐξαιρέομαι "chose". The following being could be the thrice-male child with the names spelled out and combined with Seth. He is treated as a singular and is called "the great power" (III 65,8 = IV 77,2); see also *supra*, p. 45. The double ⲦⲈⲖⲘⲀⲬⲀⲎⲖ has been inadvertently left out in III. The appearance of the great invisible Spirit next in the list is less surprising after one has seen a similar situation with the Father and the first ogdoad (see *supra*, pp. 171f). With this the climax has been reached and one would expect that the list has come to an end. This is not the case, however, for with another "and" a section is added which may originally have been independent. It interprets the four lights as the abodes of certain beings and ⲒⲰⲎⲖ as the divine archetype of John the Baptist. While "the first light" is added to the first name, this designation as a light is not continued, with the result that when the fifth name is reached it is no longer thought of as a light, but as a part of a general list. For Harmozel see ApocryJn BG 35,5ff. = III 13,3ff. = II 8,34ff. where it is the abode of Christ and Adamas while in GEgypt it is the place of the Logos and Adamas. In ApocryJn Christ has been identified with the Autogenes in contrast to GEgypt where the Logos has been identified with the Autogenes. In this passage only the designation "Autogenes" is used. III 65,14f. cannot be correct. IV 77,10f. has the correct reading. For Oroiael see ApocryJn BG 35,20ff. = III 13,17ff. = II 9,11ff., where it is the abode of Seth while in GEgypt it is also the dwelling place of "Jesus of the life" showing the close connection between Seth and Jesus in GEgypt (cf. *supra*, p. 37). For an antinomian attitude in conjunction with the idea that the world was crucified cf. Gal 6:14; Eph 2:15; Col 2:14. For Davithe see ApocryJn BG 36,2ff. = III 13,19ff. = II 9,14ff. For Eleleth see ApocryJn BG 36,7ff. = III 14,1ff. = II 9,18ff., where the inhabitants are characterized differently from GEgypt. In GEgypt a distinction is made between the sons of Seth and their souls which dwell in Eleleth; in ApocryJn the contrast is between the degrees of perfection of the inhabitants, so that Eleleth becomes the abode of the souls which have repented late.

The certainty of salvation in the present: III 65,26 - 66,8=IV 77, ?-78,10.

After the description of Seth's saving work and the list of the assistants in salvation, the author of the tractate spells out the implications for the present. Now there is the possibility of salvation for the children of Seth. The mediator is called ⲠⲞⲒⲘⲀⲎⲖ, which could be a modification or pendant of *Ποιμάνδρης* (cf. Domiel and Domedon *supra*, p. 41). This may indicate a relationship with Hermetic literature and support the idea that GEgypt originated in Egypt. If the preceding passage referred to John the Baptist, then we have here the same contrast as in Luke 16:16. There the contrast between John and the new age is expressed by *ἀπὸ τότε*, an expression which corresponds to the ϫⲚ ⲚϮⲚⲞⲨ in III 65,26. Beside Poimael stand those who are worthy of baptism and who may be considered the core of the Gnostic congregation. In IV they are worthy of "the baptisms of the renunciation (*ἀποταγή*, cf. IV 75,4) and the ineffable seals of their baptism". III combined the parallel expressions "baptisms of renunciation" and "the ineffable seals of their baptism" into a single expression in which "ineffable" was left out and the genitival connection of baptism was changed into an adverbial phrase. III added the number five to the seals perhaps due to a familiarity with five sacraments in Gnosticism (cf. H.-G. Gaffron, *Studien zum koptischen Philippusevangelium*). Likewise III further specified baptism as a baptism with running water by adding *πηγή*. The author also put the word *ἐπίκλησις* before *ἀπόταξις*. It must refer to a sacramental invocation by the believers which is part of the five sacraments, especially the spring-baptism. The subject of the sentence is "these", refering most likely to the Gnostics. We may be dealing with a separate piece of traditional material which was lifted out of its original context and thus no longer has a well-defined subject. III 66,4f. has the II Future against I Perfect in IV 78,6. Both tenses fit the context. IV views the Gnostics as having already basically received *gnosis*, while III looks upon this as an act which must continually be repeated in the future. IV says that the converted Gnostics recognize their *παραλήμπτορες* as "they have been instructed concerning them". In III ὡς is translated "as" (N̄ΘΕ). IV, where ὡς has been retained, appears to do greater justice to the context, since the causal nuance is also expressed (cf. BLASS-DEBRUNNER § 453). The unusual passive construction in this subordinate clause is also found in ApocryJn III 33,17, cf. *supra*, p. 7. N̄CΕCΟΥⲰΝΟΥ (III 66,6f.) and ΕⲀΥΕΙΜΕ (IV 78,8) can be seen as the continuation of either the main clause or the subordinate clause. IV states that the Gnostics first recognized their παραλήμπτορες and then arrived at *gnosis* by means of those whom they have known. III permits the same meaning except that the παραλήμπτορες are given as the object of the verb which no longer is used absolutely. It may be possible to see in III the introduction of a new meaning, for N̄CΕCΟΥⲰΝΟΥ can also have a passive meaning, "and they (the Gnostics) were known by them (the παραλήμπτορες)". In this case III would have a Pauline sound; cf. 1 Cor 13:12; Gal 4:9. III, then, would have first the knowing of the παραλήμπτορες by the Gnostics and then the reverse.

The result of receiving *gnosis* is freedom from death, which the Gnostic obtains already in this world. This is said in biblical language (cf. Mt 16:28 par.). Already John 8:52 does not intent a definite time, such as the coming of the Son of Man, but rather the λόγος of Jesus gives eternal immortality. The step from this to the resurrection of the Gnostic is not a large one as, for example, GPh with its interpretations of the Gospel of John, shows. Whoever has *gnosis* will not die, as GTh 1 says: "He who finds the meaning of these words will not taste death". It is most appropriate that the hymnic section of GEgypt, which speaks of the union of the Gnostic with the Eternity and the heavenly world, follows directly after these promises.

Hymnic Section (*Part I*): III 66,8-22 = IV 78,10 - 79,3.

Before the first strophe there are groups of letters that either represent glossolalia, as is also found elsewhere in gnostic writings, or secret symbols or abbreviations. The latter possibility is more likely, since ΙΕΥC̄ in III is given in IV as ΪΕCCΕΟC. In III ΙΗ which recurs in the hymn, is placed at the beginning. Nevertheless the meaning of the remaining groups of letters remains a question, especially in view of the differences between the two manuscripts.

The first part of the hymnic section can be divided into five strophes, each of which begins with "really truly" (ἀληθῶς ἀληθῶς or ἀληθὲς ἀληθῶς)! The arrangement within the strophes is more difficult, especially since one cannot assume that the Coptic translation has preserved the meter of the Greek *Vorlage*. One expects that the strophes had the same length. Here too it must not be overlooked that each repeated vowel lengthens the line accordingly.

The First Strophe.

The first strophe begins with the invocation of Yesseus, Mazareus and Yessedekeus. III has taken over the Greek vocative form, while IV has carried over the nominative of the vocalic declension. For this change from the consonantal to the vocalic declension, cf. A. Böhlig, *Griechische Lehnwörter*, pp. 117f. Three predications follow. The question is whether each predicate respectively belongs with the name to which it corresponds in the sequences. If so, one could form a strophe of two lines. One might well see in the three figures a threefold entity which possesses both the character of unity and of plurality. For the plural cf. IV 75,25f., where III has the singular in the corresponding place. It is to be noted that in this passage as well as in this hymn the designation "the living water" is used for this trinity. Here two more designations are given so that one can correctly assume that in addition to the introductory formula there are four lines:

Really truly!
  O Yesseus, Mazareus, Yessedekeus!
  O living water!
  O child of the child!
  O name of all the glories! (III: O glorious name!)

The Second Strophe.

The strophe begins in III with a Greek phrase, while in what follows the vowels of the Greek alphabet are each given four times, though, to be sure, not in the sequence of the alphabet. This raises the question of whether the vowels have a secret meaning. In IV the introductory phrase *αἰὼν ὁ ὤν* is translated with "He who exists eternally".

Really truly!
  αἰὼν ὁ ὤν (IV: He who exists in eternity!)
  ιιιι ηηηη
  εεεε οοοο υυυυ
  ωωωω αααα

The meaning is very uncertain. Perhaps it is in fact a case of glossolalia. An interpretation can only be an attempt:

Really truly!

O existing aeon!
ΙΗ! (perhaps the name of the one invoked, cf. the initial ΙΗ in III 66,8)
ϵ(ἶ or στὶν) ὁ υ(ἱός)
ω ⲁ (End and beginning; one could also consider ὦ α(ἰών) however.)

The Third Strophe.

In III the strophe begins with ΗΙ; IV reads probably ọḤ[Ι]. In light of the fact that the second and fifth strophes have the order of the vowels as ΙΗ, one could see in the ΗΙ of the third strophe a scrambled variant of ΙΗ. ΗΙ could then be the same name as in the second strophe. However, influence from the fourth strophe, where the normal sequence of the Greek alphabet is present, may also be involved here.

Really truly!
ΗΙ (for ΙΗ? cf. *infra*)
ⲁω
Thou existing One,
(Thou) who sees the aeons.

If the ο in IV 78,19 is correct, then one can take it as the article: ὁ Ἰη(σοῦς). Here the nominative could have stood for the vocative (cf. BLASS-DEBRUNNER § 147). The interpretation might be: "O Je(sus), A and O, Thou existing One who sees the aeons".

The Fourth Strophe.

The fourth strophe survives only in III. It presents the vowels, without ο and in the sequence of the Greek alphabet, in such a way that the number of occurances of each vowel increases. ⲁ is given once, ϵ twice, Η three times, Ι four times, Υ six times, and ω eight times. This gives a total of twenty-four, exactly the number of letters in the Greek alphabet. To be sure, this does not coincide with III 44,3-9 = IV 54,3-13 where each vowel occurs twenty-two times in agreement with the number of letters in the Aramaic alphabet. This would confirm the idea that here traditions of different origin are involved. As indicated before, ΙΗ or ΗΙ (once read in Greek letter order, once read in Semitic letter order) could mean Jesus. Then Yesseus would have been reinterpreted as Jesus in a composition which already through the use of the number of the letters in the Greek alphabet gave evidence of a Hellenistic character.

Really truly!
ⲁ ⲉⲉ ⲏⲏⲏ
ⲓⲓⲓⲓ ⲨⲨⲨⲨⲨⲨ
ⲱⲱⲱⲱⲱⲱⲱⲱ
He who is eternally eternal!

An attempt to make this meaningful would be as follows: α(ἰών) ϵ(ἶ) Ἰη(σοῦς), υ(ἱέ) (or υἱός), ὦ, Thou who art eternally eternal!" or *A* ἐ(στὶν) Ἰη(σοῦς), υ(ἱός), *Ω*, etc.

The Fifth Strophe.

The fifth strophe is complete in III, and partly preserved in IV, so that certain conclusions are possible. It begins with the invocation of ⲓⲏ. The ⲁ which follows in III may have been secondarily attached because of the subsequent ⲁⲓⲱ. That ⲁⲓⲱ (III 66,20) is intended as *αἰών* follows from the parallel text (ⲉⲛⲉϩ IV 79,1). The text of IV appears to presuppose a different *Vorlage* or a different understanding of the text than III.

III	IV
Really truly!	[Really truly,]
ⲓⲏ{ⲁ} αἰώ(ν) in the heart,	[ⲓⲏ] eternal who art in [the heart],
who existeth,	Thou eternal one!
υ(ἱὲ) ἀεὶ εἰς ἀεί,	[υ(ἱὲ) ἀεὶ εἰς ἀεί,]
εἶ ὃ εἶ, εἶ ὅς εἶ.	[εἶ ὃ]εἶ, εἶ ὅς εἶ.

The difference between III and IV may perhaps be explainable on the basis of a common *Vorlage*. ⲓⲏ *αἰὼν ὁ ἐν τῇ καρδίᾳ ὤν, ὁ αἰώνιος* "Je(sus), O aeon, Thou who art in the heart, Thou eternal one!" As with the rest of the hymn, we are dealing with an expression of a mystical piety. For "the aeon who is in the heart" cf. HERM. *Mand.* 12,4.3: *ὁ ἄνθρωπος ὁ ἔχων τὸν κύριον ἐν τῇ καρδίᾳ αὐτοῦ*. That "in the heart" and "he who is" are switched in III depends upon a very literal translation whereby also "he who exists" and "the eternal one" were combined and the latter expression was dropped. For "eternal God" cf. Ps 44(45 MT):7; 47(48 MT):15 etc. The phrases of the last line are a variation of Ex 3: 14: *ἐγώ εἰμι ὁ ὤν*. An interpretation of the strophe would be as follows:

Jesus, O aeon who art in the heart,
Thou eternal One
Son forever,
Thou art what Thou art, Thou art who Thou art.

In these strophes an aeon-deity is glorified and his eternal existence is the main object of praise. In mystical piety the Gnostic sees himself united with this being, who is the Son. Jesus who is clearly encountered in the second hymn, is probably the one who is invoked. Sethian reverence for Jesus is here coupled with the name of the three-fold παραστάτης (cf. III 64,10 = IV 75,25f.).

Hymnic Section (*Part II*): III 66,22 - 68,1 = IV 79,3 - 80,15.

The beginning of the second hymn points with "this great name" back to the end of the preceding section. This hymnic section may once again consist of five strophes of four lines each. Each of the first three lines has two stress-points and offers two phrases. In the fourth line the conclusion is drawn. The content of this prayer concerns the experience of salvation which has been granted to the one offering the prayer, and which will again and again be granted to him. He knows that the distant God is no longer distant from him and has even revealed his name to him. God — Father, Mother, Son — is praised here, as earlier in the tractate. Strophes two and three concern the transformation of the Gnostic, while the fifth strophe treats his union with God in the heavenly world. Unfortunately the text of IV is badly damaged. Nevertheless what remains shows that III and IV differ at many points and that one must reckon with changes based on reinterpretations. Perhaps the last copyist of III no longer considered the text rythmic.

The following reconstruction of the strophes is based on a combination of III and IV. The third strophe is so badly damaged that the wording of IV could not be established. That is all the more regrettable since here the differences appear to be considerable. In most cases IV has been preferred when extant.

The First Strophe.

a) This great name of yours is upon me
   [..........................]
b) O Perfect one who art self-begotten,
   who art autonomous,
c) O Thou who art invisible except to me,
   who art invisible to everyone!
d) For who can comprehend Thee
   with voice and praise?

The beginning of the strophe is badly damaged in IV. The second part of each of the first two lines appears to have been left out in III.

In the last line of III "and praise" has dropped out.

The Second Strophe.

a) Having known Thee I now have merged myself
with Thy steadfastness and armed myself.

b) I was armed with grace and light
(and) became light (or : enlightened).

c) For the Mother was there
because of the splendid beauty of grace.

d) Therefore I stretched out my hands
while they were folded.

The Greek participle γνούς probably began the strophe in the Greek *Vorlage*, where it occupied considerably less room than its translation as a subordinate clause in Coptic. For ⲧⲱϭⲉ (IV 79,14) cf. CRUM, *Dict.* p. 464. It may be a form of ⲧⲱⲕ "be firm" seeing that ⲧⲱⲕ "throw" in BG 38,15 is spelled ⲧⲱϭⲉ. The qualitative ⲧⲏϭ from ⲧⲱⲕ "be firm" is attested, cf. WESTENDORF, *Kopt. Handwörterbuch* s.v. Such an interpretation of the word would correspond with the ⲡⲉⲧⲉⲙⲉϥϣⲓⲃⲉ in III. The end of line 1 and the beginning of line 2 seems to have been combined in III. III 67,4-6 are missing in IV. The prayer rite makes good sense when it is referred to a person like the Mother. Having been concerned in the first strophe with the primal God from whom the Mother god came, the one who prays turns to the Mother in the second strophe.

The Third Strophe.

a) I was shaped all around with the wealth
of light that is in my bosom,

b) That which gives shape to the many begotten ones
in the light into which no complaint reaches.

c) I will declare Thy splendor truly,
for I have comprehended Thee, Jesus of [...]

d) Behold, ἀεὶ ὢ(ν)
ἀεί ἐ(στιν) ὁ Ἰησοῦς ! (?)

In IV the first words may correspond to III, but then the order appears to be completely different. IV 79,20 speaks of a "cover of riches" after which comes ⲉⲥⲕⲱⲧⲉ, that may be the translation of κύκλῳ, Coptic ϩⲙ ⲡⲕⲩⲕⲗⲟⲥ (III). ⲙⲏⲧⲣⲁ corresponds to ⲕⲟⲩⲟⲩⲛ=. Just as in the second strophe, the third strophe progresses to the next person, here Jesus, in the third line. In IV ⲓ̅ⲥ̅ is qualified by a genitival attribute. He is the Son, who forms a trinity together with the Autogenes and the Mother. The fourth line gives the content of the prayer spoken by him who has received Jesus. It is a confession of which the meaning is uncertain, if IV 79,27 has the correct order of letters ⲏⲉⲉ ⲁⲓⲉⲉ (ⲓ and ⲉ could be reversed in the second group.).

The Fourth Strophe.

a) O great(?) aeon,
O holy aeon !

b) O God of silence !
I honor Thee completely.

c) Thou art the resting place of the Son
Es(ephech), Es(ephech), the fifth !

d) Thou formless one,
who existeth in the formless ones.

This strophe is likewise badly damaged in IV, and therefore the text is dependent primarily upon III. Still a significant difference can be seen. In III the deity invoked is designated as "my resting place, the (or "O") Son", while in IV the "resting place of the Son" is mentioned. Again in the third line a new deity may have been named, although by means of a code: ⲏⲥ ⲏⲥ ⲟ ⲉ (lost in IV). Can one risk seeing ⲏⲥ as an abbreviation of ⲏⲥⲏⲫⲏⲭ? Then ⲟ could be ὁ, and ⲉ is the fifth letter of the alphabet and the sign for 5. Is ⲉ to be interpreted as πέμπτος? Esephech is fifth in the sequence of the thrice-male child, Youel, and then Esephech. Within the framework of the light-world he corresponds to the Son. IV 59,17 reports the relationship between the great Christ and these five beings. Thus the light-world with special emphasis upon Esephech can be invoked. At the same time the formless character of the light-aeon is stressed.

The Fifth strophe.

a) Since he exists, raising a man,
Thou hast purified me through him

b) Into Thy Life (and)
according to Thy imperishable name.

c) Therefore the incense of life is in him
mixed in the baptismal water of all the archons.

d) So that I live with Thee in the peace of the saints,
Thou eternal one who really truly exists.

Also in this strophe, which can largely be reconstructed in IV, there are differences between III and IV. Perhaps III 67,19 can be seen as a causative clause if IV 80,6 is correct in making ⲧ̄ⲃⲃⲟ the main verb. The use of the third person could refer back to the person in the preceding strophe. III 67,20f. ⲉϩⲟⲩⲛ ⲉ- and IV 80,7 ϩⲙ- probably both go back to εἰς. IV 80,9 ⲛϩⲏⲧϥ probably refers to "your name". III has the one who prays designate himself as the possessor of this incense which he himself mixed in the water; IV mentions here the "baptismal water of all the archons" over against III where there is a reference to the "water according to the type of all archons". The mentioning of the archons remains obscure. Perhaps the intention is to say that also false baptisms are undertaken. The meaning of the strophe as a whole is to express the certainty of salvation of which the faithful, who return to the really existing primal Father, are assured.

The first conclusion: III 68,1-9 = IV 80,15-25.

This section is very poorly preserved in IV. However, the end is still present and it suggests that we are dealing with a separate piece of tradition since there is a blank space after the colon in IV 80,25. The fact that the mountain in which the book was placed is in the plural in III 68,3 but in the singular in IV 80,17 suggests the meaning "mountain range". Prophets, apostles and preachers can readily refer to the distant past; cf. the prophets and apostles in Luke 11:49 and the title κῆρυξ for Noah in 2 Pet 2: 5 (κῆρυξ δικαιοσύνης). The reference to these groups of people means something like "from time immemorial". ⲉⲙⲛ ϭⲟⲙ in III 68,4f. is an elliptic expression which expects a verb to follow. The ⲉⲣⲟⲥ (fem.) in IV 80,25 could be a mistake due to the gender of the Greek βίβλος. Two facts are reported, the second of which is the natural consequence of the first: the placing of the book in the unreachable height, and the fact that the tractate has been hidden since time immemorial.

The second conclusion: III 68,10 - 69,5 = IV 80,26-?.

This ending, which gives the impression of being independent from the first ending, also emphasizes the authorship of Seth. This is done by giving the exact time which he needed for the composition of the work. For the 130 years see *supra*, p. 31. Also the mountain is this time specifically named. The purpose of placing it in the mountain is eschatological, for the second conclusion is specifically eschatologically orientated. It appears that Seth will come "at the end of time according to the will of the Logos, through the gift (see *supra*, p. 191) of the fatherly love". However, it makes far better sense if βίβλος, in spite of the gender, is the antecedent of ⲉϥⲉⲡⲣⲟⲉⲗⲑⲉ in III 68,19f, since ϫⲱⲱⲙⲉ is masculine. Seth appears to function as a savior here (III 68,22). For "those who dwell with him", cf. ApocAd V 74,23. The beings added on in III 68,23ff. by means of ⲙⲛ̄ continue the list begun with the race of the great savior. In 68,20-69,5 an abbreviated table of contents is given. It is difficult to assess the precise meaning of ⲙⲛ̄ in this list. The possibility must be taken into account that the beings should be separated from their appositives, which are connected with ⲙⲛ̄, to form an even larger number. One can group them more or less in the following way: 1) the great invisible Spirit; 2) his only begotten Son, the eternal light; 3) his great consort the incorruptible Sophia, the Barbelo; 4) the pleroma. Listed this way the trinity and the pleroma are the initiators of redemption. The unity of the heavenly world, also in its unified divine economy, is thus clearly visible. The concluding phrase "in eternity. Amen" is liturgical and an appropriate ending for the tractate.

The colophon: III 69,6-17.

See *supra*, pp. 8f. on the absence of the colophon in IV. There is no question that we are dealing with a colophon since it mentions the names of the scribe and his asking for *χάρις* etc. for himself and his fellow Gnostics. The name Eugnostos is interesting in that there is a tractate by that name in Codex III and V, "The Letter of Eugnostos". It is noteworthy that in addition to the spiritual name, Eugnostos, the "fleshly" name Gongessos is given. For the title ⲡⲉⲩⲁⲅⲅⲉⲗⲓⲟⲛ ⲛ̄ⲣⲙ̄ⲛ̄ⲕⲏⲙⲉ see *supra*, pp. 18ff. The style of the colophon is that of an interlinear translation. ⲛ̄ⲥϩⲁ̈ï ⲛ̄ⲛⲟⲩⲧⲉ in 69,7 corresponds to *θεόγραφος* in 69,15. The benediction "Grace ... (be) with the ..." reflects the Greek since Coptic would normally require a verb. Jesus Christ is called upon to assure the fulfilment of the prayer. The definite article is used in Coptic to indicate the vocative, except for proper names, cf. Stern, *Kopt. Gramm.* § 488. The use of the complete title *Ἰησοῦς Χριστὸς θεοῦ υἱὸς σωτήρ* (*υἱός* translated by ⲡϣⲏⲣⲉ) is remarkable. The added monogram ⲓⲭⲑⲩⲥ refers to the Greek text. The symbol of the fish was known at that time in Egyptian Christianity (cf. Clement of Alexandria, *Paid.* III 11,59.2 = p. 270,8 ed. Stählin). *θεόγραφος* at the end of 69,15 can be a reference to the holy character of the monogram or a predicate of ⲧⲃⲓⲃⲗⲟⲥ, since it is an adjective of two endings. If it is the latter then the character of the book given in 69,7 has been repeated once more at the end. It would also mean that the title following the colophon is not a mere repetition of the one at the end of the colophon, but that the latter is part of a sentence which has been translated word for word from the Greek.

BIBLIOGRAPHY

For a full listing of books, reviews, articles and dissertations on the Coptic-Gnostic library from Nag Hammadi and related subjects the reader is referred to David M. Scholer's *Nag Hammadi Bibliography 1948-1969.* (Nag Hammadi Studies I) Leiden : E.J. Brill, 1971, and Scholer's annual "Bibliographia Gnostica Supplementum" in *Novum Testamentum.*

Baer, R.A. Philo's Use of the Categories Male and Female. (Arbeiten zur Literatur und Geschichte des Hellenistischen Judentums III) Leiden : E.J. Brill, 1970.

Bauer, W. Griechisch-Deutsches Wörterbuch zu den Schriften des Neuen Testaments und der übrigen urchristlichen Literatur. Berlin : Alfred Töpelmann, 1958. English translation by W.F. Arndt and F.W. Gingrich, A Greek-English Lexicon of the New Testament and Other Early Christian Literature. The University of Chicago Press, 1957.

Baynes, Ch.A. A Coptic Gnostic Treatise Contained in the Codex Brucianus. Cambridge: The University Press, 1933.

Blass, F. und Debrunner, A. Grammatik des neutestamentlichen Griechisch. Göttingen: Vandenhoeck & Ruprecht, 1961. English translation by R.W. Funk, A Greek Grammar of the New Testament and Other Early Christian Literature. The University of Chicago Press, 1961.

Böhlig, A. Die griechischen Lehnwörter im sahidischen und bohairischen Neuen Testament. (Studien zur Erforschung des christlichen Ägyptens 2) München: Robert Lerche, 2 ed. 1958.

Böhlig, A. und Labib, P. Die koptisch-gnostische Schrift ohne Titel aus Codex II von Nag Hammadi im Koptischen Museum zu Alt-Kairo. (Deutsche Akademie der Wissenschaften zu Berlin, Institut für Orientforschung, Veröffentlichung No. 58) Berlin: Akademie-Verlag, 1962.

Böhlig, A. und Labib, P. Koptisch-gnostische Apokalypsen aus dem Codex V von Nag Hammadi im Koptischen Museum zu Alt-Kairo. Sonderband der Wissenschaftlichen Zeitschrift der Martin-Luther-Universität, Halle-Wittenberg, 1963.

Böhlig, A. "Die himmlische Welt nach dem Ägypterevangelium von Nag Hammadi," Le Muséon 80 (1967), 5-26; 365-77.

Böhlig, A. Mysterion und Wahrheit. (Arbeiten zur Geschichte des späteren Judentums und des Urchristentums VI) Leiden: E.J. Brill, 1968.

Böhlig, A. "Christentum und Gnosis im Ägypterevangelium von Nag Hammadi," in W. Eltester, Christentum und Gnosis. (Beihefte zur Zeitschrift für die neutestamentliche Wissenschaft 37) Berlin: Alfred Töpelmann (1969), 1-18.

Böhlig, A. "Zu gnostischen Grundlagen der Civitas-Dei-Vorstellung bei Augustin," Zeitschrift für die neutestamentliche Wissenschaft und die Kunde der älteren Kirche 60 (1969), 291-95.

Bonnet, H. "Seth," Reallexikon der ägyptischen Religionsgeschichte. Berlin: Walter de Gruyter, 2 ed. 1971, col. 702-15.

Crum, W.E. A Coptic Dictionary. Oxford: Clarendon Press, 1939.

Cumont, F. La cosmogonie manichéenne d'après Théodore Bar Khôni. (Recherches sur le Manichéisme I) Bruxelles: H. Lamertin, 1908.

Doresse, J. "Trois livres gnostiques inédits: Évangile des Égyptiens, Épitre d'Eugnoste, Sagesse de Jésus Christ," Vigiliae Christianae 2 (1948), 137-60.

Doresse, J. "A Gnostic Library from Upper Egypt," Archaeology 3 (1950), 69-73.

Doresse, J. " 'Le Livre sacré du grand Esprit invisible' ou 'L'Évangile des Égyptiens': Texte copte édité, traduit et commenté d'après la Codex I de Nag'a-Hammadi/ Khénoboskion," Journal Asiatique 254 (1966), 317-435 and 256 (1968), 289-386.

Gaffron, H.-G. Studien zum koptischen Philippusevangelium unter besonderer Berücksichtigung der Sakramente. Theol. Dissertation Bonn, 1969.

Gold, V.R. "The Gnostic Library of Chenoboskion," The Biblical Archaeologist 15 (1952), 70-88.

Hennecke, E. und Schneemelcher, W. The New Testament Apocrypha. Philadelphia: The Westminster Press, 1963. (Page references to the German edition are added in square brackets.)

Hommel, H. "Wahrheit und Gerechtigkeit," Antike und Abendland 15 (1969), 159-86.

Jonas, H. Gnosis und spätantiker Geist. Göttingen: Vandenhoeck & Ruprecht, 3 ed. 1964.

Kahle, P.E. Bala'izah. London: Oxford University Press, 1954.

Kasser, R. Compléments au Dictionnaire Copte de Crum. (Bibliothèque d'Études Coptes, Tome VII) Le Caire: Imprimerie de L'Institut Français d'Archéologie Orientale, 1964.

Kees, H. "Seth," Pauly-Wissowa-Kroll, Realencyclopädie der classischen Altertumswissenschaft. II Reihe 2, Stuttgart (1923), col. 1896-1922.

Kittel, G. Theological Dictionary of the New Testament IV (= *TDNT*). Grand Rapids: Wm.B. Eerdmans, 1968. (References to the German edition are added in brackets.)

Krause, M. und Labib, P. Die drei Versionen des Apokryphon des Johannes im koptischen Museum zu Alt-Kairo. (Abhandlungen des Deutschen Archäologischen Instituts Kairo, Koptische Reihe I) Wiesbaden: Otto Harrassowitz, 1962.

Kropp, A.M. Ausgewählte koptische Zaubertexte. Bruxelles: Édition de la Fondation Égyptologique Reine Élisabeth, 1930-31.

Labib, P. "Les papyrus gnostiques coptes du Musée Copte du Vieux Caire," La Revue du Caire 195-196 (1956), 275-78.

Lampe, G.W.H. A Patristic Greek Lexicon. Oxford: Clarendon Press, 1968.

Leisegang, H. Die Gnosis. (Kröners Taschenausgabe Band 32) Stuttgart: Alfred Kröner, 4 ed. 1955.

Liddell, H.G. and Scott, R. A Greek-English Lexicon, New edition by H.S. Jones. Oxford: Clarendon Press, 1968.

Nagel, P. "Die Einwirkung des Griechischen auf die Entstehung der koptischen Literatursprache," in F. Altheim und R. Stiehl, Christentum am Roten Meer I. Berlin: Walter de Gruyter, 1971.

Quecke, H. "Eine missbräuchliche Verwendung des Qualitativs im Koptischen," Le Muséon 75 (1962) 291-300.

Quecke, H. Das Markusevangelium Saïdisch, Text der Handschrift PPalau Rib. Inv. Nr. 182 mit den Varianten der Handschrift M 569. (Papyrologica Castroctaviana, Barcelona) Roma: Biblical Institute Press, 1972.

Robinson, J.M. "The Coptic Gnostic Library Today," New Testament Studies 14 (1968), 356-401.

Robinson, J.M. "The Coptic Gnostic Library," Novum Testamentum 12 (1970), 81-85.

Schenke, H.-M. Der Gott "Mensch" in der Gnosis: Ein religionsgeschichtlicher Beitrag zur Diskussion über die paulinische Anschauung von der Kirche als Leib Christi. Berlin: Evangelische Verlagsanstalt, 1962.

Schenke, H.-M. "Das Ägypter-Evangelium aus Nag-Hammadi-Codex III," New Testament Studies 16 (1969/70), 196-208.

Schmidt, C. und Polotsky, H.J. Ein Mani-Fund in Ägypten: Originalschriften des Mani und seiner Schüler. (Sitzungsberichte der Preussischen Akademie der Wissenschaften, phil.-hist. Klasse, 1933.1) Berlin, 1933.

Schmidt, C. Koptisch-Gnostische Schriften; Erster Band: Die Pistis Sophia, Die beiden Bücher des Jeû, Unbekanntes altgnostisches Werk. (Die griechischen christlichen Schriftsteller der ersten Jahrhunderte 45) 3. Auflage von W. Till. Berlin: Akademie-Verlag, 1959.

Scholem, G. Jewish Gnosticism, Merkabah Mysticism, and Talmudic Tradition. New York: Jewish Theological Seminary, 1960.

Schwyzer, E. Griechische Grammatik. (Handbuch der Altertumswissenschaft II.1) München: C.H. Beck, 1959.

Sethe, K. Amun und die acht Urgötter von Hermonopolis. (Abhandlungen der Preussischen Akademie der Wissenschaften No. 4) Berlin, 1929.

Stern, L. Koptische Grammatik. Leipzig: T.O. Weigel, 1880.

Till, W.C. Koptische Grammatik. (Lehrbücher für das Studium der orientalischen und afrikanischen Sprachen I) Leipzig: VEB Verlag Enzyklopädie, 3 ed. 1966.

Till, W.C. Die gnostischen Schriften des koptischen Papyrus Berolinensis 8502. (Texte und Untersuchungen zur Geschichte der altchristlichen Literatur 60², 2 ed. von H.-M. Schenke) Berlin: Akademie-Verlag, 1972.

Westendorf, W. Koptisches Handwörterbuch. Heidelberg: Carl Winter Universitätsverlag, 1965 ff.

Windelband, W. und Heimsoeth, H. Lehrbuch der Geschichte der Philosophie. Tübingen: J.C.B. Mohr (Paul Siebeck), 15 ed. 1957.

Wisse, F. "The Sethians and the Nag Hammadi Library," Society of Biblical Literature 1972 Proceedings Vol. 2, 601-607.

INDICES

COPTIC WORDS [1]

ⲁⲗⲟⲩ m. child III 42,6; 43,16; [44,22]; 49,26; 50,3 (bis); 53, 24; 54,[1]. 2.14; 55,24 (bis); 56,17; 62,2; 66,11 (bis). IV 51,23; 53,15; 55,12; 56,7.[21.22]; 59,18.[25].25; [61,28]; 62,[1]. <2>. [3]; [65,18]; [66,3]; [67,8.30]; 73,13; 78,[14].14.

ⲁⲙⲛⲧⲉ m. Hades III 56,25; [57,11]; 58,22. IV [68,9].

ⲁⲙⲁϩⲧⲉ : ⲉⲙⲁϩⲧⲉ possess III [50,2]; 54,1; 55,23.

ⲙⲁϩⲧⲉ III 62,6.

ⲣⲉϥⲁⲙⲁϩⲧⲉ m. IV 59,24; 62,1; [65,20]; 73,17.

ⲁⲛ negative particle III 66,24. IV 51,13.

ⲁⲛⲟⲕ 1 p.s. pronoun III 58,24.25. IV 79,13.

ⲁⲣⲏϫ⸗ end III 41,1; 54,5. IV 57,3.

ⲁⲧⲟ many III 61,17; 67,10.

ⲁⲩⲱ and III 41,[13].15.[17]; 43,3.17; 44,9; 49,5.21; 51,12.14.22; 52,3.16.22.24.26; 53,1; 54,12; 55,1.2; 56,26; 57,5.18; 58,3.23.26; 60,10.16; 61,1.6; 62,12; 63,23; 64,3.4; 68,5.9. IV 50,15.16.19.20; [51,7]; 52,9; 53,[15.21]. 23; 54,13.16.[19]; 55,23.26; 56,8.[23]; 57,23; 58,2; 59, 4.9; 60,11.19; 61,5. [13.15]. 22.25. [26]; [62,19]; 63, 3.4.6. [8.12].17.[24.25]; 64,10.11.23; 65,2.10.[28]; 66,[1]. 8. [10.13]. 14. [19]; [67,5.6]; 68,9; 69,3; 71,6.7.8. [10.19]. 27; 72,8.10.23; 73,1.[25]; 75,2.11.17.19.20.21.24; 76,14; 77,5. 14; 78,[2].9; 79,14.17.[18]; 80,[16].19.[24].

ⲁϣⲁï : ⲁϣⲁⲉⲓ multiply III 55,2.

ⲁϩⲟ : pl. ⲁϩⲱⲣ treasures IV [56,15]; 60,17.

ⲁϫⲛ- : ⲁϫⲛⲧ⸗ without III 49,12; 58,26. IV [61,13].

ⲃⲁⲗ m. eye III [58,11]. IV 61,10.

ⲃⲱⲗ : ⲃⲱⲗ ⲉⲃⲟⲗ dissolve IV 63,8.

ⲃⲟⲗ : ⲉⲃⲟⲗ ⲛ- out of, from IV 52,23; 63,1; [71,7].

ⲙⲡⲃⲟⲗ prep. outside III 66,24.

ⲥⲁⲃⲟⲗ ⲛ- except IV 79,9.

ⲉⲕⲓⲃⲉ : ⲕⲓⲃⲉ f. breast III 56,9.18. IV [68,2].

ⲉⲛⲉϩ m. eternity IV 50,7.14.

ϣⲁ ⲉⲛⲉϩ eternal III 42,9; 53,8; 65,5; 67,26; 68,26. IV 50,7.13; 51,26; 58,18. [22]; [62,20]; 65,1; 72,4; 76,25; 78,16; 79,1.2; 80,13.

ϣⲁ ⲁⲛⲏϩⲉ III 50,22; 60,22; 68,24.

ϣⲁ ⲁⲛⲏϩⲉ ⲛⲉⲛⲉϩ III 66,19.

ⲙⲛⲧϣⲁ ⲉⲛⲉϩ f. eternity III 69,4.

ⲉⲣⲏⲧ pray IV [71,5].

ⲉⲣⲏⲩ : ⲙⲛ ⲛⲉⲩⲉⲣⲏⲟⲩ with each other III 49,19.

[1] For practical reasons the word order of Crum's *Coptic Dictionary* has been followed, although we find it unsatisfactory, since it is in places incorrect.

ⲈⲤⲎⲦ : ⲈⲠⲈⲤⲎⲦ down III 59,19. IV [62,28]; 71,3.
ϣⲁ ⲠⲈⲤⲎⲦ III 49,15.
ϣⲁ ⲠⲈⲤⲎⲦⲈ III 54,15.
ⲈⲦⲂⲈ- because of III 59,4; 60,24; 61,4.10.12.13; 67,5. IV 72,[13.19.22].24.
ⲈⲦⲂⲎⲎⲦ= III 42,5; 59,9; IV 51, 24; 61,12; 63,6; 71,2.
ⲈⲦⲂⲎⲦ= IV 63,4.
ⲈⲦⲂⲈ ⲠⲀЇ therefore III 67,22. IV[80,9]. ⲈⲦⲂⲈ ⲠⲈЇ III 67,6.
ⲈⲞⲞⲨ m. glory III 41,22; 42,24; 43,12.[18]; [44,15]; 50,3.4.7; 51,1; [52,1]; 53,22; 54,[1]. 2.4.21.25; 55,14.23.24; 62,7 (bis); 67,13. IV 51,14; 53,[8].17; [54,24]; 55,[5].6; [56,14]; [57,5]; [58,1]; 59,5.8.[25].26; [60,17]; 62,2 (bis).3.[6.25]; 63, [21]; 65,16.20.21.22; 66,9.[13].29; 73,[18].18.22; [78,15].
ⲈⲐⲀ ⲈⲞⲞⲨ glorious III 56,8; 66,12.
ϯ ⲈⲞⲞⲨ give glory III 55,7. IV 59,9; 66,20.
ⲢⲈϤϯ ⲈⲞⲞⲨ IV 73,20. See ⲆⲞⲜⲞⲘⲈⲆⲰⲚ.

ⲈⲒ come III 56,12; 59,21; 60,2.9.19.26; 65,18. IV 71,[15].18.
ⲈⲒ ⲈⲂⲞⲖ III [40,14]; 41,11.17.[24]; [43,14.23]; 49,15; 51,15; 52,6; 57,9.[12]; 62,13; 65,2. IV 50,23; 51,8.24; [53,10]; 57,7; [58,23]; 60,10.30; 61,[14].16; [64,23]; 66,3.6.14; 68,9.30; [71,11]; 73,27; 76,20; 80,23.
ⲢϣⲞⲢⲠ ⲚⲈⲒ ⲈⲂⲞⲖ IV 50,4.13.29; 51,5.15; [52,13]; 53,24; 54,1; [60,1]; 63,9; [64,13].
ϬⲒⲚⲈⲒ ⲈⲂⲞⲖ m. IV 51,6.
ⲈⲒ ⲈⲠⲈⲤⲎⲦ IV [62,28]; 71,3.
ⲈⲒ ⲈϨⲞⲨⲚ IV 76,23.
ⲈⲒ ⲈϨⲢⲀЇ IV [72,12].
ⲈⲒ ϨⲒ- III 59,2. ⲈⲒ ⲈⲂⲞⲖ ϨⲒ- III 59,19.
ⲈⲒⲘⲈ know IV 78,8.
ⲈⲒⲚⲈ bring III [42,2]; 43,1.6.7; 56,9; 60,9. IV [71,19].
ⲚⲦ= IV 51,18; [53,1]; [59,1]; 75,20.
ⲢϣⲞⲢⲠ ⲚⲈⲒⲚⲈ IV [52,19].
ⲈⲒⲚⲈ ⲈϨⲢⲀЇ IV 54,14; [55,15]; 56,7; 57,13; 60,22; [61,24]; [62,16]; [65,8]; 67,4; 73,7.
ⲚⲦ= ⲈϨⲢⲀЇ IV 73,3.
ⲈⲒⲚⲈ be like IV [62,29]; 71,5. ⲒⲚⲈ III 59,5; 60,1.
m. likeness IV 79,23. ⲒⲚⲈ III 51,5; 59,20.
ⲈⲒⲞⲞⲢ : ⲀⲦϪⲒⲞⲞⲢ ⲘⲘⲞ= inaccessible IV 50,12; 65,24.
ⲀⲦⲢϪⲒⲞⲞⲢ ⲘⲘⲞ= IV 61,15.
ⲈⲒⲢⲈ : Ⲣ- make III 52,2; see : ⲢⲢⲞ; ⲞⲨⲞⲈⲒⲚ; ϨⲀⲈ.
Ⲟ† be III 41,19; 51,5; 57,3; 59,20. Ⲉ† IV 51,9.[10].13; [53, 27]; [79,8.9].
ⲈⲒⲰⲦ m. father III 40,13.18; 41,3.9.11.12. [19]; 42,[1]. 4.11.20.24; 43,5.13.[21]; 50,15; 51,2.8; 52,4.17; 53,4; 54,7; 55,9; 59,12; 63,21; 68,19. IV 63,2.
ⲒⲰⲦ III 49,13; 50,14; 54,10. IV 50,3.9.14.22.25.28; 51,[1]. 10.18.21; 52,[2].14.[18]; 53,1.[9].21; [54,18]; [55,5]; [56,24]; 58,3.26; [59,1.13]; [60,9.25]; [61,14]; 62,12.[14].26; [63,25]; [64,10.25]; [65,26.28]; [66,22]; [73,11].
ⲈⲒϣⲈ crucify IV 77,15.

ⲔⲈ- other III 66,27.

ⲕⲱ place III 68,2.12.
ⲕⲁⲁ⸗ IV 81,2.
ⲕⲁⲁ⸗ ⲛϩⲣⲁï ϩⲓϫⲛ- IV 80,16.
ⲕⲏ† ϩⲓϫⲛ- IV 52,6.
ⲕⲏ† ⲉϩⲣⲁï ⲉϫⲛ- preside over IV 55,1; 58,13; 66,26; 76,1.3.5.8.10.20.23.
ⲕⲱⲃ : ⲕⲏⲃ† fold III 67,8. IV [79,18].
ⲕⲗⲟⲟⲗⲉ f. cloud IV[61,1]; [68,10].
ⲕⲗⲟⲙ m. crown III 42,23; 50,4; 54,2; 55,24; 62,7. IV 59,26; 62,3; [65,21]; 73,18.
ⲕⲓⲙ move III 51,9; 54,11; 59,14; 61,20. IV [65,31].
ⲁⲧⲕⲓⲙ IV 63,3; [65,27]; 73,4.
ⲕⲏⲙⲉ : ⲣⲙⲛⲕⲏⲙⲉ see Proper Names.
ⲕⲟⲩⲛ⸗ bosom IV 51,19; 52,20; [53,1]; 59,2.
ⲕⲟⲩⲟⲩⲛ⸗ III 42,3; 67,10, IV 75,9. ⲕⲟⲟⲩⲛ⸗ III 43,7.
ⲕⲱⲧⲉ surround III 43,12; 50,7; 53,21; 62,10. IV 53,8; 57,25; 59,7; 62,6; [65,15]; [66,11]; 73,21; [79,21].
ⲙⲡⲕⲱⲧⲉ prep. around III 54,24.
ⲕⲟⲧⲥ f. crooked trick IV 73,1.
ⲕⲁϩ m. earth III 50,10; 57,19; 61,6. IV 62,9; [69,4]; 71,2.20; 72,15.
ⲕⲱϩ : ⲣⲉϥⲕⲱϩ jealous III [58,25].
ⲕⲱϩⲧ m. fire III [58,11].

ⲗⲁⲁⲩ anything III 49,12; 58,26. IV 61,14.

ⲙⲁ m. place III 41,13.23; 43,8; [49,1]; 50,11; 56,4; 60,13; 65,13.16.19.21; 67,5.17. IV [53,3]; 56,[6].12; 60,27; 61,1; 62,10; [71,28 (bis)]; 77,[8].12.[16].19; 80,5.
ⲙⲉ f. truth III 41,7. IV 75,22; 76,3. ⲙⲏⲉ III 40,19; 55,6; 64,15; 65,14.
ⲙⲛⲧⲙⲉ f. IV 50,10; 58,15.22; 59,21; 60,3; 66,19; 73,15; 77,10; 78,11.15.[19]; 79,25; 80,14.
ⲛⲁⲙⲉ truly IV 58,[16.22]; 59,22; 73,15; 78,12.[16.19]; 80,14.
ⲙⲟⲩ m. death, plague III 62,24; 66,8. IV [72,21]; 74,9; 78,10.
ⲙⲟⲟⲩⲧ† III 51,13. IV 63,7.
ⲙⲁⲁⲃ thirty III 68,11.
ⲙⲙⲛ- : ⲙⲛ- it is not III 41,1; 54,5; 67,11; 68,4.8. IV [61,14].
ⲙⲛⲧ⸗ not to have III 54,22.24.
ⲙⲙⲓⲛ ⲙⲙⲟ⸗ self III 61,22.
ⲙⲛ- and, with III 40,<18>.<19> : 41,22; 42,2.7.8(bis).10.20.23.[23].24; 43,10.11.12; 44,12.15.[26.27].28; 49,18.19.25.26; 50,1.2.3.4.5.6.7.8.10.16.19.21; 51,1.11.20; 53,18. 19.20.21.22(bis).23.<23>.24.25; 54,2.3.<5>.8.16.17.25; 55,1.9.10(bis).12.13.21. 22.23; 56.1.2.3.10.25;[57,11]; [58,22]; 59,3.11.12.21.22.25; 60,1.<21>.23; 61,7.9. 11.17.18.20.21(bis).25; 62,2.5.6.7.8.9(bis).10.16.18.19.20.21; 63,1.2.3.4.6(bis).7(bis). 8.9.18.19(bis).20.21.22; 64,1(bis).5.12.13.14(bis).15.16(bis).17.18.19.20(bis).21.22.27; 65,1.2(bis).3.6(bis).7.8.9.12(bis).14.17(bis); 66,2; 68,6(bis).15.17.22.23.25.26; 69,1.2. 3(bis).9.12. IV 50,9.10.20; 51,[19].25.[25]; 52,[1.14].16.17.18; [53,2.6.7.8.9.]; 54,24; [55,4.6.17]; 57,4.[5.6.22]; 58,1.[4(bis)].4.[6.7].14.16.21.24.[25].26; [59,5.8.13.14(bis).22. 24.26]; 60,12.[17]; [61,20.26.28.29]; 62,[1].2.3.[4.5].5.7(bis).[9].13.14.18.20.21.[25]; 63,[5].14; 64,17; 65,[7].12.13.14.15.16.[16.17].17.18.19.20.21.22.[24].27; 66,4.5.13. 23(bis).[23.27].28; 67,7.8.[9]; [68,8]; 71,6.[10.11]; 72,3.5.[18].21.[26]; 73,1(bis).4.5.[5]. 12.[17].18.19.20.21.22(bis).23; 74,1.3(bis).5.6.7.[8.12].14.16(bis).20.[21].22.24; 75,1.

67,22. IV [51,5.12]; 52,19; 53,[20.22.23].25.26; [55,13.14]; [56,26]; 57,13; 59,16.[18]; 60,4.7.[8]; [61,5.11.21]; 77,6. ⲡⲉ̈ϊ III 67,7. ⲡⲉⲉⲓ III 49,5. ⲉⲧⲃⲉ ⲡⲁϊ see ⲉⲧⲃⲉ-.

ⲡⲏ IV 52,6; 55,1; 62,28; 68,29; 69,2; 71,1; 74,26; 75,10.15.16; 76,1.5; 77,14.15; 78,1; 79,[8.9]. 26; 80,[14].17.

ⲧⲁϊ III 51,23; 52,14; 60,19.25; 68,1. IV [51,24]; 52,10; [56,19]; 64,8; 71,[24].30; 72,7.

ⲧⲏ III 59,23; 63,8. IV 51,22; 63,[19].21; 71,3.[8]; 72,8; 74,23.

ⲛⲁϊ III 41,9.11; 43,4; 53,2; 61,12; 62,22; 66,7. IV 50,25.29; 51,18.20; 52,[25].26; 53,22; [54,24]; 55,2; 61,12; 65,31; 72,22; 78,6. ⲛⲉⲉⲓ III [58,21]; 66,4.

ⲛⲏ IV 59,1; 66,5.27.[28]; 67,1; 74,[8]; 76,2.[8].10.19.22; 78,3.

ⲡⲉ f. heaven III 42,15; 63,25; 65,25. IV 52,6.

ⲡⲏⲩⲉ pl. IV 75,13.

ⲡⲉ copula III 41,21; 43,[4].14.21; 54,8; [57,1]; 58,8.11.12.[12].13.[13.15.17].19.20.[21]; 60,11. 13.14; 67,16; 69,12. IV 51,6.[12]; 52,23; [53,20]; [56,26]; 59,16.18; 60,[7].8; 61,9.[11.12.22]; 79,7.8; [80,2].

ⲧⲉ III 42,7; 52,15; 60,19.25; 68.1. IV 51,25; 52,3.[16]; [56,19]; 64,8; [71,21.24. 30]; 72,3.7.

ⲛⲉ III 41,9; 43,4. IV 50,25; 51,17.[20]; 52,25.26; 54,24; [55,2]; 57,5; [61,12.13].

ⲡⲉⲓⲣⲉ ⲉⲃⲟⲗ come forth, radiate III [42,17].

ⲡⲣ[ⲉⲓⲱⲟⲩ]† m. manifestation IV 63,11.

ⲡⲉⲓⲣⲉ ⲉⲃⲟⲗ m. radiance III 41,2.

ⲡⲓⲣⲉ [ⲉⲃⲟⲗ ϩⲛ-] IV 61,9.

m. III 41,10. IV 50, 19.26; [52,11].

ⲡⲱⲣϣ ⲉⲃⲟⲗ spread out III 67,7. IV [79,17].

ⲯⲓⲥ : ⲙⲉϩⲯⲓⲥ ninth III [58,18]. ⲙⲉϩⲯⲉⲓⲧ IV 70,4.

ⲡⲉϫⲉ- said III 58,24.

ⲡⲉϫⲁ= III 56,23; 57,5.[8.21].25; 58,3. IV [68,6].

ⲣⲏ m. sun III 58,17; 60,1; 65,1; 68,4. IV [71,10]; 76,21; [80,18].

ⲣⲟ : ⲕⲁⲣⲱϥ m. silence IV [52,17]; 55,19; 56,5; [58,24]; [60,26].

ⲁⲧⲕⲁⲣⲱ= silent IV 59,12; 66,22.

ⲣⲱⲕϩ m. conflagration III 63,6. IV 72,15; [74,20].

ⲣⲱⲭϩ III 61,5.

ⲣⲱⲙⲉ m. man III 49,9.10.18.21(bis); 50,13.14.20; 51,3.6.21; 55,18; 58,10.17; 59, 3(bis).15; 62,18; 64,23; 65,15; 66,1; 67,19. IV 60, [16.18].28; 61,[11].20. [22.23]; 62,11.19.[27.31]; 63,16; 67,3; 70,2; 74,3; 76,14; 77,11; 80,6.

ⲙⲛⲧⲣⲙⲙⲁⲟ f. riches III 67,9. IV [79,20].

ⲣⲟⲙⲡⲉ f. year III 56,23; 68,12. IV [68,6].

ⲣⲁⲛ m. name III 40,14; 43,19; 44,1.[11]; 49,6; [57,1]; 65,23; 66,12.22; 67,21. IV [50,4]; [53,18.25]; 60,5; 61,6; 78,14; [79,3]; [80,8]. ⲣⲉⲛ III 68,7; 69,12.

ϯ ⲣⲁⲛ name III [44,24]; 54,7. IV 55,15.

ϯ ⲣⲛ= III 60,18.

ⲁⲧϯ ⲣⲁⲛ ⲉⲣⲟ= unnameable IV [54,17]; 65,[11].25; 67,6; [73,9]; 77,6.

ⲣⲣⲟ : ⲣ ⲣⲣⲟ ⲉϫⲛ- reign over III 56,24; 57,10.

ⲣ ⲣⲣⲟ ⲉ- III 58,5.

ⲣ ⲣⲣⲟ ⲉϩⲣⲁϊ ⲉϫⲛ- IV [68,8].

ⲣⲁⲧ= : ⲁⲧⲛ ⲣⲁⲧ= untraceable III 68,18; see : ⲧⲁϩⲟ, ⲱϩⲉ.

ⲥⲁ : ⲛⲥⲁ- see : ⲧⲱⲃϩ.
ⲙⲛⲛⲥⲁ after III 56,22; 58,23. IV 68,5.
ⲥⲁ : ⲙⲛⲧⲥⲁⲉⲓⲉ f. beauty III 67,5.
ⲥⲁⲃⲉ : ⲥⲃⲱ f. teaching IV 57,8; 64,6.
ⲥⲟⲃⲧⲉ prepare IV 71,12. ⲥⲁⲃⲧⲉ III 60,3.
ⲥⲃⲧⲱⲧ= III 63,11. IV 74,26.
ⲥⲁⲃⲧⲉ m. founding III 58,23.
ⲥⲙⲏ f. voice III 43,3; 55,7; 59,1.5; 66,27. IV 52,22; [59,10]; [63,6]; [66,20]; 79, 12.
ⲥⲙⲟⲩ praise III 55,6. IV 59,9; [66,19].
m. III [44,25]; 49,23; 50,18; 53,16; 55,18; 61,24. IV 54,15; 55,16; 56,8; [57,13]; [60,22]; 61,24; [62,16]; 65,9; [67,4]; 73,8; 79,12.
ϯ ⲥⲙⲟⲩ ⲉ- give praise to III 44,10. See p. 39.
ⲥⲙⲟⲧ m. form III 57,4; 61,18.
ⲁⲧⲥⲙⲟⲧ formless III 67,18(bis).
ⲥⲓⲛⲉ ⲉⲃⲟⲗ ϩⲛ- pass through IV 59,2; [74,17].
ⲥⲛⲁⲩ : ⲥⲛⲧⲉ f. two III 57,13. IV [68,27].
ⲙⲉϩⲥⲛⲁⲩ second III 52,10.23; 53,6; 58,11; 60,17; 65,16. IV 64,[4].18.[28]; 71,28.
ⲙⲉϩⲥⲛⲧⲉ f. III 43,11. IV 52,3.
ⲙⲛⲧⲥⲛⲟⲟⲩⲥ twelve III 57,23; 58,7. IV [69,4].
ⲙⲉϩⲙⲛⲧⲥⲛⲟⲟⲩⲥ twelfth III 58,21.
ⲥⲛⲟϥ m. blood III 57,5.
ⲥⲟⲡ m. time III 49,7.
ⲥⲱⲣⲙ go astray IV 74,23.
ⲥⲟⲉⲓⲧ : ⲁⲧϯ ⲥⲟⲉⲓⲧ ⲉⲣⲟ= unheralded III 41,20.
ⲥⲓⲧⲉ : ⲥⲟⲧ= ⲉϩⲣⲁï ⲉ- sow in IV 71,1.
ⲥⲁⲧ= ⲉϩⲣⲁï ⲉ- IV 71,19.
ⲥⲧⲟⲉⲓ m. incense III 67,22. IV [80,10].
ⲥⲱⲧⲙ hear III 68,9. IV [80,25].
ⲥⲱⲧⲡ m. elect III 65,7.
ⲥⲧⲱⲧ m. trembling III 54,12.
ⲥⲟⲟⲩ : ⲙⲉϩⲥⲟⲟⲩ sixth III 58,15. IV [51,10].
ⲙⲉϥⲥⲟⲟⲩ III 41,19.
ⲥⲟⲟⲩⲛ m. knowledge III 60,24; 64,7. IV 52,17; [64,5]; 75,22.
ⲥⲟⲩⲱⲛ- know IV 78,6. ⲥⲟⲩⲛ- III 66,5.
ⲥⲟⲩⲱⲛ= III 66,7; 67,1. IV [79,12].
ϭⲓⲛⲣϣⲟⲣⲡ ⲛⲥⲟⲟⲩⲛ f. foreknowledge IV 52,1.
ⲥⲁϣϥ : ⲥⲁϣϥⲉ f. seven III 43,2.3; 58,2. IV 52,20.22.
ⲙⲉϩⲥⲁϣϥ seventh III [58,17]. IV [70,3].
ⲥⲱⲱϥ : ⲥⲟⲟϥ† defile III 59,24. IV 71,8.
ⲥϩⲁï write IV [53,17].
ⲥⲁϩ= III 68,2.10. IV 80,15.26. ⲥϩⲏⲧ= III 69,10.
ⲥⲏϩ† III [43,20].
ⲥϩⲁï m. writing III 68,11; 69,7. IV 81,1.
ⲥϩⲓⲙⲉ f. female III [42,10]. IV 52,2.
ⲥⲁϩⲛⲉ : ⲟⲩⲁϩ ⲥⲁϩⲛⲉ m. command IV 66,30.

ϯ give III 44,25; 49,23; 50,17; 53,15; 55,15.18; 61,23. IV 66,29.
ⲧⲁⲁ= III 65,24.

ϯ ϩⲓⲱⲱ⸗ put on III 64,2. ⲧⲁⲁ⸗ ϩⲓⲱⲱ⸗ IV 75,16.
ϯ m. gift III 68,17. IV 74,14.
see : ⲉⲟⲟⲩ; ⲙⲁⲧⲉ; ⲣⲁⲛ; ⲥⲙⲟⲩ; ⲥⲟⲉⲓⲧ; ⲱⲡ; ⲱϥⲧ; ϣⲱⲗϩ; ϩⲁⲡ; μορφή.
ⲧⲃⲁ m. myriad III 44,17; 54,22.24; 55,12.
ⲁⲛⲧⲃⲁ IV [55,2]; 57,26; [59,5]; 66,11.[27].
ⲧⲃⲃⲟ purify IV [80,6].
ⲧⲟⲩⲃⲟ⸗ III 67,20.
ⲣⲉϥⲧⲃⲃⲟ m. purifier IV 76,6. ⲣⲉϥⲧⲟⲩⲃⲟ III 64,18.
ⲧⲱⲃϩ ⲛⲥⲁ- pray for III 59,21.
ⲧⲁⲕⲟ destroy III 59,24.
ⲧⲁⲕⲏⲩⲧ† IV [71,8].
ⲧⲁⲗⲟ ⲉϫⲛ- rise upon III 68,7.
ⲧⲉⲗⲏⲗ ⲉϩⲣⲁї ⲉϫⲛ- rejoice about III 56,14. IV [67,28].
ⲧⲛⲛⲟⲟⲩ send III 62,24.
ⲧⲱⲡⲉ : ϫⲓ ϯⲡⲉ taste III 66,8. IV 78,10.
ⲧⲁⲡⲣⲟ f. mouth III 55,8.
ⲧⲏⲣ⸗ all, whole, every III 41,22; [44,21]; 50,9.16; 52,5.18; 54,3.4.20; 55,11; 62,11; 63,1.4; 67,16.24; 68,17; 69,4. IV 51,14; 53,22; 56,4; 57,1: 58,5; 59,3.[10.15]; 61,12.13; [62,8.14]; 64,12; 65,7.22.[23].31; 66,[7].21; [70,2]; [72,22]; 73,24; 74,13.17; 78,15; [80,12].
ⲡⲧⲏⲣϥ everything III 43,22.
ⲧⲱⲣⲉ : ϩⲓⲧⲛ- through III 49,22; 63,1.9.10.14(bis).17; 66,1; 68,17.
ⲉⲃⲟⲗ ϩⲓⲧⲛ- III 50,24; 51,10.12; 56,12.16.17; 59,6.17; 60,3.7.19.26; 61,8; 62,25; 63,12.23.25; 64,5; 66,7. IV 56,9; 60,29; 61,23; 62.24; [67,26.29]; 71,[13].16; 72,1.6.[17]; 74,10.23.25,28.30; 75,2.4.7(bis).12.14.20; 78,1.[9]; 79,17.
ⲧⲥⲁⲃⲟ instruct III 66,6.
ⲧⲥⲃⲟ⸗ IV [78,8].
ϯⲟⲩ five III 56,22. IV 68,5.
ϯⲉ f. III 53,11; 55,12; 63,3; 66,3. IV [56,25]; 58,6.[27]; 59,27; 65,3; [66,25]; 74,16.
ⲙⲉϩϯⲟⲩ fifth III [58,13]; 65,23.
ⲙⲉϩϯⲉ f. III [41,18]. IV [51,9].
ⲧⲟⲟⲩ m. mountain III 64,21; 68,3.12. IV [80,17].
ⲧⲁⲩⲟ : ⲧⲁⲩⲟ⸗ send IV 74,10.
ⲧⲱⲟⲩⲛ carry IV [71,25].
ⲧⲱⲱⲛ⸗ raise IV [63,6]. ⲧⲟⲩⲛ⸗ III 51,12.
ⲧⲱⲱⲛϥ m. rising IV 76,11.
ⲧⲟⲩⲛⲟⲥ raise III 67,19.
ⲧⲁϩⲟ seize IV 66,1.
ⲧⲁϩⲟ ⲉⲣⲁⲧ⸗ place III 56,19.
ⲧⲁϩⲟ⸗ ⲉⲣⲁⲧ⸗ III 57,14. IV 60,[19].21; 68,2.[29].
ⲁⲧⲧⲁϩⲟ⸗ incomprehensible III 49,24. IV [61,25].
ⲧⲱϩⲙ m. convocation IV 75,7.
ⲧⲱϩⲥ : ⲧⲁϩⲥ⸗ anoint III 44,23. IV 55,13.
ⲧⲁϫⲣⲟ establish III 43,17; 54,21. IV [53,15]; 66,8; 75,12.
ⲧⲁϫⲣⲉ- IV 59,4.
ⲧⲱϭⲉ : plant III 60,17.
ⲧⲟϭ⸗ IV [71,27].

ⲧⲱϭⲉ m. plant III 60,16. steadfastness IV 79,14.

ⲟⲩ who? IV 79,11.
ⲟⲩⲁ one, someone III 43,21; 56,24. IV 61,[7].7(bis).
ⲙⲉϩⲙⲛⲧⲟⲩⲏⲉ eleventh III 58,20.
ⲡⲟⲩⲁ ⲡⲟⲩⲁ each one III 58,[4].6. IV 57,24.
ⲧⲟⲩⲉⲓ ⲧⲟⲩⲉⲓ III 41,16; [57,13]. IV [51,6].
ⲟⲩⲱ : ⲁⲧⲣⲟⲩⲱ ϩⲁⲣⲱ⸗ unanswerable IV 55,23.
ⲟⲩⲟⲉⲓⲛ m. light III 40,15.16.[16].17.[18].19; 41,1.2.[15]; 43,3.13.22; 49,2.8; 50,14; 51, 3.16; 52,9.11.12.14.19.22.24.25; 53,[1].15; 55,5; 56,6.7.22.24; 57,13; 62,26; 63,21; 64,25; 65,12; 67,3.9.11; 68,26. IV 50,5.6.7.9.11(bis).12; [51,4]; 52,21;[53,10.21]; 55,11; [58,26]; 61,2.[9.10(bis)]; 62,12.[28]; 63,11; 75,10; [79,16].
ⲣ ⲟⲩⲟⲉⲓⲛ shine III 49,8; 67,4. IV [79,16].
ϣⲃⲣⲟⲩⲟⲉⲓⲛ m. fellow-light III 69,13.
ⲟⲩⲛ- it is III 61,5.
ⲟⲩⲛⲧⲉ- have III [57,13].
ⲟⲩⲟⲛ someone IV [68,7].
ⲟⲩⲟⲛ ⲛⲓⲙ everyone III 66,26. IV 72,5; [79,10].
ⲟⲩⲛⲟⲩ : ϯⲛⲟⲩ now III 65,26. IV 79,13. ⲧⲉⲛⲟⲩ III 66,27.
ⲟⲩⲱⲛϩ reveal III 68,20. ⲟⲩⲟⲛϩ† IV 60,19.
ⲟⲩⲱⲛϩ ⲉⲃⲟⲗ III 50,25; 51,10; 55,15; 56,26; 64,9. IV [55,25]; [58,8]; 60,13.18; 62,25; [66,30]; 71,31; 75,24.
ⲣϣⲟⲣⲡ ⲛⲟⲩⲱⲛϩ ⲉⲃⲟⲗ IV 53,4; [54,22]; 56,12.[21];63,5.[27].
ⲁⲧⲟⲩⲱⲛϩ ⲉⲃⲟⲗ unrevealable III 41,3; 43,19. IV 57,14.
ⲟⲩⲟⲡ : ⲟⲩⲁⲁⲃ† be holy III 49,3; 50,13; 51,3; 60,6; 63,14(bis).19.24; 65,25; 67,26; 68,21. IV [50,1]; 57,2; 61,4; 62,[11].27; [71,16.17]; [74,29]; 75,1.8.12.14; 76,13; [78,2]; 80,1.[13].
ⲟⲩⲱⲥϥ : ⲟⲩⲟⲥϥ⸗ render motionless IV 75,19.
ⲟⲩⲱⲧ single III 55,8.
ⲟⲩⲱⲧⲉ f. IV [59,11]; [66,21].
ⲟⲩⲱⲧⲃ pass through III 63,4.
ⲟⲩⲁⲧⲃ† ⲉ- surpass III 63,24; 65,25.
ⲟⲩⲟⲉⲓϣ m. time III 62,19. IV 74,5.
ⲟⲩⲱϣ m. will, love III 53,3; 57,26. IV 51,27.
ⲟⲩⲱϣⲉ III 59,11; 68,18. IV 74,12.
ⲟⲩϣⲏ f. night III 51,5; 59,20. IV [62,29]; 71,5.
ⲟⲩⲱϩⲙ : ⲟⲩⲉϩⲙ- do again IV 74,29. ⲟⲩⲟϩⲙ† III [44,17].
ⲁⲧⲟⲩⲁϩⲙ⸗ uninterpretable III 53,12.

ⲱⲙⲥ m. baptism IV 75,13.
ⲱⲛϩ ϩⲁⲧⲏ⸗ live with III 67,25.
ⲱⲛϩ ϩⲁⲧⲟⲟⲧ⸗ IV 80,12.
ⲟⲛϩ† III 41,10; 44,15; 49,3; 50,15; 55,6; 62,4; 64.1.12.17; 65,14; 66,11. IV 50,28; 52,14; [54,23]; [58,25]; 59,21; 60,2.26; 61,3; 62,13; [66,18]; [72,19]; 73,15; 75,16.27; 76,6; 77,9; 78,13.
m. life III [42,8]; 53,8; 60,22; 61,9; 65,4.17; 67,21.22. IV 51,26; 65,1; 72,4; 76,9. 24; 77,14; 80,7.[10].
ⲱⲡ : ⲏⲡ† ⲉ- belong to III 61,7.
ⲏⲡⲉ f. number III 54,22.24; 58,2; 60,11.

ⲁⲧϯ ⲏⲡⲉ without number IV 59,6.
ⲁⲧϯ ⲏⲡⲉ ⲉⲣⲟ⸗ IV 57,26; 66,12; [71,21].
ⲱϥⲧ nail III 64,3.
ϯ ⲉⲓϥⲧ IV 75,18.
ⲱϩⲉ : ⲁϩⲉⲣⲁⲧ⸗ attend to IV 75,25.
ⲱϫⲛ perish III 67,22.

ϣ- be able III 66,26; see : ϭⲟⲙ.
ϣⲁ- for, until III 49,16; 61,3; 62, 21. IV 61,17; [62,28]; [72,11]; 74,6.
see : ⲉⲛⲉϩ; ⲉⲥⲏⲧ; ϩⲣⲁï.
ϣⲁ ⲉϫⲛ- rise on III 68,4. IV [80,18].
ϣⲉ ⲉⲃⲟⲗ go forth III 58,6.
ϣⲉ ⲉϩⲟⲩⲛ ⲉ- go in III 65,4.
ⲙⲁϣⲉ ⲛⲁ⸗ imper. III 58,4.
ϣⲉ hundred III 62,14; 68,11. IV 73,28.
ϣⲓ m. amount III 60,11. IV [71,21].
ϣⲟ thousand III 56,23; IV [68,6].
ϣⲓⲃⲉ change III 67,2.
ϣⲃⲏⲣ see : ⲙⲁⲧⲉ; ⲟⲩⲟⲉⲓⲛ.
ϣⲱⲗϩ : ⲁⲧϯ ϣⲱⲗϩ ⲉⲣⲟ⸗ unmarked IV 50,16.
ϣⲙⲟⲩⲛ : ⲙⲉϩϣⲙⲟⲩⲛ eighth IV 70,3.
ⲙⲉϩϣⲏ III 58,18.
ϣⲟⲙⲛⲧ three III 42,6; [43,16]; 44,18.22; 49,7.26; 53,23; 54,13; 60,26; 62,2.
ϣⲟⲙⲧ IV 72.9.
ϣⲟⲙⲧⲉ f. III 41,8.24; 42,1.5; 43,4.5; 44,10.[18]; 63,5. IV 50,24; 51,16.17; 52,15. 25.26; [54,14]; 74,18.
ϣⲙⲧ- IV 51,23; [53,14]; 55, 3(bis).[11]; 56,6; 61,28; 65,17; 66,2; 67.8.
ⲙⲉϩϣⲟⲙⲛⲧ third III 52,12; 53,7; 56,21; 58,12; 65,19.
ⲙⲉϩϣⲟⲙⲧ IV 64,20.[29]. ⲙⲉϩϣⲟⲙⲉⲧ IV 64,5; 68,4; 77,16.
ⲙⲉϩϣⲟⲙⲧⲉ f. III 42,21.IV 52,<15>.
ⲙⲛⲧϣⲟⲙⲧⲉ thirteen III 63,18; 64,4. IV 75,6.18.
ϣⲱⲡ comprehend IV 79,<11>.
ϣⲁⲡ- p.c. receive III 50,11.
ⲣⲉϥϣⲉⲡ- ⲉⲣⲟ⸗ IV [62,9].
ϣⲱⲡⲉ become, come into being III 49,10.12.20.22; 51,8; 57,18.22; [58,26]; 59,10. 23; 61,2.6.7.11.12.14.18. IV 61,[21].22; 63,2.22; [69,3]; 72,[10].14.[16.20].22.25; 79,15.
ϣⲟⲟⲡ† be, exist III 51,24; 59,2; 60,23; 66,16.19.21; 67,18.19.26. IV 63,19; 78,16; 79,1; [80,4.9.14].
ⲣϣⲣⲡ ⲛϣⲱⲡⲉ pre-exist III 63,22.
ⲣϣⲣⲡ ⲛϣⲟⲟⲡ† IV 75,11.
ϣⲏⲣⲉ m. son III 41,9.17; 42,4.22; 51,7.20; 55,10.17; 59,3; 65,20.22; 67,17; 68,26; 69,14. IV 50,26; [51,7.21]; 52,16; [56,24]; 58,4; 59,14; 60,7.8.[12]; 63,1.15; 66,23; 67,2; 77,18; 80,3.
ϣⲟⲣⲡ : ϣⲟⲣⲡ first III [58,7]. IV 51,22; [55,25]; 61,11; 64,2.[8.14].26.
ϣⲟⲣⲡⲉ f. III 42,<5>.
ⲛϣⲟⲣⲡ before III 50,9.17; 56,3; 63,6. IV [54,20]; 73,25.
see : ⲉⲓ; ⲉⲓⲛⲉ; ⲥⲟⲟⲩⲛ; ⲟⲩⲱⲛϩ; ϣⲱⲡⲉ; ϫⲱ.

ϣⲱⲱⲧ m. deficiency III 49,16. IV 61,18.
ⲁⲧϣⲱⲱⲧ perfect III 66,23.
ϣⲧⲟⲣⲧⲣ : ϣⲧⲣⲧⲣ m. disturbance IV 66,1.
ϣⲁϫⲉ m. word III 40,19; 43,3.21; 44,21; 49,22; 53,14; 60,20. IV 50,10; 51,25; 52,23; [53,20]; 55,10; 58,26; 60,[2].21; 61,[19].23; 62,17; 65,6; [66,17]; 71,15; 72,2; 74,26; 75,16.
ⲁⲧϣⲁϫⲉ ⲙⲙⲟ= ineffable III 42,17. IV 50,15.23; 51,2; [52,10]; 54,2; 55,22; [56,2]; 60,9; 75,8; 78,5.

ϥⲓ take III 60,15.
ϥⲱⲧⲉ ⲉⲃⲟⲗ m. destruction IV 61,17.
ⲁⲧϥⲱⲧⲉ ⲉⲃⲟⲗ imperishable IV 80,8.
ϥⲧⲟⲟⲩ four III 50,24; 51,17; 53,15; 54,23; 55,4; 62,25; 64,25. IV 60,20; 62,23; 63,12; [65, 8]; 66,[10].16; 68,3; [74,11]; 76,16.
ϥⲧⲟ f. III 56,9.18. IV 63,24.
ϥⲧⲟⲩ- III 62,14. IV 73, 28.
ⲙⲉϩϥⲧⲟⲟⲩ fourth III 41,18; 52,14; 53,9; 56,20; 58,13; 65,20. IV [51,8]; 64,7.22; 65,2; 77,19. ⲙⲁϩϥⲧⲟⲟⲩ III 54,8.

ϩⲁ- under IV 77,15.
ϩⲁⲣⲓϩⲁⲣⲟ= III 42,18.
ϩⲁⲉ m. end III 68,14.
pl. ϩⲁⲉⲟⲩ deficiencies IV 71,3.
ⲁⲧⲣ ϩⲁⲉ perfect IV 79,6.
ϩⲉ : ⲛⲑⲉ as III 50,16; 55,11; 57,3; 62,11; 66,5. IV 62,15; [66,24].
ⲛϯϩⲉ thus IV [51,7]; 54,13; [56,23]; 63,[9].17; 65,2; [66,13].
ⲛⲧⲉⲉⲓϩⲉ III 41,17;[44,9]; 51,14.22; 53,10. ⲛⲧⲉⲓϩⲉ III 55,2.
ϩⲏ : ϩⲉⲃⲱⲱⲛ famine III 61,11. IV 72,21.
ϩⲓ- see : ⲉⲓ; ⲥϩⲁï; ϯ.
ϩⲓⲏ f. way III 65,1.3. IV 76,20.
ϩⲟ m. face III 57,3.
ⲛⲛⲁϩⲣⲛ- before III 66,25.
ϩⲱⲱ= even III 49,21; [58,8]; IV 71, 29.
ϩⲱⲱⲕ arm IV [79,14].
ϩⲟⲕ= IV 75,21.
ϩⲗⲗⲟ : ⲁⲧϩⲗⲗⲟ ageless III 41,4.
ϩⲙⲉ fourty III 53,11.
ⲁⲛϩⲙⲉ IV 65,4.
ϩⲙⲟⲧ m. grace III 56,15; 61,6; 67,6. IV [64,2]; [67,28]; 72,17; 79,16.
ϩⲛ- in III 41,21; 42,2; 43,[6].11.20.24; 44,1.16; 50,6.12; 51,24; 53, 3.20; 54,18.21; 55,7.8(bis); 56,12.21; 57,[4].23.26; 59,5.11; 60,5.17.20; 62,9.26; 63,12; 64,7.8; 65,18.22.24; 66,3.20.27; 67,3.8.9.11.18.20.23(bis).25; 68,3.11.12.14.15.23; 69,4.11(bis). 13. IV 50,8(bis).10; 51,[13].19; 53,2.14.19.[25.27]; 54,23; 56,15; 57,21; [58,15.22. 24]; 59,10.11.[11].21; 60,3.21.25.[27]; 61,21; 62,5; 63,19.[24]; 64,24; 66,[9.20].21.22; 67,31; 68,3; 71,[15.28].28; 72,2; 73,15; 74,[11.13].27; 75,11.16.22.23; 77,6.10.17; 78,11.15.[18]; 79,1.[11.15].25; 80,4.[7].7.9.10.12.[14]; 81,1.
ⲉⲃⲟⲗ ϩⲛ- from III 40,15; 41,2.8.9.10.[11].13.23; 42,3; 43,1.7.8.14.23; 49,[1].9.11; 51,7; 56,4.9; 57,12; [58,6]; 59,23; 60,16; [61,9]; 62,13. IV 50,[5].27; 51,1.19;

52,20;[53,1.11.22.24]; 59,2.[2].17; 60,10.18.[30]; [68,30]; 71,4.[26]; 72,9; 73,27; 74,17. 19. ⲚϨⲢⲀⲒ ϨⲚ- III [43,17]; 54,15.22; 55,4; 56,20; 57,15. IV 53,7.16.18; 65,[15]. 23; 66,16; 73,20.

ϨⲞⲨⲚ : ⲈϨⲞⲨⲚ Ⲉ- to III 49,11; 50,11; 65,4; 67,12.20. IV 76,23.

ϨⲞⲈⲒⲚⲈ : ϨⲞⲈⲒⲚ some III 60,12.15.

ϨⲀⲠ m. judgement IV 74,21. ϨⲈⲠ III 63,7.

ϯ ϨⲀⲠ condemn IV 74,8.

ϨⲰⲠ : ϨⲎⲠ† hide III 44,2; 52,1; 63,15; 69,8. IV 57,15; [63,21]; 75,2.

ϨⲢⲀЇ : ⲈϨⲢⲀЇ Ⲉ- into III 61,4. IV 66,5.6; 71,1.4.[20]; 72,13.

ϢⲀϨⲢⲀЇ Ⲉ- to III 62,23. IV [62,29]; 66,3; [74,9].

ⲤⲀϨⲢⲈ above IV 75,13.

ⲤⲀϨⲢⲈ m. III 49,15; 51,15; 54,15; 57,<17>; 59,5.8.19. IV [61,17].

ⲚⲤⲀϨⲢⲀЇ IV [63,9]; 66,3.

ⲚϨⲢⲀЇ see : ϨⲚ-; ϨⲒϪⲚ-.

ϨⲢⲞⲞⲨ m. voice IV [59,12]; 66,22.

ϨⲀⲢⲈϨ guard III 62,17; 65,6. ϨⲀⲢⲎϨ III 61,9.

ⲢⲈϤⲀⲢⲈϨ m. III 62,12. IV 73,26; 74,2; [76,27].

ϨⲰⲤ sing III 55,7. IV [59,9]; 66,20.

ϨⲎⲦ m. heart III 66,21; 68,8. IV [79,1].

ϨⲀϨⲦⲚ : ϨⲀⲦⲎ⸗ III 67,25.

ϨⲰⲦⲂ see : ϨⲰⲦⲠ.

ϨⲰⲦⲂ : ϨⲞⲦⲂ† slay IV 76,27.

ϨⲰⲦⲠ m. reconciliation III 63,9.16. IV 74,24. ϨⲰⲦⲂ IV 75,3.

ϨⲞⲞⲨ m. day III 68,5. IV [80,20].

ϨⲞⲨⲢⲒⲦ m. guardian III 61,9. IV [72,18].

ϨⲞⲨⲈⲒⲦ first III 49,9; 52,9.20.21; 53,5; 59,8.

ϨⲞⲨⲈⲒⲦⲈ f. III 52,15.

ϨⲞⲞⲨⲦ male III 42,6.10; 43,16; 44,18.19.[19].22; 49,26; 53,23; 54,13; 62,2. IV 51,23; [52,2.5]; 53,14; [54,19]; 55,[3].4.5.7.[12.17]; 56,[6].19; 59,22; 61,[27].28.29; 65,12.[18].18; 66,2; 67,7.8.9; 73,11.12.16.

ϪⲈ- conj. III 44,25; 49,6; 54,7.10; 56,24; 57,[9].22; 58,1.4.10.[14].17.[24]; 59,2; 60,13. 15.18; 61,22; 67,1.13.25; 68,13. IV 60,5; 61,6; [65,26.29]; 68,7; 70,2; 71,23.[30]; 73,6; [79,25].

ϪⲒ receive III [52,1]; 54,12; 56,17; 59,10. IV 63,21.

ϪⲒ- IV [67,31]; see : ϯⲠⲈ; εἰκών; μορφή.

ϪⲒⲦ⸗ IV 75,21.

ϪⲒ ⲈϨⲞⲨⲚ Ⲉ- III 67,12.

ϪⲞ sow III 60,5.

ϪⲞ Ⲉ- III 60,10. ϪⲰ Ⲉ- III 59,16.

ϪⲰ say III 49,6; 59,2; 60,12; 67,12. IV 60,4.5; 61,[5].6.

ϪⲞⲞ⸗ III 50,9.17; 55,11; 56,2; 63,5. IV 53,19; 55,21.

ⲀⲦϪⲰ ⲘⲠⲈϤⲢⲀⲚ unnameable III 40,14; 44,11. IV [50,4].

ϢⲢⲠ ⲚϪⲞⲞ⸗ mention before III 62,11.

ⲢϢⲢⲠ ⲚϪⲞⲞ⸗ IV [58,6]; 59,4.16.29; [62,8.15]; 66,25; 73,24; 74,19.

ϪⲰ⸗ : ⲈϪⲚ- (sic ! CRUM p.756 a; cf. ϪⲰϪ p. 799a) over, upon III 55, 13; 56,25; 57,10; 59,13; 61,19; 68,4.8.

ⲉϩⲣⲁï ⲉϫⲛ- III 56,14. IV [55,1]; 58,13; [66,26.27]; 67,28; 68,8; 73,3; 76,1. 3.5.8.10.20.23; [80,18].

ϩⲓϫⲛ- III 42,15; 58,22; 61,6; 64,14.16.19.21; 65,1.3.23; 66,23. IV 52,6; 72,15.

ⲛϩⲣⲁï ϩⲓϫⲛ- IV 80,16.

ϫⲱⲕ complete IV [63,24]; 71,2.

ϫⲱⲕ ⲉⲃⲟⲗ III 51, 22; 53, 10; 59,18. IV 56,23; 63,17; 65,3.

ϫⲏⲕ† ⲉⲃⲟⲗ III 53,11. IV 63,18; 65,4.

ϫⲱⲕ m. perfection, fulness III [40,15]; 43,4; 52,7; 59,11. IV 50,6.

ϫⲱⲕ ⲉⲃⲟⲗ m. IV [66,24].

ϫⲱⲕⲙ baptize III 65,24.

m. baptism III 64,17. IV [74,24]; 76,5; 78,3.6; 80,11.

ϫⲉⲕⲁⲁⲥ in order that III 50,24; 51,7.9.13; 54,6; [57,10]; 59,17; 68,14. IV [63,8].

ϫⲱⲱⲙⲉ m. book III 40,12. IV [50,1]; [80,15.26].

ϫⲓⲛ- since III 68,5.

ϫⲓⲛ ⲛ- from III 51,15; 54,15; 62,19.

ϫⲛ ⲛ- III 49,15; 65,26.

ⲛϫⲓⲛ (?) IV [80,19].

ϫⲡⲟ beget, give birth III 49,5; 51,17; 57,19.[20]; 60,20; 63,13. IV 61,5; 63,12; 69,4; 71,1.15.[20]; 72,2; 74,26.29.

ϫⲡⲟ= III 54,17; 59,<17>; 60,11. IV [66,6]; 75,15.

ⲣⲉϥϫⲡⲉ- III 59,25.

[ϭⲓⲛ]ϫⲡⲟ f. generation III 44,18.

ϫⲡⲟ m. begotten one III 67,11. IV 66,6.

ϫⲡⲟ ⲉⲃⲟⲗ ⲙⲙⲟ= ⲙⲁⲩⲁⲁ= m. he who begets himself (= αὐτογενής) IV 50,18; 66,4; 79,6.

ϫⲣⲟ m. strength IV [62,20].

ⲁⲧϫⲣⲟ ⲉⲣⲟ= unconquerable III 64,8. IV 56,26; 75,23.

ϫⲱⲱⲣⲉ : ϫⲟⲟⲣ† be strong IV 76,14.

m. mighty III 59,15; 64,24.

ϫⲓⲥⲉ increase IV [66,14].

m. height III 59,2.5. IV 50,5; 71,4.

ϫⲟⲥⲉ† be high III 40,15; 68,3. IV 80,17.

ϫⲟⲟⲩ : ϫⲟⲟⲩ= ⲉϩⲣⲁï ⲉ- send into III 61,4.

ϫⲱϩⲙ : ϫⲁϩⲙ† corrupt III 60,5. IV 71,4.

ⲁⲧϫⲱϩⲙ incorruptible IV 50,11.28; 51,[14].26; [54,25]; 56,27; 57,4.6; 58,2; [59,8.18]; 60,11; 61,[3].20; 62,7.[18].30; 63,[3.15].16; [65,28]; 66,[1].13.15; 67,3.30; 72,8.[23]; 73,23; 74,2; 75,9.15.23; 76,14; 77,11; 78,2.

ⲁⲧϫⲁϩⲙ= IV [54,16]; [65,10]; [67,5]; [73,8]; 77,5.

ⲙⲛⲧⲁⲧϫⲱϩⲙ f. incorruption IV [53,9]; 62,21.

ϭⲟⲉⲓⲗⲉ : ϭⲁⲗⲏⲟⲩ† ⲉ- dwell with III 68,23.

ϭⲟⲙ f. power III 41,8.16.[22].24; 42,11.16.[21]; 43,2.[5]; 44,10.14.21.25; 50,7; 53,12.21. 23; 59,11; 61,21; 62,4.10. IV 50,21.24; 51,7.[13.16]; 52,2.8.15.21.25; [53,7]; 54,14. [21].23; 55,[9].15; 56,[9].25; 57,5.[26]; 59,[7].21; 61,[2].4; 62,[6].20.[26]; 63,10. [10]; 65,[4].15.[17]; [66,12]; 73,[5].15; 74,22; 75,18.23; 77,2.

ⲙⲛ (ϣ)ϭⲟⲙ it is not possible III 68,5.8.

ϭⲏⲡⲉ f. cloud III 49,1; 56,26; 57,11.15.

ϭⲱⲣϭ ϩⲚ- mix with IV 80,10.
m. mixture IV 61,21.
ϭⲱϣⲧ ⲈⲂⲞⲖ look out III 59,6.
ϭⲱϣⲧ ⲉⲃⲟⲗ ⲉ- look out on III 57,2.
m. looking out III 59,7.
ϭⲓϫ f. hand III 67,7. IV 79,18.

GREEK WORDS

ἀγάπη love III, 53,5; 68,23. IV 64,27.
ἀγαπητικός beloved III 69,10.
ἄγγελος angel III 56,6; 57,6.9.[17].20.25; 58,[3.7].8.[24]; 60,3; 61,21; 62,15. IV 59,6; [69,1.5]; 71,12; 73,5.[28].
ἄγειν bring ⲁⲅⲉ III 64,5.
ἀγέννητος unborn III 54,16.
ἅγιος : ἅγιον holy III 60,7.
ἄδηλος unknown III 41,12.
ἀεί : ἀεὶ εἰς ἀεί III 66,21.
ἀερόδιος ethereal III 50,10. ⲁⲉⲣⲟⲥⲓⲟⲥ III 62,14.
ἀήρ air IV 62,9; [73,29].
αἴσθησις perception ⲉⲥⲑⲏⲥⲓⲥ III 52,10; 69,9. IV 64,3.
αἰτεῖν ask ⲁⲓⲧⲓ III 44,13; 50,21; 51,6; 56,3; 62,12.
ⲣⲁⲓⲧⲓ IV 56,8; [62,19.31].
ⲣⲁⲓⲧⲓ ⲛϣⲟⲣⲡ IV 54,20; 73,25.
αἰών aeon III [40,16]; 41,2.5(bis).7.[15].15; 43,10(bis).15; 44,16.[16.20]; 50,5.24; 51,13; 53,20; 54,5.23; 55,13; 56,1.20; 57,23.24; 59,16.22; 60,5.10; 61,3; 62,8.14.21; 63,18; 64,4; 66,16; 67,15(bis). IV 71,7.14; 74,7. αἰὼν ὁ ὤν III 66,13.
ⲉⲱⲛ IV 50,17.18; 51,4.[4]; 53,[5].6.[13]; 54,25.26; [55,8]; 57,22; 58,14.[21]; 59,3; [60,20]; 62,4.[23]; 63,7; 65,13.[25]; 66,10; [66,28]; 68,3; 71,1.20; 72,12; 73,19.28; 75,6.19.
ἄκλητος uncallable III 55,19. ἄκλητον III 44,12; 53,17; 61,24; 65,10.
ἀλήθεια truth III 60,21; 62,20; 64,7. IV [74,6]. ⲁⲗ⟨ⲏ⟩ⲑⲉⲁ IV 72,2.
ἀληθής : ἀληθῶς truly III 41,7; 67,13.
ἀληθῶς ἀληθῶς really truly III 66,9.12; 68,1.
ἀληθὲς ἀληθῶς really truly III 62,4; 66,15.17.20.
ἀλλά but III 41,20; 65,26. IV [51,11]; [68,5].
ἀλλογενής alien IV 50,21.
ἀλλογένιος alien III 41,6.
ἀμήν Amen ϩⲁⲙⲏⲛ III 55,16; 69,5.17.20. IV [67,1].
ἀνάπαυσις rest III 65,4.
ἀξιοῦν honor ⲁⲝⲓⲟⲩ III 67,16.
ἀόρατος invisible ⲁϩⲟⲣⲁⲧⲟⲥ III 51,2; 55,19; 65,10; 68,24.
ⲁϩⲟⲣⲁⲧⲟⲛ III 44,[1].11.23.26; 49,23; 53,16; 63,2.15; 69,16.19.
ἀπάγειν take away ⲁⲡⲁⲅⲉ III 64,6.
ἀπερινόητος incomprehensible III 49,14.
ἀπόρροια emanation ⲁⲡⲟϩⲣⲟⲓⲁ III 60,24. ⲁⲡⲟⲣⲟⲓⲁ IV 72,7.
ἀπόστολος apostle III 68,6. IV 80,21.
ἀποταγή renunciation IV 75,4; 78,4.

ἀπόταξις renunciation III 66,3.
ἀποτάσσειν renounce III 63,17.
ἀρετή virtue III 42,24. IV 52,18.
ἄρρητος ineffable ⲁϩⲣⲏⲧⲟⲥ III 63,20.
ἀρσενικός : ἀρσενική male III 44,13.27; 49,25; 50,1; 53,18.24; 55,<21>; 61,25; 62,5.
ἄρχειν rule ⲁⲣⲭⲓ ⲉϫⲛ- III 55,13.
ⲣⲁⲣⲭⲓ ⲉϩⲣⲁϊ ⲉϫⲛ- IV [66,27].
ἀρχή origin III 60,21. IV 72,3.
ἄρχων archon III 59,22; 62,22; 63,7; 67,24. IV 71,7; 74,7.21; 80,11.
ἀσήμαντος unmarked III 41,3.21.
αὐτογενής autogenes, self-begotten III 41,5; 49,17; 50,19.22; 52,8.15; 53,13; 55,5; 57,26; 62,26; 65,13; 66,24; 68,16. IV 60,2; 61,19; 62,[17].22; 64,1.9; 65,6; 66,18; 74,12; 77,9.
αὐτογένιος self-begotten III 41,6; 54,6.
ἀφθαρσία incorruption III [41,1.22]; 42,8; [43,12]; 44,15; 50,8; 55,1; 64,9; 69,13.
ἄφθαρτος incorruptible III 41,11; 49,3.18; 50,20; 51,5.20.21; 54,9.12; 55,17; 56,16; 60,25; 61,13; 62,17; 63,20.25; 65,15.26; 66,1; 68,21; 69,2(bis).
ⲁⲡⲫⲁⲣⲧⲟⲥ III 55,3. ἄφθαρτον III 51,9; 59,13; 61,19; 64,23.

βάπτισμα baptism III 63,10.24; 65,25; 66,4.
βίβλος book III 68,1.10; 69,7.16.18.

γάρ for III 49,8; 59,19; 60,20; 66,26; 67,4. IV 61,11; [71,3]; 72,2; 79,11.
γενεά race III [44,19]; 51,8; 54,8; 58,9.[16]; 59,13; 60,19.25; 61,5.7.10(bis).13.14.19; 62,7; 64,23; 68,21. IV [55,4.7]; 63,3; 65,27; 70,1; [71,31]; 72,[7].14.19.[20].23.[24]; 73,3; 74,3; 76,13.
γεννητός begotten III 54,18.
γένος generation IV 55,[3].7.
γνῶσις knowledge IV 72,6.

δαίμων demon III 57,17.[22]; 59,25. ⲇⲉⲙⲱⲛ IV 69,3.
δέ but, and III 41,12; 60,15; 61,3.12. IV 51,9.10; 52,15; [71,22]; 74,19.
διάβολος devil III 61,17; IV [72,29].
διάκονος minister III 52<20>; 64,24.
διάκων III 57,7. IV 64,14; 76,15.
διωγμός persecution III 61,20. IV 73,4.
δύναμις power III 43,11; 49,2.4; 50,21; 51,1.15; 54,25; 56,5; 63.7; 64,3.8; 65,8.

ἑβδομάς hebdomad III 51,23. IV 63,18.
ἔγκλημα complaint ⲉⲛⲕⲗⲏⲙⲁ III 67,11.
εἰκών image ϩⲓⲕⲱⲛ III 55,8; 59,4.6.7. IV 59,11; 66,21.
ϫⲓ ϩⲓⲕⲱⲛ receive shape III 50,12. IV [62,10].
εἶναι : εἶ ὁ εἶ III 66,22. IV [79,3]. εἶ ὅς εἶ III 66,22. IV 79,3.
εἶ ἕν ϊⲉⲛ III 49,5.6. ὤν see αἰών.
εἰρήνη peace ⲓⲣⲏⲛⲏ III 53,7; 67,25. IV [64,28]; [80,13].
εἷς : ἕν see εἶναι.
ἐκκλησία church III 55,4. IV [66,15].
ἑνδεκάς eleven III 52,2. IV [63,22].
ἐνέργεια activity ⲉⲛⲉⲣⲅⲓⲁ III 61,16. IV 72,29.
ἔννοια thought III 42,7. IV 51,25.
ἐξουσία authority III 53,22; 59,22; 63,8. IV 65,17; 74,22; 79,7.

ἐπειδή for ⲉⲡⲓⲇⲉ IV 61,8.
ἐπιγέννιος self-producing III 41,6.
ἐπίκλησις invocation III 66,2.
ἐπίκλητος f. convocation III 63,19.
ἐπιτροπή command III 55,15.
ἑρμηνεύειν : ⲁⲧⲣϩⲉⲣⲙⲏⲛⲉⲩⲉ ⲙⲙⲟ⸗ uninterpretable IV 50,21; 52,8; 55,24; 65,5. ⲁⲑⲉⲣⲙⲏⲛⲉⲩⲉ ⲙⲙⲟ⸗ III 42,16.
εὐαγγελίζεσθαι : ⲁⲧⲉⲩⲁⲅⲅⲉⲗⲓ ⲙⲙⲟ⸗ unproclaimable III 41,4.
εὐαγγέλιον gospel III 69,6.
εὐδοκεῖν agree, approve ⲉⲩϫⲟⲕⲉⲓ III 42,19. ⲉⲩϫⲟⲕⲓ III 59,13.
εὐδοκία good pleasure, approval III 53,3; 59,12; 63,2.

θέλημα will III 42,9; 62,26; 68,15.
θέμισσα Justice; see : Proper Names.
θεόγραφος god-written III 69,15.
θρόνος throne III 43,[11].18; 50,6; 53,20; 54,21; [57,14]; 62,9. IV [53,6.16]; 57,22; 59,5; 62,5; 65,14; 66,9; 73,20.

ἱερός : ἱερά holy III [40,12]; 69,7.16.18.
ἵνα in order that IV [62,24]; 63,[1].23; [65,25]; 71,2.

καιρός moment ⲕⲉⲣⲟⲥ III 62,20; 68,15.
κάλυμμα veil IV 79,20.
καλυπτός hidden IV 57,16.
καρπός fruit III 56,9.11; 62,18. IV 74,3.
κατά according to III 67,21. IV [80,8].
κατάβασις descent III 59,4.
κατακλυσμός flood III 61,1; 63,6. IV 72,11; 74,20.
καταλύειν dissolve ⲕⲁⲧⲁⲗⲩ III 51,14.
κατανεύειν nod approval ⲕⲁⲧⲁⲛⲉⲩⲉ III 52,3.16.
κερᾶν mix ⲕⲉⲣⲁ III 67,23.
κῆρυξ preacher III 68,7.
κόλπος bosom III 43,1; 63,20.
κόσμος world III 51,4; 57,24; [58,5.23]; 59,20; 61,1(bis).4; 63,9.16(bis).17. IV 62,29; 71,4; 72,[9].13; 74,24; 75,3.4.5.
κρίνειν condemn ⲕⲣⲓⲛⲉ III 62,22.
κριτής judge III 62,23. IV [74,8].
κύκλος circle III 67,8.
κυροῦν establish ⲕⲩⲣⲟⲩ III 63,23; 64,5.

λογογενής logos-begotten III 60,6; 63,10; 64,1.
λόγος word, logos III 42,7; 49,17.20; 50,18; 53,13.
λοιμός plague III 61,11.

μέρος part III [57,2]. IV 79,4.
μετάνοια repentance III 59,10.
μήτρα womb IV [79,22].
μνήμη memory III 53,4.

μονάς monad III 57,12.
μονογενής only begotten III 68,25.
μορφή : ϪΙ ΜΟΡΦΗ take shape III 67,8. IV 79,19.
ϯ ΜΟΡΦΗ give shape III 67,10.
μυστήριον mystery III 44,1; 51,24; 63,12. IV 52,2; 55,1; 56,16; [57,14]; [58,7.8]; 63,19. 20; 74,27.

νοεῖν : ⲀⲦⲚⲞⲈⲒ ⲘⲘⲞ= unknowable III 49,14. ⲀⲦⲢⲚⲞⲈⲒ ⲘⲘⲞ= IV [61,16].
νόμος law III 65,18. IV 77,15.
νοῦς mind III 42,9. IV 51,27.

ὀγδοάς ogdoad IV 51,17.22; 52,3.15.26; 63,23.24.29; [64,9]; 65,3.
ϨⲞⲄⲆⲞⲀⲤ III 42,1.5.12.21; 43,5; 52,2.7.15; 53,11.
ὅλως at all III 68,7.
ὀνομάζειν name ⲞⲚⲞⲘⲀⲌⲈ III 49,5.
ⲀⲦⲞⲚⲞⲘⲀⲌⲈ ⲘⲘⲞ= unnameable III 54,6; 55,20; 65,10.
ὁπλίζειν arm ϨⲞⲠⲖⲒⲌⲈ III 64,6; 67,2.
ὅπλον armor III 64,7; 67,3. IV 75,22; [79,15].
ὅταν when IV 66,2.
οὐδέ nor III 68,4.
οὔτε nor III 68,8. IV 80,18.

παραλήμπτωρ receiver III 64,22; 66,5.
ⲠⲀⲢⲀⲖⲎⲘⲠⲦⲰⲢⲞⲤ IV 76,12.
ⲠⲀⲢⲀⲖⲎⲘⲀⲰⲢⲞⲤ IV 78,7.
παραστατεῖν assist ⲠⲀⲢⲀⲤⲦⲀⲦⲈⲒ III 57,20.
παραστάτης attendant ⲠⲀⲢⲈⲤⲦⲀⲦⲎⲤ III 64,10.
παρθενικός : *παρθενικόν* maidenly III 44,12; 49,24; 53,17; 55,20; 61,25; 65,11. IV [54,17]; [56,10]; 60,24; 61,26; 65,11; [67,6]; 73,10.
παρθένος virgin III 42,12; 44,27; 49,25; [50,1]; 53,18.24; 55,22; 56,8.18; 60,4; 62,1.5; 63,13. IV 52,4; 54,19; 55,18; 56,19; [59,23]; 61,27.[29]; [65,12.19]; 67,[7].9; 68,1; 71,13; 73,11.16; 74,28.
ⲠⲀⲢⲐⲈⲚⲎ III 44,13.
παρουσία parousia III 63,5. IV 74,18.
πείθεσθαι trust ⲠⲒⲐⲈ III [58,26].
πειρασμός temptation IV [72,25]. ⲠⲒⲢⲀⲤⲘⲞⲤ III 61,14.
πηγή spring III 56,10.11; 64,15; 66,4. IV 62,13; 71,26; 76,3.
πλανᾶσθαι go astray ⲠⲖⲀⲚⲀ III 63,8.
πλάνη falsehood, error III 61,15.22. IV 72.26; 73,6.
πλάσμα creature III 59,9.
πλάσσειν form ⲠⲖⲀⲤⲤⲀ III 59,8.
πλήρωμα pleroma III [44,21]; 50,8.16.23; 52,5.18; 53,14; 54,3.4; 55,10; 56,2; 62,10; 63,1.4; 68,17; 69,3. IV 52,24; [55,10]; [58,5]; 59,15.28; 62,[7].14.[22]; 63,[26].29; 64,12; 65,7.22.23; 73,23; 74,13.16.
πνεῦμα Spirit III 69,19. ⲠⲚⲀ III [40,13]; 44,11.24.26; 49,25; 53,17; 55,21; 57,19; 60,7; 61,25; 63,3.14; 65,12; 68,25; 69,11.17. IV [50,3]; 54,18; [55,14.17]; 56,10; 58,25; 60,[11].24; [61,26]; [65,12]; 67,7; 69,4; 71,16; [73,10]; 74,15.[30]; 77,7.
πνευματικός : *πνευματική* spiritual III 55,3. IV 66,15.

πρόγνωσις foreknowledge III 42,10.
προελθεῖν come forth **ⲠⲢⲞⲈⲖⲐⲈ ⲈⲂⲞⲖ** III 41,7.13; 42,6.19; 43,8; 44,2.14; 49,13; 52,19; 53,2; 54,14.18; 55,1; 68,19.
πρόνοια providence III 40,17; 42,2; 43,6; 63,22. IV 50,8; 51,20; [53,2]; [58,23]; 75,11.
προφάνεια manifestation **ⲠⲢⲞⲪⲀⲚⲒⲀ** III 51,17.
προφήτης prophet III 61,8.15; 68,5. IV 72,18.27; 80,20.
πρύτανις ruler III 65,5.
πύλη gate III 64,19. IV 76,8.
πύξος tablet III 43,20. IV [53,19].

σάρξ flesh III 69,11.
σιγή silence III 40,[17].18; 41,10.12; 42,2.[22(bis)].23(bis); 43,23; 44,14.15.28(ter); 50,15(bis); 51,11; 65,12; 67,15. IV 50,8.9.[28]; 51,1.19; 52,14.16; 53,2.23.[24].26; 54,[22.23]; [55,19(bis)]; 56,5.18; [58,24]; [59,19]; 60,9.12.[12.24].25.26; [62,13(bis)]; 63,5; 77,7; [80,2].
σκεῦος vessel III 60,6. IV 71,15.
σοφία III 57,1; 69,3.
σπορά seed III 54,9.10; 56,3.17; 59,21.25; 60,8.10.22; 62,13. IV 65,30; 67,31; 71,6.10.[14].17.19.[27]; 72,4; 73,26.
σταυροῦν crucify **ⲤⲦⲀⲨⲢⲞⲨ** III 65,18.
στρατηγός leader III 55,14; 64,12. **ⲤⲀ†ⲄⲞⲤ** IV 66,28; 75,27.
σύζυγος consort **ⲤⲨⲚⲌⲨⲄⲞⲤ** III 52,6.20; 53,2; 69,1. IV 63,28, 64,24
σύμβολον symbol III 44,1; 63,15. IV 53,27; 75,1.
σύνεσις understanding **ⲤⲨⲚϨⲈⲤⲒⲤ** III 52,11; 69,8.
συνευδοκεῖν be well pleased **ⲤⲨⲚⲈⲨⲆⲞⲔⲈⲒ** III 52,4.17.
συντέλεια consummation **ⲤⲨⲚⲦⲈⲖⲒⲀ** III 61,3; 62,21. IV 72,12; [74,6].
σφραγίς seal III 55,12; 63,3; 66,3. IV 56,25; 58,6; 59,1.28; [66,26]; 74,16; 78,4.
σῶμα body III 63,11. IV 74,25.
σωτήρ savior III 68,22; 69,15.

τέλειος : *τελεία* perfect III 51,23.
τολμᾶν : **ⲦⲞⲖⲘⲀ Ⲉ-** act against III 61,22.
ⲢⲦⲞⲖⲘⲀ Ⲉ- IV 73,6.
τόπος place III 60,17.
τότε then III 44,22; 49,16; 53,12; 54,11.13; 55,16; 56,4.13; 57,11.[17]; 59,1; 60,2.9; 61,16.23; 62,13.24. IV 55,11; 56,11.20; 58,23; 60,[17].30. 61,18; [62,30]; [65,5.30]; 67,2; 71,11.[18]; [72,27]; 73,7.27; 74,9.
τύπος example, model III 61,2; 67,24. IV [72,11].

ὑλικός : *ὑλική* hylic III 57,1.
ὑπομένειν persevere **ϨⲨⲠⲞⲘⲒⲚⲈ** III 60,23.
ⲢϨⲨⲠⲞⲘⲒⲚⲈ IV 72,5.
ὑπόστασις nature III 59,1.
ὑστέρημα deficiency III 59,18.

φορεῖν bear **ⲪⲞⲢⲈⲒ** III 55,14. **ⲢⲪⲞⲢⲒ** IV [66,29].
φρόνησις prudence III 52,13; 69,9.
φύσις physis IV 60,3.

φωνή voice III 51,11.
φωστήρ light III 51,18; 52,6; [57,8]. IV 63,[12].27; 64,2.4.6.7.13.16.18.20.22; 65,8; 66,17; 68,4.[7]; 74,11; 76,16; 77,8.

χάος chaos III 56,25; 57,[3].10; [58,22]. IV 68,8.
χαρίζεσθαι grant ⲭⲁⲣⲓⲍⲉ III 56,15.
χάρις grace III 52,9; 69,8.
χρόνος time III 68,15. IV 74,5.
χωρεῖν comprehend ⲭⲱⲣⲓ III 66,27. ⲣⲭⲱⲣⲓ III 67,13. IV [79,25].

ψυχή soul IV 76,27. pl. ⲯⲩⲭⲟⲟⲩⲉ III 65,7.21.

ὡς as IV 78,7.

PROPER NAMES [1]

ⲁⲃⲉⲗ III [58,17]. IV [70,3].
ⲁⲃⲣⲁⲥⲁⲝ III 52,26; 53,9; 65,1. IV 64,21; 65,2; 76,19.
ⲁⲇⲁⲙ III 60,1. IV [71,10].
ⲁⲇⲁⲙⲁⲥ III 49,8.19; 50,20; 51,6.21; 55,18; 65,15. IV 61,8.[20]; 62,19.31; [63,17]; 67,3; 77,12.
ⲁⲇⲱⲛⲁⲓⲟⲥ III 58,13.
ⲁⲉⲣⲟⲥⲓⲏⲗ III 62,16. IV 74,1.
ⲁⲑⲱⲑ III [58,8].
ⲁⲓⲛⲟⲛ III 44,25. IV [55,15].
ⲁⲕⲓⲣⲉⲥⲥⲓⲛⲁ III 58,18. IV [70,4].
ⲁⲕⲣⲁⲙⲁⲛ III 65,7. IV 77,1.
ⲁⲣⲙⲟⲍⲏⲗ III 52,10. IV 63,13; 64,3.[16]; 77,8. cf. ϩⲁⲣⲙⲟⲍⲏⲗ.
ⲁⲣⲭⲉⲓⲣ ⲁⲇⲱⲛⲉⲓⲛ III [58,20].
ⲃⲁⲣⲃⲏⲗⲟⲛ III 42,12; 62,1; 69,3.
ⲃⲁⲣⲃⲏⲗⲱ IV[52,4]; [54,20]; [61,27]; 73,12.
ⲃⲉⲗⲓⲁⲥ III [58,21].
ⲅⲁⲃⲣⲓⲏⲗ III 52,23; 53,6; [57,7]; 64,26. IV 64,17.28; 76,18.
ⲅⲁⲗⲓⲗⲁ III [58,12].
ⲅⲁⲙⲁⲗⲓⲏⲗ III 52,21; 53,5; 57,6; 64,26. IV [64,27]; 76,17.
ⲕⲁⲙⲁⲗⲓⲏⲗ IV 64,15.
ⲅⲟⲅⲅⲉⲥⲥⲟⲥ III 69,12.
ⲅⲟⲙⲟⲣⲣⲁ III 56,10.12; 60,16.
ⲅⲟⲙⲟϩⲣⲁ III 60,14. IV 71,24.[26].
ⲇⲁⲩⲉⲓⲑⲉ III 51,19; 52,13.25; 56,22; 65,19. IV [63,14]; 64,6.21; 68,5; [77,16].
ⲇⲟⲙⲉⲇⲱⲛ ⲇⲟⲝⲟⲙⲉⲇⲱⲛ III 41,14; 43,9.
ⲇⲟⲝⲟⲙⲉⲇⲱⲛ III 43,15; 44,20; 50,5; 53,19; 56,1; 62,8. IV 53,5.12; 55,9; 62,4; [65,13]. ⲇⲟⲝⲟⲙⲉⲇⲱⲛ ⲇⲟⲙⲉⲇⲱⲛ (?) IV 51,2f.
ⲉⲇⲱⲕⲗⲁ III 60,20. IV 72,1.
ⲉⲗⲁⲓ̈ⲛⲟⲥ III 64,21. ⲉⲗⲉⲛⲟⲥ IV 76,11.

[1] Personified concepts are listed in the word indices.

ⲉⲩⲣⲩⲙⲉⲟⲩⲥ IV 76,22. cf. ϩⲉⲩⲣⲩⲙⲁⲓⲟⲩⲥ.
ⲉⲩⲅⲛⲱⲥⲧⲟⲥ III 69,10.
ⲏⲗⲏⲗⲏⲑ III 51,19. IV 63,14; 64,8.23; 68,7; 77,19.
ⲏⲗⲉⲗⲏⲑ III 52,14; 53,1; 56,24; 65,21.
ⲏⲥⲏⲫⲏⲭ III 50,2; 53,25; 55,22; 62,6. IV 56,22; 59,24; 62,1; 65,19; 73,17.
ⲑⲉⲙⲓⲥⲥⲁ III 60,<21>; 62,20. IV 72,3; 74,6.
ⲑⲉⲟⲡⲉⲙⲡⲧⲟⲥ III 64,13. IV 75,28.
ⲓ̈ⲁⲕⲱⲃ IV 75,28.
ⲓ̈ⲁⲕⲱⲃⲟⲥ III 64,13.
ⲓ̈ⲉⲥⲥⲉⲩⲥ : ⲓ̈ⲉⲥⲥⲉⲟⲥ IV 78,10.
ⲓ̈ⲉⲥⲥⲉⲟⲥ ⲙⲁⲥⲁⲣⲉⲟⲥ ⲓ̈ⲉⲥⲥⲉⲇⲉⲕⲉⲟⲥ IV 78,12.
ⲓ̈ⲉⲥⲉⲁ ⲙⲁⲥⲁⲣⲉⲁ ⲓ̈ⲉⲥⲥⲉⲇⲉⲕⲉⲁ IV 75,25.
ⲓ̈ⲉⲥⲥⲉⲁ ⲙⲁⲍⲁⲣⲉⲁ ⲓ̈ⲉⲥⲥⲉⲇⲉⲕⲉⲁ III 64,10.
ⲓ̈ⲉⲥⲥⲉⲩ ⲙⲁⲍⲁⲣⲉⲩ ⲓ̈ⲉⲥⲥⲉⲇⲉⲕⲉⲩ III 66,10.
ⲓⲏⲥ III 64,1.
ⲓⲥ III 65,17. IV 75,15; [77,13]; 79,26.
ⲓⲥ ⲡⲉⲭⲥ III 69,14.
ⲓ̈ⲟⲩⲃⲏⲗ III [58,18]. IV 70,4.
ⲓ̈ⲟⲩⲏⲗ III 50,2; 53,25; 55,22; 62,6. IV [56,20]; 59,23; [61,29]; 65,19; [67,9]; 73,16.
ⲓ̈ⲥⲁⲟⲩⲏⲗ III 64,14. IV 76,1.
ⲓ̈ⲱⲃⲏⲗ III 58,13.
ⲓ̈ⲱⲏⲗ III 44,27; 65,23. IV [55,18].
ⲕⲁⲓ̈ⲛ III [58,15].
ⲕⲏⲙⲉ : ⲣⲙⲛⲕⲏⲙⲉ Egyptian III [40,12]; 69,6. IV [50,2].
ⲙⲏ̣ⲡ̣[..]ⲏ̣ⲗ IV 76,2.
ⲙⲓⲝⲁⲛⲑⲏⲣ III 65,5.
ⲙⲓⲕⲝⲁⲛⲑⲏⲣⲁ IV 76,25.
ⲙⲓⲣⲟⲑⲟⲏ III 49,4.
ⲙⲓⲥⲉⲩⲥ IV 76,9; cf. ⲙⲓⲭⲉⲩⲥ.
*ⲙⲓⲭⲁⲛⲱⲣ : ⲙⲓⲭⲁⲛⲟⲣⲁ III 65,6. IV 76,26.
ⲙⲓⲭⲁⲣ III 64,15.20. IV 76,4.10.
ⲙⲓⲭⲉⲩⲥ III 64,20. cf. ⲙⲓⲥⲉⲩⲥ.
ⲙⲓⲭⲉⲁ III 64,15. IV 76,4.
ⲙⲛⲏⲥⲓⲛⲟⲩⲥ III 64,16. ⲙⲛⲏⲥⲓⲛⲟⲩ IV 76,4.
ⲛⲉⲃⲣⲟⲩⲏⲗ III 57,18.22. IV 69,2.
ⲟⲗⲥⲏⲥ III 65,2. IV 76,21.
ⲟⲣⲟⲓ̈ⲁⲏⲗ III 51,18; 52,11.24; 57,8; 65,16. IV 63,13; 64,4.[18]; 77,12.
ⲡⲗⲏⲥⲓⲑⲉⲁ III 56,6.
ⲡⲟⲓⲙⲁⲏⲗ III 66,1. ⲡⲓⲙⲁⲏⲗ IV 78,2.
ⲥⲁⲃⲁⲱⲑ III 58,14.
ⲥⲁⲕⲗⲁ III 57,16.21.[26]; 58,24. IV 69.1.
ⲥⲁⲙⲃⲗⲱ III 53,8; 64,27. IV 64,19.[29]; 76,18. ⲥⲁⲙⲗⲱ III 52,25.
ⲥⲉⲗⲇⲁⲱ III 64,21. IV 76,11.
ⲥⲉⲗⲙⲉⲭⲉⲗ III 62,16. ⲥⲉⲗⲙⲉⲗⲭⲉⲗ IV 74,1.
ⲥⲉⲥⲉⲅⲅⲉⲛⲃⲁⲣⲫⲁⲣⲁⲅⲅⲏⲥ IV 76,7.
ⲥⲉⲥⲉⲅⲅⲉⲛⲫⲁⲣⲁⲅⲅⲏⲛ III 64,18.
ⲥⲏⲑ III 51,20; 54,11; 55,17; 56,13.14; 59,15; 60,2.8.9.14.15; 61,16.23; 62,4.19.24;

REFERENCES

7,23ff. 44
7,23-8,4 44
9,24ff. 32
10,23 191
11,15ff. 32; 179
11,16 191
11,22ff. 33; 180
12,2ff. 180
12,17ff. 191
12,21 191
12,25 191
13,3ff. 179; 196
13,11ff. 177
13,17ff. 196
13,19ff. 182; 196
14,1ff. 196
14,9ff. 33
15,16ff. 183
16,20ff. 183
18,20ff. 184
21,17f. 29; 184
33,17 7; 198
III,*3* Eugnostos the Blessed
81,23ff. 185
82,7f. 185
85,10f. 185
85,11f. 185
87,15 191
III,*4* The Sophia of Jesus Christ
102,12f. 44
IV,*1* The Apocryphon of John
49,27f. 20
V,*2* The Apocalypse of Paul
18,7 46
V,*3* The First Apocalypse of James
41,16ff. 41
V,*4* The Second Apocalypse of James
46,10 10
V,*5* The Apocalypse of Adam
64,6ff. 41
64,24ff. 186
64,29ff. 34
69,19ff. 34
71,10ff. 36
74,10f. 186
74,23 206
75,9ff. 189
75,21ff. 195
75,22ff. 180
76,11ff. 186
76,17ff. 34
77,27ff. 192
79,2 194
84,5 195
84,5f. 195
84,6 195
85,30f. 16; 194
85,31 194
VI,*2* The Thunder: Perfect Mind
13,19ff. 182
VI,*3* Authoritative Teaching
35,23f. 20
VII,*2* 2nd Treatise of the Great Seth
53,30f. 184
70,11f. 20
VII,*3* The Apocalypse of Peter
70,13 20
84,14 20
VII,*5* The Three Steles of Seth
118,10-12 20
118,10-127,27 35
119,12 176
119,12f. 176
120,15 176
120,29 44
121,8 44
125,23 176
VIII,*1* Zostrianos
2,9 46
6,10 195
6,11f. 195
6,16 195
6,30 176
8,11 178
9,2ff. 178
9,4ff. 178
13,4f. 46
18,14 170
29-30 34
30,14 176
45,2 48
45,11 48; 178
47,2 195
47,3 196
47,5f. 194
47,9ff. 186